Film Noir FOUNDATION™

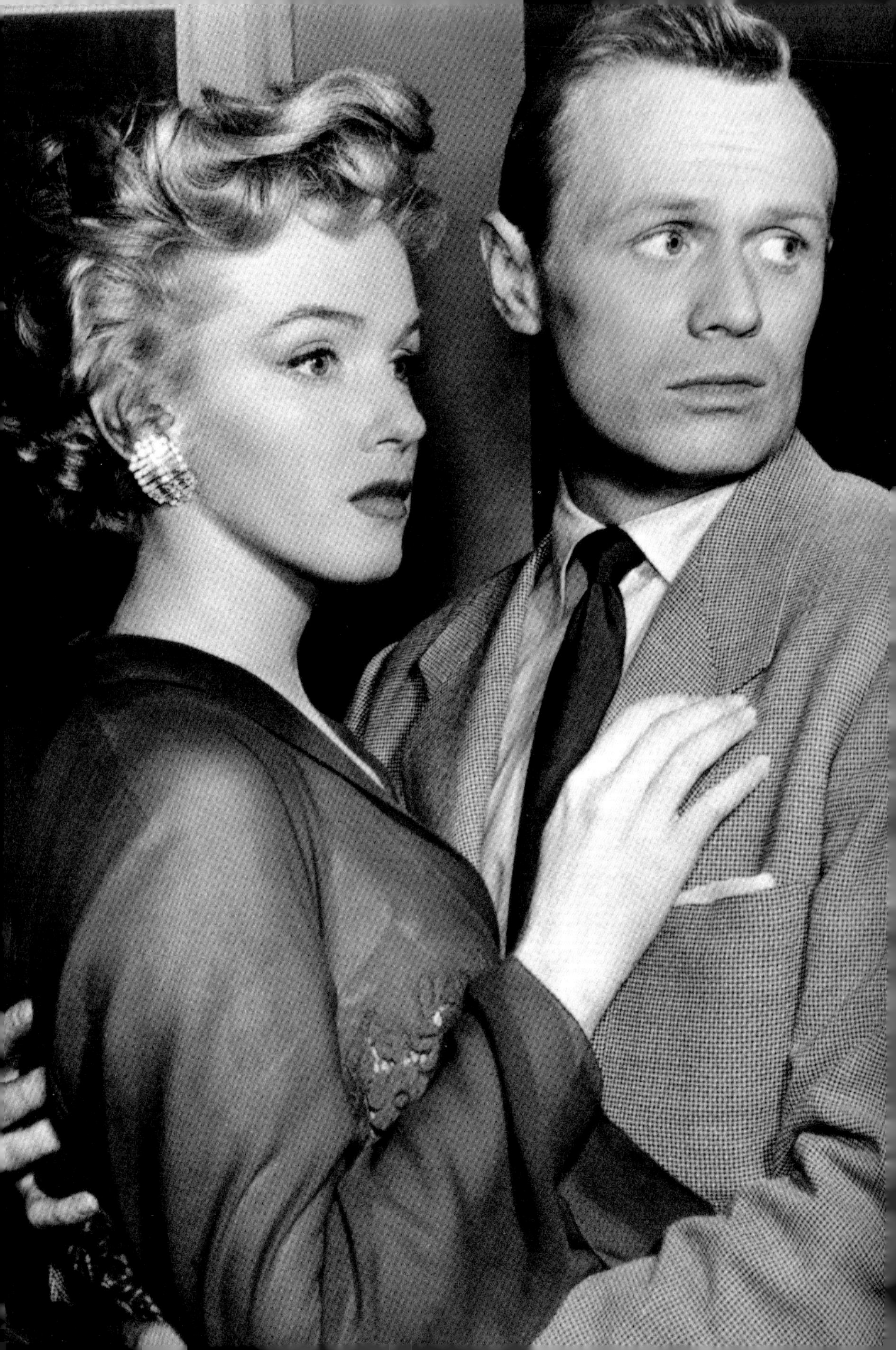

NOIR CITY®

OFFICIAL MAGAZINE OF THE FILM NOIR FOUNDATION

ANNUAL TEN

The Best of **NOIR CITY** e-magazine

2017

PUBLISHED BY THE FILM NOIR FOUNDATION
San Francisco | Los Angeles | New York

NOIR CITY ANNUAL 10: The Best of NOIR CITY 2017

All proceeds from the sale of this book go directly to the non-profit Film Noir Foundation's mission to find and preserve *films noir* in danger of deterioration, damage or loss, and to ensure that high quality prints of these classic films remain in circulation for theatrical exhibition to future generations.

Interested in contributing to *NOIR CITY e-magazine*? Contact us at mailbox@filmnoirfoundation.org. Accepted submissions are published with the permission of the authors and the Film Noir Foundation claims no exclusive rights to the material.

FIRST EDITION

Cover and book design by Michael Kronenberg

ISBN 978-0-692-98068-2

FRONT COVER: *Somewhere in the Night* (1946), three-sheet poster

FRONTISPIECE: Marilyn Monroe and Richard Widmark in *Don't Bother to Knock* (1952)

BACK COVER: *Le Samouraï* (1967), Japanese poster

INTRODUCTION

I've been holding this rant in for more than a year, so excuse me while I blow off some steam. Last year our series of NOIR CITY film festivals, presented by the Film Noir Foundation, featured the theme "The Big Knockover: Heists, Hold-ups, and Schemes Gone Awry." The idea was to provide a chronological survey of international heist movies, decade by decade, from the 1940s to present day. Just to make sure I wasn't forgetting anything, I went online and searched for "greatest heist movies of all-time." The first thing that came up was from an online journal called Complex, posted by a young man named John Flynn. It is, of course, a list—because that's all the 'net seems to be interested in. Lists. The 10 this, the 50 that. Mr. Flynn's list comprised the "25 Greatest Heist Movies of All-Time."

I'm sure you see where this is going ...

Eighteen of the films on this list were made after 1987, and it included such "all-time" heist classics as *Bad Santa* (2003), *Ant-Man* (2015) and *Fast Five* (2011), which placed, respectively, numbers 17–19. Amazingly, two films on the list were also included in our NOIR CITY 2017 programs: *Rififi* (1955, #7) and *The Killing* (1956, #4). But before you give Master Flynn a pass for that modicum of good taste, understand that *The Asphalt Jungle* is nowhere to be found, and *Ocean's 11* (2001) is #1. And note that, *Rififi* aside, every movie listed is an English language film. Jean-Pierre Melville turns in his grave.

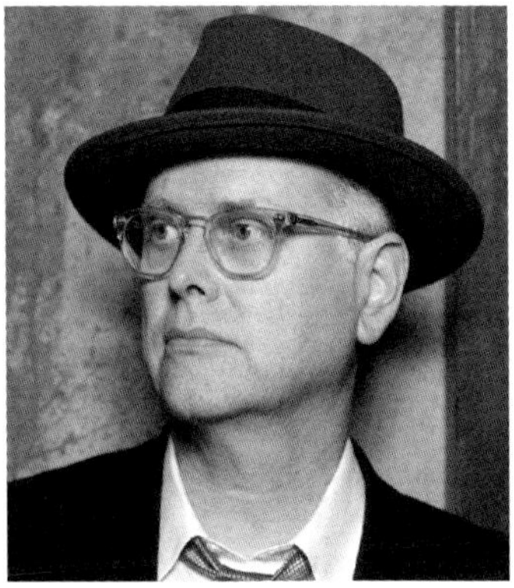

Who knows, maybe Master Flynn will go on to be one of the most erudite and sophisticated cinema reviewers in America. You know, I too used to make silly lists of "The 100 greatest movies of all-time" when I was 18 years old (I think *Where Danger Lives* was #27 back then)—but the difference is that my lists didn't circulate globally via Google and top the "hit list" for people doing legitimate research.

Understand, this is not a screed against movies made after 1987. I like pretty much all the films on Flynn's list (especially *Bad Santa*!)—this is a screed against a ludicrous and untrustworthy internet culture that allows ill-informed bloggers to proclaim anything the "greatest of all-time." Which, I suppose, is one of the lesser sins of a contemporary media culture, "social" or otherwise, that relentlessly erodes the public's remaining intelligence.

But I suppose I'm preaching to the choir. If you've purchased this volume—I thank you for supporting the Film Noir Foundation's restoration efforts (even if you didn't know that's what your money is doing)—then you must already have a craving for substance and style in your cinema scholarship. That's what we are dedicated to providing in our quarterly *NOIR CITY e-magazine*, which we proudly boast has the finest stable of writers of any film periodical on the planet.

This tome represents the crème of last year's crop of essays, interviews, and appreciations, all crafted from experience, perspective, insight, and exceptional writing. You won't find a list in the bunch.

Darkly,

Eddie Muller

***Eddie Muller**, known as "The Czar of Noir," is a writer, cinema historian, and film preservationist. As founder and president of the Film Noir Foundation, he has led the campaign to rescue and restore dozens of at-risk films. He produces and hosts NOIR CITY film festivals in nine U.S. cities and is a frequent guest at international festivals and cinematheques. Muller programs, writes, and hosts the weekly "Noir Alley" series on Turner Classic Movies. In addition to numerous non-fiction books, Muller also writes crime fiction; his 2002 book* The Distance *was named Best First Novel by the Private Eye Writers of America.*

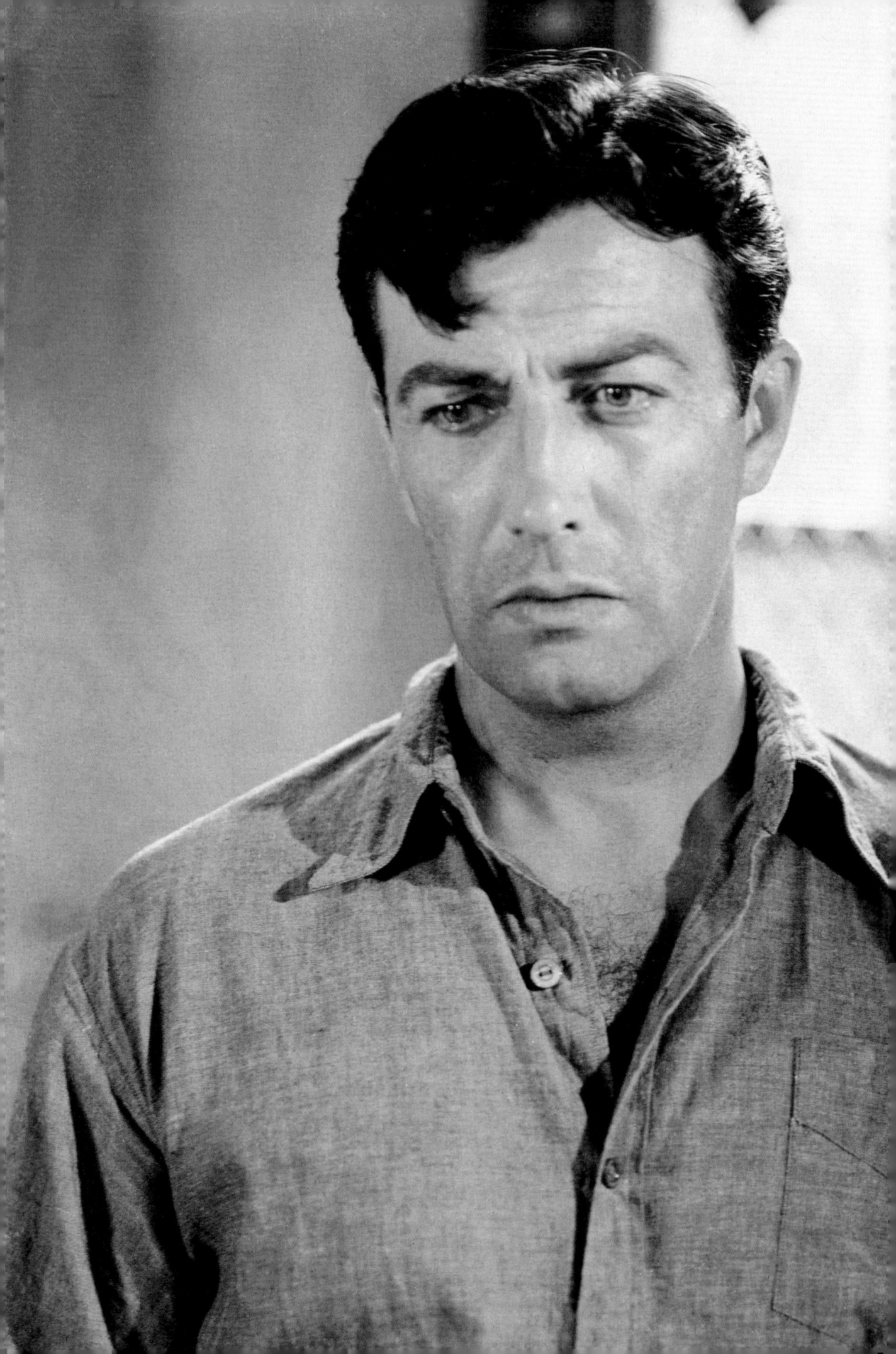

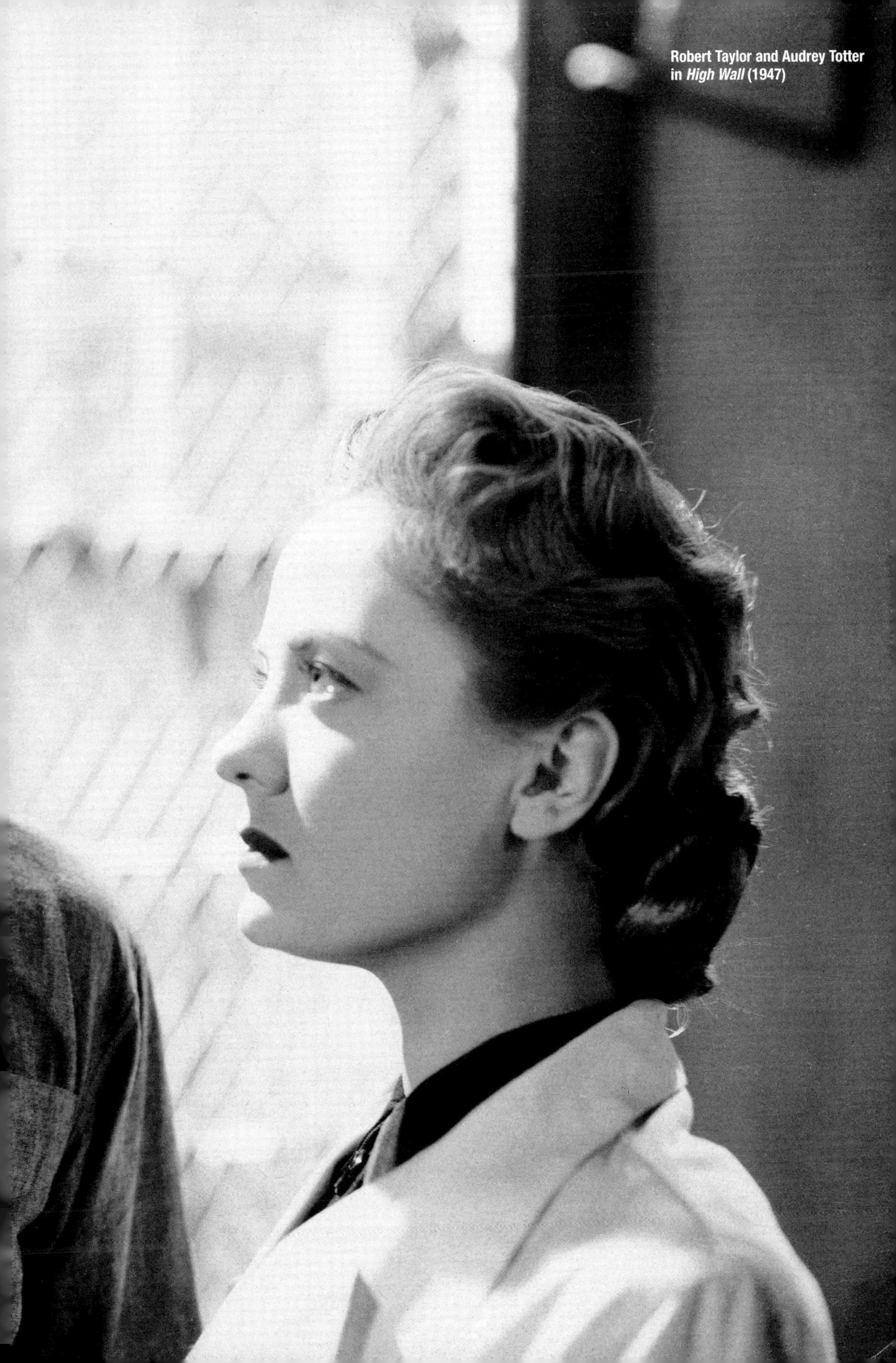

Robert Taylor and Audrey Totter in *High Wall* (1947)

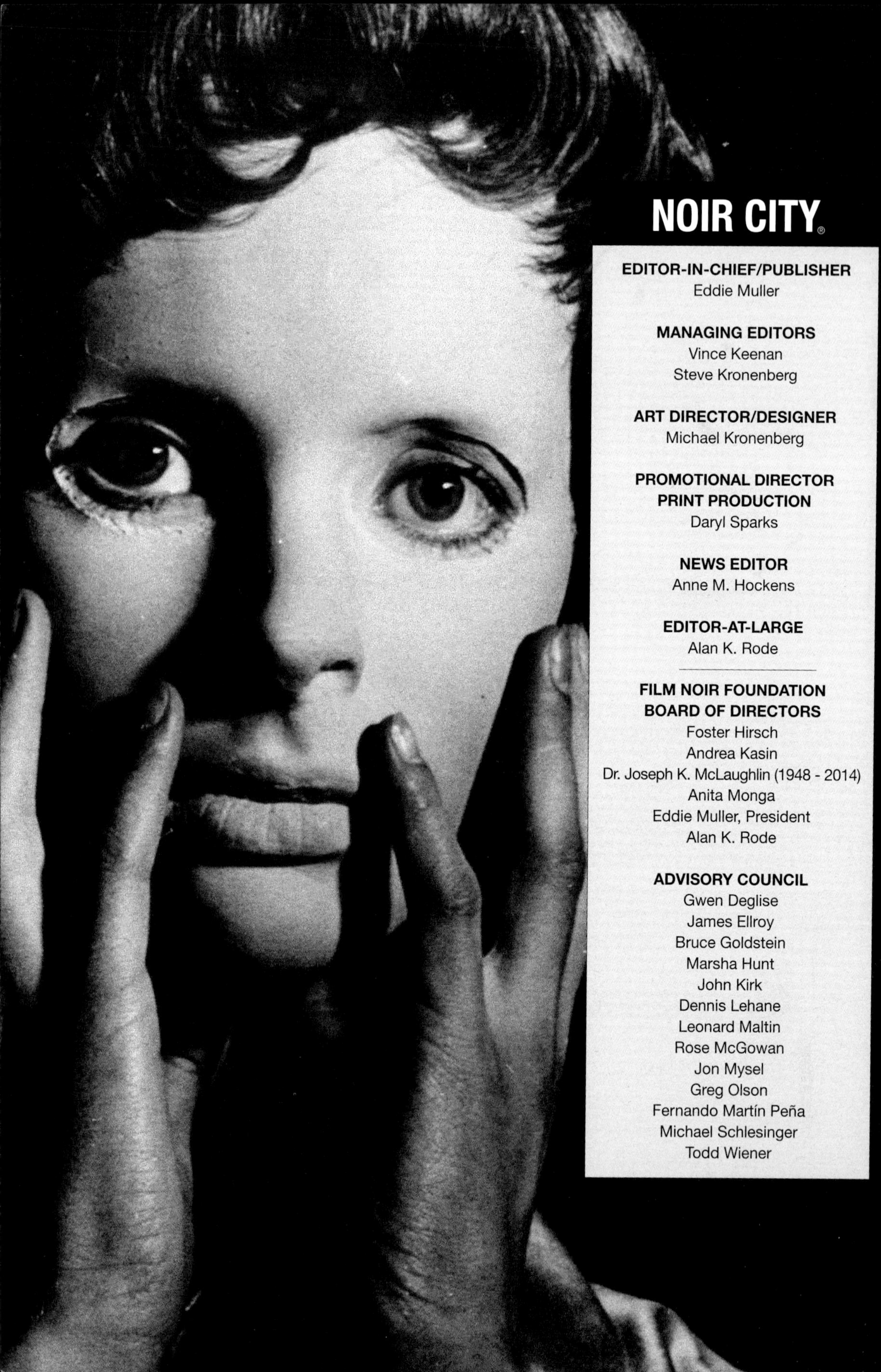

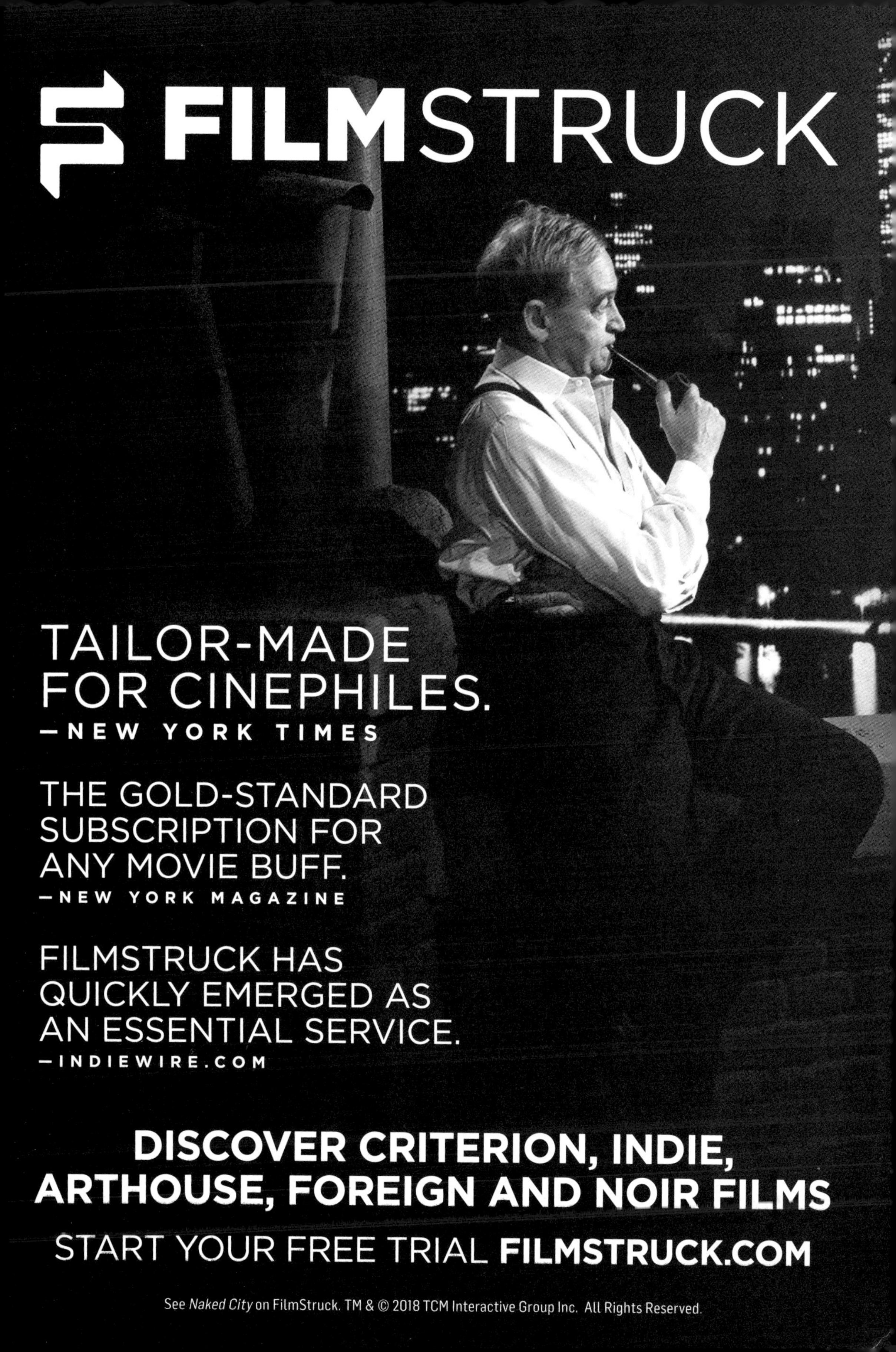
FILMSTRUCK
TAILOR-MADE FOR CINEPHILES.
—NEW YORK TIMES
THE GOLD-STANDARD SUBSCRIPTION FOR ANY MOVIE BUFF.
—NEW YORK MAGAZINE
FILMSTRUCK HAS QUICKLY EMERGED AS AN ESSENTIAL SERVICE.
—INDIEWIRE.COM
DISCOVER CRITERION, INDIE, ARTHOUSE, FOREIGN AND NOIR FILMS
START YOUR FREE TRIAL FILMSTRUCK.COM
See Naked City on FilmStruck. TM & © 2018 TCM Interactive Group Inc. All Rights Reserved.

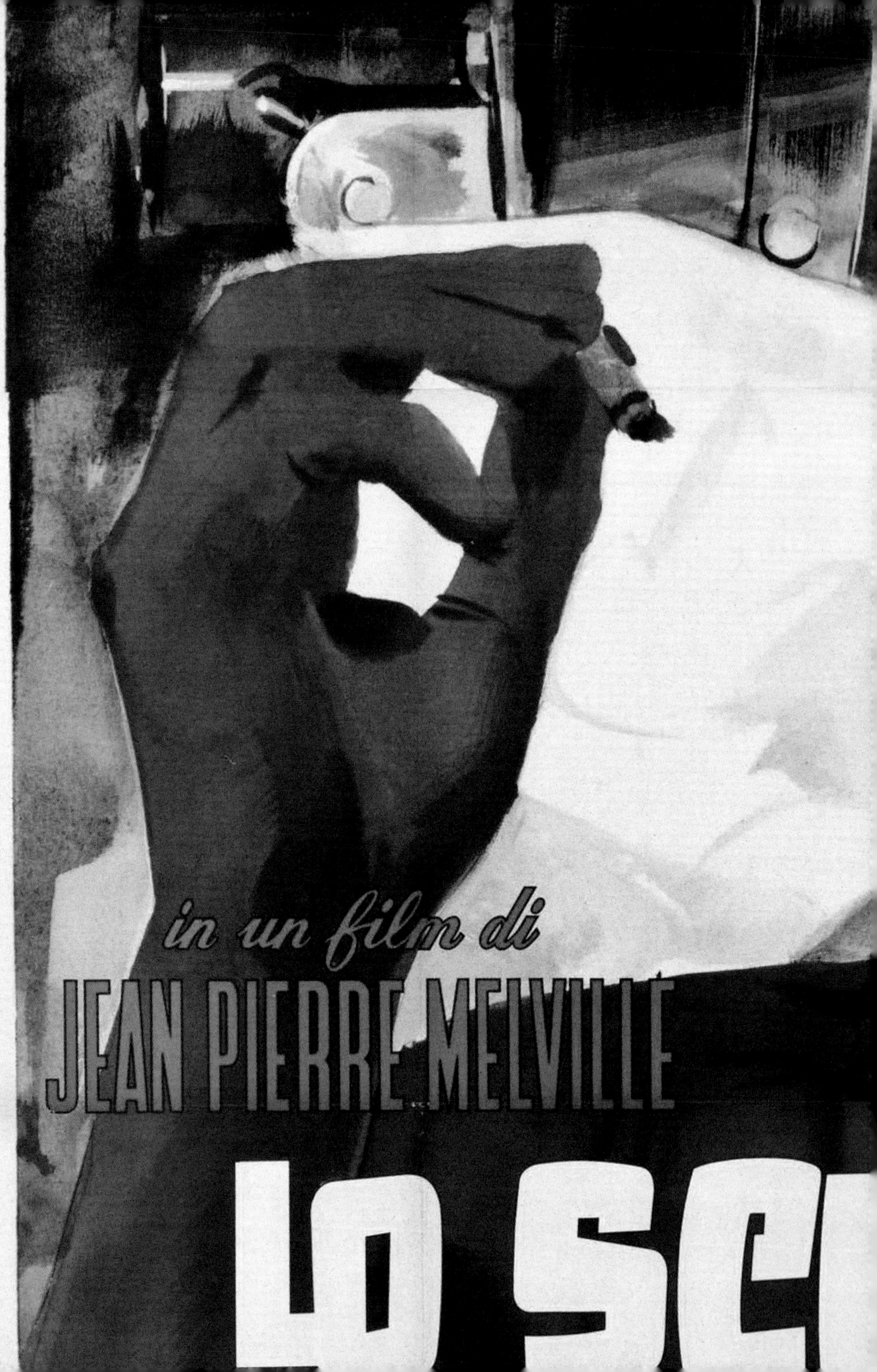

in un film di
JEAN PIERRE MELVILLE
LO SC

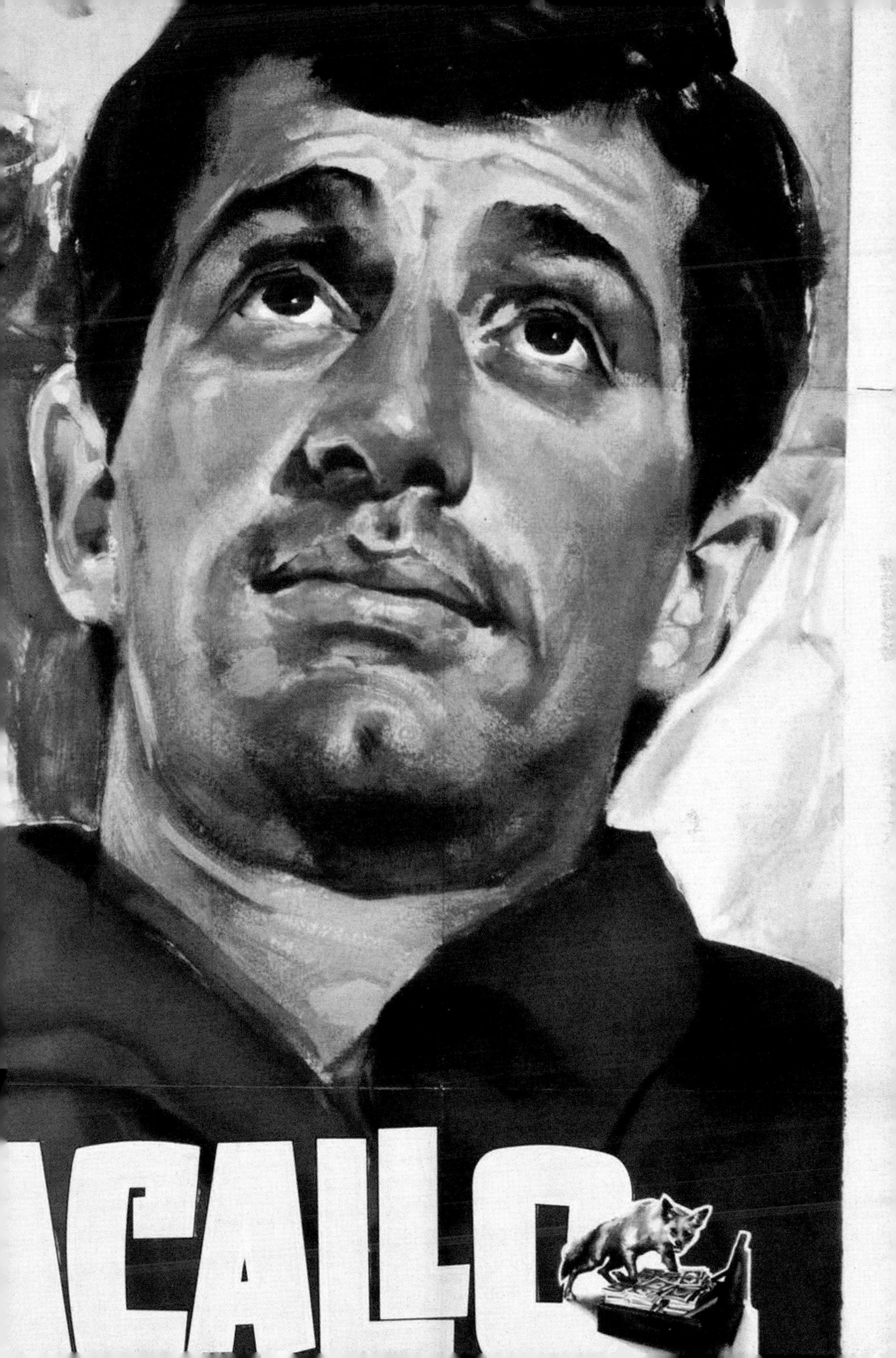
CALLO

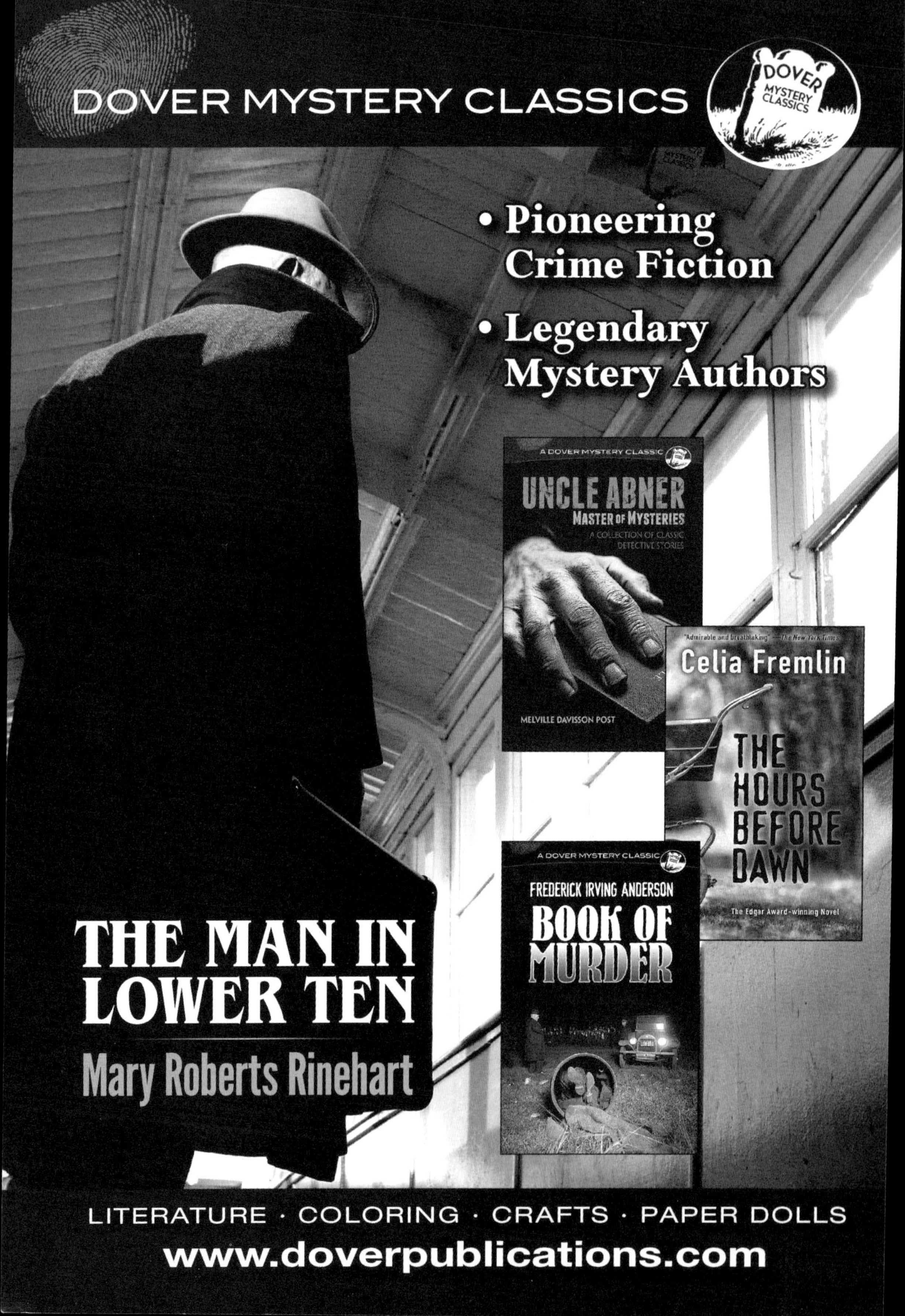
DOVER MYSTERY CLASSICS
• Pioneering Crime Fiction
• Legendary Mystery Authors
A DOVER MYSTERY CLASSIC
UNCLE ABNER
MASTER OF MYSTERIES
A COLLECTION OF CLASSIC DETECTIVE STORIES
MELVILLE DAVISSON POST
"Admirable and breathtaking" —The New York Times
Celia Fremlin
THE HOURS BEFORE DAWN
The Edgar Award-winning Novel
A DOVER MYSTERY CLASSIC
FREDERICK IRVING ANDERSON
BOOK OF MURDER
THE MAN IN LOWER TEN
Mary Roberts Rinehart
LITERATURE · COLORING · CRAFTS · PAPER DOLLS
www.doverpublications.com

TABLE OF CONTENTS

ESSAYS

PROFILES

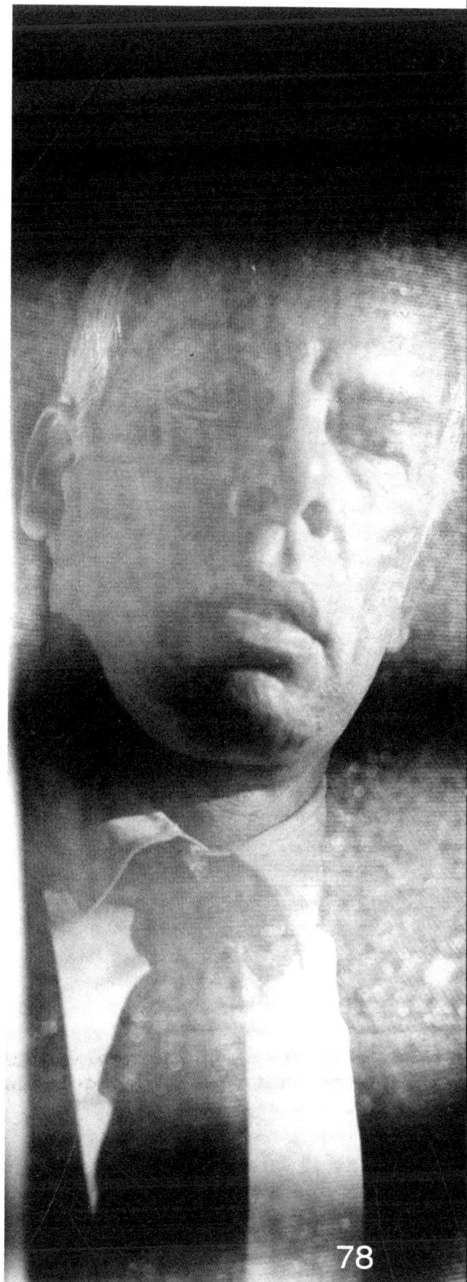

78

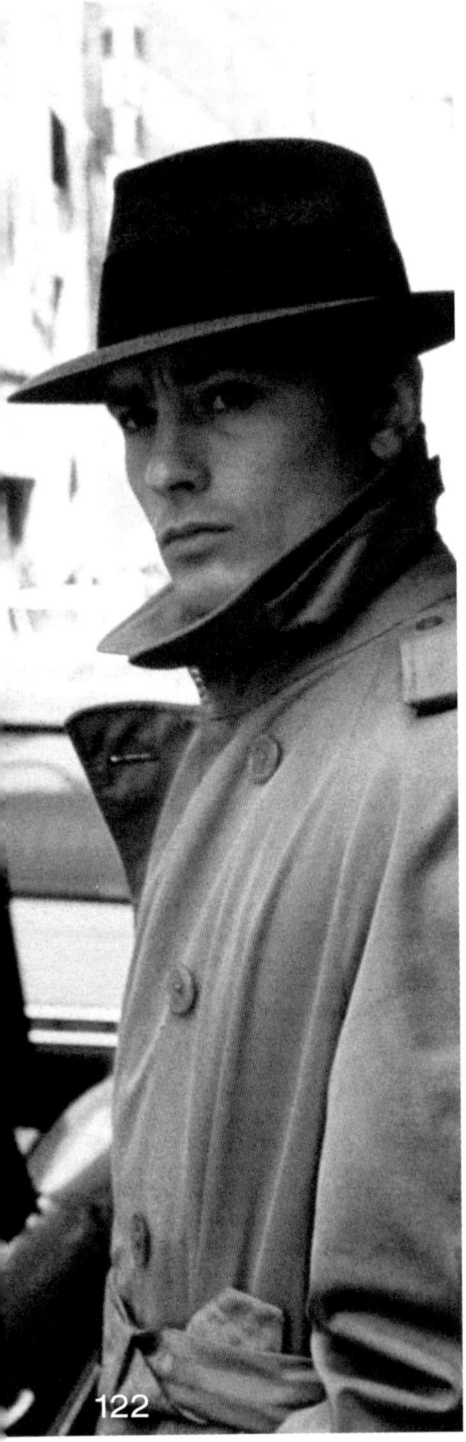
122

INTERVIEWS

APPRECIATIONS

BOOK vs. FILM

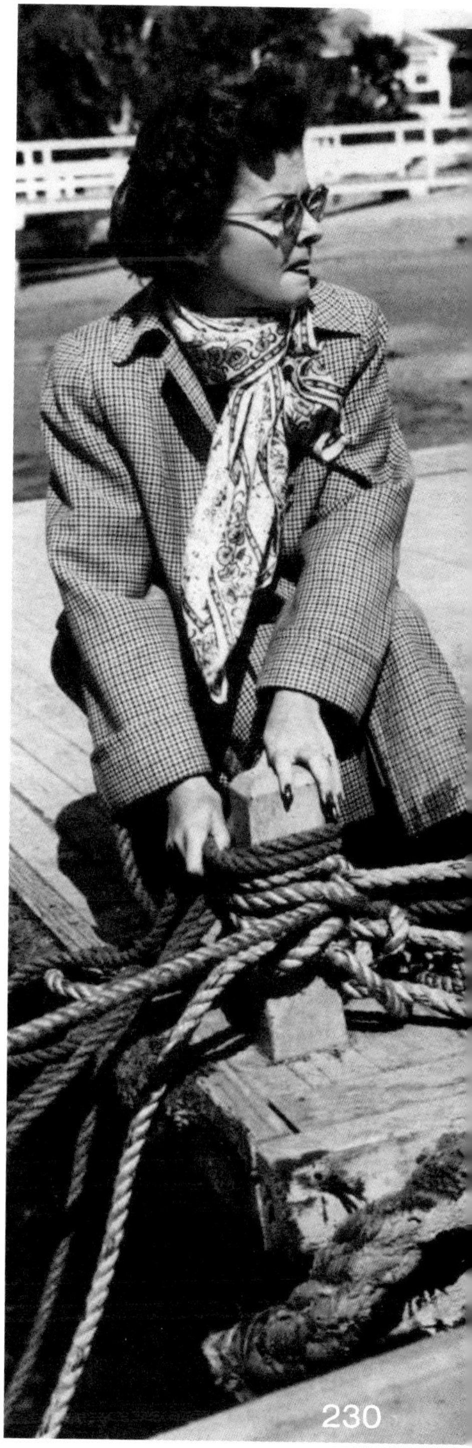

230

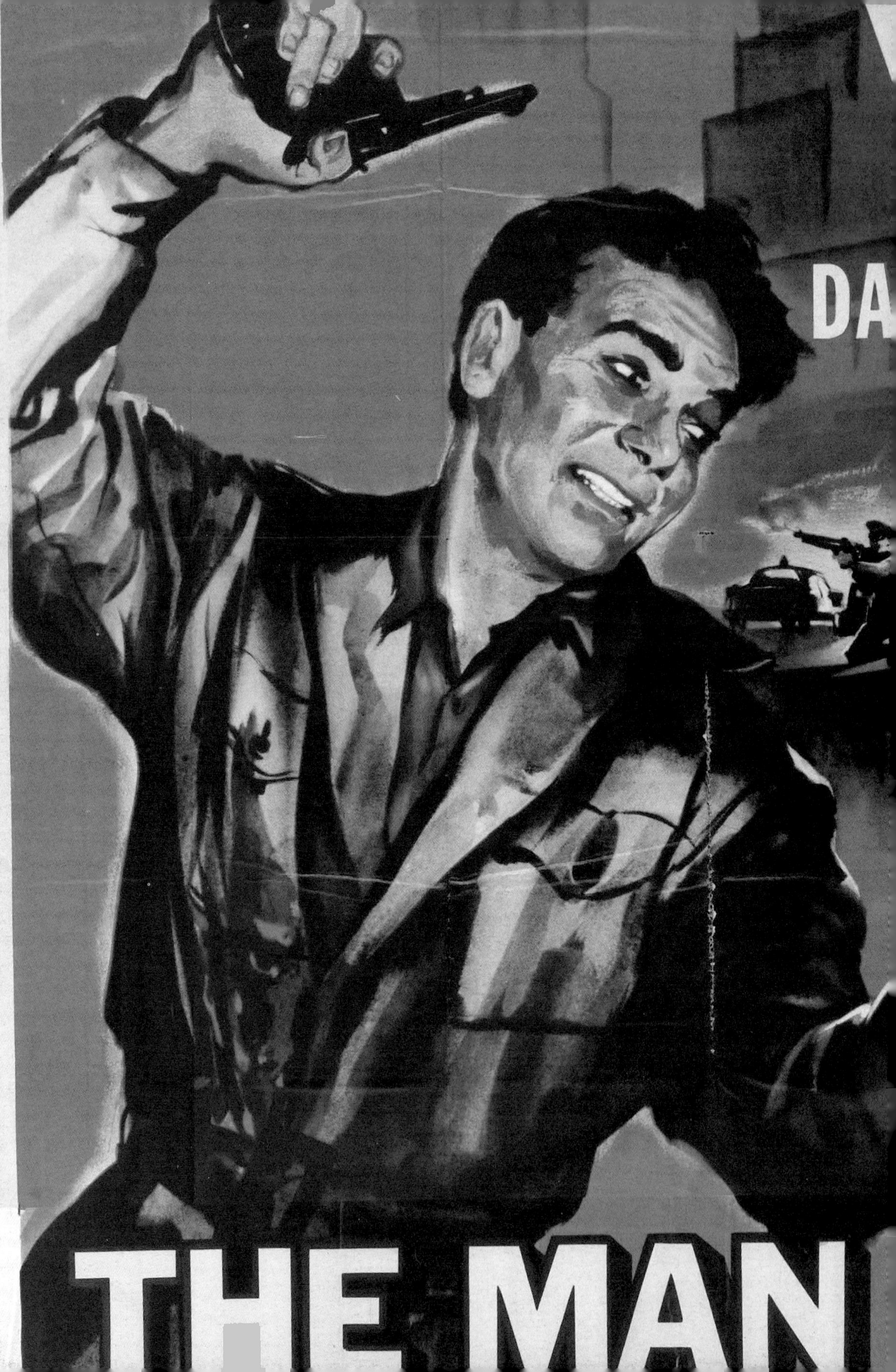
DA
THE MAN

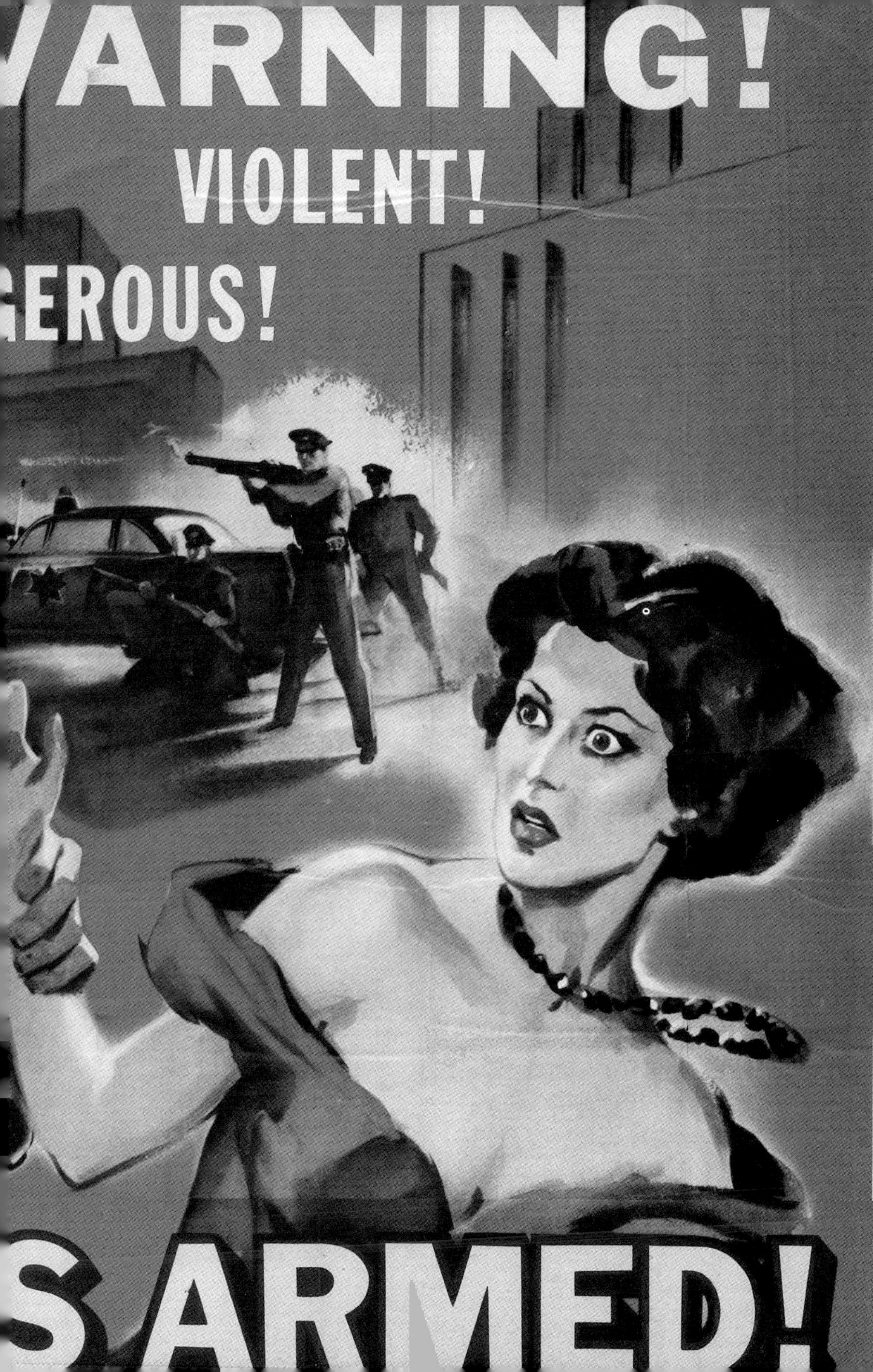

VARNING!
VIOLENT!
GEROUS!
S ARMED!

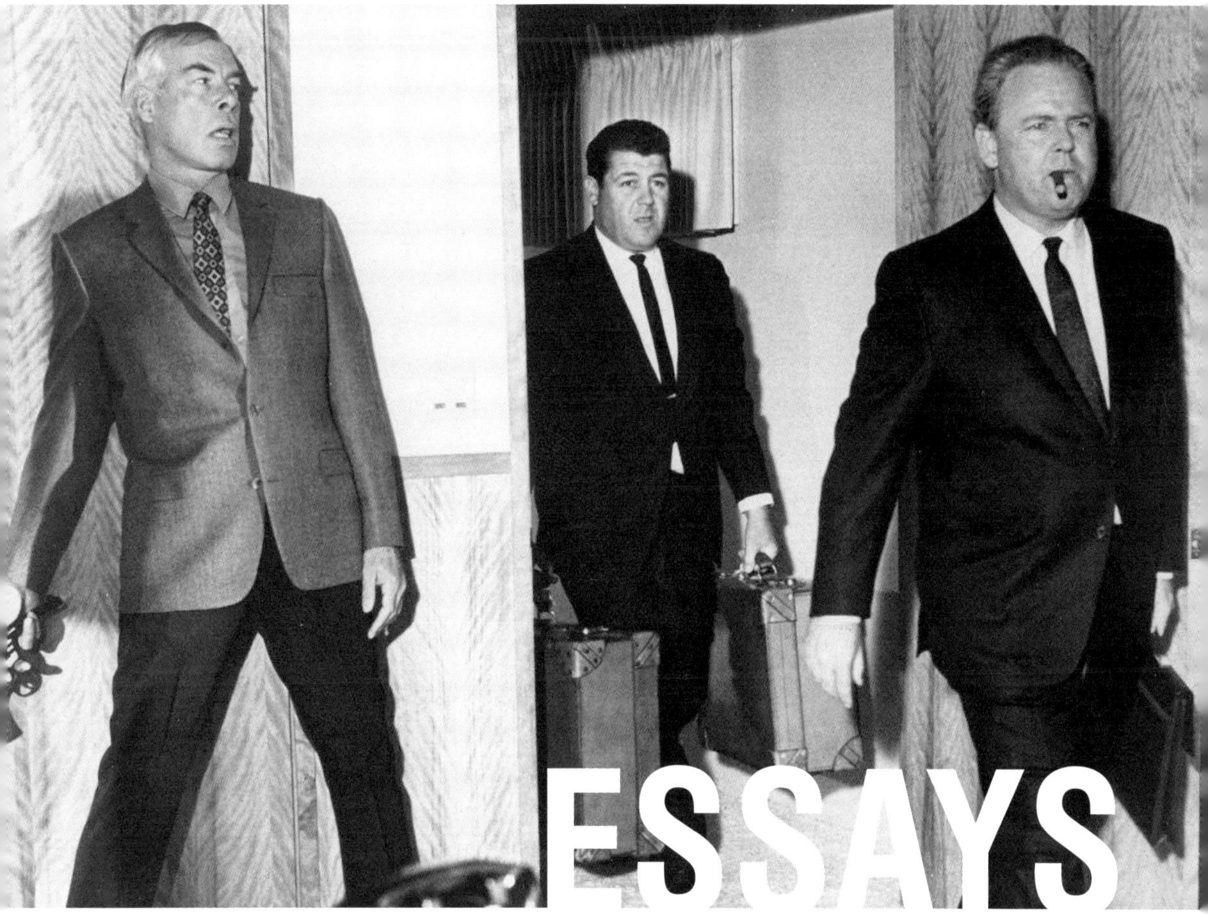

ESSAYS

SECTION ONE

HEADSHRI

PSYCHIATRISTS AS VILLAINS, ON

Sharon Knolle

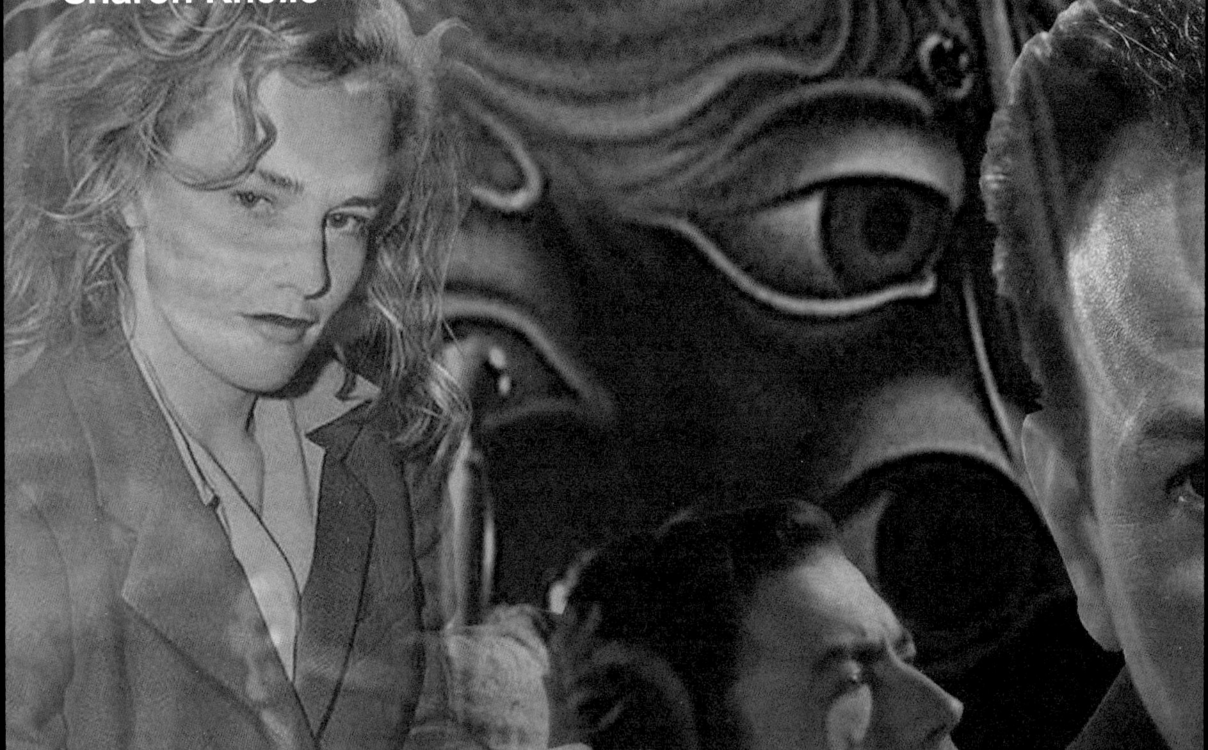

"Nothing appears more desperately urban than psychoanalysis, that theory and therapy invented by and for citified bourgeois," wrote Sigmund Freud's biographer Peter Gay. Freud's theory of what lurks in the darkest parts of the psyche forever changed what humans thought of themselves and their fellow man. The idea that we are secretly ruled by our subconscious would become an integral part of film noir. Neurotic murderesses and sociopaths with Oedipal complexes, like *White Heat*'s Cody Jarrett, ran wild in the noir landscape, the id writ large.

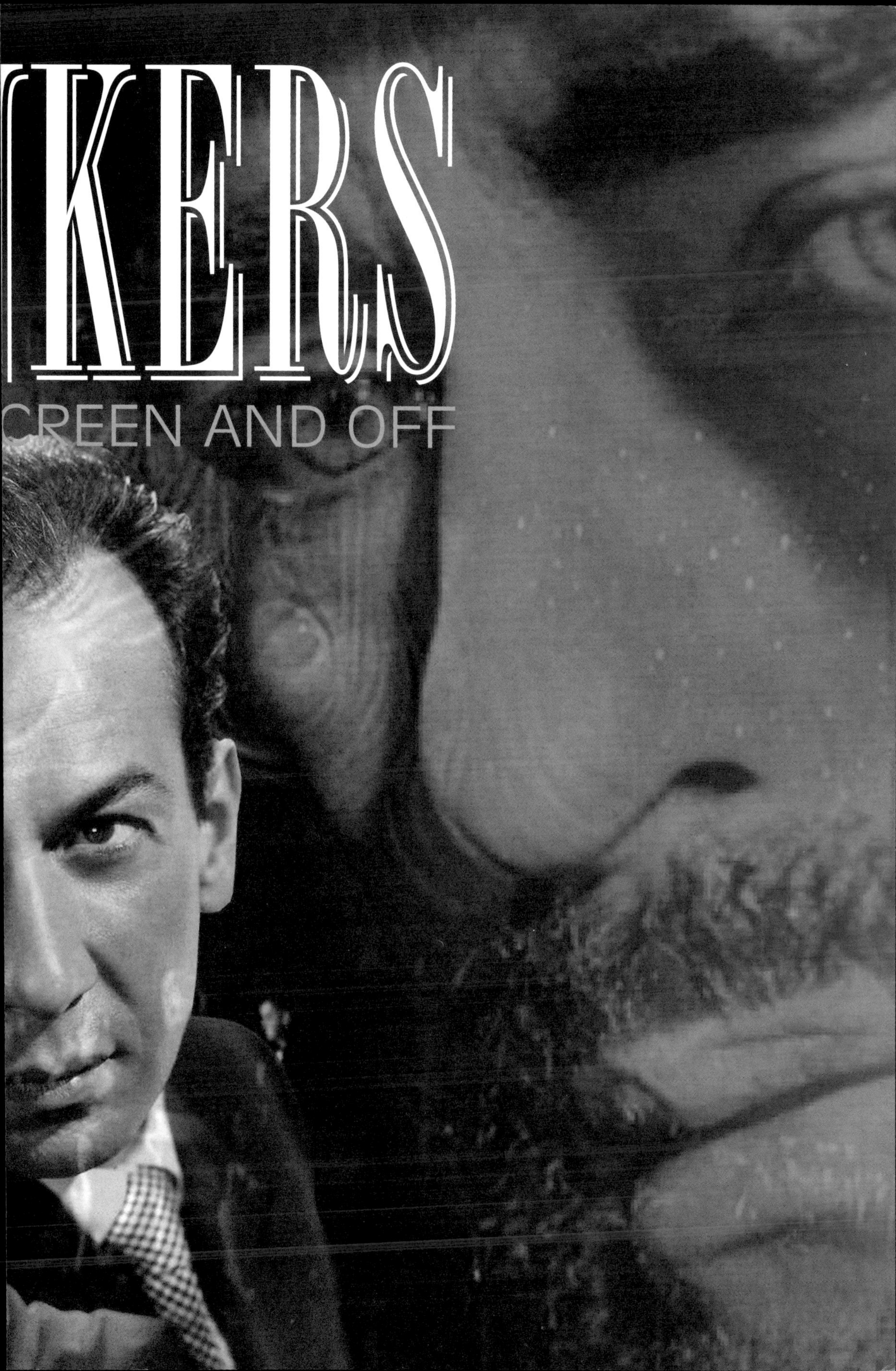
KERS
CREEN AND OFF

Freud would not only start a revolution in psychiatry, psychoanalysis would become so popular in the mid-twentieth century that it became unthinkable for an actor to *not* be in therapy. Rod Steiger, who played an analyst trying to rehabilitate a pedophile in 1961's *The Mark*, declared, "In 1950s New York, if you didn't go to an analyst, you were sick. Everybody had to go so they could sit at Sardi's and say, 'My analyst is better than your analyst.'"

Postwar Hollywood seized upon the psychoanalytic trend: Directors used psychoanalysis to get young actresses into bed and actors such as Kirk Douglas eagerly shared the details of their latest sessions during romantic trysts. Studios used analysts to keep wayward actors in line. During the Red Scare of the '50s, therapists who knew their patients' darkest secrets reportedly encouraged them to rat on their friends.

Within the wave of European émigrés who fled the Nazis, such as Fritz Lang and Conrad Veidt, came a wave of displaced psychoanalysts, many of them to be embraced by the Hollywood elite.

One of the early adopters of the cult of psychoanalysis was Adeline Jaffe Schulberg, the well-connected sister of agent Sam Jaffe and mother of Budd Schulberg, Oscar®-winning screenwriter of 1954's *On the Waterfront*. At her Hancock Park mansion, "moviemakers and analysts would regularly rub elbows at lavish dinner parties and intimate soirees," according to *Hollywood on the Couch* (by Stephen Farber and Marc Green).

Quick to join the Freudian flock were *Citizen Kane* screenwriter Herman Mankiewicz and his producer-director brother Joseph. Herman saw Ernst Simmel, a protégé of Freud's and an expert on addictive behaviors. Herman, at first, found analysis helped his alcoholism and jealousy of his brother Louis, but eventually he walked away "the same neurotic, self-destructive alcoholic" he had been when he started therapy. According to his nephew Tom, he quit Simmel with a flourish, declaring, "You're a quack. And, oh, by the way—I never mentioned that I have a sister and I hate her, too."

The most well-known psychoanalysts were nearly as famous as their clients, and often far more colorful. In the late '40s, after a series of failed romances, Celeste Holm saw Frances Deri, who was referred to as "Madame Deri." Holm recalled, "She looked just like a Buddha. She had that German hairdo that's really a Marine cut—straight across the top. She smoked cigarettes with a long wire holder in that German way. I came in to see her and her first words were, "You don't need to be entertaining in here."

Then there was Ukrainian Gregory Zilboorg, who wore a black cape and sported an enormous mustache. The leader of the New York Psychoanalytic Association, he was called "a first-class phony" by his colleagues. He eventually was investigated for unethical practices, but the charges were dropped, partly because no one wanted to give the burgeoning movement a bad name. He was adored by patients, however, including George Gershwin and Lillian Hellman, who named her poodle after him.

The 1941 Broadway musical *Lady in the Dark*, in which a career woman undergoes analysis and learns her trouble is that she has no man in her life—was allegedly based on Moss Hart's sessions with Zilboorg. Other sources put Hart in therapy with Zilboorg's biggest rival, New York-born Lawrence S. Kubie, whose specialty was "curing" homosexuality. Hart, who eventually married and had children, was Kubie's greatest "success story," although associates claimed Hart was miserable. Said Celeste Holm, "Moss was a homosexual and didn't want to be—and when he was through with Dr. Kubie, he wasn't."

Among the biggest power players in the headshrinking set was Russian-born May Romm, who included producer David O. Selznick among her clients. He credited her for curing his depression after seeing her daily for several weeks. In 1944, he produced

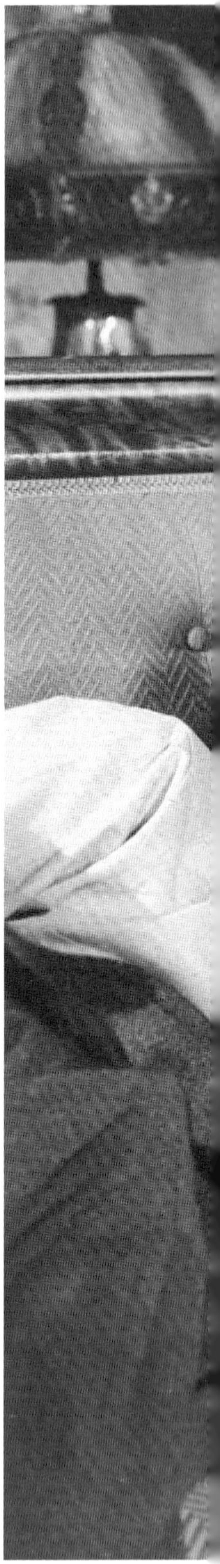

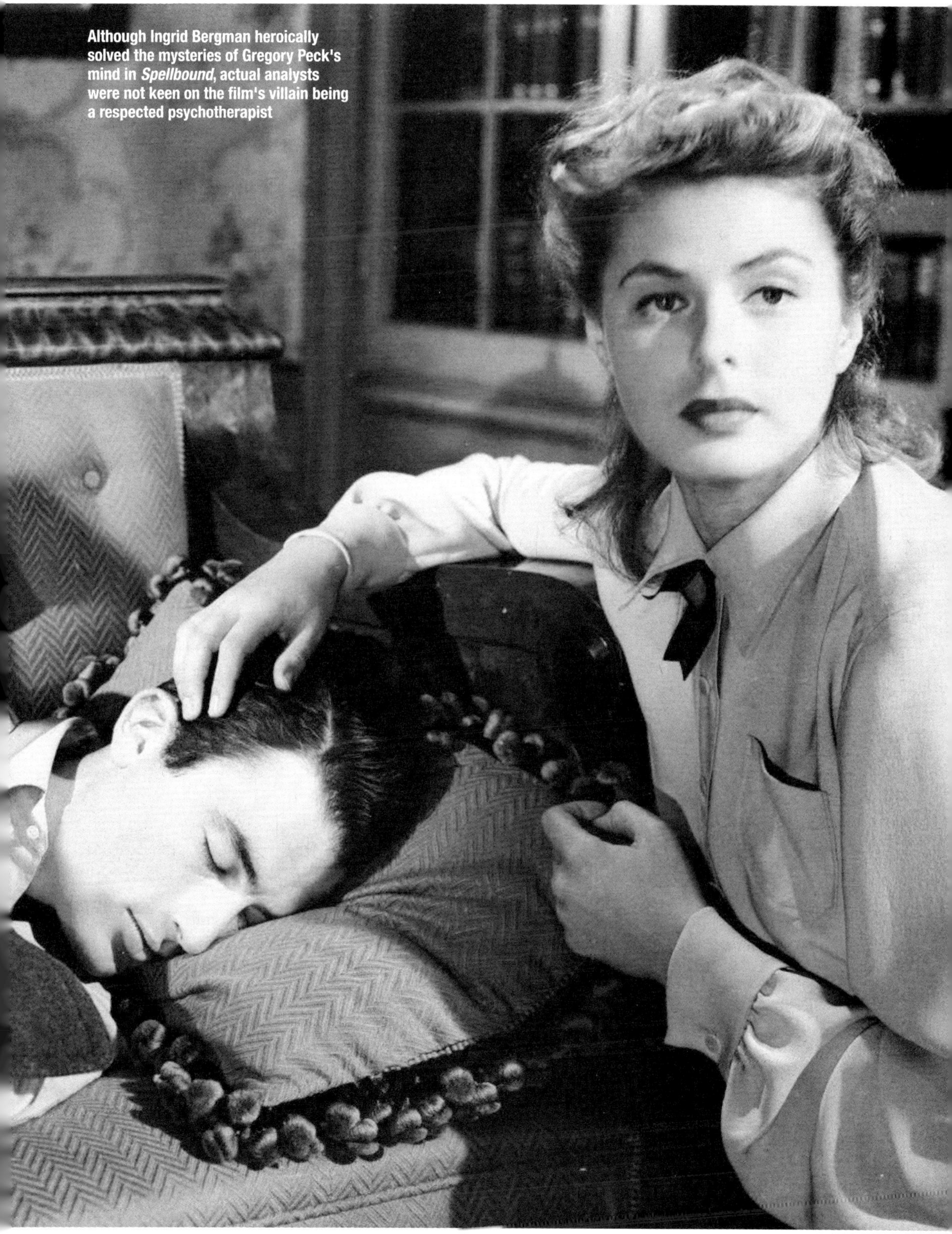

Although Ingrid Bergman heroically solved the mysteries of Gregory Peck's mind in *Spellbound*, actual analysts were not keen on the film's villain being a respected psychotherapist

Alfred Hitchcock's ode to psychoanalysis, *Spellbound.* Romm received credit as "Psychiatric Advisor."

"Her influence sometimes rivaled that of the actors, directors and producers she was treating... she was the first analyst to be embraced as a crony by the Tinseltown rajahs," note Farber and Green. Her clients included Robert Taylor, Ava Gardner, Edward G. Robinson, and Jennifer Jones, Selznick's second wife.

Although Ingrid Bergman heroically diagnoses the root of Gregory Peck's neurosis in *Spellbound* and reveals the true murderer, the psychiatric community and its adherents were appalled when the real killer was revealed to be a respected analyst.

Famed bandleader and ladies' man Artie Shaw adored Romm, but disapproved so strongly of her lending her name to *Spellbound* that, according to Farber and Green, he stopped seeing her. Although that may have simply been an excuse to quit therapy since she intended to talk him out of marrying Ava Gardner, which Shaw admitted after the marriage to Gardner fell apart.

Joseph L. Mankiewicz was so incensed about Romm's involvement with *Spellbound* that he alerted one of the Grand Poobahs of Hollywood shrinks, Karl Menninger, who fired off blistering memos to Romm and Selznick. Romm defended her participation, arguing, "Had I not done so, it would have been produced in a much more undesirable form than it is now."

Dr. Frederick Hacker, a Viennese émigré, received the warm backing of Joseph Mankiewicz after he befriended the director's wife while in training at the Menninger Clinic in Kansas, where recalcitrant actors and offspring were often shipped for straightening out. Once in Beverly Hills, he founded the Hacker Clinic and was knee-deep in well-heeled clients. "Hacker was the first analyst to become a millionaire," said rival Dr. Martin Grotjahn, whose clients included Vivien Leigh, and who advocated group therapy for actors—as long as there was only one *star* per group.

Robert Mitchum was sent to Hacker after declining to prosecute the manager who had drained his bank account. "My mother and sister, doubting my sanity, implored the cooperation of my wife in suggesting a visit to a psychiatrist," recalled the actor. And so he found himself on the couch of Dr. Hacker, who reminded him of character actor Walter Slezak.

According to Mitchum's biographer Lee Server, Hacker's advice may have been partially responsible for the actor's famous "Baby, I don't care" attitude: "You suffer from a state of over-amiability, in which failure to please everyone creates a condition of self-reproach," Hacker told the actor. "You are addicted to the good will of people and I suggest that you risk their displeasure by learning to say, 'No.'" Once home, Mitchum told his family: "He said I should tell you all to go shit in your hats."

Hacker's ministrations proved fatal for another client, Robert Walker. Despondent after wife Jennifer Jones left him for David O. Selznick, Walker took to drinking heavily and his behavior became wildly erratic. In 1948, he was arrested for drunk and disorderly conduct. Dore Schary, head of production at MGM where Walker was under contract, gave him an ultimatum: If he did not submit to psychiatric treatment at the Menninger Clinic in Kansas, he would be fired. He agreed to the treatment, then returned to California and began sessions with Dr. Hacker.

On August 28, 1951, Hacker arrived at Walker's Brentwood home and found the actor ranting incoherently. He administered a shot of sodium amytal to calm him down. Walker immediately went into shock and died. Hacker had previously given Walker the same injection, but according to Farber and Green's account, the doctor had failed to determine the level of barbiturates already in Walker's system.

Shockingly, there was no investigation. Dr. Alex Rogawski, a prominent analyst who had grown up with Hacker in Vienna, was less circumspect: "Hacker killed Robert Walker. He actually killed him. But a doctor could get away with it back then. Today you would have a nice lawsuit."

Adds Dr. Leo Rangell, "That case didn't do Hacker any harm. It almost worked to his advantage, on the premise that any publicity is good publicity." (Rangell went on to write *The Mind of Watergate: An Exploration of the Compromise of Integrity* about the American public's tendency to be "gullible or easily seduced, and susceptible to leaders of questionable character.")

Walker's devastated son, then 11, was—unimaginably—sent to therapy with none other than Frederick Hacker, the man who'd given his father the fatal shot. "I didn't know Hacker had anything to do with my

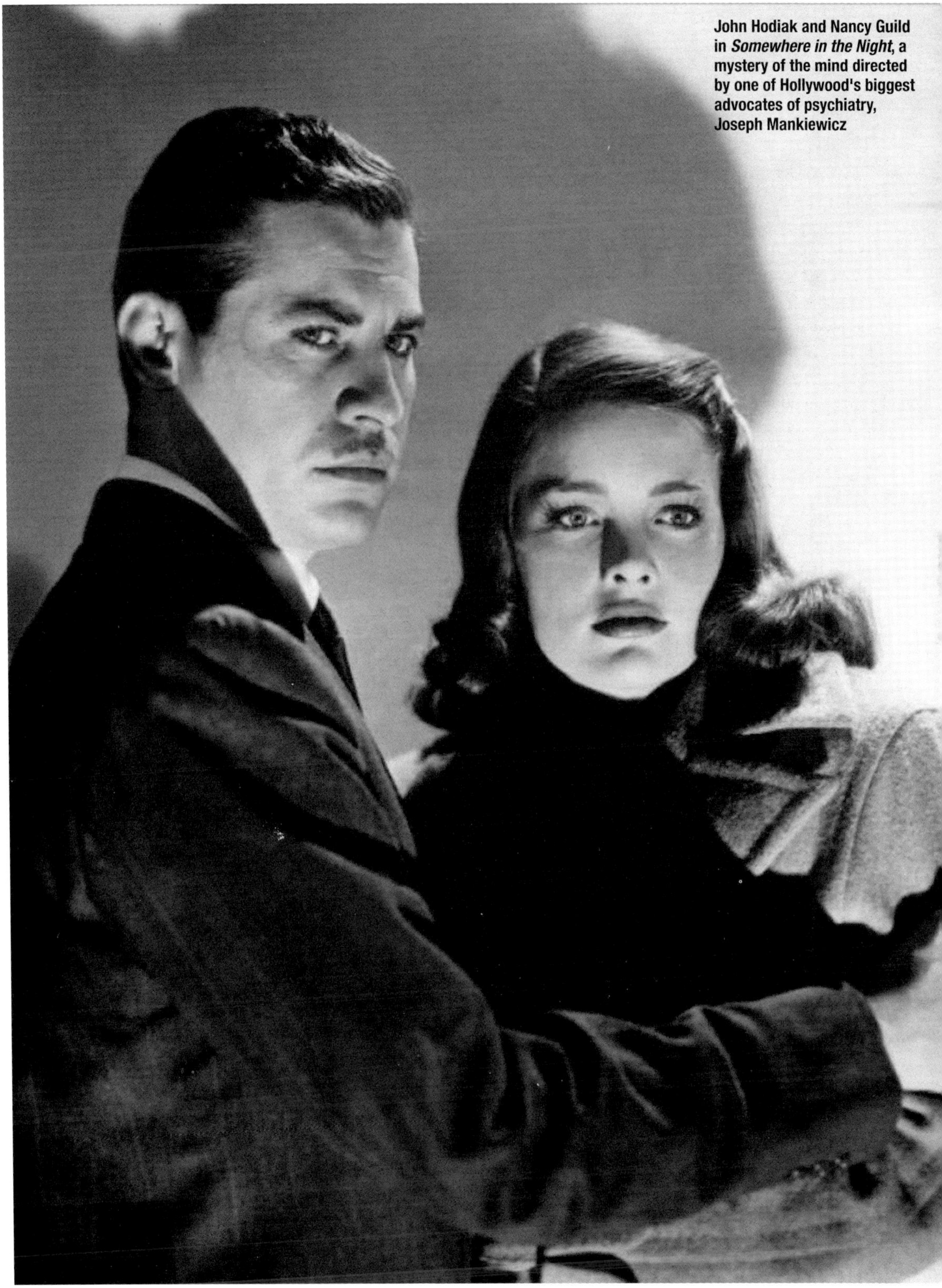

John Hodiak and Nancy Guild in *Somewhere in the Night*, a mystery of the mind directed by one of Hollywood's biggest advocates of psychiatry, Joseph Mankiewicz father's death," Walker Jr. said. "He gave me a few psychological tests. I remember thinking even then that he seemed like a pompous know-it-all. But I don't blame him for what happened to my father. I just feel he didn't know any better."

The line between professional and private lives was crossed regularly: Artie Shaw briefly dated Dorothy Colodny, the daughter of his analyst, May Romm. Romm also analyzed Selznick's wife, Irene, who revealed in her autobiography that Romm saw nothing wrong in breaking client confidentiality and discussing her other clients, including Irene's sister. The two were very cozy: Romm was always at the Selznick's—so much so that son Daniel said, "I assumed all psychiatrists were like a part of the family."

According to son Christopher, Joe Mankiewicz' years of analysis not only failed to cure his philandering, but became a technique to seduce women. Among the actresses he persuaded to try psychiatry were Judy Garland, with whom he had an affair in the '40s. First, he bought her books on Freud, then he introduced her to Karl Menninger. Eventually, she ended up in therapy with Ernst Simmel, but preferred Dr. Herbert Kupper who made house calls.

Christopher Mankiewicz told Farber and Green, "My father believed passionately in Freud and in psychiatry. He once confessed to me that he actually wanted to be a psychiatrist but couldn't pass the premed courses at Columbia. So he became a director instead, which was the next best thing. Psychiatry was his only religion."

The director of *All About Eve* (1950) and *Five Fingers* (1952) also applied psychoanalytic techniques while directing: Nancy Guild, whom he directed in the 1946 amnesia noir *Somewhere in the Night*, recalled that he spent a few months with her before production learning the intimate details of her childhood and teenage years. When a problem arose on set, the director "would sit with me for half an hour reminding me of things I'd told him about myself... He was psychoanalyzing me all through the picture, breaking down my inhibitions."

Evelyn Keyes, star of *The Prowler* (1951) and *99 River Street* (1953), began therapy on the suggestion of lover Kirk Douglas. As she wrote in her autobiography, "Kirk was responsible for two very important decisions in my life: I went to a psychoanalyst and I broke my contract with Columbia. Kirk, just parted from his wife, with two small sons to worry about,

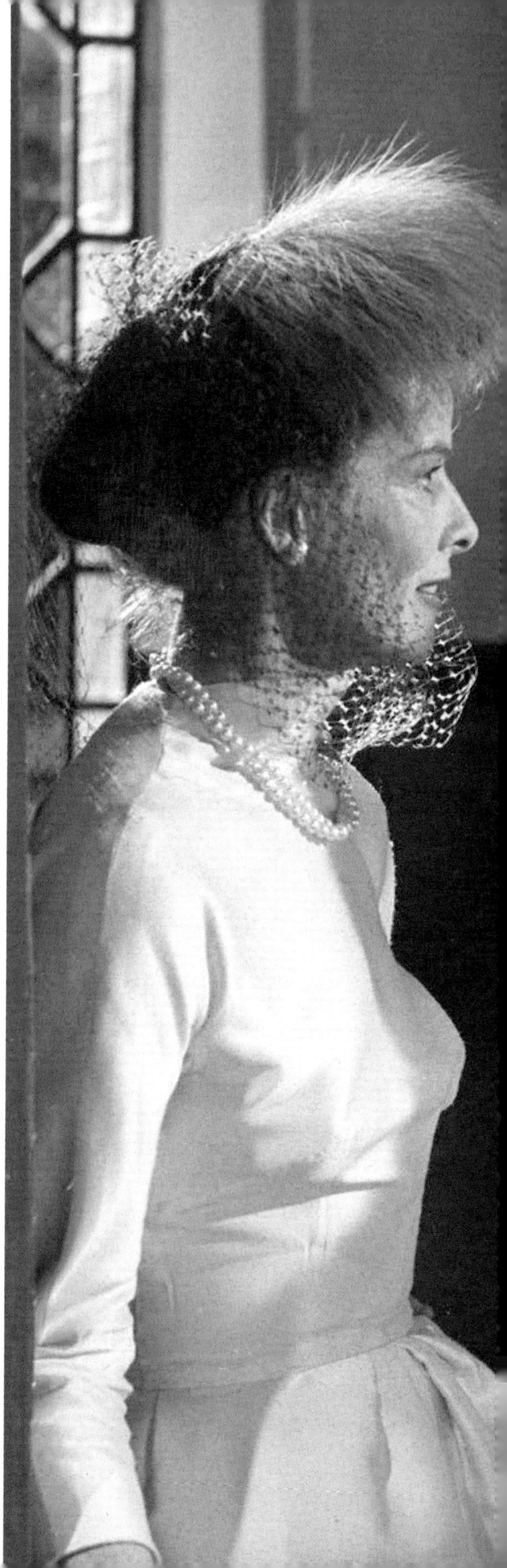

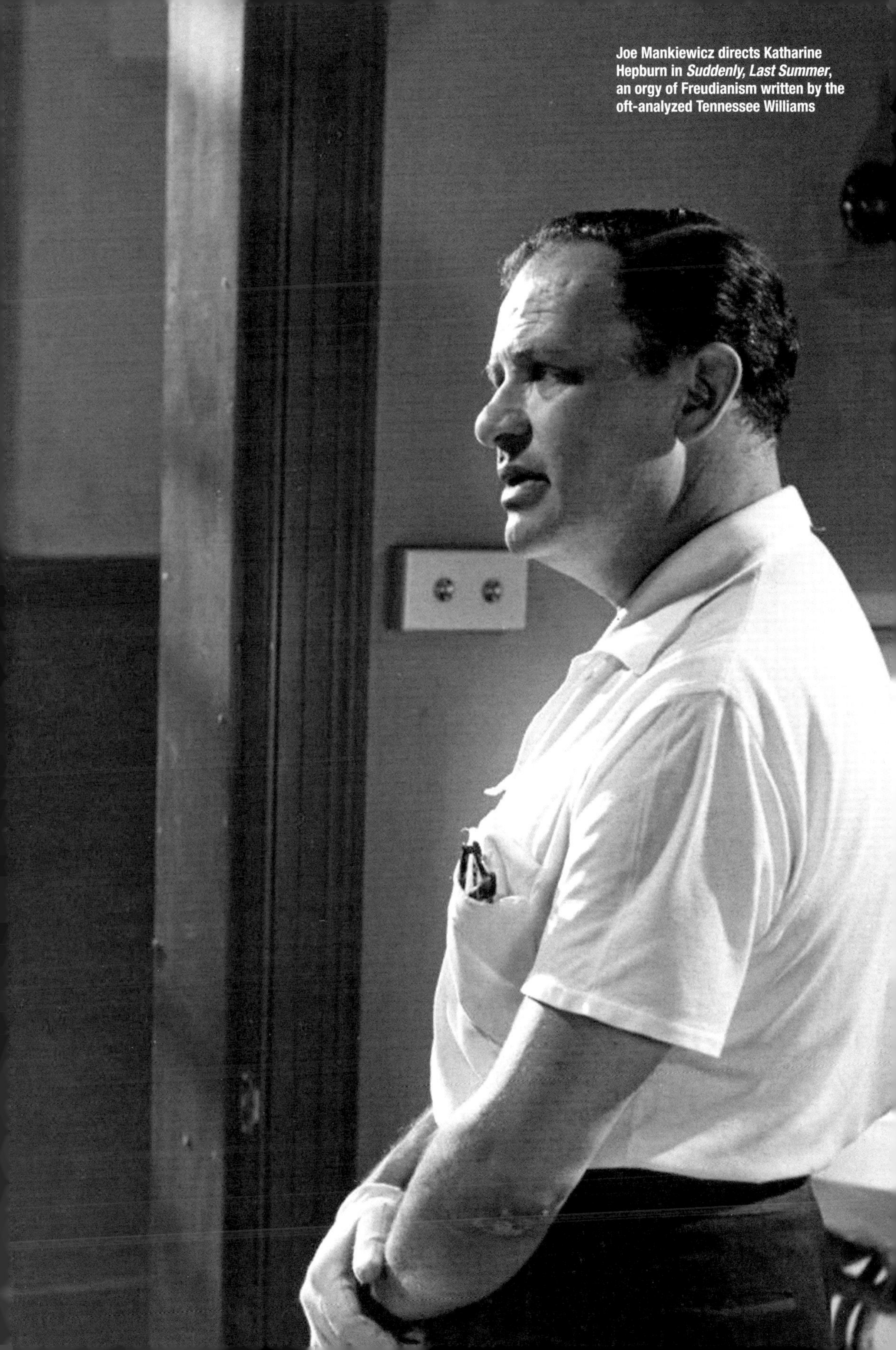

Joe Mankiewicz directs Katharine Hepburn in *Suddenly, Last Summer*, an orgy of Freudianism written by the oft-analyzed Tennessee Williams already knowing that success wasn't synonymous with happiness, was looking for it on an analyst's couch. I somehow became an extension of his treatment." She relates how he'd go to her place and discuss his session with her, then bring her comments back to his analyst. "I envied him the doctor to talk to," she noted wryly.

She was less happy with her own therapy. "Going to the analyst didn't offer the relief I had anticipated, nor the joy I thought to have talking about myself to a paid listener. On the contrary. The way he asked the simplest questions was like an attack, as if he were after me. How do you feel about your mother? Brother? Sisters? Well, how should I feel, I love them, no? Doesn't everybody?"

Evelyn finally quit analysis when offered a role in another country: "Having got rid of my original roots, three husbands and one studio, one lousy doctor was a cinch."

Soul-searching was an integral part of The Method created by Lee Strasberg at the Actors Studio in New York. Bruce Dern, who studied with Strasberg in the '50s, recalls, "When Lee would do his comments on a scene, and he would sense a resistance in dealing with certain emotions, he would literally write vocal prescriptions for analysis... He would say, 'You should see a doctor.... Or he might ask, 'Are you in therapy? Are you going to a psychiatrist? Who is it?' Then Dane Clark or Eli Wallach might raise his hand and ask, 'Is he on Fifty-Seventh Street?' At the time I hadn't been in analysis and I wasn't sure if it was an intrusion or an invasion of an actor's privacy."

"Analysts came to our sessions," Frank Corsaro, who followed Strasberg as the director of the Actors Studio told Farber and Green, "and I remember one of them said, 'You get results much more quickly than we do.' Some actors come to the Actors Studio almost for therapy."

Anne Bancroft, who filmed noirs *Don't Bother to Knock* (1952), *The Naked Street* (1955), and *Nightfall* (1957) before netting an Oscar for 1962's *The Miracle Worker*, credited her success to the Actors Studio and her six years of psychoanalysis, saying, perhaps only half jokingly, "The only men in my life from now on will be my father, my agent, my press agent and my psychiatrist."

Kubie, the doctor who had "cured" Moss Hart of his homosexuality, also counseled Tennessee Williams in 1957. He didn't succeed in rewriting the playwright's sexual orientation, but he did get Williams to break up with the love of his life, Frank Merlo. Screenwriter Arthur Laurents says, "I don't think Tennessee ever got over the guilt of abandoning him."

Williams talked about his analysis in a 1958 *New York Herald Tribune* interview, crediting therapy with dramatically diminishing his claustrophobia and panic attacks. After the failure of his play *Orpheus Descending*, his depression was so great that friends Marlon Brando, Elia Kazan, and Irene Selznick urged him to consult a psychoanalyst.

He underwent therapy 50 minutes a day, five days a week at the office of his analyst. Williams put his experiences into the 1958 play *Suddenly, Last Summer,* which became the 1959 Joseph Mankiewicz film starring Elizabeth Taylor, Montgomery Clift, and Katharine Hepburn. The shocking play contained references not just to homosexuality, but death by cannibalism and one of the most Oedipal mother-son relationships ever written, yet somehow it made it past the censors to the big screen.

At the film's crux is rich matriarch Hepburn's wish to have "babbling" niece Taylor lobotomized so the truth about her son's gruesome death will be kept hidden forever. The scenario recalls the sad true story of Frances Farmer, who shared the same bogus diagnosis—"dementia praecox"—with Taylor's character. (Popular legend has it that Farmer *was* lobotomized, a fate Taylor's character avoids thanks to the good doctor Clift and a dose of truth serum, but no one has been able to verify that the procedure was ever actually performed on the doomed actress.)

Tragically, Williams had more than Farmer's tabloid story to draw from: His own sister, Rose, underwent a lobotomy at his mother's orders. In a 1975 *New York Times* interview, Williams shared:

"[My sister] could have become quite well by now if they hadn't performed that goddam operation on her; she would have come back up to the surface.... My mother panicked, you know, because she said my sister had begun using four-letter words. 'Do anything! Don't let her talk like that,' mother cried."

The playwright explained, "But Rose wasn't doing that. Oh, she said things that four-letter words

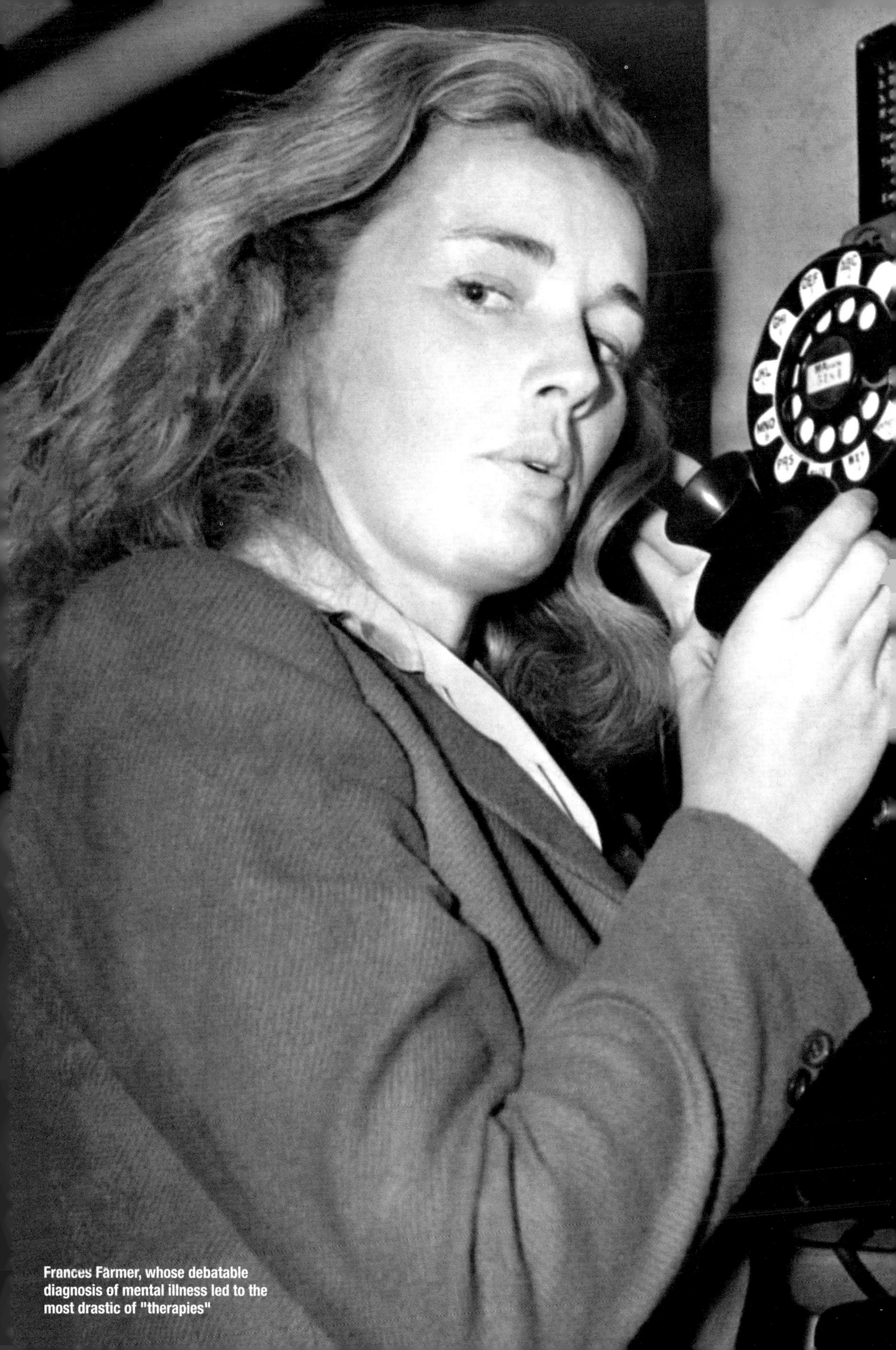

Frances Farmer, whose debatable diagnosis of mental illness led to the most drastic of "therapies"

say, but she put them in elegant language, like this: 'Mother, we girls at All Saints used to abuse ourselves with candles we stole from the chapel.' Mother couldn't bear it!" He added, dryly, "Mother's ninety now, and an inspiration to us all."

Williams ended the therapy after six months and later told his mother why he stopped seeing Kubie: "He hit me where it hurt most. He said I wrote cheap melodrama and nothing else."

Like Williams, Patricia Highsmith, the author of *Strangers on a Train* and the many Tom Ripley novels, sought therapy to "cure" being gay. The details of her short-lived analysis came to light with the release of *Carol*, the 2015 Todd Haynes film based on *The Price of Salt*, a lesbian love story she wrote under a pseudonym. The inspiration for the story came in 1948 when she took a job at the toy counter of Bloomingdale's in Manhattan to pay for her psychoanalysis. At the time, she was engaged to an author named Marc Brandel and was, as she later wrote, trying to "get myself into a condition to be married."

At the time, being gay was not only illegal, but was believed to be just as subversive—or possibly more so—than being a Communist. Senator Joe McCarthy not only targeted suspected Communists, but forced 91 suspected homosexuals to resign from the State Department. The year *The Price of Salt* was published, the first edition of the *Diagnostic and Statistical Manual of Mental Disorders* listed homosexuality as a "sociopathic personality disturbance."

One of the oddest—and shadiest—chapters in psychoanalysis concerns Ernest Philip Cohen, whose clients included Lloyd Bridges, John Garfield, and screenwriter Sylvia Richards. According to *Naming Names* author Victor Navasky, Cohen was also an FBI informant who talked his clients into cooperating with the HUAC hearings in the '50s. Navasky described Cohen, a former Communist, as "a master of manipulation operating at the murky crossroads where the mystique of Freud met the mystique of Marx."

Force of Evil director Abraham Polonsky firmly believed that Cohen had betrayed his clients: "I know he was reporting confidences to the FBI. There's no question about that. And he was turning patients into stool pigeons," he told Navasky.

Richards, whose credits include the 1947 noirs *Possessed* and *Secret Beyond the Door*, recalls that she got the same message from her boss, her therapist, and her lawyer: Cooperate with HUAC. "I was the sort of person who wanted to please my friends, please my analyst... I thought I was choosing my friends," she said of her decision to become an informant.

Sterling Hayden was likely talking about Cohen in his 1964 memoir *Wanderer* when he included a conversation with a doctor whom he blames for persuading him to name names: "If it hadn't been for you I wouldn't have turned into a stoolie for J. Edgar Hoover. I don't think you have the foggiest notion of the contempt I have had for myself since the day I did that thing."

In his book *Inquisition in Eden*, Hollywood Ten screenwriter Alvah Bessie wrote that two years after consulting an analyst, he learned the man "had worked with a great many Hollywood writers and actors ... at least six of his patients turned up at subsequent investigations of the industry and every one of them was a stool pigeon. It also appeared that the man was not a psychiatrist at all; he was not even a psychologist, but apparently he was an FBI man."

William Wheeler, the HUAC chief investigator, told Navasky that Cohen never shared his patients' names, but promised their full cooperation. According to Wheeler, Cohen said: "If you subpoena one of my patients, I'll try to condition him to testify."Navasky ask for clarification: "Condition or convince?"

"What's the difference? It was part of the therapy. The whole thing," Wheeler replied.

If the psychiatric community had been up in arms over *Spellbound*, its swoony romance and famous Salvador Dali dream sequence certainly helped make psychoanalysis more accessible to the masses. Freudian therapy had already provided the framework for light-hearted comedies, including 1938's *Carefree*, in which Ginger Rogers invents elaborate dreams to keep seeing analyst Fred Astaire, and Ernst Lubitsch's *That Uncertain Feeling* (1941), where Merle Oberon's socialite undergoes analysis to cure a case of the hiccups—but with noir it became serious stuff.

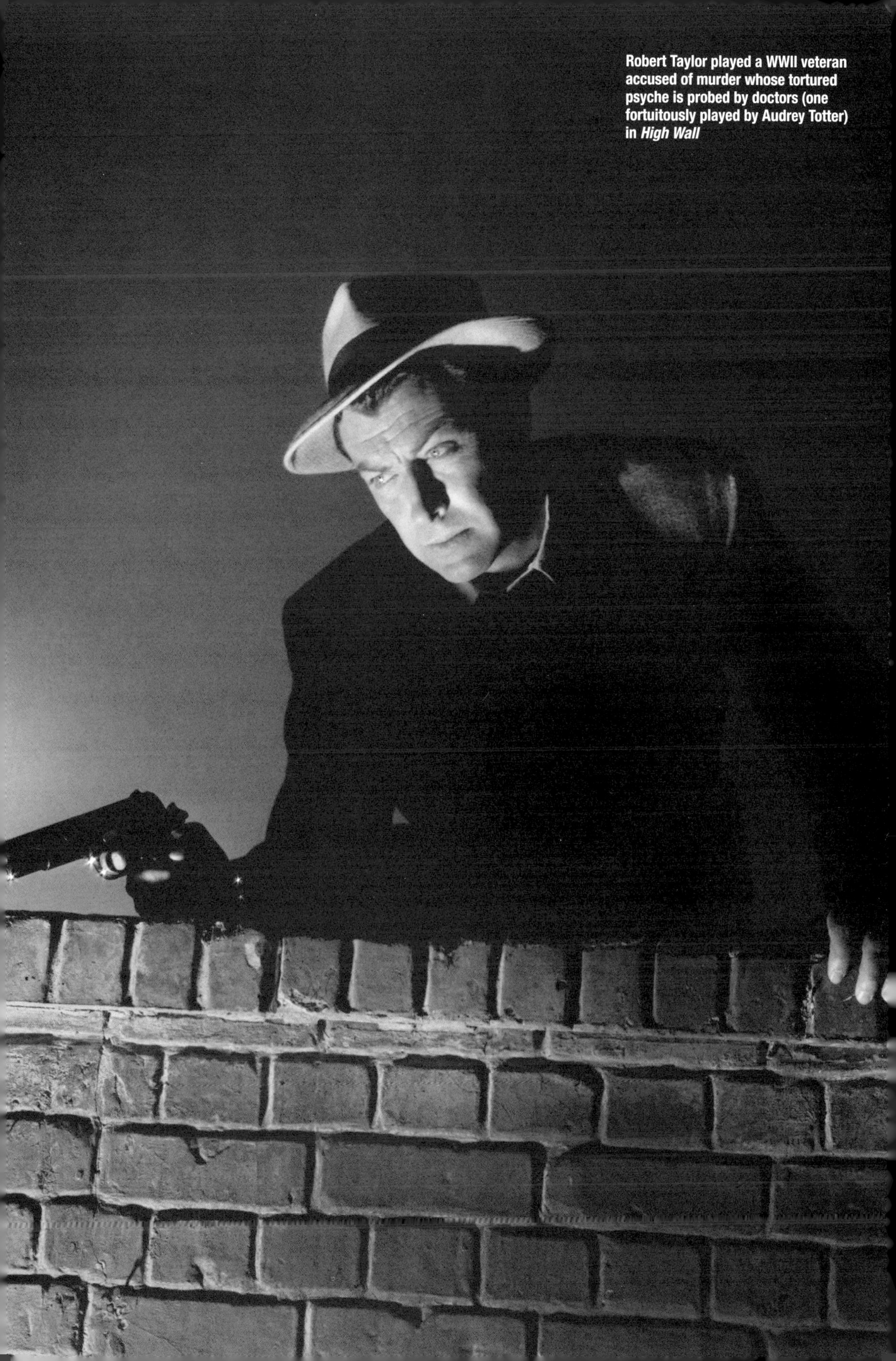

Robert Taylor played a WWII veteran accused of murder whose tortured psyche is probed by doctors (one fortuitously played by Audrey Totter) in *High Wall*

Now every psychoanalyst was a cop and every cop had to be a psychoanalyst. As Police Inspector Burgess (Thomas Gomez) says in Robert Siodmak's *Phantom Lady* (1944), "We used to talk about 'the criminal type.' Criminal type my eye. It's not what a man looks like, it's how his mind works." The man he's hunting, Jack Marlow (Franchot Tone), is the new breed of killer, one who doesn't know why he's driven to kill, he's simply compelled to do it. Like the child murderer in *M* (1931) or the loner in *The Sniper* (1952), many of these killers are so pathetic they almost warrant sympathy—they *cannot* stop, try as they might.

Some film shrinks were "dream detectives," like Lee J. Cobb in *The Dark Past* (1948), who successfully psychoanalyzes gangster William Holden in a single evening while held hostage; Audrey Totter, who employs narcosynthesis to prove Robert Taylor's innocence in 1947's *High Wall*, and Lew Ayres, who determines good twin Olivia de Havilland from her murderous twin in *The Dark Mirror* (1946). That many of these analysts were in love with their patients might be bad for the ethics committee, but hardly bad for the box office. In the movies, science was ever aided by romance.

But for every kind, decent psychoanalyst, there was a charlatan using his power for evil: In *Shock* (1946), doctor Vincent Price attempts to drive insane the lone witness to a murder, and, in *Nightmare Alley* (1947), Helen Walker's analyst admits her business is really no different—just more respectable—than Tyrone Power's carny sideshow. "Takes one to catch one," she admits.

And then there are the hypnotists—such as the mysterious, Freud-reading killer of *Nightmare* (1956) who sets up suggestible musician Kevin McCarthy for a murder in a mirrored room. And as Richard Conte's lawyer says of dubious doctor José Ferrer in Otto Preminger's *Whirlpool* (1950), "The fellow's a hypnotist, among his other shady practices." Among those other practices? Blackmail, swindling, and murder! While he frames his kleptomaniac client Gene Tierney for murder, he's created his own perfect alibi: He's just had his gall bladder out and is lying helpless in a hospital bed. Cue the crazy finale in which Ferrer hypnotizes himself to ignore his blinding pain and retrieve incriminating evidence. Now *that's* psychiatry!

After the success of 1957's *The Three Faces of Eve*, the 1960s saw a new, socially conscious incarnation of the hero-psychiatrist, with prison shrink Sidney Poitier analyzing violent neo-Nazi Bobby Darin in *Pressure Point* (1962), Rod Steiger working with pedophile Stuart Whitman in the wildly optimistic *The Mark* (1961), and call girl Anne Francis undergoing therapy in *Girl of the Night* (1960).

The latter was based on the bestseller by Harold Greenwald, *The Call Girl*, in which he interviewed 16 prostitutes, six of whom were in analysis with him. The film ends on an optimistic note, with Francis leaving "the life" and starting over. *Pressure Point* was drawn from a case in *The Fifty-Minute Hour* by Robert Lindner. The film ends with Poitier being overruled by prison authorities who decide to release Darin despite Poitier's warnings. A postscript tells us that Darin's character ultimately beat an old man to death, proving Poitier's instincts correct. Not everyone can be saved.

The '60s also gave us the prescient *The Manchurian Candidate* (1962), in which a soldier is brainwashed into becoming an assassin and his entire platoon conditioned to consider him "the kindest, bravest, warmest, most wonderful human being" they've ever met. As the sinister Chinese hypnotist says of poor Raymond Shaw (Laurence Harvey), "His brain has not only been washed, as they say... It has been dry cleaned." Angela Lansbury, as the controlling mother who sacrifices her own son and kisses him on the lips, is quite possibly the most "Freudian" mother in all of cinema.

1962 was also the year John Huston brought his docudrama *Freud: The Secret Passion* to the screen, starring Montgomery Clift as the father of psychoanalysis. The pinnacle of Huston's wartime documentaries between 1942 - 1946 was *Let There Be Light*, about the treatment of WWII soldiers who'd had mental breakdowns. "Making that film was like having a religious experience," Huston said of the project, which inspired his lifelong fascination with analysis.

John Huston envisioned Freud's career as "as a kind of thriller, a mystery of a special sort" as he developed his radical Oedipus complex theory. The director's only choice for the role of Freud was Clift, who'd just completed co-starring in Huston's *The Misfits* (1961). Co-star Marilyn Monroe said

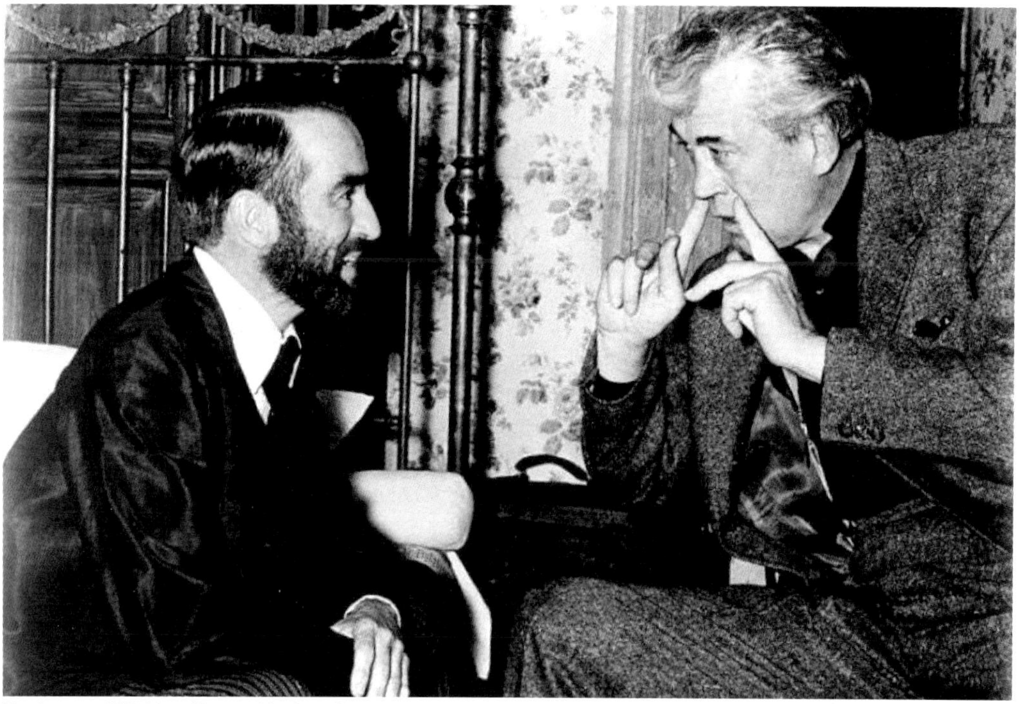

Montgomery Clift, himself a psychiatric patient, portrayed the field's most famed practitioner for director John Huston in *Freud*

of Monty Clift, "He's the only person I know who's in worse shape than I am." The only person who didn't seem to see it was Huston.

According to Clift biographer Patricia Bosworth, sometime in mid-shoot—when Clift and Huston had begun to clash and Clift was having difficulty memorizing his ever-changing lines—a hypnotist named Dr. Black arrived as one of Huston's advisors, "presumably to coach Susannah York, who played the hysterically repressed Cecily. Dr. Black made an unsuccessful attempt to hypnotize [Clift]. Monty told people he thought Black was treating him like a patient and he didn't like it. Later, a story got around Hollywood that Monty had been hypnotized into memorizing his lines by Black. When he angrily confronted Huston with the story, the director shrugged, 'You're paranoid, boy.'"

While the film was well-enough received by critics, it's more famous for the conflicts between Huston and Montgomery Clift, as well as the lawsuit Universal filed against Clift for cost overruns—all serious issues derailing what was left of Clift's career. Clift acquits himself quite well, considering he was suffering from hypothyroidism, alcoholism, and cataracts during filming. The surreal dream sequences, one of which includes Freud attending his father's funeral, anticipate Fellini's *8½*, which was released six months later.

Monty Clift did the film as a tribute to his own analyst, William Silverberg, with whom he had a relationship so intimate, Farber and Green describe it as "verging on *folie à deux*." As they note, "Silverberg was [also] gay and in addition to socializing frequently, the two men sometimes vacationed together ... Silverberg was completely ineffectual at treating Clift's crippling alcoholism. When Clift's medical doctor urged the actor to seek treatment at the Menninger Clinic, Dr. Silverberg vetoed the idea: he could not bear to lose his hold on the magnetic star. In their sessions together toward the end of Clift's life (according to the actor's secretary, Lorenzo James), Dr. Silverberg spent as much of the hour confiding his own problems as he did listening to [Monty's]."

May Romm's daughter Dorothy Colodny told Farber and Green, "I know some very good psychiatrists who were marvelous with patients, and you never hear their names... the big wheels who treated famous people were usually not the good therapists.... I think that is why so many of the important Hollywood people didn't get good care, which is very sad because a lot of them needed it." ■

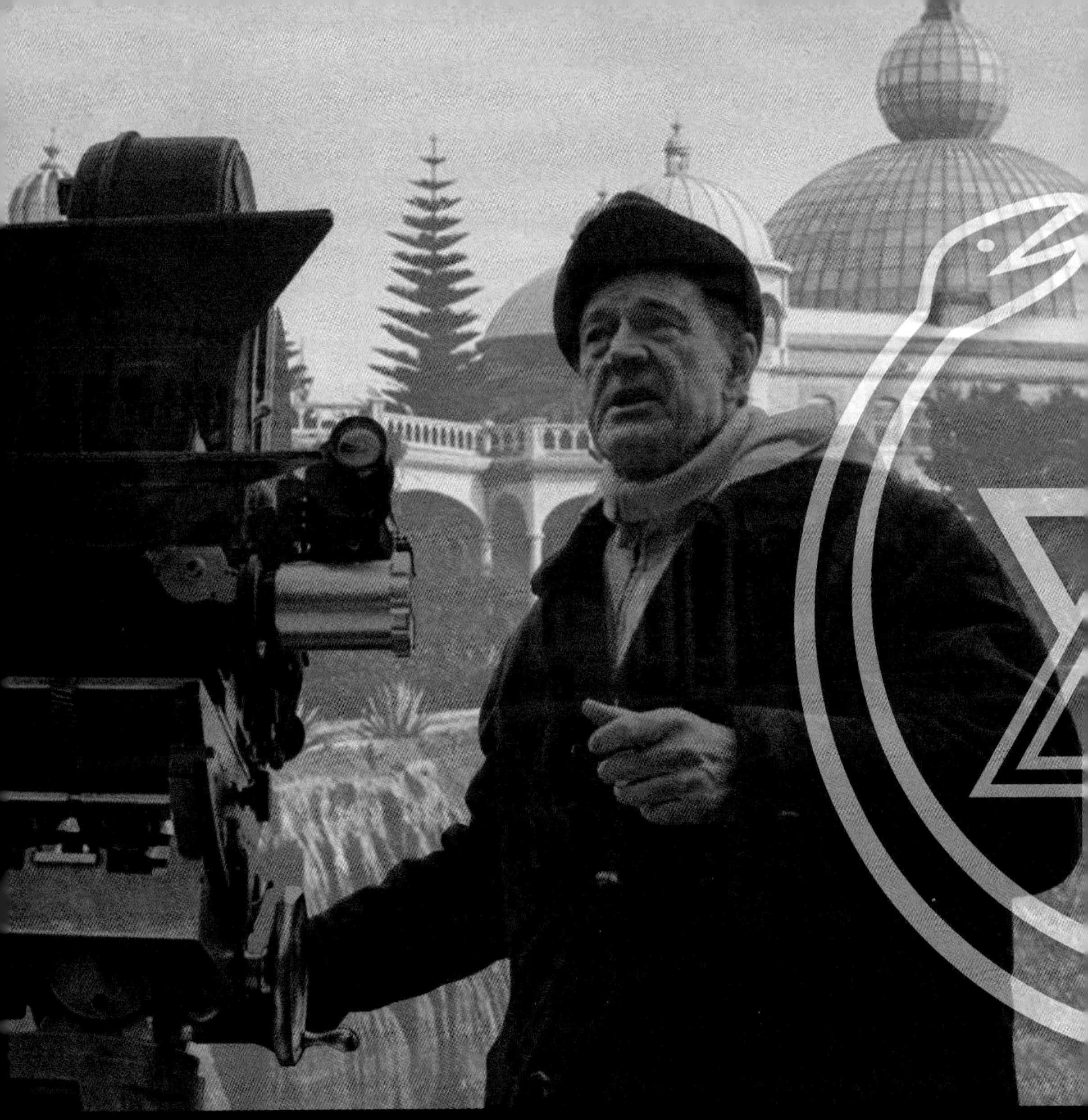

UNCOMMON GROUND

ANTHONY MANN, GEOFFREY SHURLOCK, AND THE CULT OF THEOSOPHY

John Wranovics

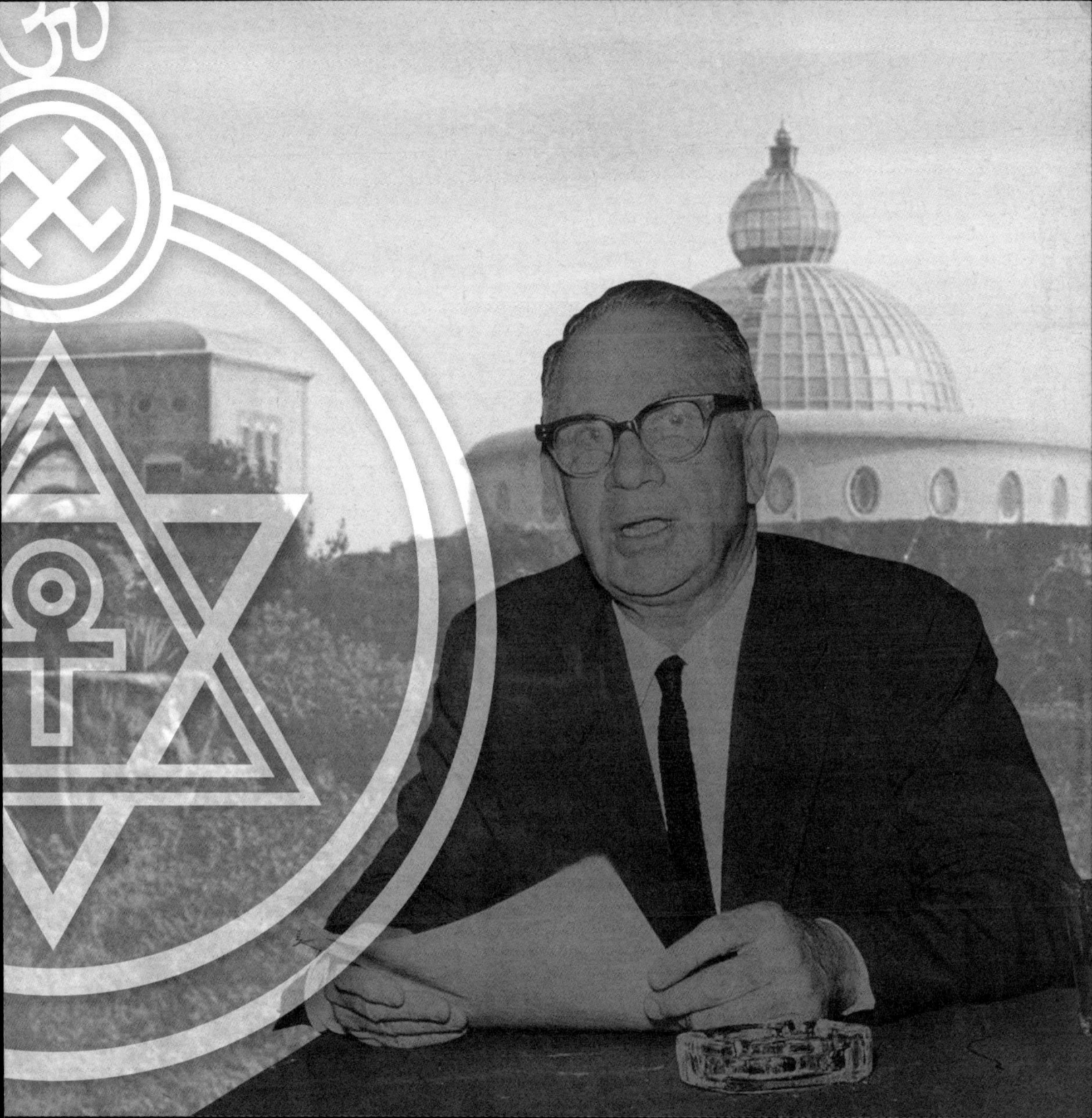

Throughout his career, Anthony Mann pushed the envelope regarding what could be shown on screen. With unprecedented acts of violence, such as Raymond Burr throwing molten Cherries Jubilee in Chili Williams' face in *Raw Deal* (1948), George Murphy slashed to pieces by a motorized harrow in *Border Incident* (1949), or Alex Nicol firing a bullet through Jimmy Stewart's hand in *The Man from Laramie* (1955), Mann constantly tested the limits. He didn't shy away from controversial sexual subjects either, filming adaptations of James M. Cain's *Serenade* (1956) and Erskine Caldwell's *God's Little Acre* (1958), stories that for years had been stalled by censors and branded as unfilmable.

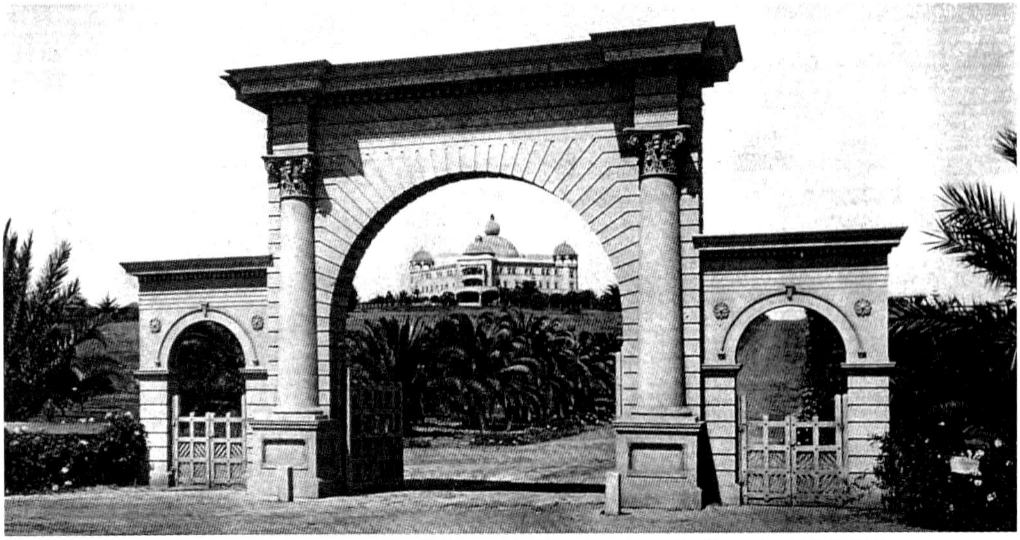

In 1900, Katherine Tingley founded the International Theosophical Headquarters, aka "Lomaland," in Point Loma, a seaside community in San Diego, California

As he moved from Poverty Row to major studios, Mann routinely battled the Production Code Administration (PCA), the industry's self-policing censorship office, headed by Irish-Catholic Joseph I. Breen. From its inception in 1932 until 1954, Geoffrey Manwaring Shurlock served as Breen's right-hand man. Shurlock even ran the PCA during Breen's brief stint as general manager of RKO from 1941-1942. He formally took the reins when Breen retired in '54, serving as America's chief film censor until his own retirement in January 1968, when introduction of the ratings system made the PCA superfluous.

"The code is a set of self-regulations based on sound morals common to all peoples and all religions."

—Geoffrey Shurlock

"Shakespeare was the most violent writer that's ever been. Heads roll. The most gruesome. Even in King Lear when he gouges Gloucester's eyes out with his spurs...but this is true of great drama, that it needs violence...it's been used in all the Miracle Plays, it was used in every form of theatre."

—Anthony Mann

It's now known that during the first two decades of the 20th century, Anthony Mann was raised in a bizarre utopian commune known as "Lomaland," run by the Universal Brotherhood and Theosophical Society. It was located on 350 acres of Point Loma, a peninsula bordering San Diego Bay. What has remained unexplored, however, is the intriguing coincidence that Mann's nemesis at the PCA, Geoffrey Shurlock, also spent his youth at Lomaland.

Founded on the precepts of notorious Russian occultist Helena Petrovna Blavatsky, and run by Katherine Tingley, the community at its peak boasted 500 residents, of which 300 were children. Mann, an only child, was born Emil Anton Bundsmann on June 6, 1906 on the grounds of the commune. There, he attended the theosophist Raja Yoga school, participated in the community's famed productions of ancient Greek and Shakespearean tragedies and ornate pageants, and toiled in its avocado groves. At the insistence of his aunt, he was removed from Lomaland at the age of 14, and moved with his mother to the relative normality of life in Orange, New Jersey. According to Mann's daughter Nina, up until that time, he had never seen money.

Geoffrey Shurlock, 12-years older than Mann, was born in Liverpool, England. He arrived in Lomaland in 1901, at the age of seven, in the company of his parents and two younger siblings. Deemed one of the commune's most promising youngsters, Shurlock lived in the commune until 1918, graduating from the Raja Yoga College and the School of Antiquity, Lomaland's equivalent of a graduate-level theology school.

"Any one who lives in a Raja Yoga school has plenty of chances to study character...This is the magic of Raja Yoga. The effect of Raja Yoga is not only seen in a child's physical improvement, but also in his mantle and moral improvement, which is more important...We are all taught not to have mean or unclean thoughts...Every thought we think influences our body, so that bad thoughts produce diseases in our body...We believe that there are two 'people' inside of us, that one is a god and the other a demon, that each is trying to get ahead of the other, and it depends on us which is to gain mastery."

—Geoffrey Shurlock
"The Effect of Raja Yoga on Character"

"Actually, I think the real reason why people like violence, particularly in pictures or in drama, is they can look at it and they see this terrible thing, and they say it's not happening to me. I can understand it, and I feel it, and I'm excited by it, but I'm not doing it, it hasn't happened to me. And really, the same thing in my own life. I'm very mild mannered, but I like to impress. I like to do something violent to make people to talk and to make people say, well that's a fascinating thing. That's why I use it."

—Anthony Mann

Mann's father, Emile Bundsmann, was born in Rositz, Bohemia, in 1869. He emigrated to the U.S. in the spring of 1891, settling in Macon, Georgia. With a Chemical Engineering Ph.D. earned in Vienna, Emile found work at a cotton mill owned by the locally prominent Hanson family. In 1898, a year after becoming an American citizen, the *Atlanta Constitution* reported: "Emile Bundsmann, superintendent of the dye works in the East Macon factory of the Bibb Manufacturing Company, left this morning for Europe to be gone several months...while away [he] will deliver a series of lectures on 'Theosophy.' He is one of the best read members of the Macon Theosophical Society."

In 1900, Emile married Bertha Waxelbaum, daughter of a wealthy textile and dry goods merchant, described in the local press as "one of the most beautiful brides of the season." Four years earlier, the death of Sol Waxelbaum, Bertha's father, had been major news. Known as the "merchant dry goods prince of Georgia" and the "best businessman in Macon," Sol's fortunes collapsed when his business, Waxelbaum & Son, was destroyed in a fire big enough to be reported 900 miles away by the *New York Times*. His death the following year was attributed to a "sinking attack" following "a collapse of the nervous system."

Bundsmann's employer, Walter T. Hanson, was a leading figure in Macon's Theosophical community and likely the major influence on Emile's involvement with the group. Heeding Katherine Tingley's call, Hanson moved his entire family west to Lomaland in 1900. The Bundsmanns followed suit one year later. The kibbutz-like Lomaland community had been founded by Katherine Tingley, head of the dominant branch of the Theosophical Society that emerged in the U.S. following the death of Madame Blavatsky in 1895. Major funding for the development of the Point Loma property came from a core group of wealthy followers, including Albert Spalding, famed pitcher for the Chicago White Stockings baseball club, renowned for popularizing the use of a mitt and founding the eponymous sporting goods company.

The Theosophist religion had been founded a couple of decades earlier by Madame Blavatsky and one-time newspaper reporter Henry Steel Olcott, following a meeting in Vermont at the home of two boys who, it was claimed, had the ability to levitate. In 1896, Katherine Tingley seized the reins

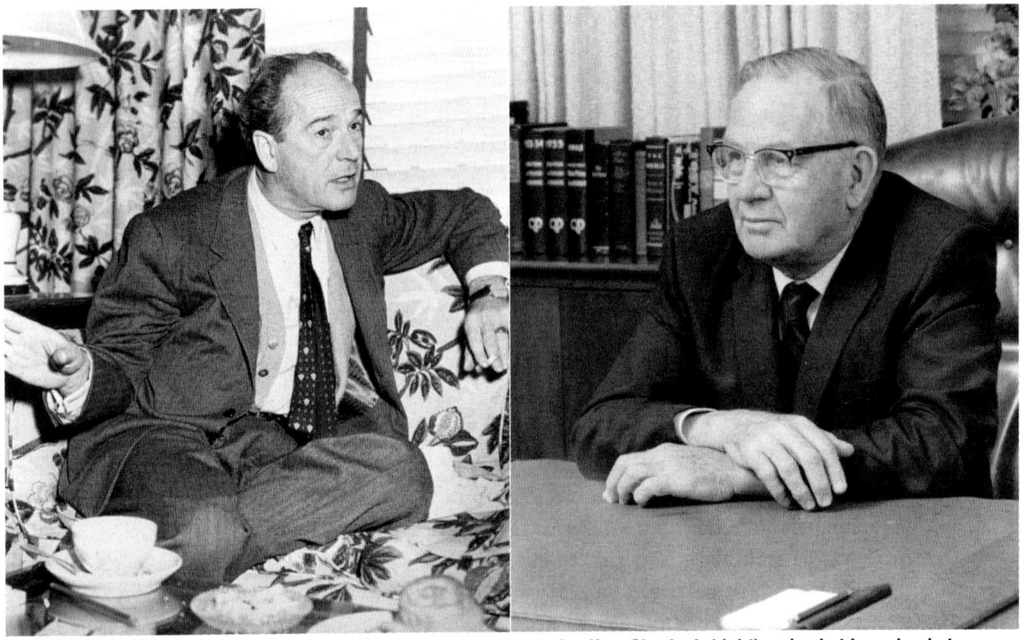

Anthony Mann (left), born in Lomaland, lived there until he was 14. Geoffrey Shurlock (right) arrived at Lomaland at age seven and left there at the age of 24

of the Theosophical Society in America following the death of her mentor, W. Q. Judge. Tingley's main rival, Annie Besant, retained control of Theosophical lodges in the UK, Europe, and India. The highly disciplined Lomaland community, which embraced a blend of Hindu, Buddhist, and Neo-Platonist thought—intermixing concepts of spiritualism, reincarnation, and karma—was purportedly directed by an unseen Great White Brotherhood of "Mahatmas," ancient advanced souls living in Nepal, who only communicated with adepts like Blavatsky and Tingley.

Geoffrey Shurlock's father, Captain Charles Shurlock, born in 1847, was a master mariner in the merchant navy and the great-grandson of John Russell, a notable portrait painter and member of the Royal Academy famed for his deeply religious lifestyle. For most of his career, Capt. Shurlock sailed cargo ships from Liverpool along the coast of South America and the U. S. In 1890, he married Frances Hallawell, an active Theosophist in England. Geoffrey Shurlock was born in Liverpool in 1894. Seven years later, the couple and their three children, Geoffrey (7), Alan (6), and Olive (3), moved to Lomaland.

The Century Path, one of the group's numerous publications, reported on November 2, 1902, that "Mr. and Mrs. Shurlock, who are so well known in England, are moving into their new home, which occupies an exceptionally charming position midway between the Homestead and the Bay, and commanding an exquisite view of both."

Childhood in Lomaland was unusual. Children were raised by the entire community. After a few months with its mother, a baby was placed into a common nursery. Parents were allowed to visit the child for a few hours, only on Sunday. Once old enough, children moved from the nursery into a gender-segregated group home, overseen by surrogate mothers. The uniformed children were marched to classes and forbidden to speak in class or at mealtimes, unless absolutely necessary. Their day was divided between school work and field work, in which they tended the community gardens. In their early teens, classes were separated by gender. According to one alumnus of the Raja Yoga school, "When we got to be dangerous teenagers, we were kept pretty much apart."

Dramatic performances were integral to Lomaland, and Tingley oversaw construction of the first open-air Greek amphitheater in the U.S. In the evenings, children attended orchestra or theater rehearsals. Preparations for a play preempted the regular schedule as the entire community focused on making cos-

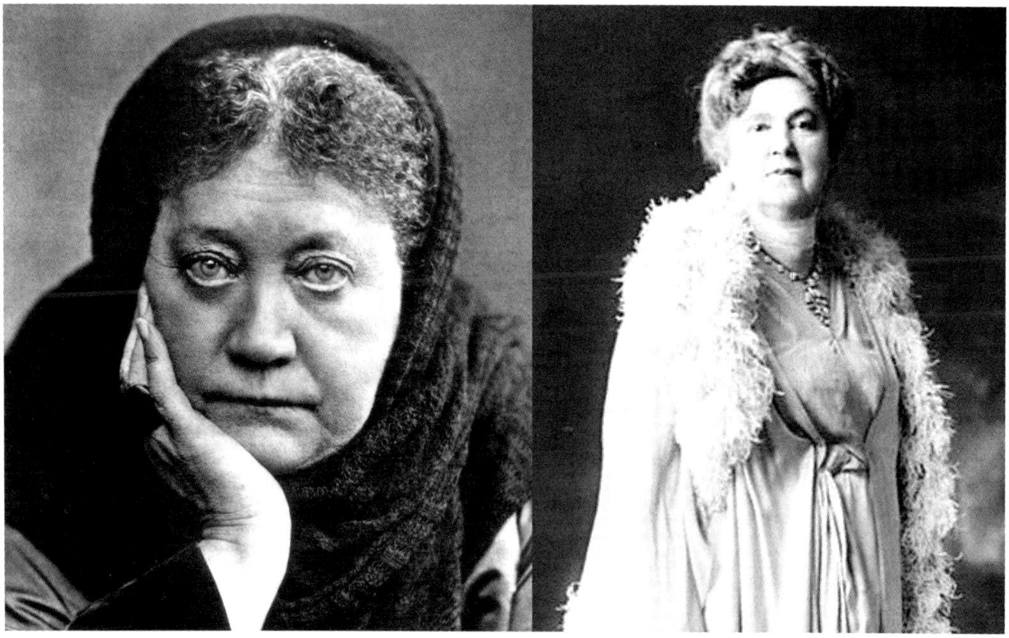

Following the death of Madame Blavatsky (left), the Theosophical Society splintered with Katherine Tingley (right) taking the reins of the U.S.-based lodges in 1896

tumes, building sets, and rehearsing. Significant for Tingley was the ancient Greek drama *The Eumenides*. She considered Aeschylus, the "intellectual Sphinx" and Shakespeare a teacher of ancient wisdom.

> "*Theosophy teaches the very antithesis of [Calvinism]. It declares that we are dual in nature; that we are born for a high purpose; that our souls and our spiritual natures are splendid with all the infinite possibilities of human life; that the soul is the Knower, the Inspirer; that the soul is immortal, and the physical is mortal. So the physical has its weaknesses, its passions, its greed, its deceit, its imperfections; it is on this plane for the purpose of self-evolution; it is not evil, it is only undeveloped good. And so we have the soul the Inspirer, the protector; and the mind the vehicle, receiving the inspiration from this higher source as far as it is able to.*"
>
> —Katherine Tingley

While at Lomaland, Anthony Mann's father created several new dyes and granted the patents to Tingley. He was listed in the faculty as a teacher of German, Mathematics and Science, and Engineering, and Mann's mother was listed as a Dramatic Instructress in the Isis Conservatory of Music and Drama. Around 1912, Emile Bundsmann fell seriously ill and his wife squired him back to Austria, leaving their son, six-years old, behind—essentially an orphan for the two years they were away.

In 1918, at the age of 24, Shurlock left school to help his mother run the family business in San Diego, a steam laundry. Three years later, the entire Shurlock family returned to England for 18 months. In 1922, Geoffrey and his sister Olive reconnected with Katherine Tingley and accompanied her on a lecture tour of Europe. Shurlock later recalled, "We traveled around with them in Germany and in Holland." The Lomaland newspaper described "two big public meetings in Nürnberg in the old Katharinebau ... the hall was packed with a larger crowd than it had ever known before, according to the statement of many of the citizens. The Theosophical Leader's work in Nürnberg was a tremendous triumph in every respect."

Later that year, the Shurlocks returned to San Diego. Geoffrey worked briefly as a journalist before becoming a research secretary for Rupert Hughes. Hughes, a popular novelist and screenwriter and

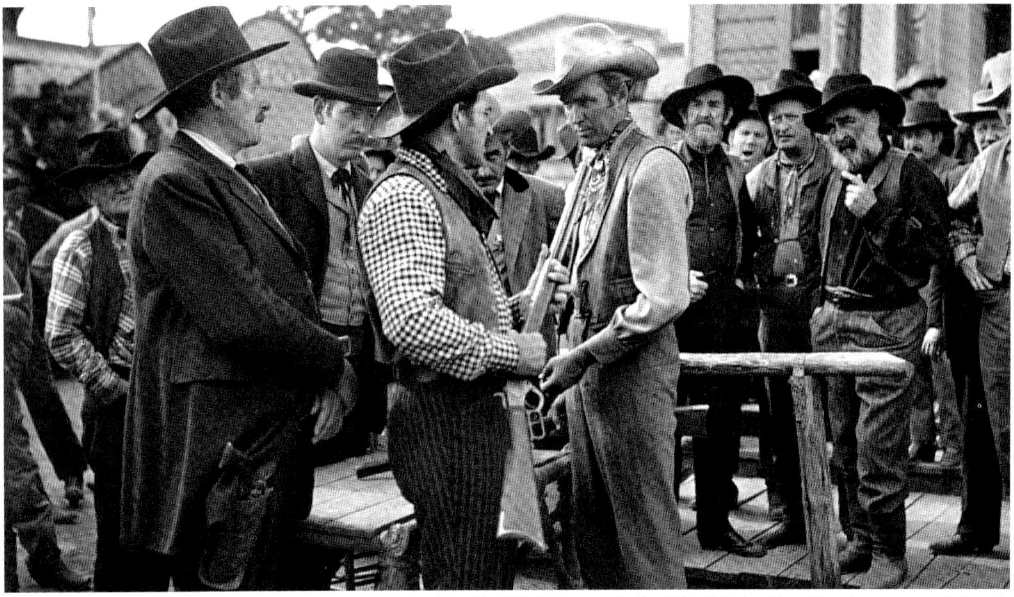

"In *Winchester 73,* he went out to destroy the man who killed his father… So he killed his brother. This is as powerful and strong a yarn as you can tell." —Anthony Mann

the uncle of Howard Hughes, needed someone fluent in French to help him research his novel *The Golden Ladder*. Hughes' novel about the film industry, *Souls for Sale*, was published in 1922 and filmed in 1923. *The Theosophical Path* magazine noted in its July 12, 1923, edition that Hughes was among recent "notable visitors" to Lomaland. Shurlock worked with Hughes for four years—quitting once he discovered that Hughes' chauffeur was more highly paid.

Upon leaving Hughes in 1926, Shurlock co-wrote an unproduced play, *The Painted Man*, with Joseph Jackson, who also helped him get hired by Paramount's story-reading department. Shurlock worked as a script editor before getting a chance to produce. In 1929, he produced Paramount's last silent film, the Western *Stairs of Sand*, starring Wallace Beery. He oversaw the production of ten sound films made for the foreign market, but later that year, Shurlock was fired from Paramount. The following year, he became a naturalized U. S. citizen, and, in 1932, he went to work for the Motion Picture Association of America, a lobbying group advocating for the six major studios. In later years, Shurlock was frequently described in the press as an Episcopalian, setting him apart from the Catholic-dominated PCA. It's unclear if Shurlock purposely obfuscated his Theosophical background. Several film history books falsely state that Shurlock graduated Phi Beta Kappa from Dartmouth College. In his memoir, *See No Evil*, Jack Vizzard, a member of the PCA staff, described Shurlock, perhaps with a knowing wink: "Geoff Shurlock ... passed for Episcopalian, even though he was an eclectic, and in the deepest currents of his soul, a theosophist."

No hard evidence exists that Anthony Mann and Geoffrey Shurlock ever acknowledged each other as fellow Lomalanders during their careers in the movie business. Shurlock, though, had a prince-like status at the commune during Mann's time there, and his sister, Olive, was a celebrated musician. It is highly unlikely that Mann wouldn't remember or recognize Shurlock from his childhood. It would also not be surprising if both men chose to hide their unusual and potentially controversial upbringings. After all, the magazine that Madame Blavatsky published in London was entitled *Lucifer*.

It remains for researchers to tease out any evidence of theosophical tenets in Mann's movies and Shurlock's censorship. One may notice, for example, how often the first shot of a Mann film is of a mountain peak—a theosophical metaphor for the struggle and progress a soul makes towards its next incarnation. In interviews, both Mann and Shurlock frequently refer to ancient Greek playwrights and Shakespeare, and the dramas they were raised on, to make points about aesthetics or the value of cathartic violence. Mann argued that one of the things he liked about Westerns was that the characters "can be more primitive: they can be more Greek, like *Oedipus Rex* or *Antigone*." Unfortunately, Mann died before realizing one of his great ambitions—a Western based on *King Lear*.

"I don't think we're here to preach. I don't think we're here to sermonize or moralize or even socialize...I don't try to bring out moral issues."

—Anthony Mann

Another area of potential exploration for researchers is Shurlock's antipathy toward any depiction of homosexuality. As social attitudes shifted in the second half of the 20th century, one taboo after another fell by the wayside. Shurlock was often given credit for his reasonable stewardship of the PCA, displaying a markedly more liberal reaction to the rapid cultural changes of the early 1960s. Adultery, narcotics, prostitution, and violence all found a way onto movie screens, but the last taboo against which Shurlock held fast was the depiction of gay relationships.

Mann, on the other hand, helmed several projects during his career that featured homosexual characters (though typically dialed down by the PCA), ranging from the character Rick Coyle in *Raw Deal*, the admittedly bowdlerized version of *Serenade*, all the way to *Spartacus*, from which Mann was fired after the start of production. Shurlock had rejected the dialogue in the bath scene between Laurence Olivier and Tony Curtis about those who "eat oysters and those who prefer snails." Although the scene was filmed, it was removed from the film and not restored until 1991 (with Anthony Hopkins looping the late Olivier's lines).

Shurlock's bulwark against homosexuality is especially interesting when one considers that Katherine Tingley's most aggressive weapon against her great rival in the Theosophical world, Annie Besant, head of the Adyar Society, was propaganda, widely distributed in a series of tracts, that denigrated Besant for the continued support within her organization of reputed pederast Charles Webster Leadbeater. To articulate the distinction between the American lodges and those led by Besant in the UK, Europe and India, Tingley vociferously campaigned against Besant's harboring of an admitted homosexual. One early historian of Point Loma wrote that Tingley "doubtless hoped to establish in the public mind a distinction of Point Loma as the center of 'pure' Theosophy and Adyar as the disseminator of an 'unpure' brand."

Like the two brothers in Mann's *Winchester 73* (1950), the righteous Lin McAdam (James Stewart) and the outlaw Dutch Henry Brown (Stephen McNally), Mann and Shurlock followed divergent paths, but their unusual and intense upbringing inevitably brought them into fundamental conflict. In its day, the Theosophical movement had a strong presence in Hollywood. The Krotona colony, founded by followers of Annie Besant, was established on 10 acres in lower Beachwood Canyon in 1912, and, in 1924, moved to a 115-acre property in Ojai. That same year, Thomas Ince, "father of the Western", after dying mysteriously (in some reports, he was shot by William Randolph Hearst), was given a Theosophist funeral. Talbot Mundy, writer of "King of the Kyber Rifles" and "Her Reputation," lived on the grounds of Lomaland from 1922-1927, and there wrote the Blavatsky-influenced "Om: The Secret of Ahbor Valley." With the passing of time, the Theosophist movement has seen a great decline and mostly faded from public awareness. The religion's influence remains to be discovered in the works of those filmmakers who embraced it. Undoubtedly, future researchers will similarly look back to investigate how the teachings of Scientology, arguably the Theosophy of today in Hollywood, may be infused in the films made by its adherents. ■

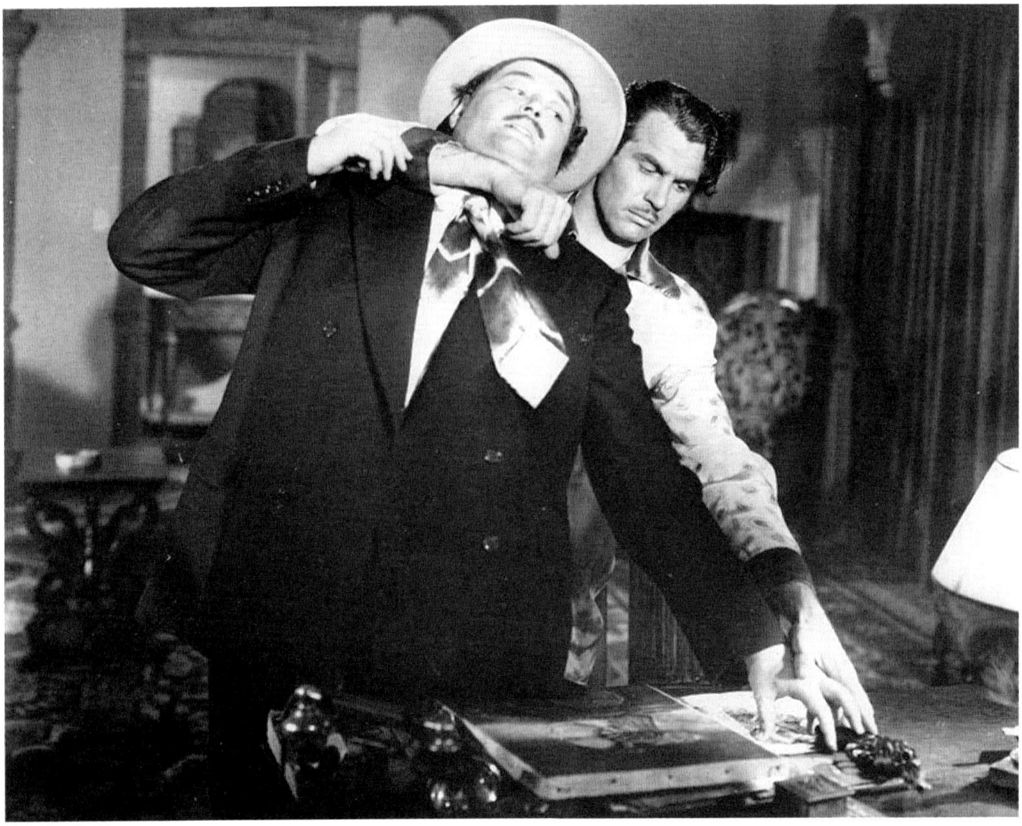

The Falcon (John Calvert) puts the arm on Jack Reitzen who's hoping to cash in some stolen paintings in *Appointment with Murder*

In this one, Martin's ability to tender complicated plotlines that don't end up chasing their own tails is front and center. Though Martin was willing to make daredevil bets with his storylines, they nearly always paid off, and *Appointment with Murder* comes through big enough.

Search for Danger (1949), Director: Jack Bernhard

Waring has been hired by club owners, Kirk (Albert Dekker) and Gregory (Ben Welden) to trace their missing business partner, "Larry Andrews," who's embezzled $100,000 from the club. Waring follows Andrews to a cheap hotel in Santa Monica and lets his clients know where their runaway associate can be found. When they brace Andrews, he tells them Waring has the money. Waring knows nothing about it, of course, and returns to the motel to find Andrews dead. Waring realizes he's been set up. The question is why, and by whom?

Martin's screenplay for *Search for Danger* is the best of the three *Falcon* titles featuring Calvert. It's mind-bendingly complex, but every twist and turn comes with its own reward and the ending is a genuine surprise. The series had begun to hit its stride with Martin as producer and Jack Bernhard (*Decoy* [1946], *Violence* [1947], *The Hunted* [1948]) in the director's chair for the second time. Unfortunately, *Search for Danger* was The Falcon's last case.

Destination Murder (1950), Director: Edward L. Cahn

Coed Laura Mansfield (Joyce Mackenzie) sees her father gunned down at the front door by someone in a messenger-boy's uniform. She picks ferret-faced Jackie Wales (Stanley Clements, ex-Mr. Gloria Grahame) out of a police line-up, and, while she suspects he's the killer, she can't give a positive ID. Laura, who's unknown to Jackie, tracks him down and sweet-talks him into revealing his connections:

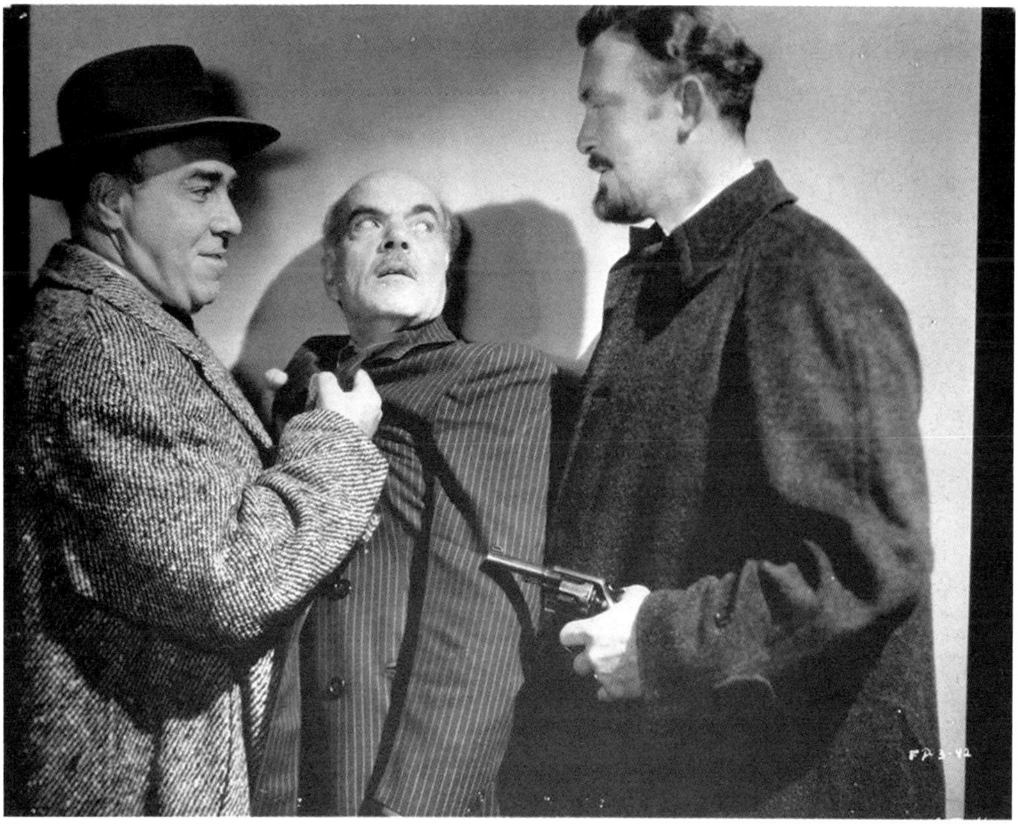

Albert Dekker gets the drop on his cohorts in another of the Martin-penned Falcon movies, 1949's *Search for Danger*

nightclub owner Armitage (Albert Dekker) and club manager Stretch Norton (Hurd Hatfield). She then gets herself hired at the club, to the annoyance of Alice Wentworth (Myrna Dell) who sees her as a rival for the boss' affection. Nothing is as it seems and Laura begins to understand she's not in Kansas anymore.

Produced by RKO, the crime thriller was a step up the studio ladder for Martin, and he made good with an offbeat and clever original script. Like notorious B-noirs such as *Night Editor* (1946) or *The Big Combo* (1955), the film challenged the PCA with some suggestive material and snuck it by, knowing that the censors often overlooked things given their usual disregard for low-budget Bs. Thus, we have the sadistic Armitage, who refers to himself only in the third person and who revels in violence as Beethoven's 'Moonlight Sonata' plays full volume on the pianola; also, the homoerotic relationship between Armitage and Norton is revealed as something more when Norton proclaims, "Haven't you heard? I don't like women!" Martin's story fuses culture, deviance, and brutality in exhilarating, outré B-noir style. And while it doesn't rate with the best of the Bs, *Destination Murder* does rank among the better ones.

Shakedown (1950), Director: Joseph Pevney

Shutterbug Jack Early (Howard Duff) is desperate to make it big. He'll watch a man drown or urge a woman to jump from a burning building if it means getting the photos that will land him a job at a major daily. Jack also sees advantage in cozying up to local mobsters Nick Palmer (Brian Donlevy) and Harry Colton (Lawrence Tierney) to set one against the other. He blackmails Colton while secretly romancing both Palmer's wife, Nita (Anne Vernon), along with Ellen Bennett (Peggy Dow), the newspaper's comely photo editor. Early's reckless ambition forces his friends to turn their backs on him and his enemies to look to kill him.

Shakedown (working title: *The Magnificent Heel*) gave Martin the opportunity to work with a major studio (Universal) and a better director, Joe Pevney. The film also aimed to deliver a much bigger emotional punch with a greater emphasis on its main character, one of the most unscrupulous and unsympathetic protagonists in film noir: a self-serving, self-pitying *homme fatale*. Martin Goldsmith (*Detour* [1945], *The Narrow Margin* [1952]) wrote the final draft, which became one of the postwar period's most unflinching noirs and a B-budget bookend to Billy Wilder's coruscating picture from 1951 *Ace in the Hole*.

The Deadliest Sin aka *Confession* (1955), Director: Ken Hughes

Mike Nelson (Sydney Chaplin) returns home to the UK from America with a suitcase full of stolen cash. His partner Corey (Patrick Allen) then turns up wanting his share, but he's accidently killed by Mike's friend, Alan Pool (Peter Hammond). Tormented by grief, Alan goes to his priest to confess the crime, but Mike, afraid that Alan knows too much, shoots him in the confessional. Scotland Yard investigates and soon enough Mike is suspected of the overseas robbery *and* the killings, though the evidence is circumstantial. Mike doesn't know that, however. The police set a trap, figuring Mike will try to kill the priest if he's convinced the Church will allow the clergyman to testify.

The Deadliest Sin aka *Confession* was the collaboration between Martin (on whose theatrical play the film was based) and British director Ken Hughes (*Wicked as They Come* [1956], *The Long Haul* [1957]). Produced by the UK's Merton Park Studios, the film's reach exceeds its no-budget grasp thanks to Hughes' atmospheric direction, a savvy British cast, and the challenging moral and ethical provocations of Martin's carefully balanced screenplay.

Double Jeopardy (1955), Director: R. G. Springsteen

Property developer Emmett Devery (John Litel) is being blackmailed by a former business partner, Sam Baggott (Robert Armstrong) and his gold-digging wife, Marge (Gale Robbins). Meanwhile, Marge is planning something more with her car salesman lover, Jeff Calder (Jack Kelly). It all goes wrong and Devery ends up framed for murder. Devery's lawyer and son-in-law-to-be, Marc Hill (Rod Cameron) and Devery's daughter, Barbara (Allison Hayes), work to clear him, but with the police treating it as an open-and-shut case, where do they even start?

A late-period title from Republic Studios, *Double Jeopardy* is the kind of fast-pulsed thriller beloved by film noir fans. It was this kind of story—compact, unpretentious, unpredictable—that Don Martin seemed most eager and well-equipped to tell. While director Springsteen doesn't provide much visual excitement, Martin's hard-charging screenplay and performances by veteran players Tom Powers, Minerva Urecal, John Gallaudet, and Dick Elliott—all of whom appear to be relishing their roles—deserve to get *Double Jeopardy* taken off those lists of "overlooked" noirs.

No Man's Woman (1955), Director: Franklin Adreon

Carolyn Ellenson Grant (Marie Windsor), a willful, self-obsessed art dealer, has any number of people around her who would happily see her dead: her estranged husband, Harlow Grant (John Archer); Louise Nelson, the woman he wants to marry (Nancy Gates); Harlow's father (Douglas Wood); gallery assistant Betty (Jill Jarmyn); Betty's boyfriend Dick Sawyer (Richard Crane); and art critic Wayne Vincent (Patric Knowles). In fact, all fall under suspicion after Carolyn is murdered, with her husband being the prime suspect. Grant sets out to clear his name since it doesn't appear the cops are going to make much of an effort, but what of the others?

As she did in most of her films, including *The Narrow Margin* (1952) and *The Killing* (1956), Marie Windsor plays her part to the hilt, and with Carolyn gone by mid-point, *No Man's Woman* loses much of its propulsion. We know someone killed her, but we don't really much care whodunnit. It's a shame (and a surprise) how soon the air goes out of the balloon. Martin, who wrote the story,

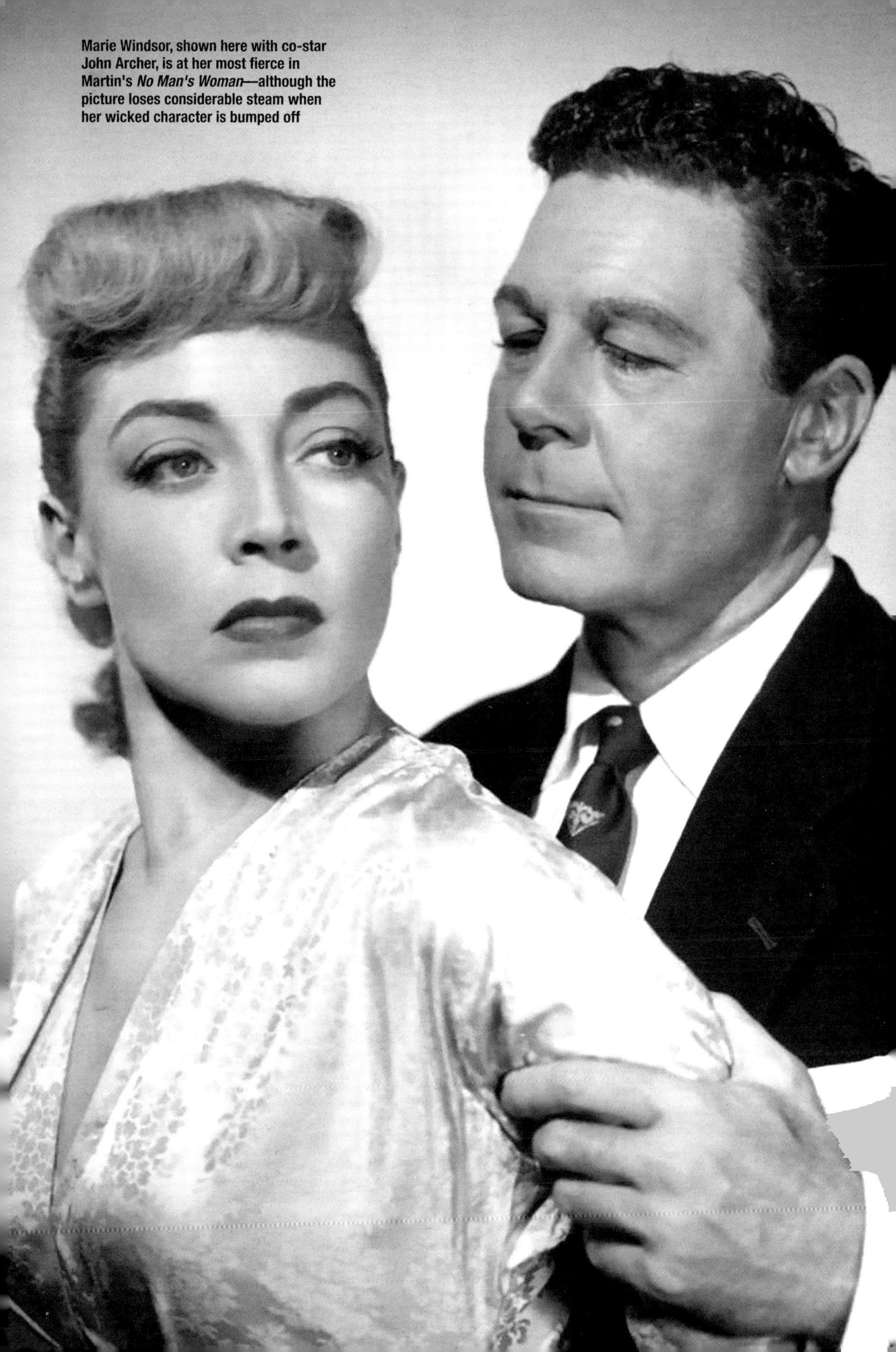

Marie Windsor, shown here with co-star John Archer, is at her most fierce in Martin's *No Man's Woman*—although the picture loses considerable steam when her wicked character is bumped off usually torqued the suspense right 'til the end. Unfortunately, things can happen betwixt and between as productions go through the agonies of birth. *No Man's Woman* at least has Marie Windsor and lots of luminously bitchy dialogue, which make the film worth watching.

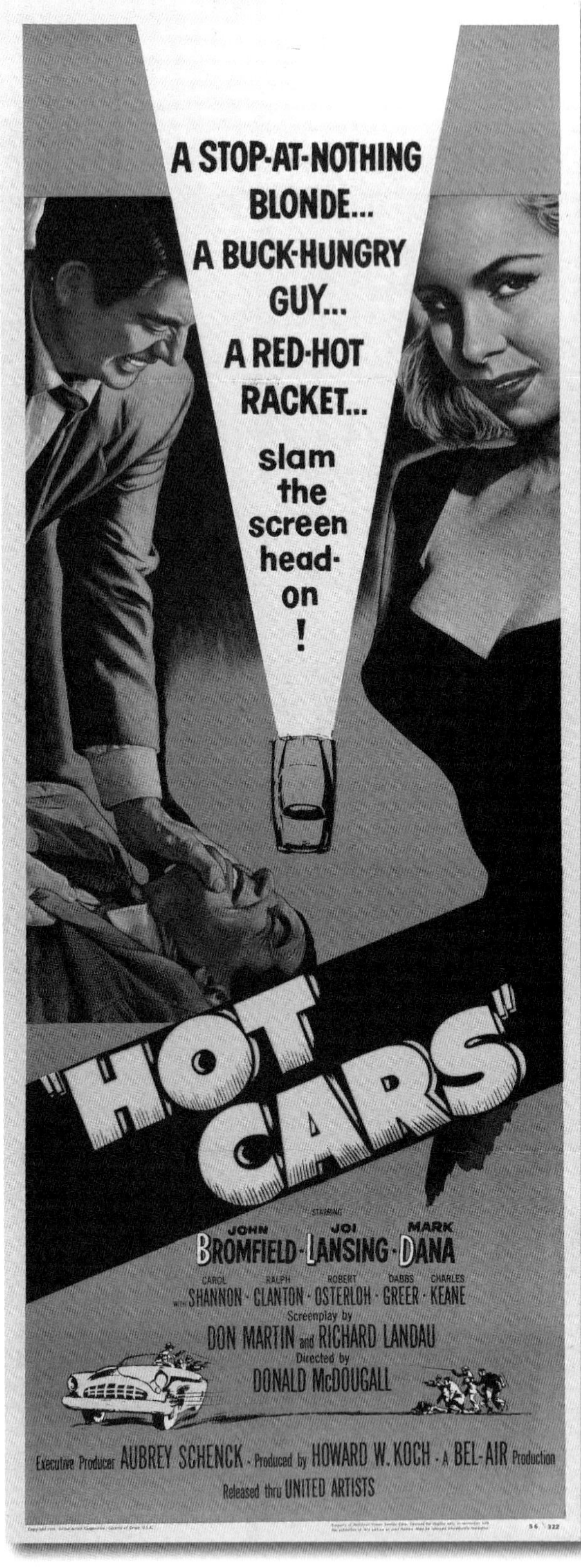

The Man Is Armed (1956)

Director: Franklin Adreon

Johnny Morrison (Dane Clark) is released from San Quentin after having taken the fall for his boss, Hackett (William Talman). Johnny wants to go straight, but Hackett wants him in on a half-million-dollar armored car heist. Meanwhile, detective Dan Coster (Barton MacLane) has Johnny pegged for the death of a fellow truck driver who went off the top of a building the day after Johnny's release. Truth be told, Johnny's never had a break in his life and nothing is going to change. His fate is never really in doubt, even though his girl, Carol Wayne (May Wynn), desperately clings to hope. Carol's wishful "love is all you need" won't come close to saving him.

With *The Man Is Armed*, Martin was back in top form. The story, though dire, is wound tightly until the last frame, even though Johnny Morrison is doomed from the start. The part is an ideal one for Dane Clark, a brooding, ill-at-ease actor who often played characters not as tough as they wanted or needed to be. William Talman is almost as terrifying a presence here as he was in *The Hitch-Hiker* (1953), which is really all you need to know.

Hot Cars (1956)

Director: Don McDougall

Nick Dunn (John Bromfield) is a used car salesman who's fired for giving customers the straight goods. He ends up working for a rival dealer that's a front for moving stolen cars. Nick plays along because he needs money for his infant son's surgery. Helping keep Nick on the line is the boss' curvaceous blonde girlfriend, Karen Winter (Joi Lansing). When a nosy cop (Dabbs Greer) gets too close to the action, the boss kills him, then frames Nick for the murder.

Martin's screenplay for *Hot Cars* was more than good enough to anchor a bigger production budget with a marquee cast. As it is, the movie is a hugely entertaining crime drama and noir morality tale, with Bromfield and Lansing giving star-turn performances. Lansing was a better actress than she ever had the chance to show, and this part is as good as it got for her. Plenty of period Los Angeles locations and a heart-pounding finale hoists *Hot Cars* up with some of the better end-of-the-era noirs.

Violent Road (1958), Director: Howard W. Koch

Mitch Barton (Brian Keith) leads a truck convoy racing against time to deliver a load of explosive rocket fuel to a new plant after the old facility is mothballed. Avoiding population centers, the convoy must navigate dangerous desert terrain and treacherous mountain roads. Barton's toughest job is keeping his crew in line. A bunch of desperate last-chancers, most of whom are their own worst enemy. Barton couldn't care less about any of them—he only wants the big payout of which he'll end up earning every cent.

Violent Road is not *The Wages of Fear* (1953), but then Don Martin never aspired to be Georges Arnaud, and Howard W. Koch was no Henri-Georges Clouzot. *Violent Road* is a gripping B-actioner from Warner Bros. with a workhorse supporting cast that includes Dick Foran, Arthur Batanides, Efrem Zimbalist Jr., and Perry Lopez. Also onboard is Ann Doran as Sarge's suffering wife and Merry Anders, a not-so-dumb blonde Mitch picks up one night, no strings attached. Just as well—Mitch is a Man's Man who says things like, "I knew a woman once," and "I'm not allergic to a buck" before heading on his way.

Following *Violent Road*, Martin, like many Hollywood writers of the period, took nearly full-time to television, which he'd gotten into in the early '50s, writing for a few short-lived shows. He later contributed teleplays to anthologies like *Schlitz Playhouse, Lux Video Theater,* and *Celebrity Playhouse,* the productions often featuring noir favorites such as Edmond O'Brien, Kent Smith, Arthur Franz, Alexis Smith, Scott Brady, Angela Lansbury, and Howard Duff.

IN 1957, MARTIN WAS RECRUITED to write for the TV series *Official Detective*, based on the true crime magazine of the same title (as well as a radio program which ran from 1950 to 1956). The show, riding on the coattails of popular police shows such as *Dragnet* and *M Squad,* was hosted by Everett Sloane as the "Official Detective Investigator." Of the available episodes, several contain Martin's signature tangled, violent plotlines, notably *Hostages,* an episode starring Robert Blake as one of a trio of escaped convicts who hold two teenage sisters hostage in a derelict house in downtown Los Angeles. Other Martin-scripted episodes feature an array of noir-stained supporting veterans, including Ted de Corsia, Dabbs Greer, Wayne Morris, John Doucette, and Mike Mazurki, as well as young gun Mike Connors.

After *Official Detective*, Martin shifted his attention to Western series, including *U.S. Marshal* (1958 – 1960) with John Bromfield, *The Texan* (1958 – 1960) featuring Rory Calhoun, and *Bronco* (1958 – 1962) starring Ty Hardin. Typically, Martin had come well prepared having earlier written several well-received "Westerns": Jacques Tourneur's *Stranger on Horseback* (1955) with Joel McCrea, *Quincannon, Frontier Scout* (1956) starring Tony Martin, The *Brass Legend* (1956) headlining Hugh O'Brian, and *The Storm Rider* (1957) with Scott Brady.

Don Martin was nothing if not versatile, and he ranks among the most productive and reliable writers to toil in the take-no-prisoners world of Hollywood B-movie and television production. No matter what the genre or the medium, he would forever stay faithful to "the story." Don Martin passed away in Woodland Hills, California, in 1985, at the age of 74. ■

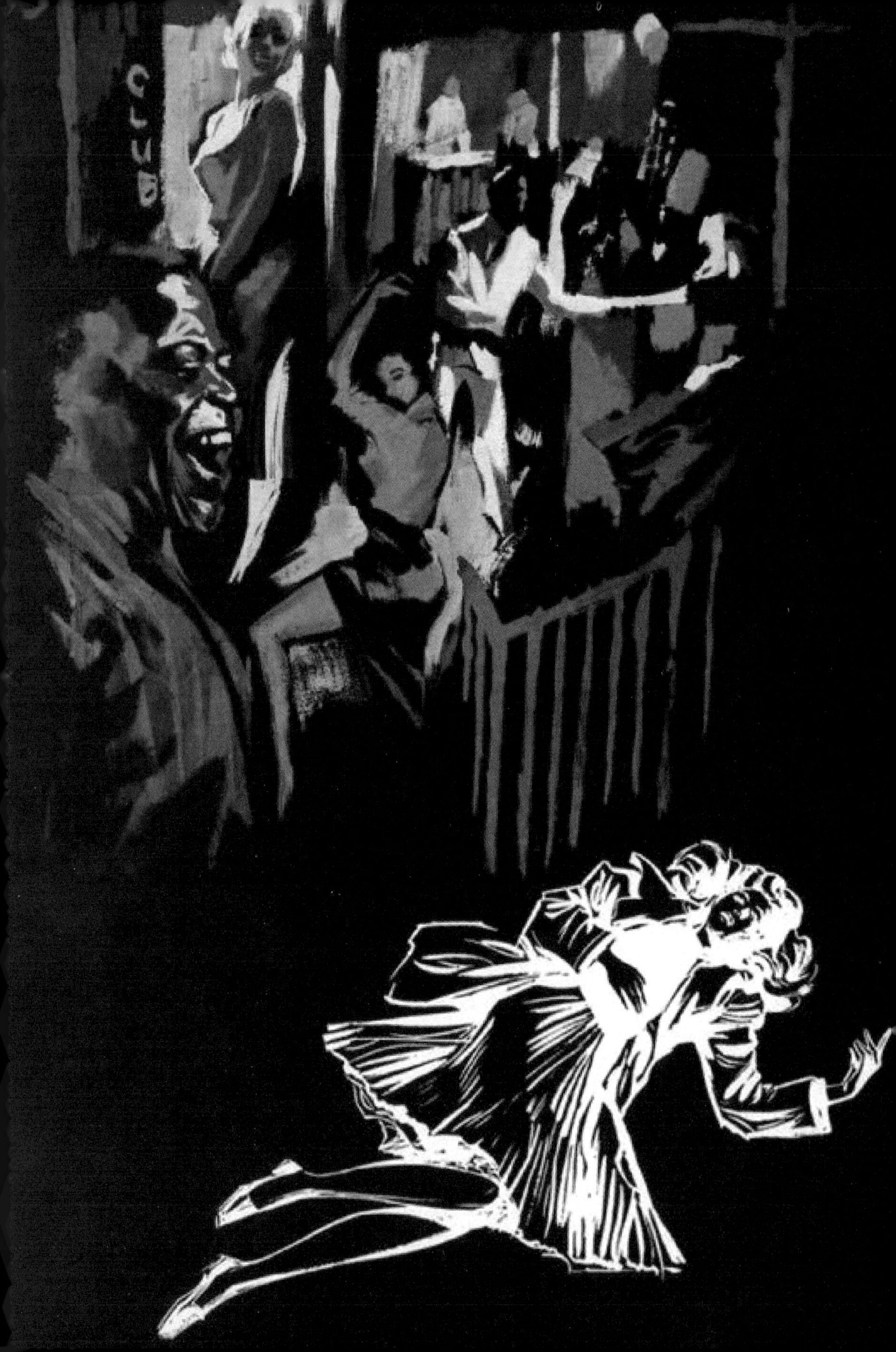
CLUB

Windrush Noir

Racism in *Pool of London* and *Sapphire*

Ray Banks

"Passenger Opportunity to United Kingdom"

Tuesday 22nd June, 1948. The HMT *Empire Windrush*—once a German cruise ship named *Monte Rosa*, now a prize of the Second World War—docked at Tilbury with just under 500 passengers aboard. Britain was still reeling from the war, and The British Nationality Act of 1948 aimed to fill the gaps in the labour market with Commonwealth citizens—mostly from the Caribbean—some of whom had fought for the "mother country" only three years before. For many, the £28 ticket was the promise of a new, better life.

Over at Ealing Studios, screenwriters T. E. B. Clarke and John Eldridge had been assigned *Pool of London*, a slice-of-life drama set on that dingy stretch of the Thames between London Bridge and Cuckold's Point. The Pool was once the centre of the merchant shipping trade and a hive of criminality—the very first police force was formed at the end of the 18th century as a direct response to the theft and fraud in the Pool—but by the beginning of the 1950s, the docks were already in decline. It would be the perfect setting for the kind of gritty, realist drama Michael Balcon had pioneered in his tenure as head of the studio.

But Clarke had other ideas. Much to Balcon's chagrin, he turned Eldridge's outline into a heist comedy about a Bank of England drone who relieves his employer of a fortune in gold bullion. Balcon assigned the new script—now titled *The Lavender Hill Mob*—to Charles Crichton, and reassigned *Pool of London* to Jack Whittingham, who had just written the crime melodrama *Cage of Gold* for Basil Dearden and Michael Relph. Dearden and Relph were already familiar with the setting—the Pool had featured in a key scene in their first film as director-producer team, *The Bells Go Down* (1943)—and they were keen to revisit the documentary techniques that had informed their biggest hit to date, the police drama *The Blue Lamp* (1950). *Pool of London* would be an opportunity to show the underbelly of London, racial tensions and all.

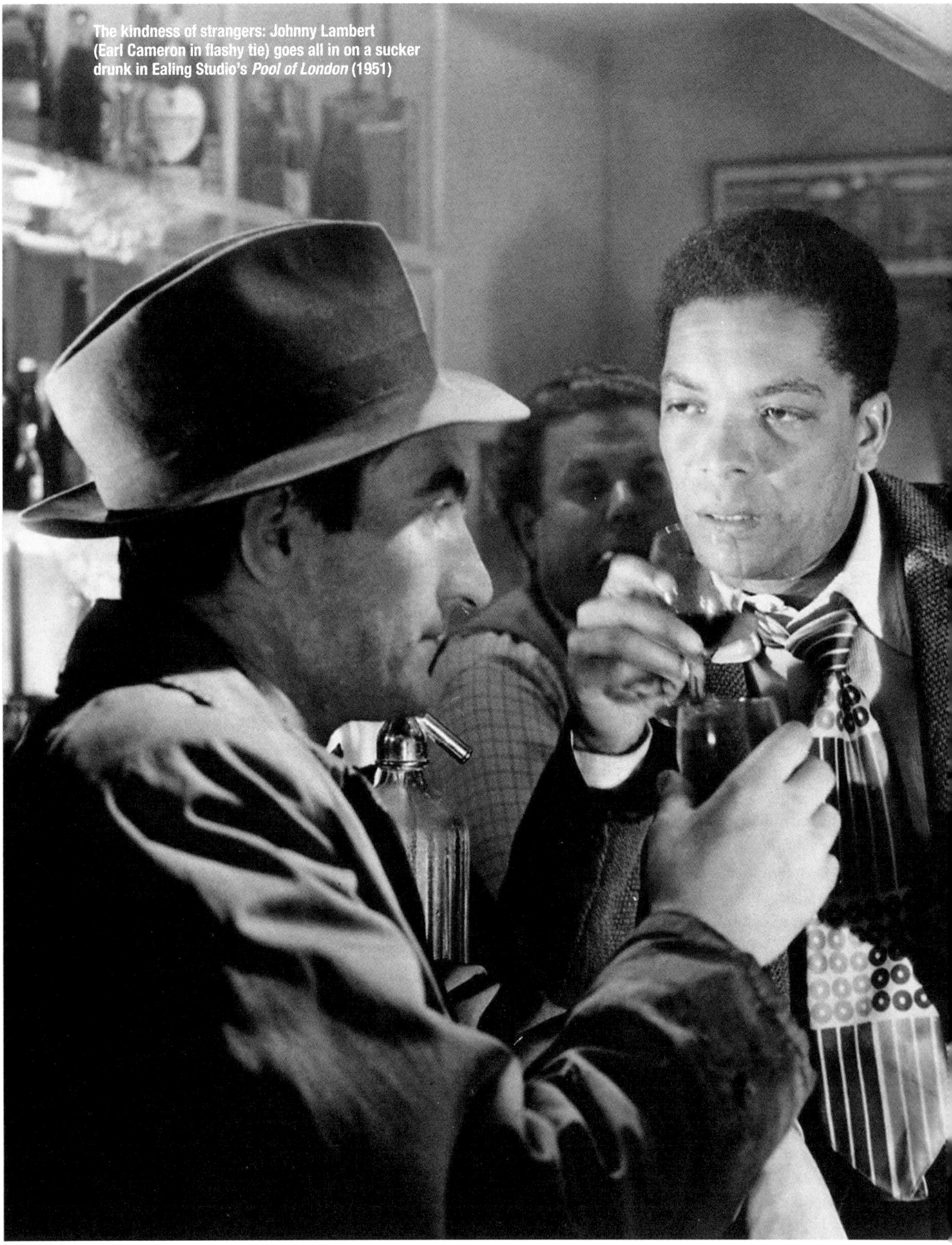

The kindness of strangers: Johnny Lambert (Earl Cameron in flashy tie) goes all in on a sucker drunk in Ealing Studio's *Pool of London* (1951)

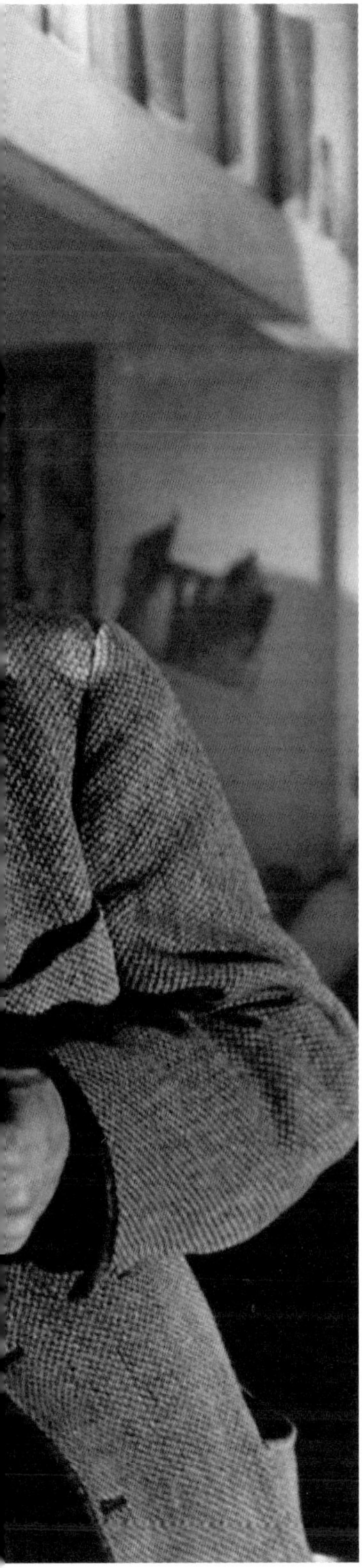

spread through the white community that a black man had raped a white girl. Mobs of 500 and more took to the streets, smashing windows and bellowing racist slurs. It wasn't until a group of mostly Jamaicans retaliated with Molotov cocktails that the white mob retreated and the police moved in to make arrests. Despite the violence, there were no deaths, but the Notting Hill Riots were a local and national event thanks to television, and became a defining moment in post-war Britain. And while the disturbance was just as much a product of grinding poverty as it was overt racism, it was the latter that shouted loudest. Britain had once united with its colonies to fight the fascist menace; now it was growing its own. The "mother country" was a myth.

By 1958, Ealing Studios was a studio in name only—the facilities had been sold to the BBC in 1955, and MGM had effectively taken over production duties at Borehamwood. The Free Cinema movement of the mid-1950s made Ealing's drama-documentaries seem quaint by comparison, and what Kenneth Tynan once called Ealing's "patriotic realism" would be downright unfashionable in the age of Angry Young Men and the burgeoning British New Wave. Though Dearden and Relph were involved with the last of Ealing's output (Relph directed the sentimental Harry Secombe vehicle *Davy* with Dearden producing, and Dearden did uncredited work on Ealing's only true noir movie *Nowhere to Go*), they had already moved over to Rank, where they had recently completed Britain's gritty response to *The Blackboard Jungle*, the Liverpool-set juvenile delinquency drama *Violent Playground*. After the Notting Hill Riots, there was only one topic Dearden and Relph wanted to explore. "We plan to show this prejudice as the stupid and illogical thing it is," they said in a production feature for *Kine Weekly* in December 1958. That production would take a deep, disturbing dive into the fears of white Britain, this time masquerading as a whodunit.

"Would you be pleased with a brass sovereign, Superintendent?"

Sapphire (1959) opens with the discovery of the eponymous young woman's body on Hampstead Heath. She has been brutally stabbed to death. Superintendent Hazard (Nigel Patrick) and Inspector Learoyd (Michael Craig) first suspect Sapphire's student boyfriend David (Paul Massie), but he has an alibi for the night in question. Further complications arise: the autopsy reveals that Sapphire was three months pregnant, and when her brother Dr. Robbins (Earl Cameron) arrives at the station, the police learn that Sapphire was mixed race, passing for white with her university friends by day and trawling the black jazz clubs at night. This apparently promiscuous double life throws up another suspect in the form of Johnnie Fiddle (Harry Baird), her former dance partner. Johnnie's subsequent flight from the law and his possession of what looks like the murder weapon would appear to confirm his guilt, but Hazard's suspicions lie elsewhere, especially when David's alibi starts to crumble and it becomes clear that David's nice middle-class family are hiding a bloody secret.

If *Pool of London* whispered its criticism of Britain's bigotry, then

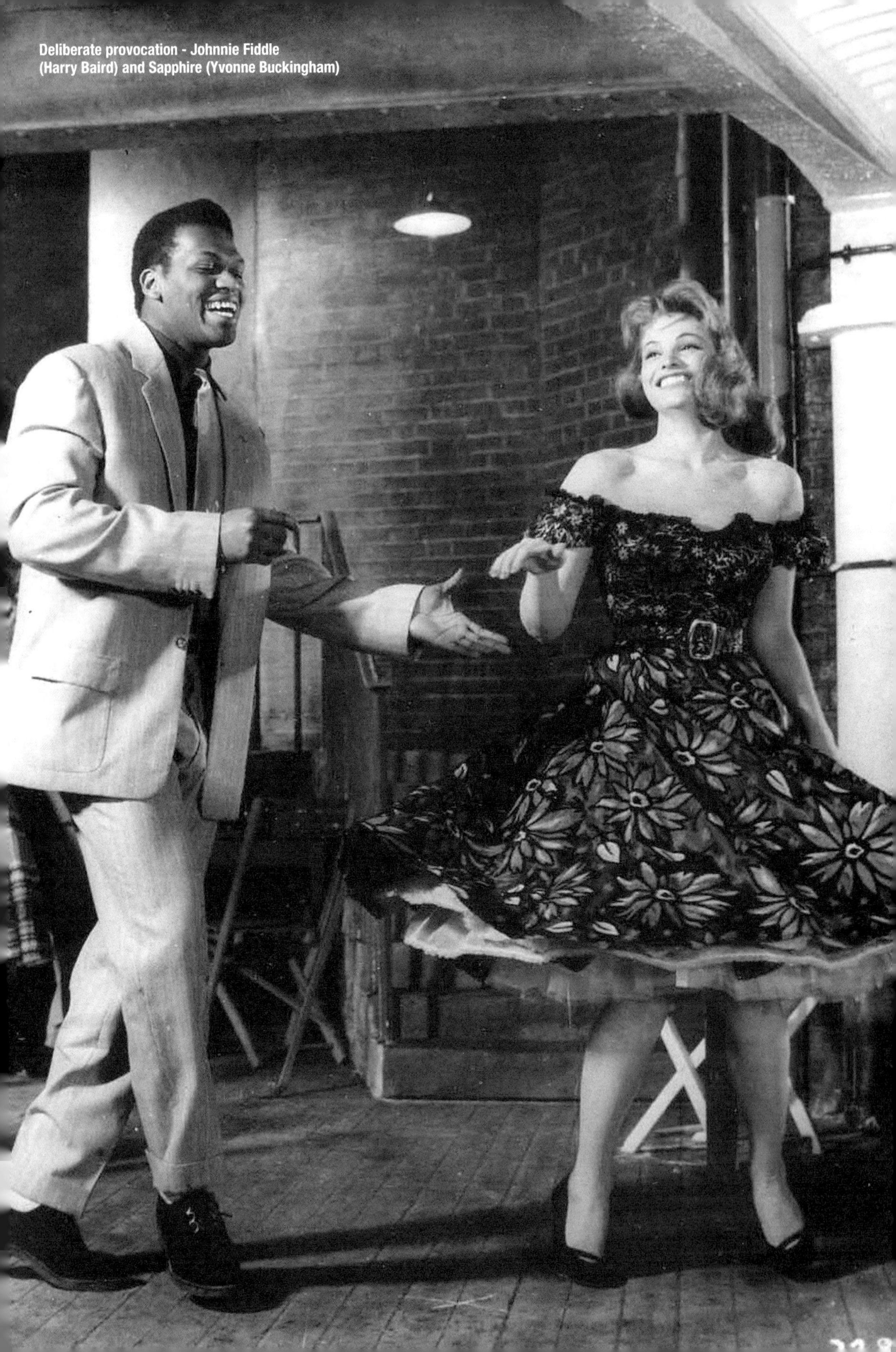

Deliberate provocation - Johnnie Fiddle (Harry Baird) and Sapphire (Yvonne Buckingham)

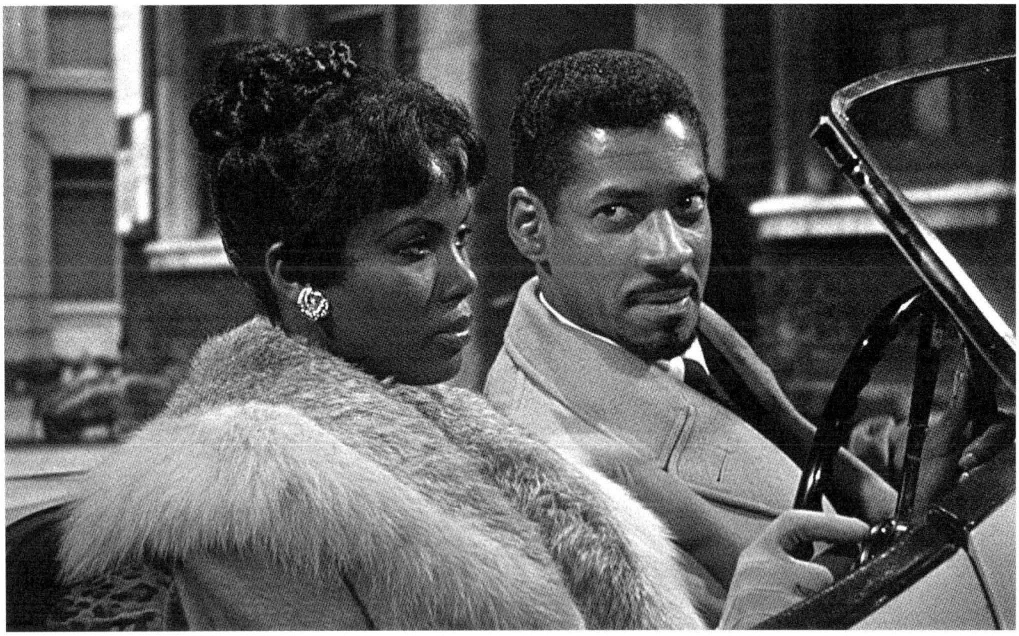

Gordon Heath as Paul Slade, the seething counterpart to Dr. Robbins in *Sapphire*

Sapphire delivers its condemnation in a full-throated roar. Seven years later, racism is no longer confined to the unsympathetic underclass who populate the Pool, but has become an integral feature of an aspirational middle-class. Screenwriter Janet Green's previous work included the woman-in-peril crime dramas *Cast a Dark Shadow* (1955), based on her play *Murder Mistaken*, and *Eyewitness* (1956), as well as the police thrillers *Lost* (1956) and *The Long Arm* (1956), and she elegantly weaves the two genres together in *Sapphire* to explore and expose a white community's terror of miscegenation, first through the character of Sapphire herself, and then in the characterisation of the black male.

"She wasn't any delicate flower, you know."

Sapphire is barely seen and never speaks, and yet her presence haunts the film. She is the offspring of a white doctor and a black dancer—her parents a clear mix of respectable middle-class and exotic *other*—and represents the archetypal tragic mulatto, at once attractive to white men and doomed by her heritage. From her original status as victim, she swiftly becomes defined by her sexuality. Her murder is seen as a tragic (if somewhat inevitable) outcome of her apparent promiscuity, signalled by her red taffeta petticoat, her visits to jazz clubs, and her independence. A visit to the Tulip's Club confirms the bias—the "lily skin" girls frequenting the mostly black club appear as slaves to the "beat of the bongos." Most of the male clientele go by the name of Johnnie (Johnnie Rags, Johnnie Tiger, Johnnie Fiddle) and so become a seething mass of sexual predation. It would be terrifying enough if they were strangers, but these men are sailors on shore leave; they are a permanent fixture of a settled community.

The racial violence in *Sapphire* is palpable. The police pursuit and apprehension of Johnnie Fiddle is notable for the problems it caused censors at the time. Dearden and Relph were instructed to cut scenes of Teddy Boys attacking a shop where Johnnie takes brief refuge—uncomfortably echoing recent events—and to lower the volume of the interrogation, which comes dangerously close to coercion, especially when the racist Learoyd takes the lead. An hour into the film, it's easy to believe that *Sapphire* could end with the hanging of an innocent man.

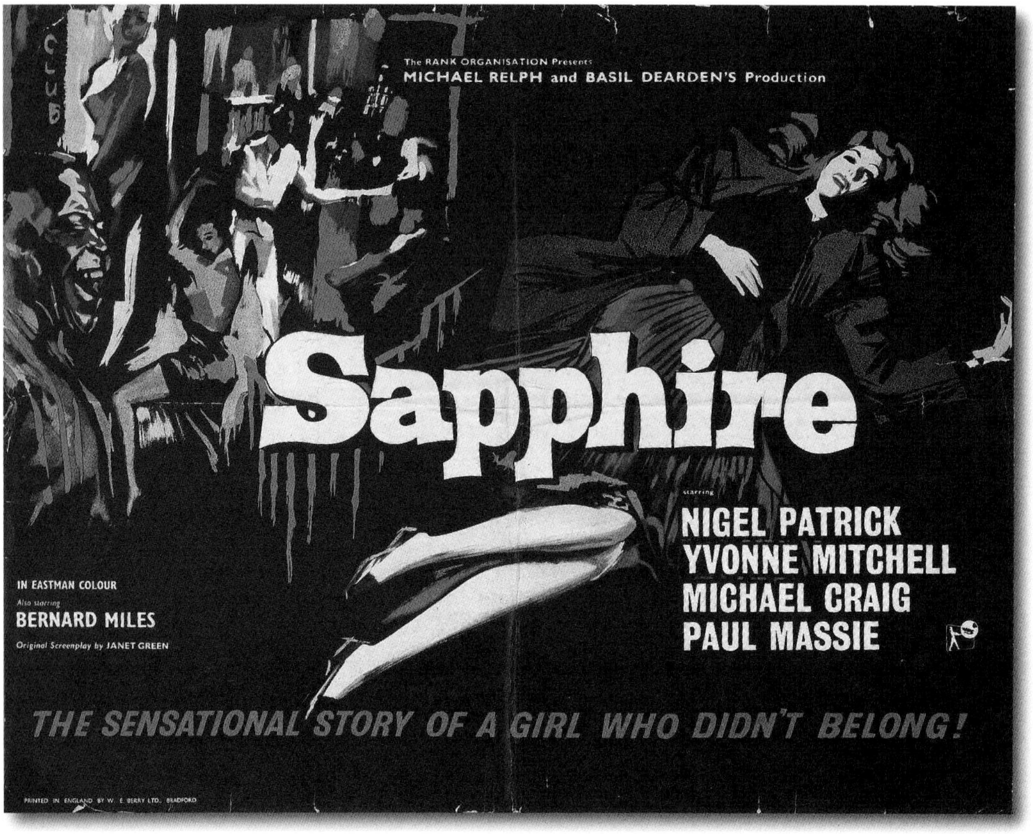

"There's no assurance for me and my kind, Superintendent. I've been black for thirty-eight years. I know."

Because even the innocent black male is a destructive force. His skin colour functions as deliberate provocation. Earl Cameron's Dr. Robbins—apparently made up to be "as dark as possible to get the contrast"—may be a respectable, educated member of the black middle-class, but his presence acts as a catalyst for prejudice wherever he goes. The most devastating example of this catalyst effect comes at the end of the film, where Robbins' handling of a doll prompts a hysterical reaction from the murderer. And it's here that the previous characterisation of the black community is revealed as canny misdirection.

Just as Learoyd's simpleminded bigotry clouds his investigative skills, so the audience's assumption of black guilt is challenged when the murderer is revealed to be a doting mother of two, driven temporarily insane by the prospect of a "yellow brat" in the family. By placing the violence squarely within a (somewhat) relatable middle-class home, the film demands that the audience question their own bias. Although there are mitigating circumstances—David's sister Mildred is clearly unhinged, and Yvonne Mitchell's screen persona comes with the echoes of previous long-suffering roles—the message remains the same: unchecked prejudice leads to tragedy.

This message ultimately denies the audience the catharsis of resolution. The murderer might have been exposed and arrested, but the suspicion remains that at least one other member of the family knew about the crime, and may even have helped to dispose of the body. Order cannot therefore be restored while racism exists. And while Learoyd insists the mystery is solved, Hazard believes otherwise: "We didn't solve anything, Phil. We just picked up the pieces."

Sapphire's ambiguous approach won the film a BAFTA, but any glory was short-lived. In the following years, the rise of the British New Wave and the auteur theory further diminished Dearden and Relph's reputations; they were dismissed as exemplars of safe, bureaucratic British studio cinema, too squeamish to challenge the establishment of which they were a part. But without that establishment, there would be no British New Wave. Michael Balcon's preference for British social realism over Hollywood tinsel established documentary verisimilitude as a key aesthetic of mainstream British cinema. He would also co-found Bryanston Films, which was instrumental in the release of *Saturday Night and Sunday Morning* (1960), *A Taste of Honey* (1961) and *The Loneliness of the Long Distance Runner* (1962). For their part, Dearden and Relph remained committed to making realist drama that reflected experiences other than their own, and would continue to break ground with their exploration of criminalised homosexuality in *Victim* (1961) and the battle between medical ethics and religious fundamentalism in *Life for Ruth* (1962).

Horace Ové would eventually break through with *Pressure* (1975), widely regarded as Britain's first feature film to document the black experience. Until then, Dearden and Relph's *Pool of London* and *Sapphire* represented earnest, considered attempts to challenge audience prejudice. While some critics have accused Dearden and Relph of political timidity for presenting the problem rather than answering it, both films portray racism as a learned behaviour—most notably in *Sapphire*, where the children are prejudice-free—and both acknowledge that any answer to the "race problem" would be trite at best. Instead, they take a position echoed by Dr. Robbins: "I see all kinds of sickness in my practice, Superintendent. I've never yet seen a kind you can cure in a day." Ultimately, Dearden and Relph felt that their duty was to provide the diagnosis; it was up to society to treat itself. ■

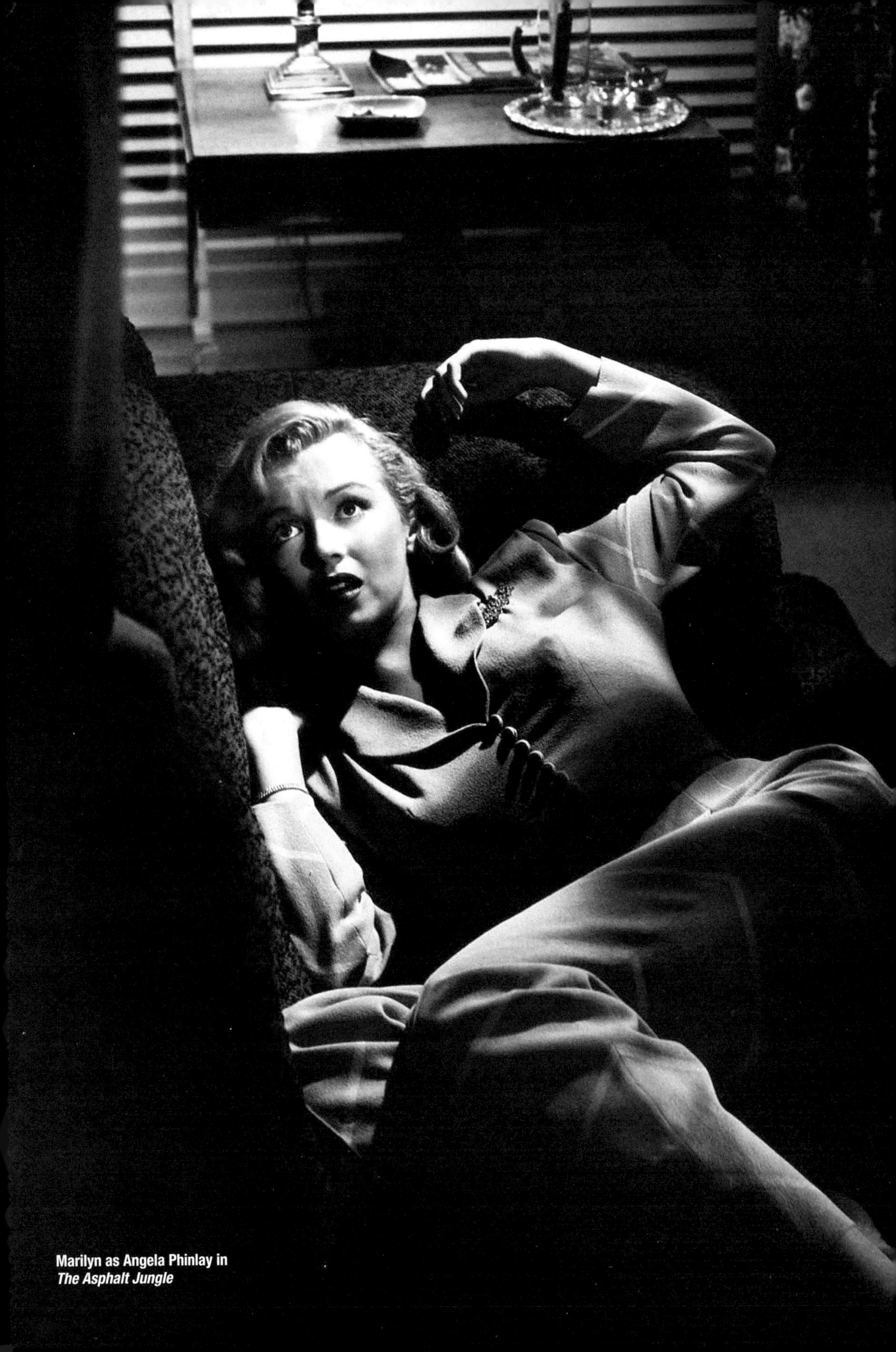

Marilyn as Angela Phinlay in
The Asphalt Jungle

Marilyn Noir

The Dark Roots of Hollywood's Blonde Bombshell

Jake Hinkson

For most of her career, Marilyn Monroe's sex appeal was literally a joke. Her biggest hits were light comedies, often with Monroe playing the naïve bombshell, the laughs arising from the way her guileless exhibitionism manages to upend the social order of any situation she happens to jiggle into. The key to these roles was the Marilyn character's seemingly innocent obliviousness to her own potent sensuality. Even when her character was in on the joke, her sexual power never posed any real threat to the men around her. For all the taboo-breaking impact of her on-screen sensuality, for most of her career, Marilyn Monroe played her characters as sweet goofballs. One of the screen's great comic forces, she was, in a word, lovable.

One place where this wasn't true was in the handful of noirs Monroe made early on in her career, before her screen image solidified. These crime films and dark dramas presented her sexual appeal as a source of danger, allowing the actor to explore the limits of her charisma. They offer a fascinating glimpse at the career Monroe might have had if she hadn't become a comedy phenomenon.

Certainly, her early life was more drama than comedy. Born Norma Jean Mortenson, she never knew the identity of her father, and her mother, a negative cutter at Consolidated Film Industries, was diagnosed with paranoid schizophrenia and committed to the state hospital when the girl was still young. For most of her childhood, Norma Jean was passed around between family friends and foster parents, including a two-year stay in the Los Angeles Orphan's Home. Married at 16 and divorced by 20, the ambitious young woman knew only one thing for sure: she wanted to be a movie star. Before long, she had hustled her way into a contract at 20th Century–Fox and changed her name to Marilyn Monroe.

After a few bit parts in small pictures, her contract at Fox was terminated in 1947, but she grabbed her first substantial role the following year at Columbia in the B-musical *Ladies in the Chorus* (1948). The modest film has director Phil Karlson's usual energy and pacing, but while Marilyn herself is affable and pretty in the role of an up-and-coming showgirl, it's easy to see why this film didn't immediately catapult her into better and bigger parts. She's good without being great, adequate without being particularly interesting. Nothing about her performance lingers after the film is over.

The Marilyn Monroe that we all remember really began in 1950, in John Huston's *The Asphalt Jungle* (made, of all places, at MGM). Adapted from W. R. Burnett's novel, the script by Huston and Ben Maddow is an urban crime epic populated by jewelry thieves, hooligans, bookies, bent cops, and steely-eyed getaway drivers. From top to bottom, the film is impeccably cast and ably performed by noir stalwarts like Sterling Hayden, Sam Jaffe, and Marc Lawrence. Even in this sprawling menagerie of great character actors, Monroe stands out. Playing Angela Phinlay, the young mistress of corrupt lawyer Alonzo D. Emmerich (Louis Calhern), she seems fully possessed for the first time on-screen.

Huston gives her a star's entrance into the film, with Emmerich watching Angela, bathed in white light, sleeping on a sofa. When she wakes up, she teases him, "What's the big idea staring at me like that, Uncle Lon?"

"Don't call me Uncle Lon," he says.

"I thought you liked it," she says defensively.

"Maybe I did," he replies. "I don't anymore."

The interplay between Monroe and Calhern is perfect. There's an edge to the way she delivers the line "I thought you liked it," (which leaves little doubt they're talking about more

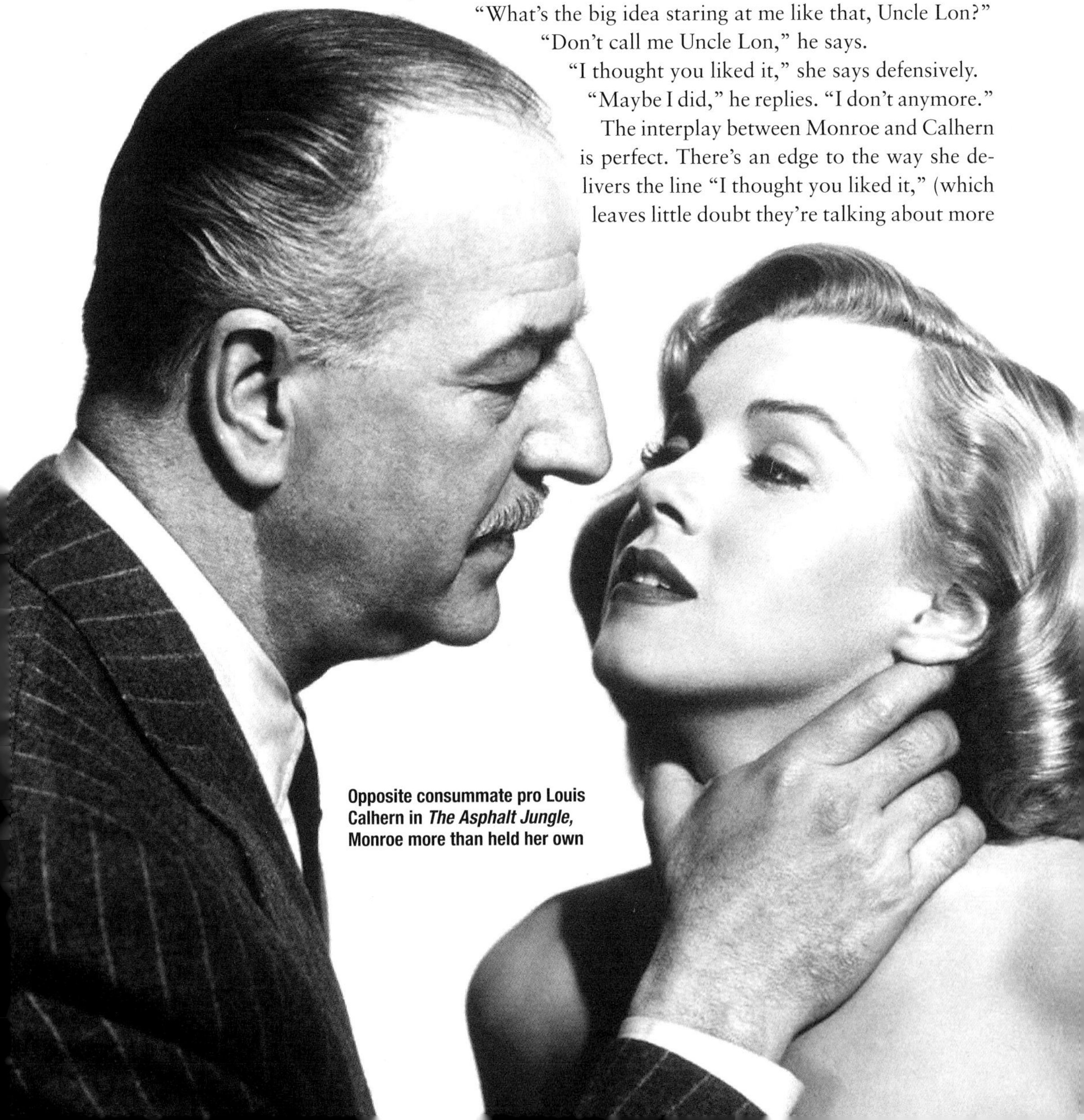

Opposite consummate pro Louis Calhern in *The Asphalt Jungle*, Monroe more than held her own

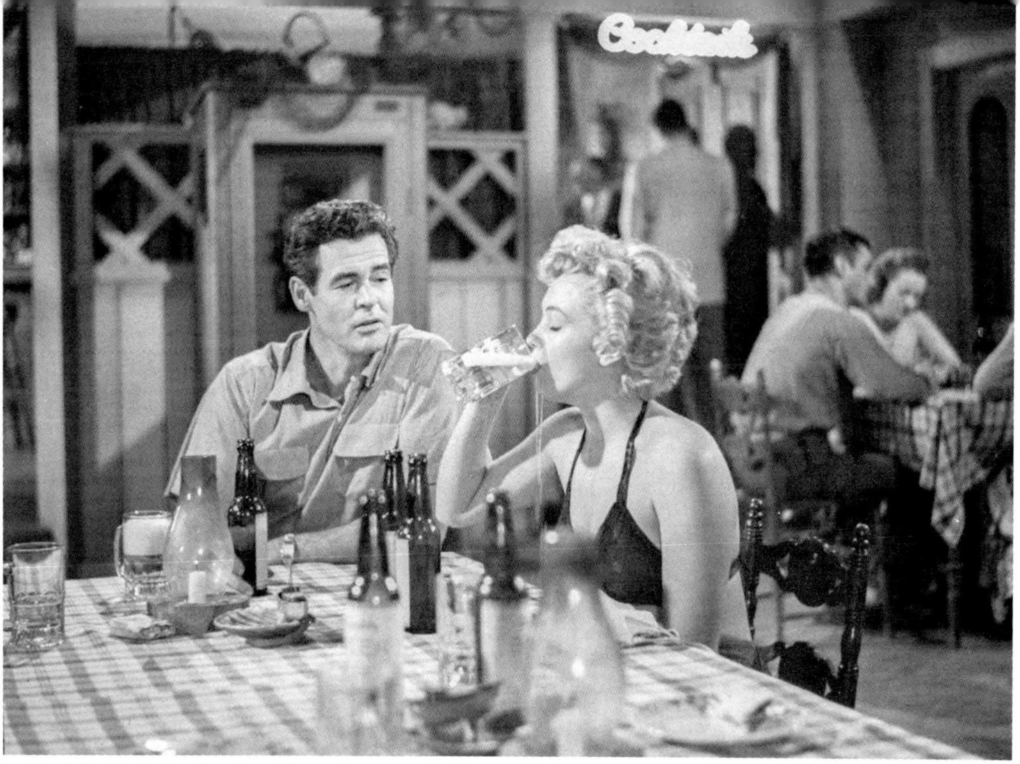

In *Clash by Night*, Marilyn found herself surrounded by top-flight actors Barbara Stanwyck, Paul Douglas, and Robert Ryan (pictured)—yet she left the most indelible impression. A star is born

than a nickname) and there's shrewdness in the way she looks him over and switches the subject. She knows what the score is. As played by the excellent Calhern, Emmerich is a man in the grip of a crushing midlife crisis. He's latched onto Angela in the hopes that her youth and sexuality will work whatever restorative magic such men hope to find in the arms of younger women (Calhern was 54 when the film was made, while Monroe was 23). We see her only in the context of Emmerich's world, and her position in the film, alone among all its characters (including the female characters played by Jean Hagen, Teresa Celli, and Dorothy Tree), is based on sex, and sex of a particularly transactional kind. The kept woman of an older man, Angela clearly thinks of her "Uncle Lon" as a bank account.

After the film's central jewelry heist has gone spectacularly wrong, we see Emmerich with Angela again, making plans to send her off on a vacation to Cuba—a vacation the ruined older man must know is a pipe dream. Once the cops arrive, Angela hurries off to hide in her bedroom. When the hard-nosed police commissioner (John McIntire) sends a detective (Don Haggerty) to retrieve her, she sizes up the young cop and pouts, "Do I have to go talk to him? Couldn't I just stay here and...talk to you?"

Later, under harsh questioning from the commissioner, she drops the sex appeal and plays the small, scared animal instead. Collapsing into tears, admitting she learned the phony alibi "by heart," she sells Uncle Lon up the river. "I'm sorry," she tells her doomed lover as the police lead her away. "I tried."

Following her good notices for *The Asphalt Jungle*, Marilyn was rehired by Fox, which then quickly loaned her out to RKO for a supporting role in Fritz Lang's sweaty adultery drama *Clash by Night* (1952). Adapted from the play by Clifford Odets (with a script by Alfred Hayes), the film is a tortured romantic triangle showcasing the three stars at its center (Barbara Stanwyck, Paul Douglas, and Robert Ryan), yet it is Marilyn who pops off the screen and very nearly steals the picture. This would mark a turning point in her career.

As the film starts, cynical Mae Doyle (Stanwyck) returns to her hometown and marries a goofy lug named Jerry D'Amato (Douglas). Soon, however, Mae finds herself irresistibly attracted to Earl

Pfeiffer (Ryan), a hard-drinking misogynist and all-around nasty piece of business. While Mae heads for disaster with Jerry and Earl, a pretty cannery worker named Peggy (Monroe) works out her own heated dynamic with Mae's domineering brother Joe (Keith Andes).

Marilyn lights up the screen in this movie, both as a star on the ascent and as an actor perfecting her craft. She's luminously beautiful, and even though most of her scenes are with beefy-but-bland Keith Andes, she has enough charisma for both of them. In some respects, Peggy might be the scrappiest woman Monroe ever played on-screen. Joe is as much a misogynist as Earl, and he and Peggy have a tense, violent dynamic. In one scene, Joe and Peggy are drinking at a beach bar —him bare-chested and her in a bikini top—and Joe gets jealous when Peggy calls Earl "exciting." Irritated, Joe pretends to strangle her with a towel until she agrees that he's the one who is "exciting" (an image of rough play that would figure into the movie's advertising without the scene's "playful" context). When he releases her, she punches him in the jaw. It's a good punch, too. (Monroe really clocks Andes.) Their subplot ends by Joe demanding, and receiving, Peggy's capitulation to his manly authority, but Monroe's performance hints at unhappiness sure to come later on in their relationship. Though her role here was small, her performance showed that Monroe could hold her own with heavyweights like Stanwyck and Ryan, and that she would blast a lightweight like Andes right off the screen.

The studio took notice. The brass at 20th Century–Fox (in particular, studio chief Daryl F. Zanuck, who had hitherto paid her scant attention) finally realized that Marilyn Monroe wasn't just some busty knockoff of Betty Grable. In addition to *The Asphalt Jungle* and *Clash by Night*, she'd also performed a small but showy role in Fox's own 1950 hit *All About Eve*, and by 1951, the studio began taking an active interest in developing her as a star.

The first starring role that Monroe was assigned by her home studio was *Don't Bother to Knock* (1952), a tense thriller adapted from the excellent novel *Mischief* by Charlotte Armstrong. The film casts Marilyn as Nell, a disturbed young woman enlisted by her Uncle Eddie (Elisha Cook Jr.) to babysit at the hotel where Eddie works as an elevator operator. Nell is hired to look after Bunny (Donna Corcoran), the young daughter of Peter and Ruth Jones (Jim Backus and Lurene Tuttle) who are in town for an awards banquet.

Once Nell is in charge, however, she banishes Bunny to bed, rummages through the Jones' things, and tries on Ruth's négligée and perfume. When she spies a handsome stranger across the hotel courtyard, she invites him over for a drink.

The stranger is Jed Towers (Richard Widmark), and he's in for a hell of a night. He's just broken up with his girlfriend (Anne Bancroft), so when the voluptuous young Nell gives him the come-on, he grabs a bottle and licks his lips and rushes over like an idiot. What Jed doesn't know is that the delusional young woman thinks he's her dead boyfriend.

While Charlotte Armstrong's source novel expertly merges the tawdry babysitter-gone-wrong storyline with an astute probe of latent maternal guilt, director Roy Ward Baker (*Inferno*) and screenwriter Daniel Taradash (*From Here to Eternity*) merely do a workman-like job of adapting her book to the screen. Reducing, in both importance and size, the role of the mother, they focus almost entirely on the Nell-Jed part of the story. This refocusing is predictable, if still unfortunate, but more mystifying is the way they tone down the central storyline. Downplaying the innately trashy thrill of the naughty-gone-nutty babysitter storyline, the filmmakers give Nell a tragic backstory which overexplains her actions and softens her culpability, thus making her less of an id unleashed and more of a case study. Likewise, they make Widmark's Jed too stolid. In the film's tensest moments, his discomfort never rises to the level of panic and perspiration; at his most distressed, Jed mostly seems irritated. The resulting movie shakes out as less of a nightmare and more of a morality tale. Nell is just a confused girl, and Jed is just a man who needs to learn his lesson, and that's that.

The saving grace of the film is the central performance by Monroe. She enters the movie looking as dowdy as she ever appeared on-screen (which is to say that she looks beautiful), dressed in a loose sweater over a high collar, with her light brown hair pulled back under a little hat. On her next film,

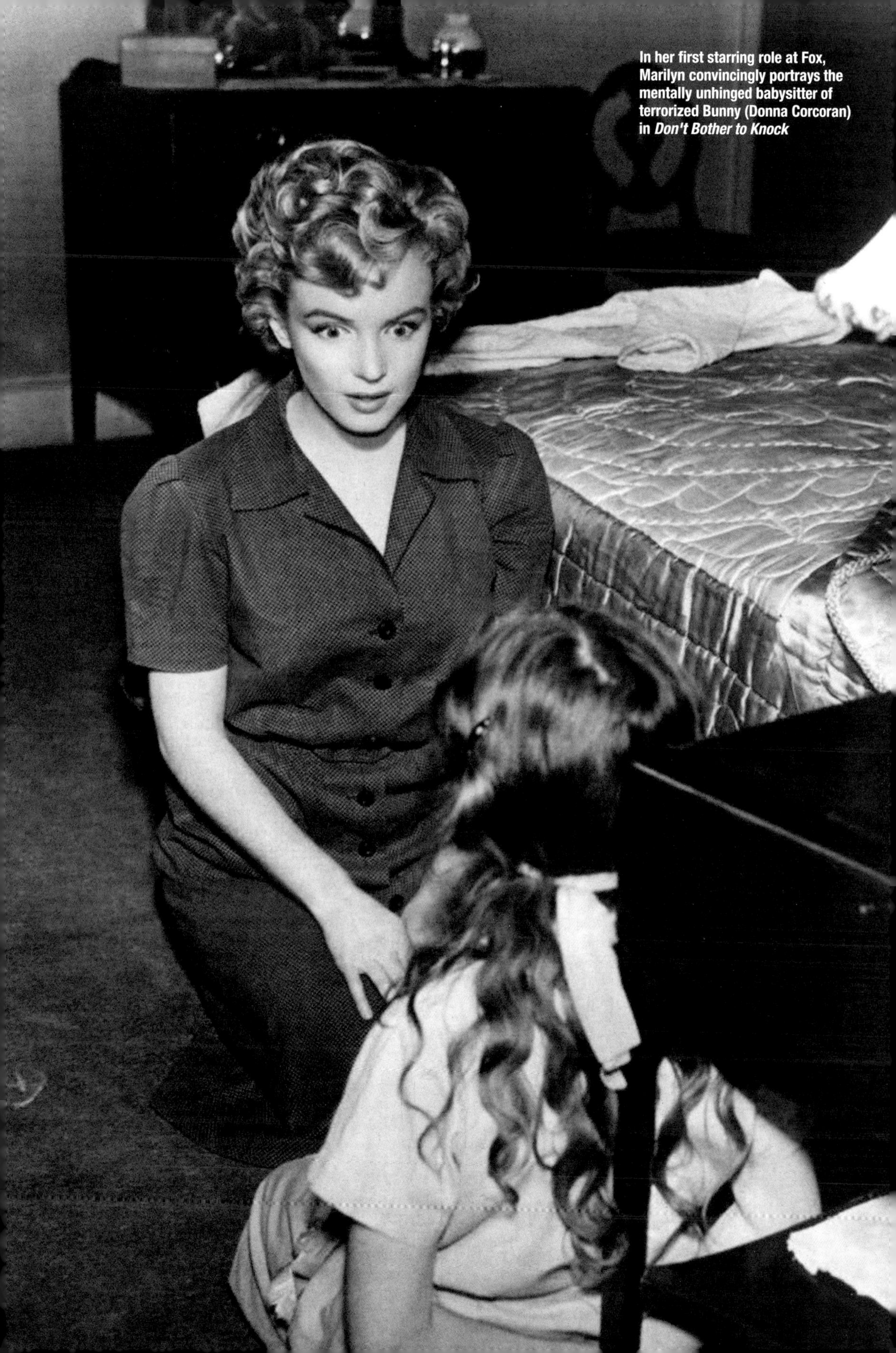

In her first starring role at Fox, Marilyn convincingly portrays the mentally unhinged babysitter of terrorized Bunny (Donna Corcoran) in *Don't Bother to Knock*

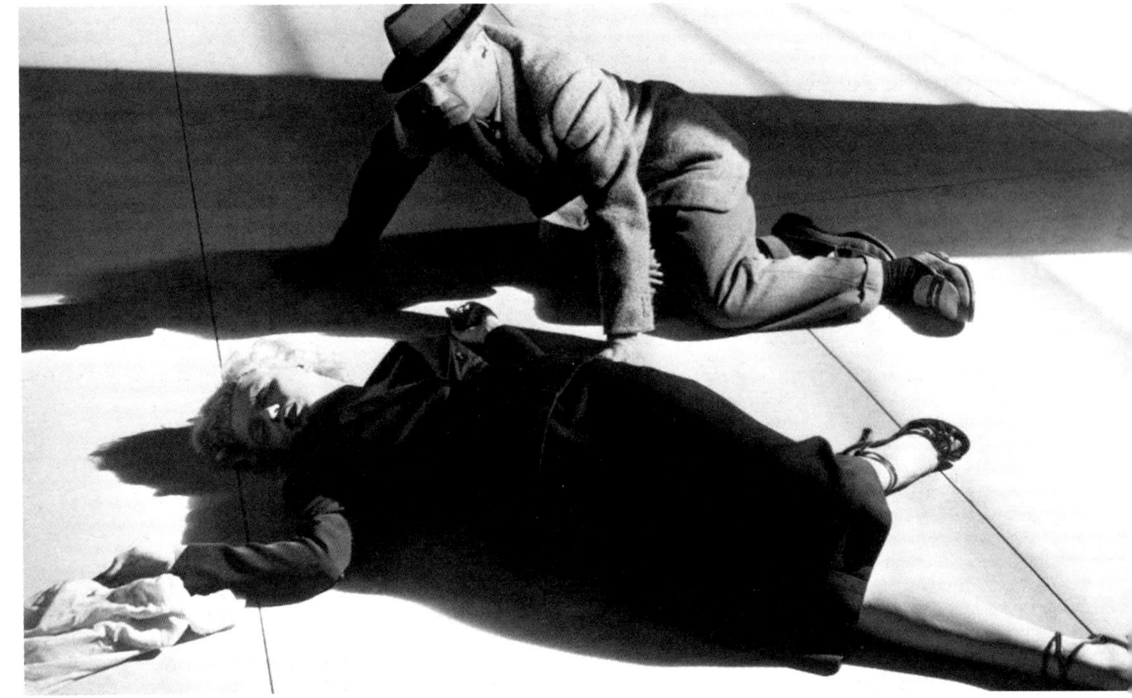

In the lush Technicolor noir *Niagara*, Marilyn is literally too sexy to live; she's done in by the jealous husband who could never satisfy her, played by Joseph Cotten

Monroe would develop one of the most distinctive walks in movies, a voluptuous sway that would become as famous as John Wayne's macho swagger, but here she moves tentatively, hands clutched in front of her. Her early interplay with Widmark is nicely offbeat—they're never having quite the same conversation at the same time—and quickly something happens that would rarely happen again in a Marilyn Monroe movie: she loses her control over a man. The promise of sex gets Jed into the hotel room, but Nell's lies are sloppy and her evasions are transparent. She starts to creep him out a little. "Half the time, I don't know what you're talking about," he tells her. When Bunny wakes up, Nell becomes convinced that the little girl is ruining her chances with Jed. ("It's wicked to come between people," she hisses at the child.) After almost pushing Bunny out the window, she binds and gags the girl while Jed paces in the next room. When her Uncle Eddie shows up unexpectedly, Nell clubs him in the head with a standing ashtray. Then, she threatens to kill herself with a razor.

The filmmakers don't do as much with this story as they could have, but, in the context of Monroe's career, *Don't Bother to Knock* marks a unique milestone. It's the first time Marilyn was an actual threat to a man. When Jed enters her hotel room, he thinks he's getting an early version of the Marilyn Monroe that would soon become a sensation: the laughing good-time girl cooing baby talk while displaying her cleavage. What he gets instead is Psycho Marilyn, the blithe sexpot's dark twin sister, a woman whose sexual allure masks trauma, rage, and violence.

Impressed by *Don't Bother to Knock,* and even more certain that Marilyn should be cast in some film that did more to glamorize her on-screen image, the studio rushed her into another noir, Henry Hathaway's *Niagara* (1953). At last, this was the A-list, with an experienced noir director like Hathaway (*Kiss of Death*) at the helm, a talented cinematographer like Joseph MacDonald handling the film's lush Technicolor visuals, and writers like Charles Brackett working on the script.

Niagara casts Monroe as Rose Loomis, the bored wife of a very upset man named George Loomis (a suitably maladroit Joseph Cotten). They're vacationing at Niagara Falls when they meet Polly and Ray Cutler (Jean Peters and Max Showalter), a young couple on their honeymoon. Polly Cutler immediately notices that Mister and Missus Loomis are as miserable as any couple can make each other—both her boredom and his neediness reek of pathology. Intrigued, Polly gets drawn further into their lives when she catches Rose kissing another man under the Falls and planning George's murder. When a body washes up under the waterfall, Polly fears it's George. When the body turns out to be Rose's boyfriend, Rose takes off, trying to escape her vengeful husband. She won't get far.

Niagara presents a fascinating Marilyn Monroe, one with all the glamour of a major star, but one untethered to a preexisting notion of what it means to be *Marilyn Monroe*. Blonde and tan, her blue eyes sparkle in vivid Technicolor. Packed into beautiful dresses and in high heels, she saunters seductively, the on-screen birth of the Marilyn walk. For the first time, she doesn't just look beautiful. She looks larger than life.

Yet what makes *Niagara* compelling is that it allows Monroe a kind of freedom she rarely got again. Rose Loomis was the only *femme fatale* she ever played, and her performance is a distinctive characterization. In most noirs, the *femme fatale* uses sex as a way to induce the man to other forms of sin, like theft and murder. In *Niagara*, sex isn't a tool to get something else. It's the source of the conflict. Driven largely out of contempt, Rose torments her husband by withholding sex, as a form of punishment. Since Monroe's every moment in the movie is suffused with her sensual allure, the weaponizing of her sensuality is particularly potent. The more she withholds her body from him, the more he wants her, and the less she thinks of him.

Though the film presents her as a villain, Rose Loomis was also one of the few grown-up women that Monroe ever got to play. The famous introductory shot of her smoking naked in bed, legs splayed open under one sheer white sheet, is a brazen image of sexual maturity, about as brazen as she ever got. The other side of the coy sexpot in *The Asphalt Jungle*, this is the image of a woman bored with her life, ready to move on, pondering her options. Tellingly, she's alone. *Niagara* gives Monroe a lot of time alone on-screen, thinking, scheming, panicking. Her scenes opposite Polly Cutler are even more telling. Marilyn's the older, wiser woman, jaded and amused by the younger woman's domestic happiness, and what can one say about Monroe's performance except that she does indeed seem to have seen it all?

At the end of *Niagara*, George Loomis takes his revenge on Rose, strangling her in a moodily shot sequence in a bell tower. Since she tried to have him murdered so she could run off with her lover, her killing is presented as a kind of justifiable homicide. In a sense, though, at the end of *Niagara*, Joseph Cotten is murdering the Noir Monroe. Though the movie was big hit, *Niagara* would be her final film noir, and after this, Marilyn would never again play a character with as much fierce sexual autonomy. It was almost as if Hollywood recognized her power and flinched. The woman who would become *the* sexual icon of her age couldn't be allowed to wield her sexuality for dangerous purposes. She could woo a man and win a man, but she couldn't be allowed to threaten a man.

Niagara was quickly followed that same year by two even bigger hits, *Gentleman Prefer Blondes* and *How to Marry a Millionaire*, both of which began the process of codifying her on-screen persona as essentially light and comic. 20th Century–Fox had intended 1953 to be the year that announced her as a star, and she had succeeded beyond anyone's expectations. By the end of 1953, Marilyn Monroe was the hottest movie star in the world.

She would spend the rest of her life chasing down exactly what it meant to be *Marilyn Monroe*. One reason her film noirs remain interesting is because she never played the same role twice. In each of her four noirs, Monroe played a different female archetype prominent in the genre: the fallen angel (*The Asphalt Jungle*), the good girl (*Clash by Night*), the psycho (*Don't Bother to Knock*), and the *femme fatale* (*Niagara*). It's a testament to her talent that she was good in all of these roles. In the years to come, she would complain mightily about the studios typecasting her in musicals and romantic comedies as the goofy sexpot or the lovable gold digger. She would always say she was capable of more. Her film noirs show she was right. ■

NOIR...OR NOT?

KNIFE TO MEET YOU

THE *GIALLO* CINEMA OF MARIO BAVA

Steve Kronenberg

"In my entire career, I made only big bullshits." That's how Mario Bava summarized his extensive filmography. His fans knew better. Over the course of 34 years, Bava transcended low budgets and lent his considerable directorial skills to comedies, Westerns, horror films, and sword-and-sandal "epics." Still, his greatest contribution to film may have been the development of *giallo* cinema, an Italian crime genre that plunged viewers into a world of perversity and madness, soaked in kaleidoscopic color. Devoid of supernatural elements, most *gialli* aren't really horror films—but are they noir?

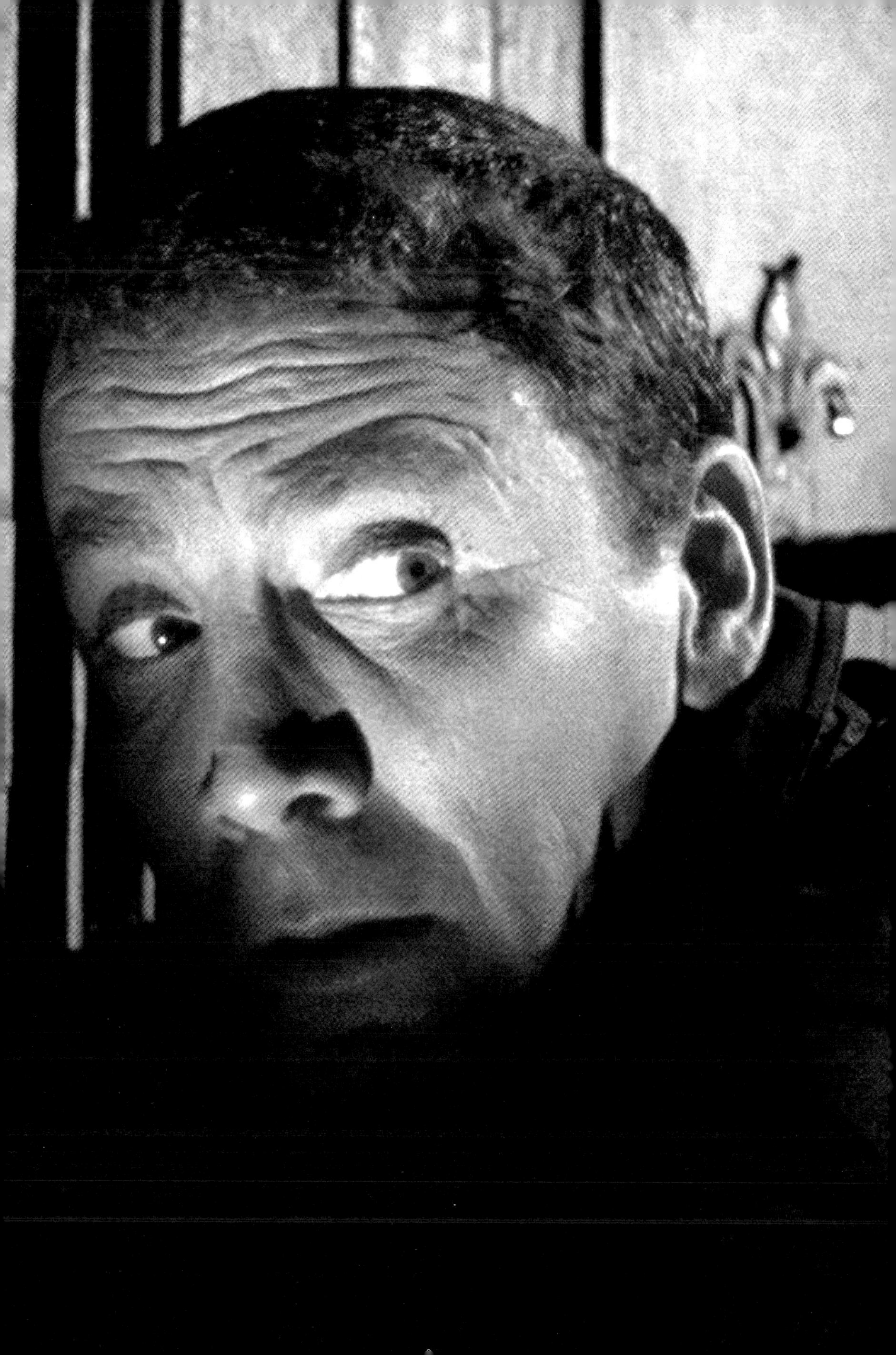

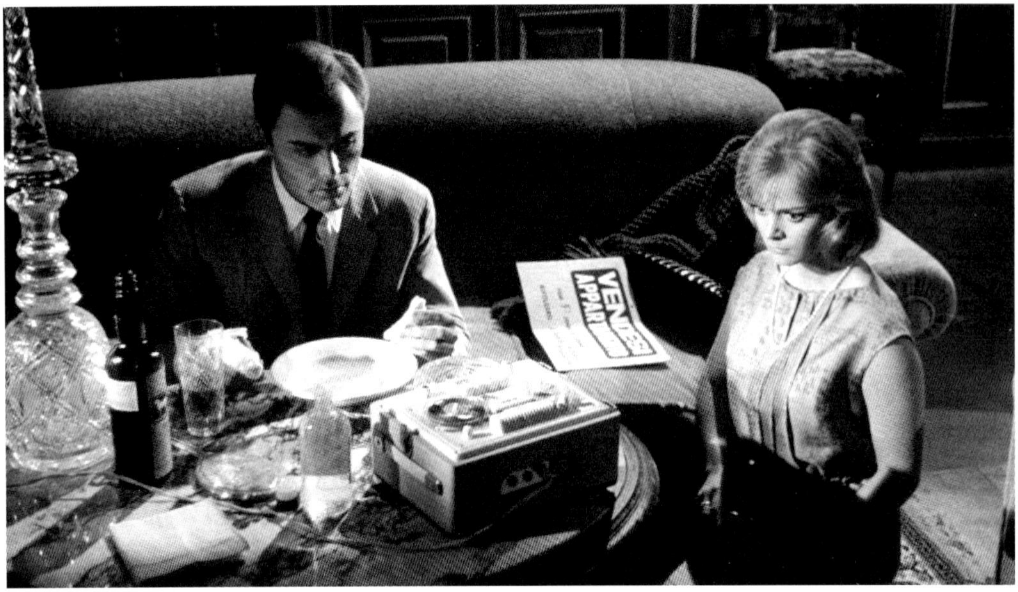

A vintage Chianti barely provides a respite for Letícia Román and John Saxon as they investigate a series of grisly murders in *The Girl Who Kew Too Much*

Giallo (English translation: "yellow") originated in 1929 when Italian publisher Arnoldo Mondadori introduced a series of paperbacks translating the works of renowned American and British crime novelists. The books, which bore yellow covers and lurid art, became enormously popular—an Italian version of the French *Série Noir* published by Éditions Gallimard. Other publishers followed Mondadori's lead and eager readers were soon devouring yellow-jacketed works by Agatha Christie, Edgar Wallace, Raymond Chandler, and Erle Stanley Gardner. Italy's first *giallo*-based film was Luchino Visconti's *Ossessione* (1943), an unlicensed adaptation of James M. Cain's *The Postman Always Rings Twice*. The books, as well as Visconti's film, were banned by Benito Mussolini's fascist regime for their "corrupting" influence.

After World War II, *giallo* literature once again thrived, and Bava took notice. *Giallo* films, named after their paperbacked forebears, focus on the depravity of the human soul, augmented by strikingly stylish cinematography, jarring musical scores—and generous helpings of grue. *Giallo* protagonists are usually menaced by masked murderers garbed in dark clothing and black leather gloves. The killings are grisly and savage, yet filmed in a peculiarly baroque and beautiful style. *Giallo* cinema reflected Italy's cultural turmoil during the mid-1960s and '70s, much as American film noir mirrored postwar upheavals in the United States. *Gialli* incorporate Italy's obsessions with fashion, gender identity, urban malaise, repressed sexuality, and bourgeois ennui. Few characters are sympathetic or likeable. Writer Gregory Small succinctly described *giallo*'s twisted aesthetic: "In *giallo*, everybody has some dirty secret, everybody has something to hide. The *giallo* world is one of cynicism, greed, sexual depravity, and violence."

Mario Bava is generally considered the godfather of *giallo* cinema. From his birth in 1914, Bava was destined for a career in film. His father, Eugenio, was one of Italy's earliest and most innovative cinematographers. Educated in the fine arts, Bava's passion for painting led to an interest in cinematography, nurtured under his father's tutelage. In 1939, aided by his father's connections, the budding filmmaker began lensing short subjects for Roberto Rossellini. In the late 1940s and early '50s, Bava shot several of Gina Lollobrigida's early films, and collaborated with Orson Welles on *Portrait of Gina*, a 1958 documentary on La Lolla (the actress hated the film and successfully enjoined its stateside release). Later, he photographed low-budget pictures for elder cinema statesmen Jacques Tourneur and Raoul Walsh (who

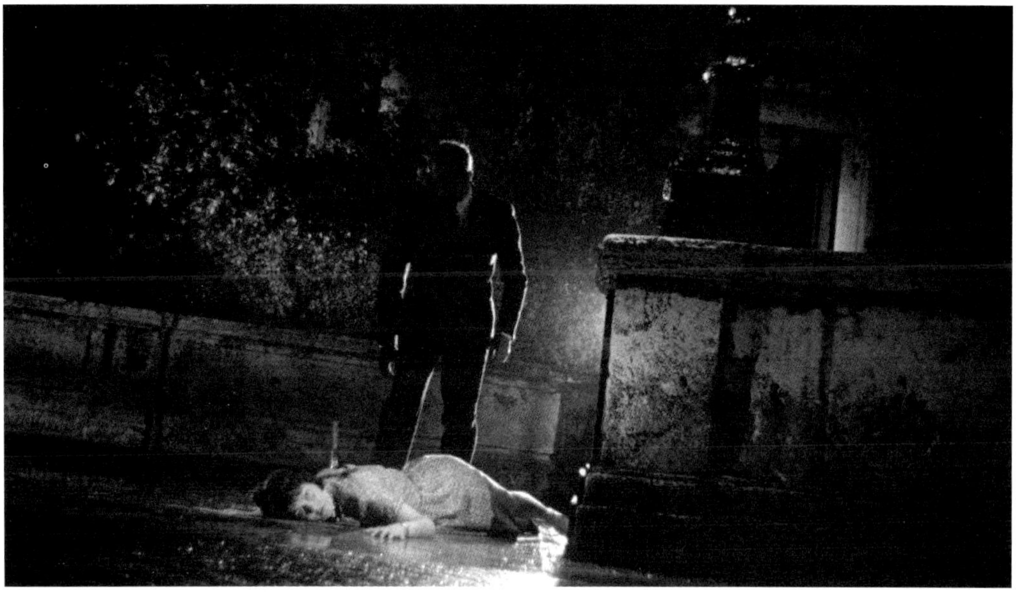

When in Rome... Letícia Román's Italian vacation is disrupted when she witnesses a brutal murder in *The Girl Who Knew Too Much*

called Bava "a genius who knew all about cinema technique"). In 1959, Bava reluctantly found himself doing double duty, photographing and then supervising films begun and abandoned by other directors.

He made his full-fledged directorial debut with the Gothic horror classic *Black Sunday* (1960). The film was a critical and financial success, and Bava was determined to meld its graphic style with the mood and mystery of film noir. Inspired by the work of Fritz Lang and Alfred Hitchcock, Bava birthed *giallo* cinema with *The Girl Who Knew Too Much* (1963). With its derivative title and intriguing story, *Girl* is a shadowy homage to Hitchcock in particular and film noir in general. Nora Davis (Letícia Román) a devotee of *giallo* novels, is en route to Rome to visit her aunt (during the flight she reads a yellow-covered mystery titled *The Knife*). Soon after her arrival, she witnesses a murder and realizes she's now targeted by the killer, a psychopath known as "The Alphabet Killer." With Hitchcockian aplomb, the young woman decides to solve the crimes with the help of a young doctor (John Saxon) and her aunt's breezy neighbor (Valentina Cortese). Aided by Ubaldo Terzano's atmospheric photography, Bava infuses the film with dread. The picture's black-and-white palette, an obvious nod to noir, is dappled with swatches of darkness and high key lighting: Nora's nocturnal elevator ride to an abandoned apartment; her disorienting descent down a brightly lit corridor illuminated by rhythmically swinging light bulbs; the startling subjective shots of the killer's violent attacks, recalling the voyeurism of *The Spiral Staircase*, *Peeping Tom*, and *Psycho*. Rome's exteriors are filmed in a gritty, grimy haze, reminiscent of the menacing tone of Fritz Lang's *M*. Letícia Román ably conveys Nora's mounting paranoia. As she closes in on the killer's identity, ever one becomes a suspect. The police wonder if she's read too many *gialli* (in one scene, she calls on her "old friends Agatha Christie and Mickey Spillane" to help her unmask the murderer). *The Girl Who Knew Too Much* established several *giallo* tropes: elaborately orchestrated murders, disarming close-ups, animated camerawork, plucky American tourists playing amateur detective, silhouetted stalkers clad in black.

Bava didn't think too much of *The Girl Who Knew Too Much*. "I thought the film was too preposterous," he declared. "Perhaps it would have worked with James Stewart and Kim Novak." As usual, the director was too modest. *Girl* is a crisp, beautifully photographed exercise in mood and madness, paving a path for *giallo* cinema while paying tribute to noir's uniquely sinister style.

Girl may have created the template for *giallo*, but Bava's bold *Blood and Black Lace* (1964)

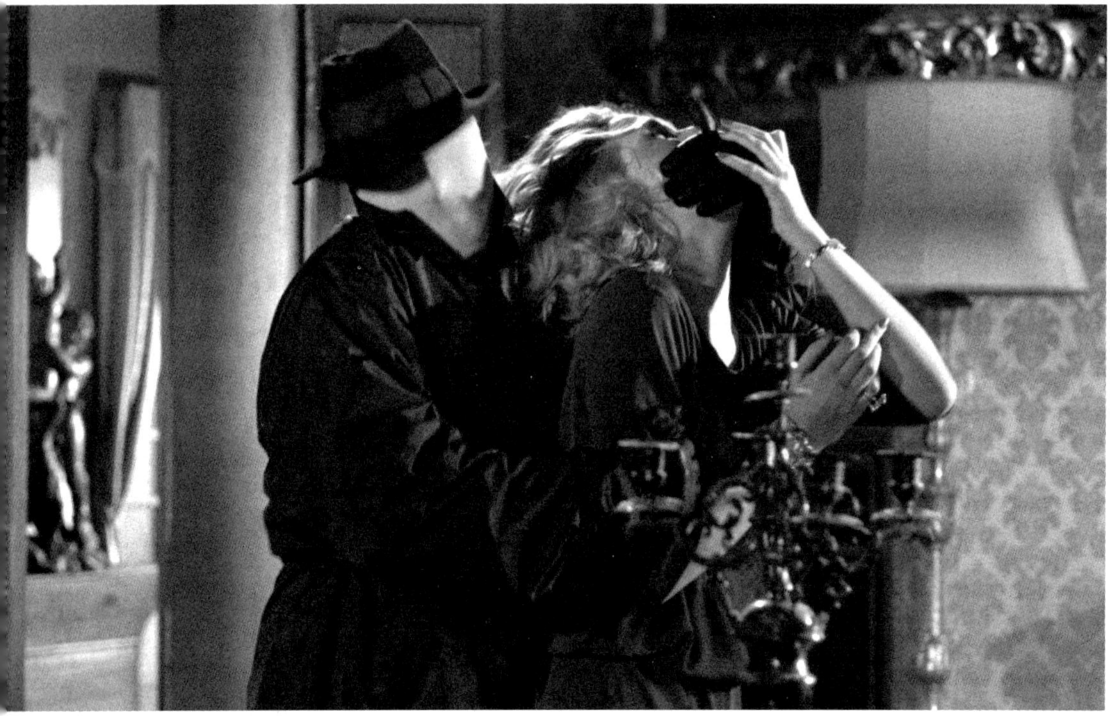

Murder and mayhem by a masked maniac mark Bava's groundbreaking *Blood and Black Lace*

permanently codified the genre. With its rich colors and bravura style, *Blood* represented a sea change for Bava. The action takes place in a fashion salon where a black-gloved, masked psychopath is stalking and brutally eliminating a group of models, one of whom kept a diary filled with scandalous secrets about her friends and co-workers. The body count mounts as the killer seeks to find and destroy the diary. The salon's petulant owner (Eva Bartok) and scowling manager (Cameron Mitchell) are determined to apprehend the murderer, but Bava is more concerned with the mayhem than the mystery. Each murder becomes an elaborate, ornate set piece. Assaultive color clashes with the icy gleam of knives and razors. A shiny hooked gauntlet slowly descends on a woman's face. Another victim has her wrists slit in a bathtub, the bright water slowly consumed by crimson (Martin Scorsese cited the scene as a favorite cinematic moment). Ubaldo Terzano's mobile camera delivers startling close-ups of each attack, but he also blurs the boundary between reality and illusion (in what may be the film's most memorable scene, a corpse, pulled by the killer's unseen hands, appears to float into darkness). Bava imbues these scenes with an operatic, nearly erotic beauty. We wince, but we can't look away. Yet there is relatively little blood in *Blood*. Bava eschews the actual gore by wrapping the proceedings in a rich tapestry of scarlet, from the salon's draperies, to the models' lipstick and nail polish, to the leather cover of the poisonous diary. Reddest of all are the herrings Bava tosses us. Each character has a motive for murder; the diary holds sinister secrets about everyone. Eva Bartok and Cameron Mitchell give the film a noirish chill, icy enough to freeze half of Rome. The elegance of the fashion salon is merely a façade, its underbelly riddled with betrayal, blackmail, and backstabbing. The theme here is the corruptibility of beauty, the darkness belied by a veneer of chic affluence. The sanguinary stew is occasionally peppered with dollops of *Diabolique* and *Double Indemnity*. The movie's lurid blend of reds and blues recalls such Technicolor noirs as *Rear Window* and *Vertigo*, while prefiguring Michael Mann and *Miami Vice*. *Blood and Black Lace* is film noir painted in oils.

Bava shot *Blood* in six weeks with a minuscule budget and limited equipment. Dolly shots were accomplished by attaching the camera to a child's (appropriately) red wagon. Crane shots were

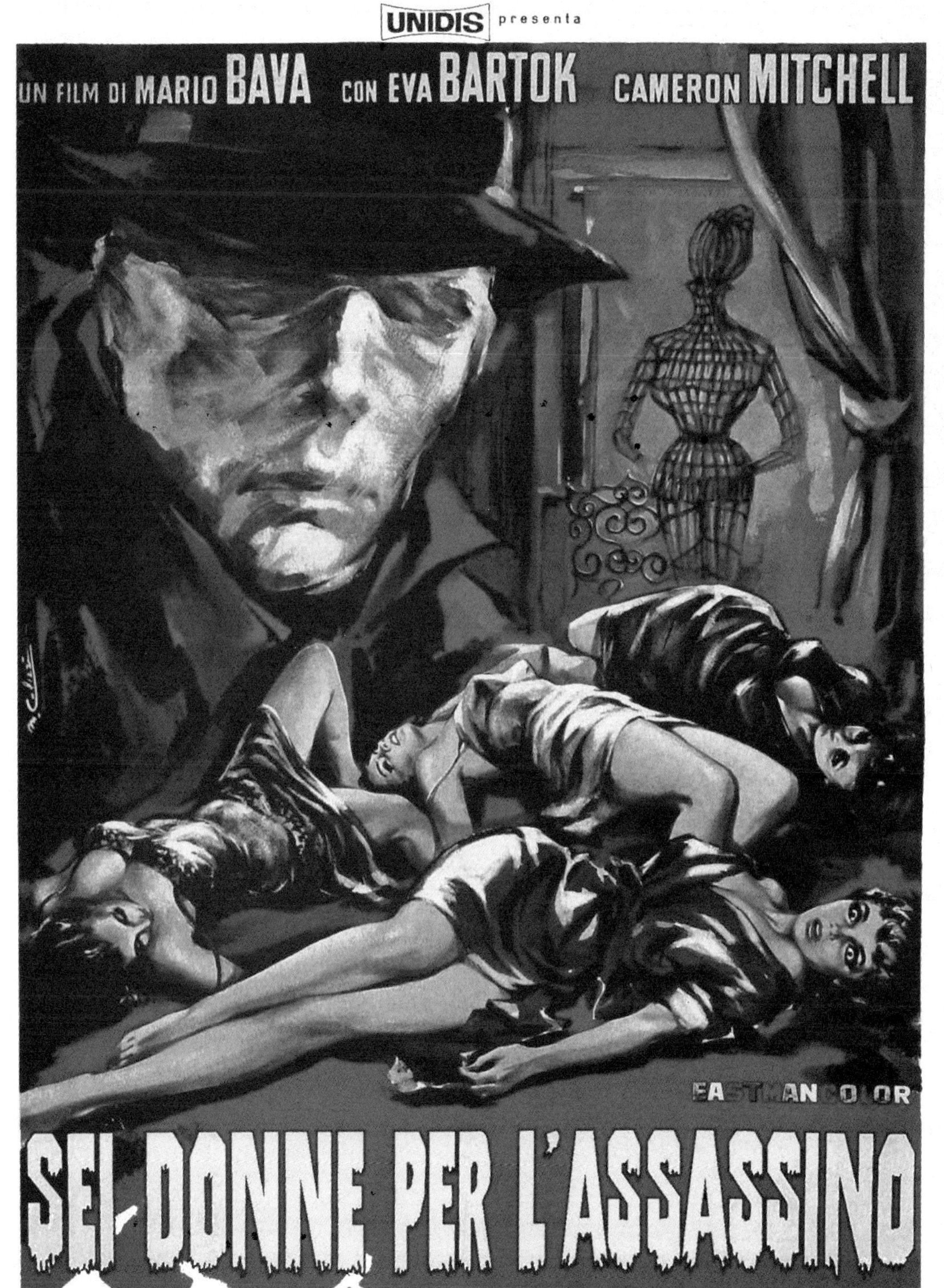
UNIDIS presenta
UN FILM DI MARIO BAVA CON EVA BARTOK CAMERON MITCHELL
EASTMANCOLOR
SEI DONNE PER L'ASSASSINO
THOMAS REINER CLAUDE DANTES DANTE DI PAOLO
PRODUZIONE EMMEPI CINEMATOGRAFICA

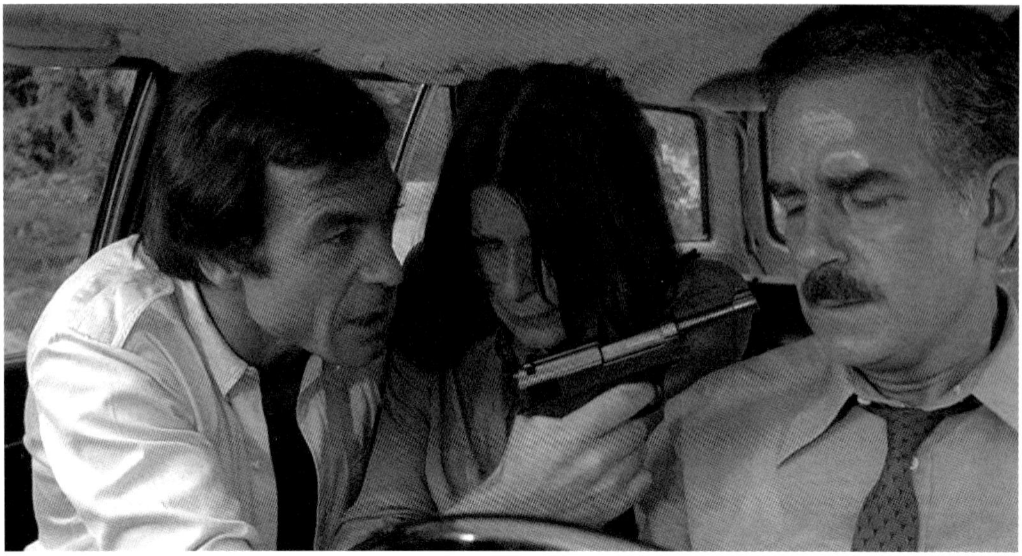

Leader of the pack Maurice Poli threatens Riccardo Cucciolla as a helpless Lea Lander looks on in *Rabid Dogs*

managed by Bava aiming his lens from the ascending side of a see-saw. "We had to do everything ourselves and to solve problems using only our brains and our enthusiasm," he recalled. "It was the result that mattered, not the money." In an interview with film historian Tom Weaver, Cameron Mitchell applauded the director's ingenuity:

"I loved Mario Bava; in some ways he may have been the best director—certainly the best I've worked with in Europe, and maybe the best of them all. I've worked with Kazan. I've worked with Orson Welles. I've worked with John Ford. I've worked with the best. Bava's right up there. And when I think of the limited money he had and the corners he had to cut, it's unbelievable! ... He did incredible things with nothing. He was so clever!"

Blood and Black Lace scored with Italian filmgoers, but its bold style didn't resonate with critics. Bava's final cut was butchered and diluted for American distribution (Arrow Video has restored and remastered the picture for Blu-ray release). Fortunately, its place in crime cinema is secured. Writer Troy Howarth observed that "... *Blood and Black Lace* is the first full-blooded *giallo* and its remorseless cruelty and embittered cynicism mark it as a film that was very much ahead of its time." Bava scholar Tim Lucas noted the film's influence on "... legions of filmmakers from Dario Argento to Martin Scorsese to Quentin Tarantino."

After *Blood and Black Lace*, Bava continued to direct *gialli* (*Five Dolls for an August Moon*, *Hatchet for the Honeymoon* [both 1970], *Twitch of the Death Nerve* [1971]). His influence was keenly felt by young directors like Dario Argento and Lucio Fulci, who refined the Master's *giallo* blueprint and dominated the genre well into the 1980s.

In 1974, Bava took a stab at straight crime with his startling slash-and-dash heist film *Rabid Dogs*. Though the movie draws on noir films as diverse as *The Asphalt Jungle*, *The Hitch-Hiker* and *The Getaway*, its violence and depravity are firmly rooted in *giallo*. Based on Ellery Queen's 1951 short story *Kidnapped*, the plot is deceptively simple: a violent gang commits a daring robbery, abducts a woman hostage, and escapes by carjacking a man en route to the hospital with his ailing son in the back seat. At a lean 92 minutes, *Dogs* is a tight, taut ride. Bava's hand-held camera veers between dashcam views of the desolate highway and the sweaty, claustrophobic confines of the getaway car. The picture is propulsively paced, marked by relentless tension and a rock-solid cast. Riccardo Cucciolla delivers a subtle performance as the carjacked driver Riccardo, controlling his desperation as he watches his son dying at the hands of his captors (ironically, Al Lettieri, who played the ride-along thug Rudy in *The Getaway*, was originally cast in the role before being fired for his alcohol abuse). Maurice Poli adopts a serpentine restraint as the gang's icy leader, "Doc" (Bava's nod to Steve McQueen's "Doc" in *The Getaway* and Sam Jaffe's "Doc" in *The Asphalt Jungle*). "Doc's" vicious cohorts cause most of the movie's mayhem. The knife-wielding "Blade" (Don Backy) sadistically threatens Riccardo's helpless son with some of the film's most toxic dialogue ("It's amazing how long a person can survive with a slit throat. Especially *children.*") George Eastman, the Timothy Carey of Italian cinema, nearly steals the film as the twitchy, psychotic "Thirty-Two" (nicknamed for the size of his bulging love muscle). He spews most of his venom at the abducted Maria (Lea Lander), taunting her with a steady stream of humiliation and the threat of rape. In her scenes with Eastman, Lander effectively strikes a balance between fear and outright terror.

The pall of anxiety that hangs over *Rabid Dogs* is exceeded only by its jaw-dropping conclusion—a rib-cracking sucker punch that seems to come out of nowhere. Some viewers will want to head for the shower after riding with these dirty *Dogs*. Others may be tempted to revisit Bava's *Dog* house to search for clues that tip off the shocking finale.

The film's backstory is as twisted as its fictional plot line. *Dogs* was nearly consigned to the cinematic scrapheap. Before post-production began, the picture's producer and backer went broke. Bava's work print was confiscated by an Italian bankruptcy court and remained in limbo for 20 years. He was unable to finish the film before his death in 1980. Co-star Lea Lander finally bought the rights to *Rabid Dogs* and used Bava's editing notes to complete the picture for European release in 1996. In 2000, Lander sold the film's rights to producer Alfredo Leone, who enlisted Bava's son Lamberto to supervise a new edit. The revision was re-titled *Kidnapped* and released in 2002. Lamberto Bava tampered with the film's musical score, but *Dogs*' impact remained intact. Tim Lucas has commented that "*Rabid Dogs* is to Bava's career what *Detour* is to the filmography of Edgar G. Ulmer, a minimalist noir masterpiece that shows how much drama he was capable of conjuring on screen with little or no means."

Whether black-and-white or saturated with color, Mario Bava's films reveal a jaundiced world consumed by greed, cynicism, and corruption. He once declared that "the only monsters are the ones within ourselves."

Bava knew noir. It was in his blood. ■

The following references were invaluable in preparing this article: Troy Howarth's So Deadly, So Perverse: 50 Years of Italian Giallo Films, Volume One (Midnight Marquee Press, 2015) *and* The Haunted World of Mario Bava (Midnight Marquee Press, 2014); *and excerpts from Tim Lucas' comprehensive* Mario Bava: All the Colors of the Dark (Video Watchdog, 2007).

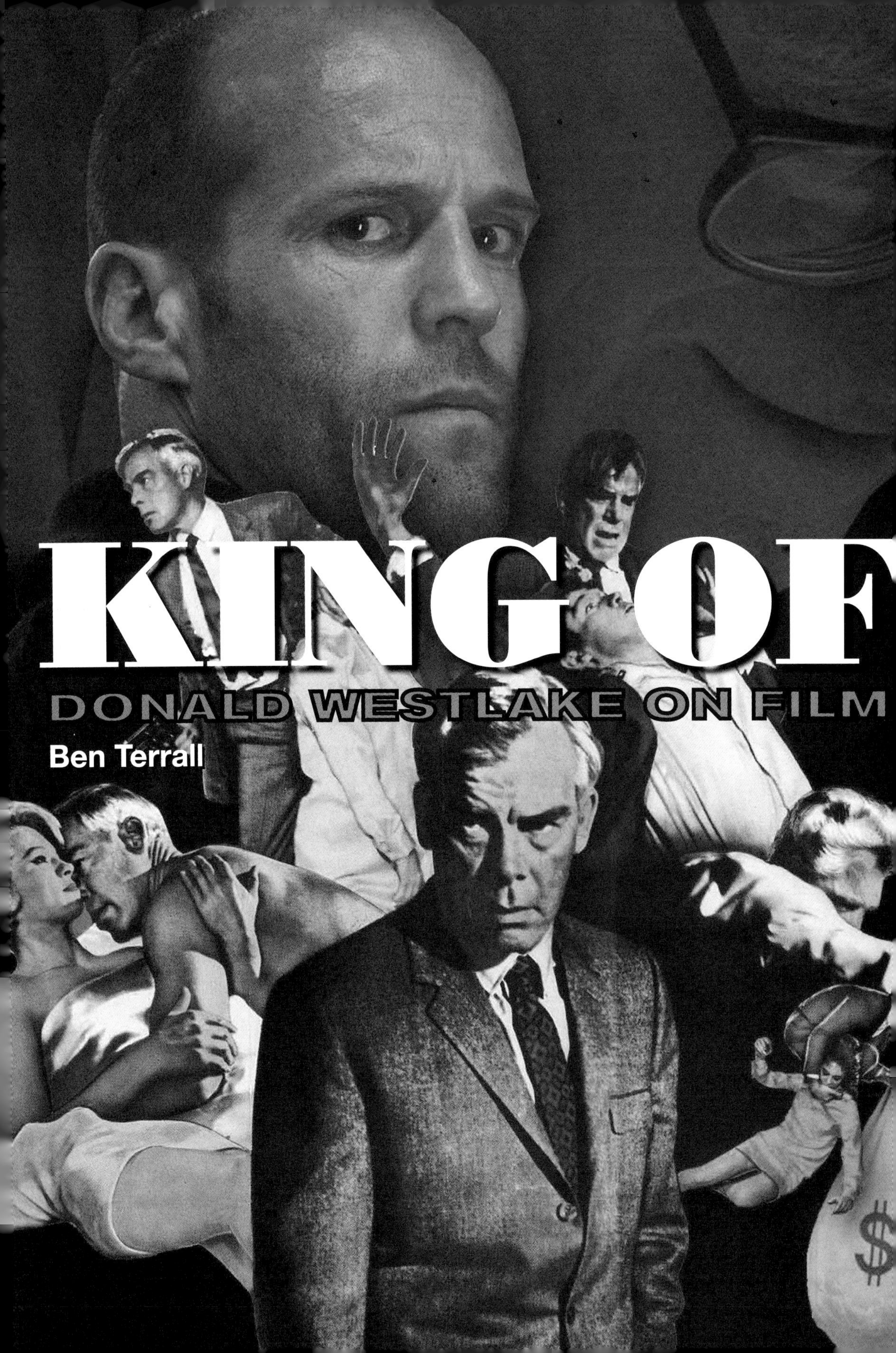
KING OF
DONALD WESTLAKE ON FILM
Ben Terrall

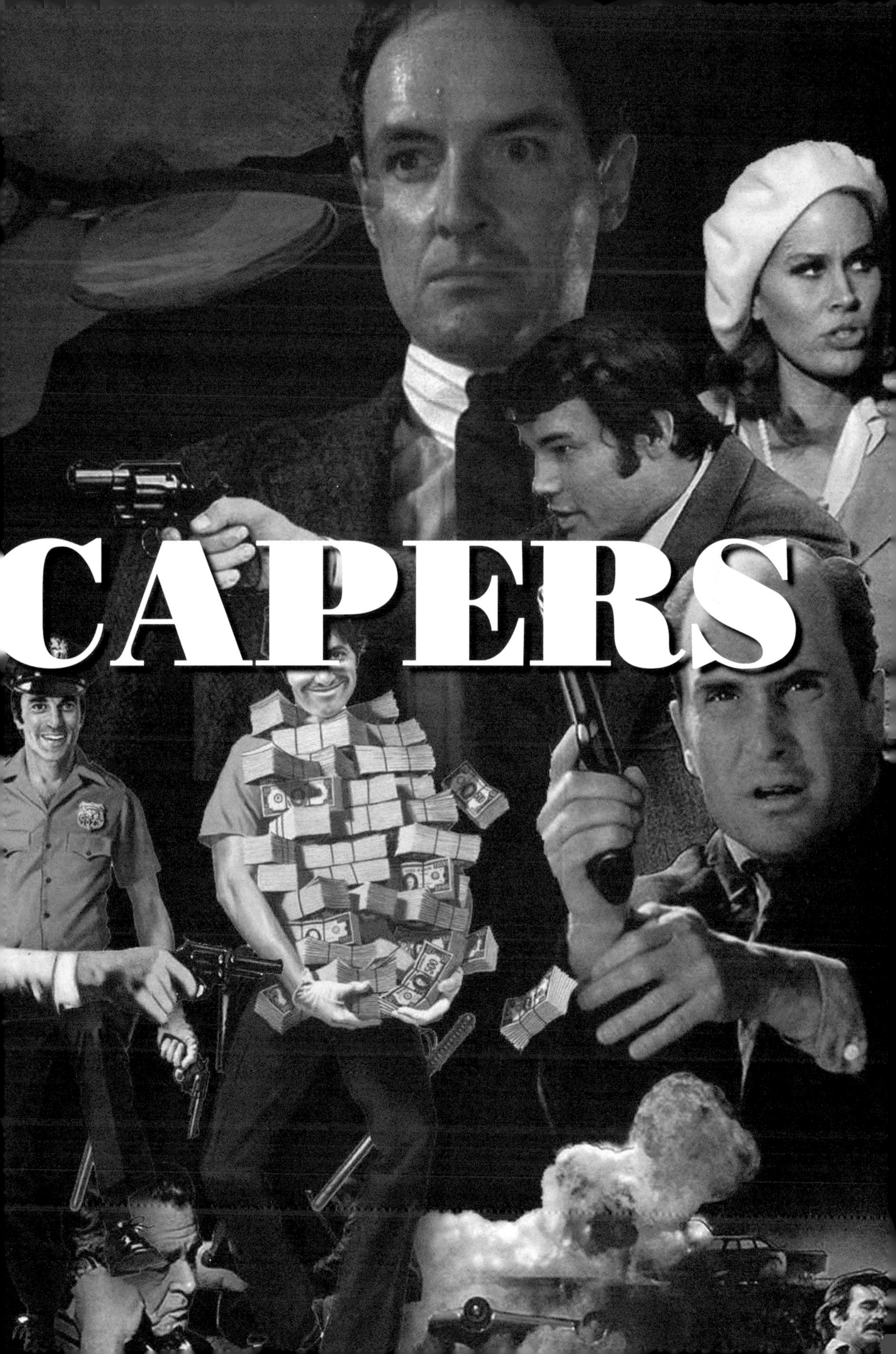
CAPERS

When it comes to compulsively readable and wildly entertaining crime fiction, few authors can match the work of Donald E. Westlake. His remarkable career encompassed short stories, a long list of novels, and several popular series with recurring characters. His two most famous protagonists, John Dortmunder and Parker (the latter's adventures written under the pseudonym Richard Stark), appeared in several film adaptations; movies have also been made from Westlake's non-series work. Throughout his prolific career, the author kept a low profile and, inexplicably, never wrote a bestseller.

Westlake was as much appreciated by his fellow writers as his readers. His friend Lawrence Block wrote that his colleague "[has] never written a bad sentence, a clumsy paragraph, or a dull page." Westlake won Edgar Awards in three different categories, and was voted a Grand Master by the Mystery Writers of America.

He also wrote numerous screenplays and teleplays, many never produced, and he sold film rights to at least ten books that were never made into movies. While he never got rich from his Hollywood sales, Westlake made far more money from the film industry than he did writing novels. In the late 1990s, Westlake wrote, "From time to time I'd be hired to write a screenplay about something or other. The movie industry needs writers, but ignores writers as a matter of principle; it is the perfect place for a writer who didn't want to be noticed." Westlake didn't want visibility because "I wanted to write whatever came into my head, and not worry about it."

The Richard Stark books live up to that pseudonym (the first name came from Richard Widmark, a favorite of Westlake's). They are stripped-down, high-adrenaline stories that deliver pure action with plenty of satisfying plot twists. The novels are admired by other crime writers—Dennis Lehane called Parker "the greatest antihero in American noir"—as well as more rarefied types; Man Booker Prize winner John Banville called the Parker books "... among the most poised and polished fictions of their time and, in fact, of any time."

Other than one novel in which Parker goes to jail, this professional thief never gets caught, and despite complications, he usually walks off with the money. Westlake wrote that "Parker is a Depression character, Dillinger mythologized into a machine." These narratives definitely lean toward the noir end of the spectrum, though sticklers might argue that hardboiled is a more appropriate descriptor. Author Jack Bludis has made the distinction "hard-boiled = tough, noir = screwed." By that definition, the Parker books fit either category: Parker himself is plenty tough, but the people who cross him are definitely screwed. "I think hard-boiled and noir are both a little past their sell-by date," Westlake noted in 2006, "Hard-boiled is what the [WWII] vets brought back with them, and noir is the world they found when they came home. I think hard-boiled is still possible, but noir today is another word for artsy."

IN 1966, JEAN-LUC GODARD shot *Made in U.S.A.*, which the director claimed was based on *The Jugger*, a 1965 Richard Stark novel—not that the film's producer actually purchased rights to the book. Godard's film was made on the fly and seems to have been mostly an excuse to show off Anna Karina playing with a gun in various brightly colored outfits. Film critic Gilles Jacob wrote that in *Made in U.S.A.* Godard "has managed to disincarnate the object," which is only slightly more comprehensible than most of the film's dialogue. Godard's *Breathless* (1960) and *Alphaville* (1965) both worked as, among other things, an oddball aesthete's tribute to U.S. crime novels and films, but *Made in U.S.A.* is just a pretentious mess. The film does include a radiant Marianne Faithfull singing "As Tears Go By," which doesn't particularly fit into what passes for a story, but which does make a strong impression.

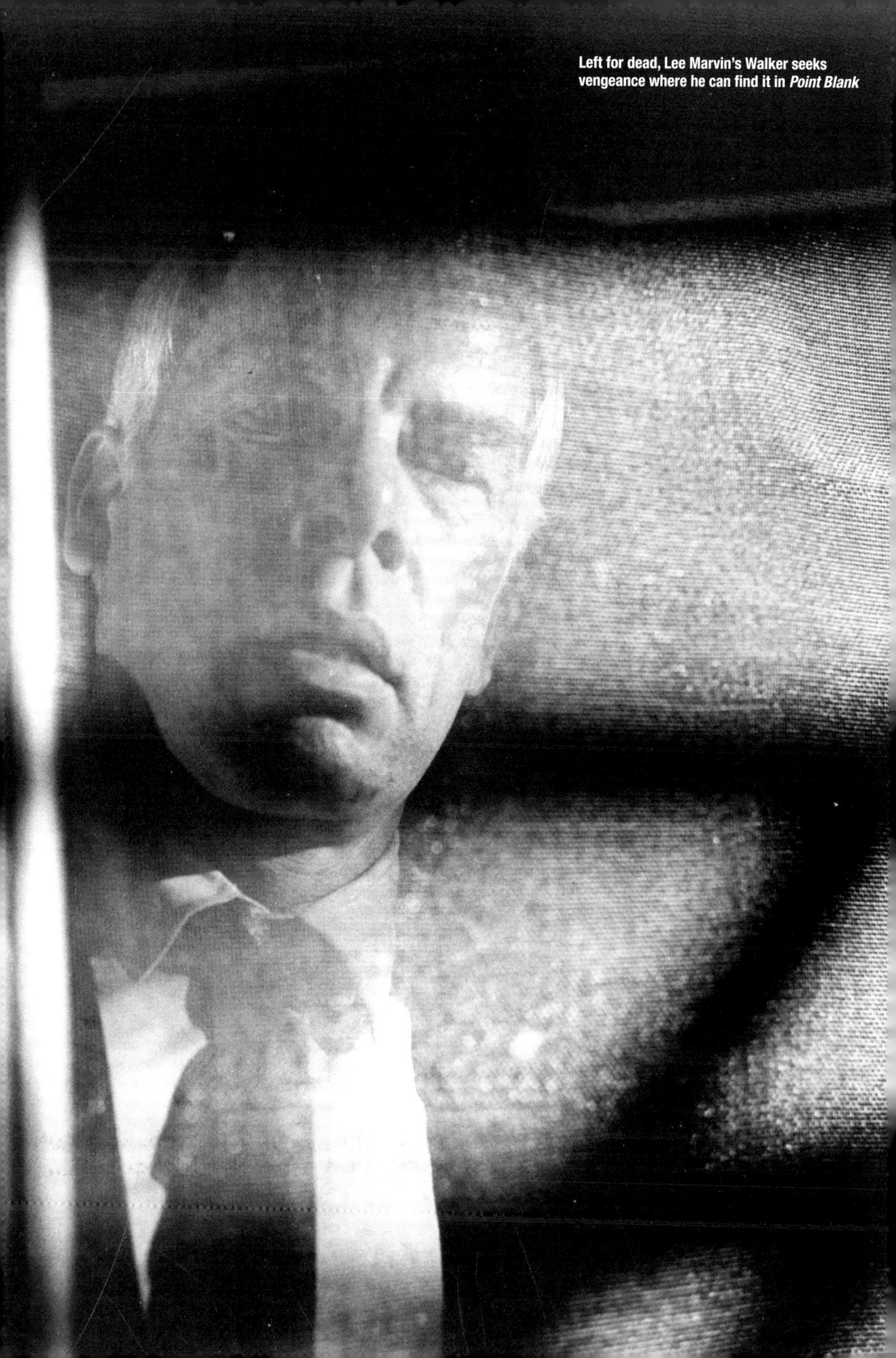

Left for dead, Lee Marvin's Walker seeks vengeance where he can find it in *Point Blank*

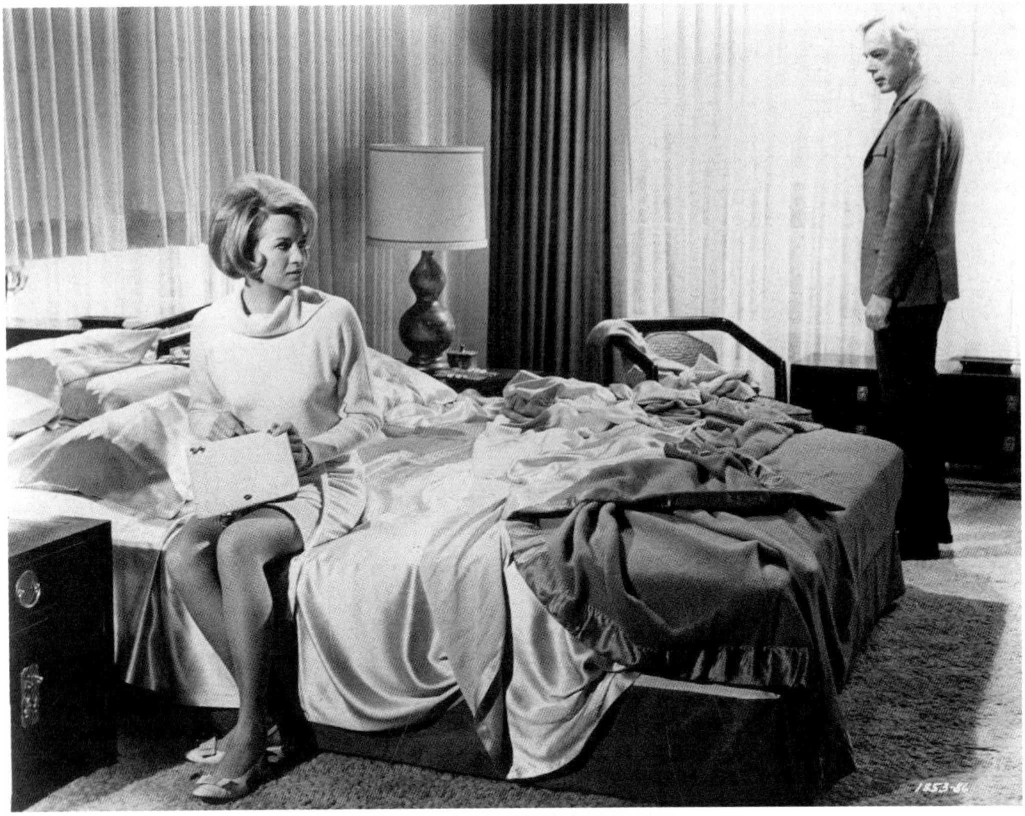

Angie Dickinson gets recruited into Walker's payback plan in *Point Blank*

The first noteworthy adaptation of a Westlake book was *Point Blank* (1967), based on the initial Parker book, *The Hunter* (1962). *The Hunter*'s opening sentence sets the tone: "When a fresh-faced guy in a Chevy offered him a lift, Parker told him to go to hell." The antihero tough guy then lights his last cigarette and walks across the George Washington Bridge. Parker is broke after being left for dead by his wife and an accomplice in their stickup of international arms smugglers. Scraping together a stake by pulling petty scams, Parker is driven by an all-consuming desire for revenge. After tracking down his wife, he tells her what he will do to his former partner-in-crime, Mal: "I'm going to drink his blood. I'm going to chew up his heart and spit it into the gutter for the dogs to raise a leg at. I'm going to peel the skin off him and rip out his veins and hang him with them."

When Parker finally get his hands on Mal, though, his anger is not sated. "Mal wasn't enough, he was easy, he was too easy, he was the easiest thing that ever happened." Mal also doesn't have the share of the robbery loot he stole from Parker, since he used it to pay off a debt to the Outfit, a Mafia-like organized crime network. So, after dispatching Mal, Parker moves on to target Outfit operatives.

Westlake told an interviewer he didn't do anything to make Parker "reader-friendly." This one-man force of nature has no use for small talk or patience with anyone he feels is wasting his time. He gets no pleasure from killing, but won't shy away from it if he decides it's his best option. Unlike the film adaptations of *The Hunter*, in the novel Parker planned to kill Mal before Mal beat him to the punch because he saw his ex-cohort as a coward and a "weak link." As Westlake noted, "[There is] no socially redeeming quality in this guy at all."

In *Point Blank*, Parker becomes Walker, and Lee Marvin brings to the role an unrelenting ferocity. Critic Luc Sante wrote that *Point Blank* "takes major liberties with the plot, but brings out the latent modernism of the series. It is all noon light and harsh edges, in striking contrast to the shadows

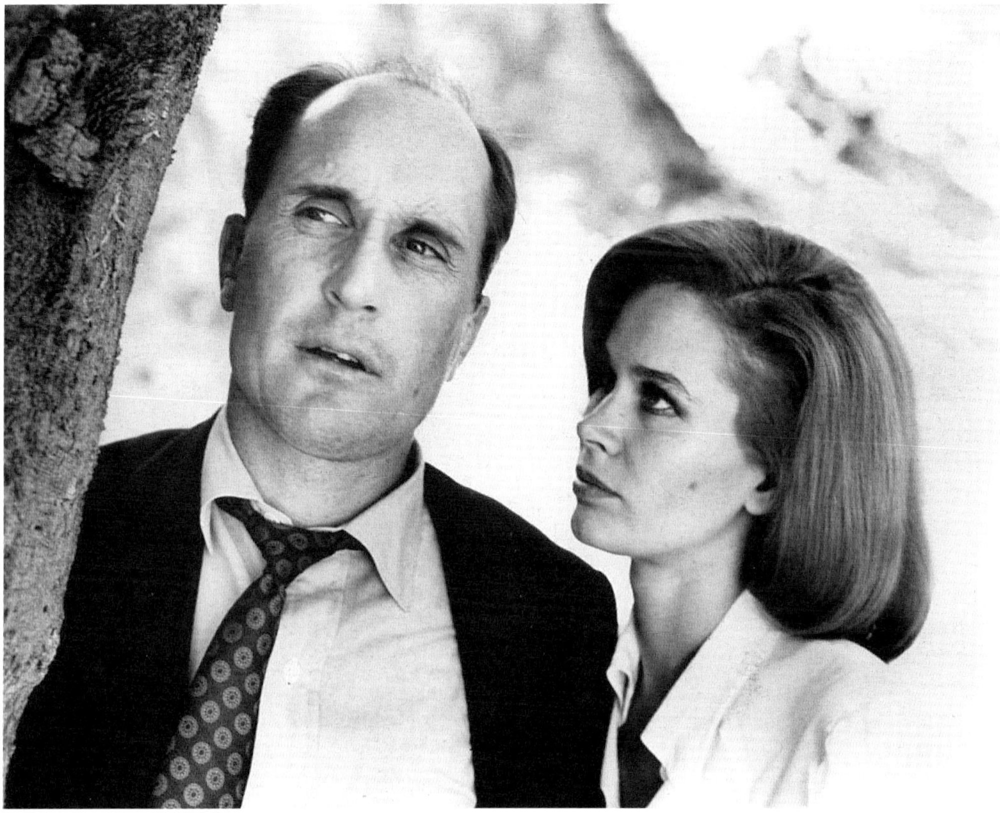

***The Outfit*, from the Westlake novel of the same name, starred Robert Duvall and Karen Black**

and melancholy of *film noir*." The film was director John Boorman's first major feature after helming the 1965 Dave Clark Five vehicle *Having a Wild Weekend*, and the British filmmaker went all out with elaborate cutting, multiple flashbacks, and a variety of striking visual touches, such as having cinematographer Philip H. Lathrop shoot each scene in a specific color scheme.

At Lee Marvin's insistence, Boorman had final cut on the film. The director later said in a DVD commentary Marvin agreed to do the picture only if they threw out the existing script. In Boorman's words, "we went back to the book, of course," but, in an interview with author Michel Ciment, Boorman said, "You know, I've never read the book!" Certainly the original script by David and Rafe Newhouse was much closer to *The Hunter*. The final screenplay is credited to Alexander Jacobs and the Newhouses.

Point Blank changed locations from its source material and added characters, including a memorable Angie Dickinson as a quasi-love interest who moves quickly from bashing Walker's head with a pool cue to lustily climbing all over him. The film successfully rendered Parker's unstoppable quest, the sole purpose of which he sums up in four frequently repeated words: "I want my money." Marvin, who Boorman called "a master of gestures" and "very intuitive," is entirely convincing as Walker. It's one of his best performances, and one of the reasons the film holds up so well after repeated viewings.

The more recent adaptation of *The Hunter* is, to say the least, far more predictable. Though it follows the novel more closely than did *Point Blank*, the Mel Gibson vehicle *Payback* (1999) is underwhelming at best. If you're not a Mel Gibson fan, the film is quite skippable.

The Outfit (1973), based on a Stark novel of the same name, stars Robert Duvall as a Parker stand-in named Earl Macklin. Macklin is released from prison in the film's opening sequence, shot in an actual correctional facility. Bett Harrow (Karen Black), who is waiting to drive him to freedom, tells Macklin that his brother has been gunned down in retribution for the brothers robbing an Outfit-controlled bank. Macklin recruits his old buddy Jack Cody (Joe Don Baker) to wage a full-scale assault on the Outfit's operations, starting with a card game where Macklin takes on Menner (played to perfection by the great Timothy Carey). From there, the mayhem continues until the entire organization is brought to its knees.

The character of Cody did not appear in Westlake's novel; in the book, Parker wields a network of freelance heisters instead of going after his adversaries with only Cody and Bett. There are other differences between the book and the movie, but, overall, director John Flynn and cinematographer Bruce Surtees remain faithful to the book's tone with its largely rural locations providing a nice alternative to run-of-the-mill urban Hollywood crime fare. The lone sour note comes in an unfortunate scene where Macklin engages in a stereotypical and unnecessarily prolonged slapping of Bett.

Westlake judged *The Outfit* to be "quite good," telling an interviewer, "It is a ... small movie with every B-movie actor you've ever thought of in it." The cast is indeed rich in veteran character actors, including Elisha Cook Jr., Marie Windsor, Jane Greer, Henry Jones, Richard Jaeckel, and, most indelibly, Robert Ryan as the mob boss, Mailer. Anita O'Day even has a cameo singing in a deserted club.

Director Taylor Hackford's 2013 film *Parker*, mostly based on the novel *Flashfire* (2000), is a diverting entertainment that doesn't ascend to the giddy heights of *Point Blank* or equal the stripped-down momentum of *The Outfit*. Working from a script by John J. McLaughlin, Hackford opens the film with a robbery at the Ohio State Fair that is exciting, visually impressive, and much more elaborate than the opening bank robbery in *Flashfire*.

After the revisionist kick-off, McLaughlin's screenplay mostly follows the book, from the betrayal of Parker by his crew to the final campaign of Parker's retribution. Though it's at first off-putting to hear Parker with a British accent, Jason Statham is suitably cool and unstoppable in the title role. He's not Lee Marvin or Robert Duvall, but then he isn't as awful as some critics implied (especially the ever-catty Rex Reed who wrote, "Mr. Statham is to acting what Taco Bell is to nutrition"). He's certainly more appropriate for the part than Mel Gibson. The worst part of Statham's performance is his unfortunate attempt at a Southern accent when Parker impersonates a wealthy Texan scouting for Florida real estate.

In *Flashfire*, the real estate agent Leslie Rogers is described as "a round-faced blonde" who is "one of an interchangeable half dozen of such women" in her "spacious cool office." Not exactly the famously heart-stopping Jennifer Lopez, who plays her in the film. The sexual tension between Leslie and the typically disinterested Parker is non-existent in the book, while in the movie Statham and Lopez share a mutual attraction and even kiss briefly. Statham's Parker is also more noble than in the book; in *Parker*'s opening robbery, Statham announces to a roomful of civilians he is holding at gunpoint, "I don't steal from people who can't afford it, and I don't hurt people who don't deserve it."

Flashfire is one of the Stark books in which Parker's lover Claire appears. Claire mostly serves as a backup to help Parker out of jams, and in *Flashfire* she remains at a distance from the main action. She's not a hardened moll, but a woman with her own life who doesn't want to know too much about Parker's work. In *Parker*, Claire, played by Emma Booth, is a nurturing presence who shows up to tend to Parker's wounds while Leslie looks on enviously. Booth's character is young and more than a little vapid, which makes Parker's loyalty to her—despite Ms. Lopez' readiness for romance—highly improbable.

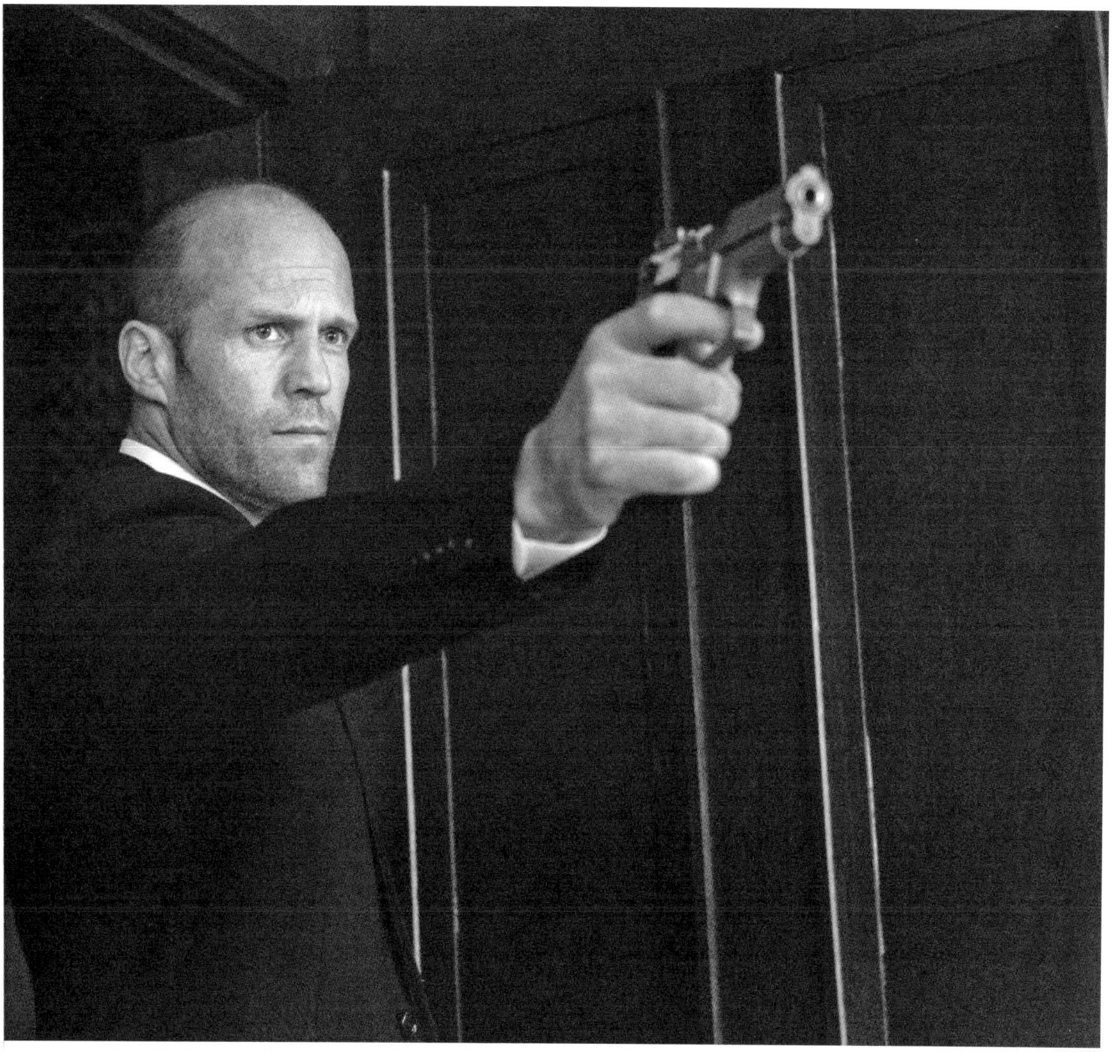

When Stark revived the character of Parker, Jason Statham finally got to use the name

The main difference between the film *The Split* (1968) and the novel *The Seventh* (1966) is that the movie's protagonist is black. Though Westlake wrote few African-American characters, much of his '60s fan mail came from young black men who enjoyed reading about the exploits of an outsider looting establishment institutions. The casting of the lead was a brilliant stroke: Jim Brown, former NFL superstar, plays Parker surrogate McClain. Who better to rob a football stadium while a game is underway than a former pro? Brown brings new meaning to the word "hulking," and box-office revenue was no doubt increased by having the actor repeatedly taking off his shirt.

Brown was joined on-screen by an impressive roster of 1960s–1970s actors, including Ernest Borgnine, Donald Sutherland, Warren Oates, Jack Klugman, and Gene Hackman. Gordon Flemyng isn't an especially memorable director (he worked mostly in TV), but Burnett Guffey's cinematography is first rate. Visually, this vehicle is very much a 1968 period piece with sharp outfits and what passed for hip dialogue in Hollywood at that time, but the screenplay, aside from the actual robbery (the highlight of the movie), makes a hash of Westlake's book. It's easy to see why Donald Westlake had nothing positive to say about this cinematic outing, which is best viewed for cheap laughs and Ernest

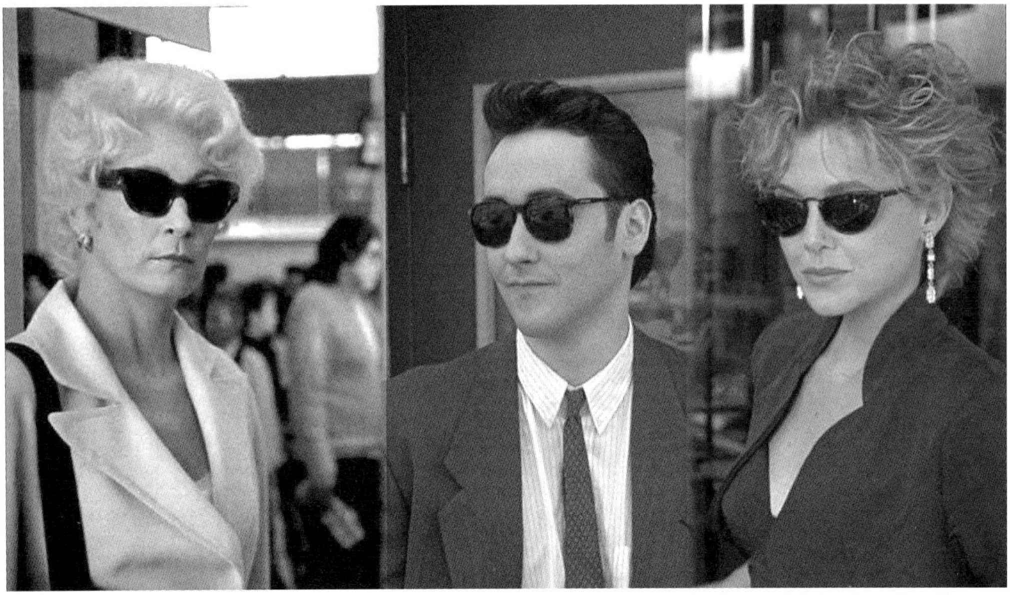

A triptych of trouble ready to tangle: Anjelica Huston, John Cusack, and Annette Bening in Westlake's adaptation of Jim Thompson's *The Grifters*

that he write a screenplay. Once he committed himself to the project, though, Westlake remained true to Thompson's pitch-black vision. When producer Martin Scorsese asked Westlake how the writing was going, Westlake replied, "I'm doing damage on every page." The script is extremely faithful to the novel, including its startling ending which Westlake insisted remain. The three leads, Anjelica Huston, John Cusack, and Annette Bening, all fought for inclusion of Thompson's dialogue; Westlake later noted, "... it's nice that they were defending the writer. Everybody had this feeling that we were doing something good."

Westlake created a brilliant opening which placed the three main characters, Roy Dillon (Cusack), his mother Lilly (Huston), and the seductive hustler Myra Langtry (Bening), on equal footing. The leads appear in a triptych, each walking purposefully in what Thompson biographer Robert Polito called "a dazzling bit of invention" which "[Thompson] would have loved."

IN ADDITION TO HIS GIFT for dark stories, Westlake was also a brilliant comic writer. Even in his darkest stories, he's funny in a wonderfully off-kilter way. He doesn't go for predictable sit-com humor, but with single-talent characters trying to make a larcenous living on minimal skills, unpredictable situations often build toward comic outcomes. Through a series of hilarious novels, the bumbling thief John Dortmunder manages to make every mistake Parker avoids: he misjudges people, others get the drop on him, he fumbles his follow-throughs. Dortmunder rarely gets away with any proceeds from his criminal endeavors and Murphy's Law is the constant.

Though Robert Redford might have been an odd choice to play Dortmunder, *The Hot Rock* (1972), adapted from a Westlake novel of the same name, is a hugely entertaining caper movie. It's packed with great comic actors, primarily Ron Leibman as Murch, the gearhead driver of Dortmunder's crew, and Zero Mostel as an uncle of one of Dortmunder's accomplices. Aside from the addition of Mostel's character and a change in the ending, the movie hews closely to the book. Westlake liked the film and its scripter, William Goldman, calling him "the best living screenwriter." Several other attempts to capture Dortmunder on-screen turned out badly, but this one hit the mark.

One last film worth noting is *Cops and Robbers* (1973), which Westlake scripted. Westlake also wrote a book of the same name—after the film was made. "I did the screenplay first," Westlake noted, "so that became a kind of extended outline for the novel, and I could put into the novel what I wished the actors had done. But generally, I think the writer of the book is going to try to keep in things he loved in the book that are wrong for the movie."

Cops and Robbers has two excellent leads in Cliff Gorman and Joseph Bologna playing frazzled cops who decide to pull a heist to finance early retirement. Bologna described Westlake as "a super guy" who "embraced my ideas for the character." The actor also recalled, "This movie was plain joy, it was fun every day to go to work." John P. Ryan is also excellent as a Mafioso to whom Gorman and Bologna arrange to sell millions in stolen securities. His character is all lethal arrogance, a formidable opponent the two protagonists almost don't vanquish.

The other major reason to watch the movie is New York City circa 1973, where the film was shot on location. For anyone who wonders what the borough of Manhattan looked like before Wall Street and Walt Disney transformed it into the upscale, spic and span island it is today, look no further. ■

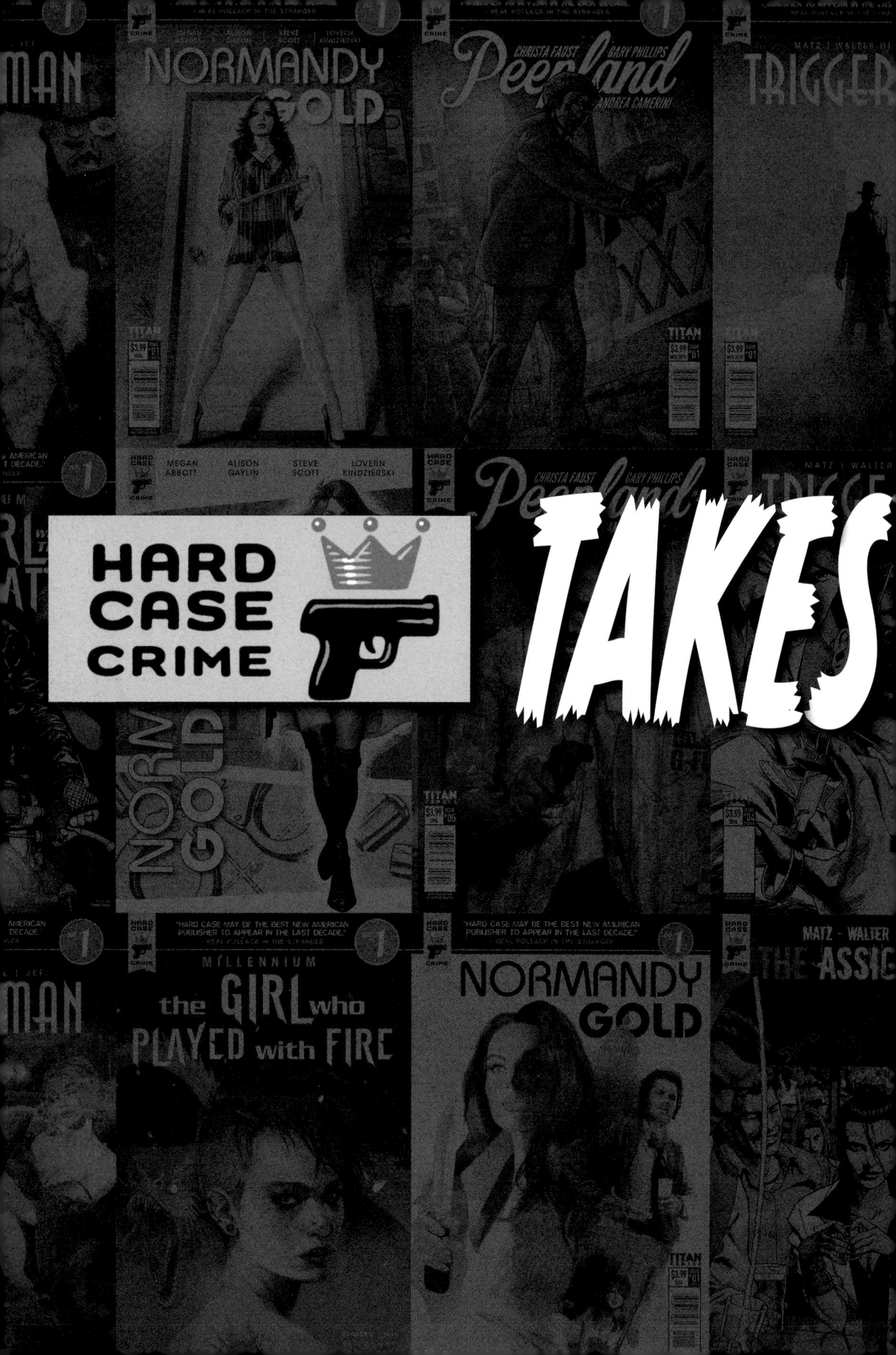
HARD CASE CRIME
TAKES

ON COMICS

Nathalie Atkinson

Since its founding in 2004, publishing throwback Hard Case Crime has presented the prose of Donald E. Westlake, Harlan Ellison, Michael Crichton, and Stephen King, all with gorgeous book jackets done in high-pulp style. That visual care with art and illustration now extends to the pages *between* the covers.

The companies that eventually became DC Comics and Marvel began as publishers of pulp; Mickey Spillane started out as a writer for Timely Comics, Hard Case Crime publisher Charles Ardai is keen to remind readers, especially now, as he launches the company's new imprint Hard Case Crime Comics, in partnership with Titan Comics and working closely with consulting editor Tom Williams.

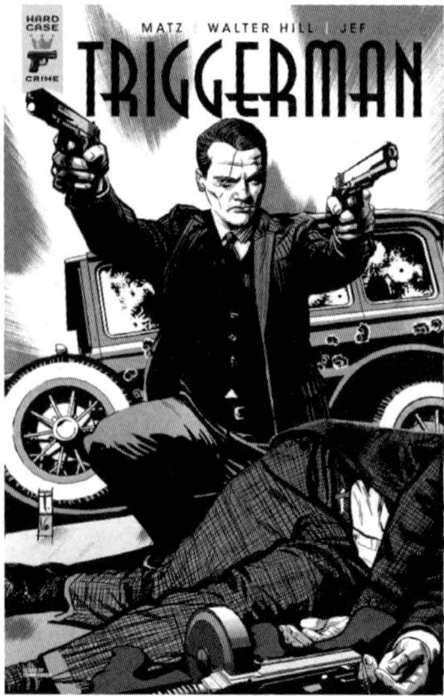

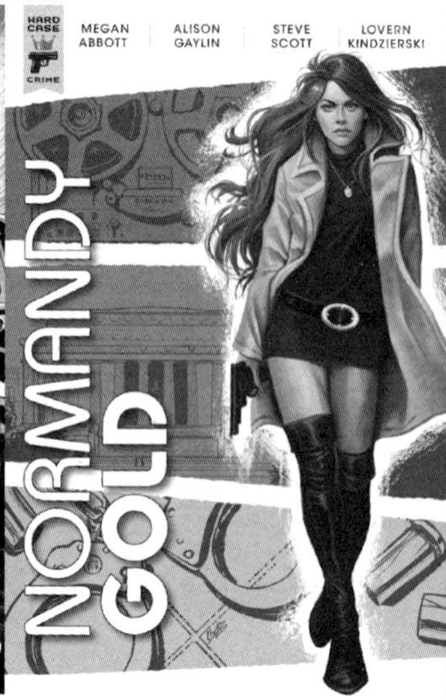

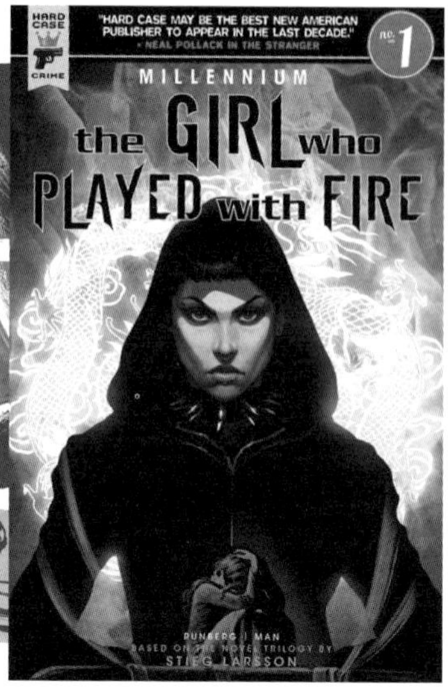

Learning the specific strengths (and weaknesses) of the comics medium has been eye-opening, according to the co-founder and publisher. Ardai is a writer himself, winner of the 2004 Shamus Award for Best First Novel (*Little Girl Lost*, penned under the clever *nom de plume* Richard Aleas). He recently penned the novelization for Shane Black's *The Nice Guys*, and prior to that he learned screenwriting while working on television shows like *Haven*. Comics lie somewhere in between all this, and he's enthusiastic about the hardboiled possibilities of the medium—and not just because "we go back and forth on how high the G-strings should be in a peepshow," he laughs, referring to the script instructions of *Peepshow*, one of the imprint's new titles. "Where the art is concerned, when people are supposed to be naked there will be no flowering plant," he promises.

"Words are mediating. Visual media [is] more immediate," Ardai says of comics' immersive quality and their ability to put all-important atmosphere into a reader's mind more directly with accuracy and fidelity. "Done well, telling any story, not just crime, in panels can convey setting, costume, gesture, facial expression, sex appeal in a way that prose doesn't," he adds. "It's visceral."

Like many, Ardai was an avid reader of comics as a child, a fan of EC's crime comics and Charlton's E-Man and Nova Kane, who bantered like Nick and Nora Charles. "Some Batman comics emphasized the Dark Knight detective and crime-fighting aspect a little bit more. In the 1940s and 1950s, he was wearing a cape and cowl, but really he could have been wearing a trench and fedora." In crime comics' modern incarnation, Ardai credits Max Allan Collins' *Road to Perdition* ("all the flavor of hardboiled comics from the old days") and its successful film adaptation as well as indie comics like the David Mazzucchelli experimental literary adaptation of Paul Auster's *City of Glass* with reviving interest in the medium.

After buying the first half-dozen titles, Hard Case Comics launched in October 2016. Although series like Max Allan Collins' *Quarry* and playwright Cynthia von Buhler's Jazz Age gumshoe Minky Woodcock released in the fall of 2017, Ardai keeps it tightly edited by design. "It's small in terms of number, because I want each book to be a success." When it comes to their originals and matching established writers with complementary artists, Ardai says they look for up-and-coming comics talent, "not famous, and we go through a few dozen portfolios to pick the one that's right for the property."

The imprint is a combination of licensed translations from France like *The Girl with the Dragon Tattoo* and Walter Hill's *Triggerman* and *The Assignment*, along with originals commissioned from established crime writers—most of whom happen to be women.

"It's hard to find reprints from the '40s and '50s of women to do," Ardai admits of Hard Case's main prose line. He says he was very conscious of the fact that Christa Faust was the first Hard Case female

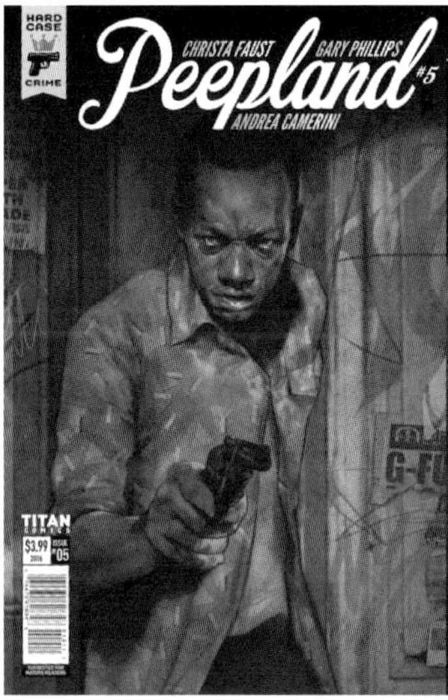

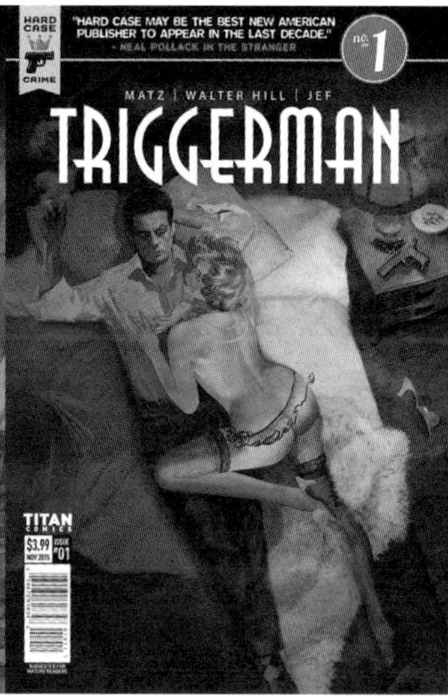

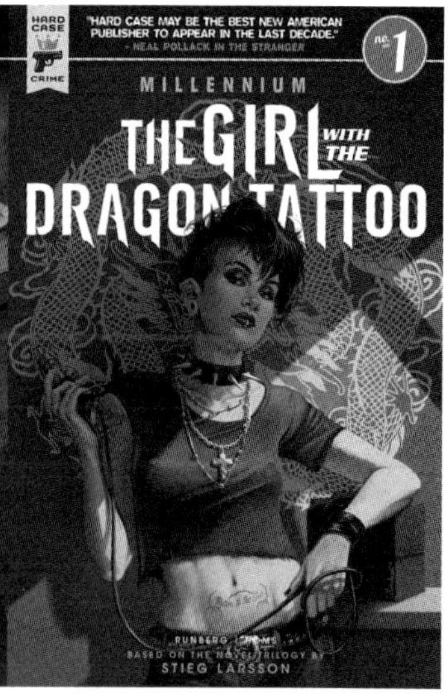

writer—"and that was forty books in! So, when we started the comic line, I wanted to get it off to a good start. It's ended up being more estrogen-heavy than the prose side, but that wasn't calculated."

The *Normandy Gold* series, for example, is both female-centric and female-led. It's the creation of acclaimed authors Alison Gaylin and Edgar-winning Megan Abbott (*Queenpin, Dare Me*), who is also a writer on David Simon's 1970s HBO series *The Deuce,* which premiered September 2017.

In the 1970s-set series, a tough female sheriff heads to Washington, D.C. to find out what's happened to her kid sister, and descends into the world of politics and prostitution. To give you an idea: the titular brash and battle-hardened Gold glares out from the book's cover with legs akimbo in a sheer negligée, brandishing a necktie like a whip.

"So much of noir is in comics since they came of age at the same moment—so many of the classic comics have a noir bent," the co-writers explain, Abbott beginning and Gaylin finishing the thought. They trace the idea for *Normandy Gold* back to 2008's Bouchercon in Baltimore. "We met when we were both nominated for the best first novel Edgar at the same time and what we got out of that was a really great friendship," Gaylin recalls. "We both love movies so much and talk about even our books rather cinematically—we started talking about '70s movies, how great they are especially the vigilante ones, and we were imagining a female vigilante and conspiracy thriller," Abbott adds. "Blaxploitation, Pam Grier, that's the world we wanted to dip into. Raquel Welch was our first thought!" Initially they sold the idea to DC's Vertigo crime line before it was shut down; then there was small-screen interest. "We had this adventure in TV-land with it," Gaylin laughs. "We were so insistent that [our female protagonist] not talk a lot, but that was very foreign to television producers for a female character. It's still really hard as a culture for them to understand a noir female heroine. But Lee Marvin, Charles Bronson—they didn't have to speak, and that really mattered to us."

"It's a very, very visual story, and Normandy's a really interesting character because she doesn't say a lot, but through the voiceover we get to hear her extensive thoughts," Gaylin says. Hard Case Crime's comics line launch came at just the right time.

Besides Abbott and Gaylin growing up obsessive *Archie* and *Tales from the Crypt* fans, respectively, the dynamic duo makes no pretense of being experts. "In our script, we dropped a few movie stills in there just to give the idea of the way we wanted our characters to look," Abbott says. "Stills of Season Hubley from *Hardcore*—that Paul Schrader movie was a big influence in having Normandy not being humiliated by the things she does." Reference material also included stills from *The Parallax View* and *The Conversation*, of Angie Dickinson in *Dressed to Kill*, and Mark Ruffalo in *Zodiac.*

From this combined script and materials, artist Steve Scott illustrated pages with the amber-washed

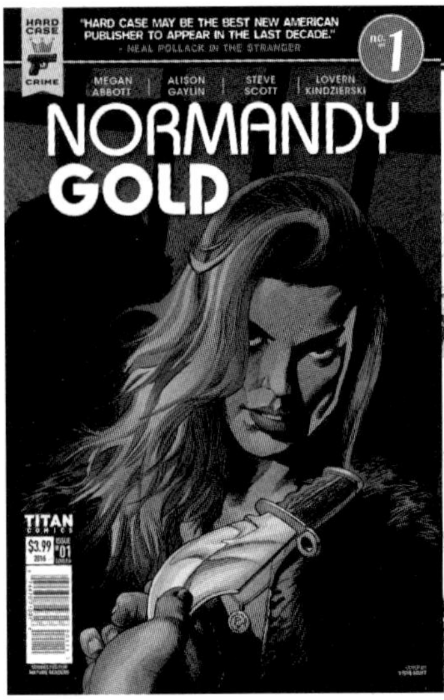

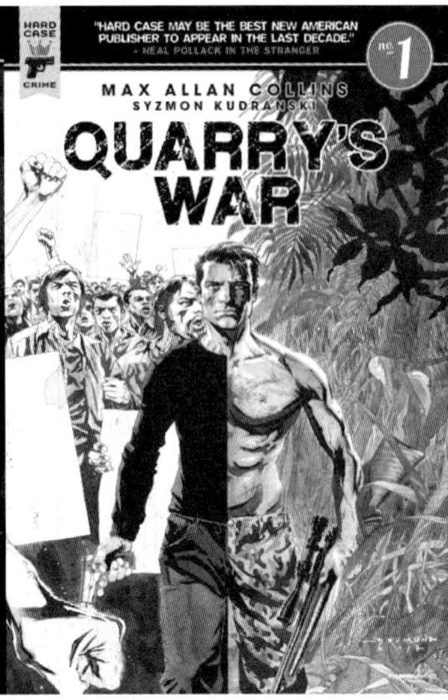

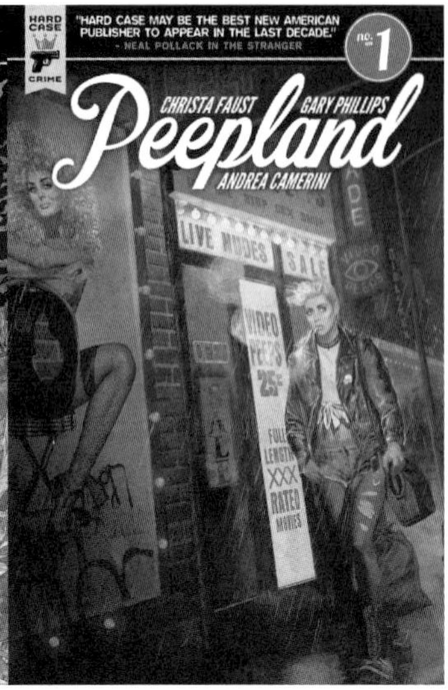

and desaturated tones of a New Hollywood indie. "It was inspired by movies more than anything," Abbott explains, before rhyming off a list. "*Taxi Driver*, conspiracy thrillers, and Brian De Palma movies. We were building these set pieces which were perfect for comics."

"We wanted a gritty, cinematic, and pulpy look," she says. "It's essential to the story. And there's a real danger to something like this looking cartoonish or *Scooby-Doo*." That includes the "specifically 1970s nudity, in an age before breast implants," Abbott adds. "Small-breasted women who had imperfections, who didn't look like centerfolds or like we often see now in these fantasies."

Normandy Gold's Washington D.C. plot and political milieu also provide all-too-timely parallels of their own. "All the structures we believed in—it's no longer a question of whether figures of authority *might* be corrupt; they are proven to be," Abbott says. "It's after the fall, which is definitely a different kind of noir. There's no expectation that anyone should be trusted. And the suspicion of the opposite sex operates very differently. That is often the most retro part of original noir—the complicated gender stuff—and that's not there in the 1970s."

The dirty, disturbing, and perverse government activity continues as *Normandy Gold* progresses, too. "It's kind of shocking that we wrote it and so much has come true."

Peepland, another comic in the line, takes place elsewhere and at another time—the crime-infested New York City of the 1980s—yet it unwittingly explores some of the same prescient terrain. The series follows peepshow worker Roxy Bell as she investigates the murder of a pornographer with her punk ex-boyfriend Nick in tow, moving through the seedy types that operate in the city's underbelly and Park Avenue apartments alike.

To transform her own experience of growing up in Hell's Kitchen and her memories of working in a Times Square peepbooth, Christa Faust teamed up with Italian artist Andrea Camerini and co-wrote with fellow crime writer Gary Phillips (*Angeltown*, *The Rinse*), a California activist and community organizer turned author, because of his depth of experience working in comics for Oni and Vertigo. "Gary was the wily veteran to my mouthy rookie," she jokes.

Faust was the first female author Hard Case Crime published back in 2008 (her books include the Angel Dare series, in which a former adult film star is a feminist vigilante). Like their prose siblings, the women in *Peepland* are neither vixens nor victims—instead, Faust and Phillips play with another binary—that of client and service provider. In this case, sex worker. "There is a literal plate of glass between the viewer and the viewee—the booth girl and the client," Faust explains. "Normally the story being told is that of the observer, men observing women. We flipped it and wanted to tell the story from the other side of the glass."

"I really felt a visual component was going to be crucial to telling the story because the version of New York City I grew up in—that meant so much to me back then and contributed both to the persona and the writer I later became—that's *gone* now," Faust says of choosing comics as the medium for this long-simmering tale. "So, I didn't want to just tell it, I wanted to show it." It became an elaborate work of reconstruction—of NYC in the early 1980s before Giuliani or the Disneyfication of Times Square, or even before Patrick Bateman's worshipping at the altar of Gordon Gekko and Donald Trump 1.0 ("Greed ... is good.").

"When you are a writer, you tend to cannibalize your life and experience—a mill inside your mind where you take the memories that affect you, grind them and put them out in a different way," Faust says. "We didn't want to make it just a *roman à clef*, an exact replica of events that took place, but we took the flavor of those events and gave them a new life."

That said, Faust admits she "made people crazy with my diagrams" depicting the layout of the actual peepbooths. "I have never seen online or in a movie the way one of the real booths was laid out, which is like a Siamese twin phone booth. *That* had to look exactly the way it did back then."

But *Peepland* also reconsiders and reframes a cultural moment that, until the recent presidential election, had been all but forgotten. Namely, rounding out the antagonists are newly prosperous and powerful property developer Simon Went and his Eastern European-born wife Oksana, who are protecting their son Rob. The plot also remixes aspects of historic true crimes like the Central Park Five and the so-called 'rough sex' Preppie Murder.

"This is only one particular area of New York at some point, and we've talked about this," Phillips says. "Rap is happening at the same time over in the Bronx. That whole scene doesn't even leak into our story, but we have designs to go there." Their sliver of Times Square, functioning as a waystation with the transient nature of clients and staff providing subplots, is hopefully just the beginning.

It's a tentacled and potentially sprawling premise that could tackle the changing face and human cost of the gentrifying city throughout the five boroughs, since *Peepland* fleshes out even its peripheral characters—women, the economically disadvantaged, the immigrant and working class—who might, in another story, be one-note or exist merely as plot devices.

And as Ardai intended, the series stay true to the pulp ethos. The comics don't pull punches with the medium's inherently more explicit treatment of lurid material—violence and sexuality. "We wanted to be trashier, in the best way," Gaylin chimes in. "We indulge our more pop sensibility that we just wouldn't put in our books and I mean that with love because I *love* De Palma movies—he has no fear of being bad. And you can let your libido fly in comics."

"Anything that causes someone to pick up a book is good—and I'm not embarrassed to publish books that have sexy women on them," Ardai says. But the hardboiled and often sexy milieu *Peepland* and *Normandy Gold* depict in their panels are only part of the draw. "And then to force male readers to confront the inside of a woman's mind while they're at it," he adds, alluding to the irony of an ostensibly racy *Normandy Gold* scene that is only titillating if you don't read the text. "The narration is a wonderful counterpoint to what's happening. Her *client* sure isn't reading what she's thinking in those panels." ■

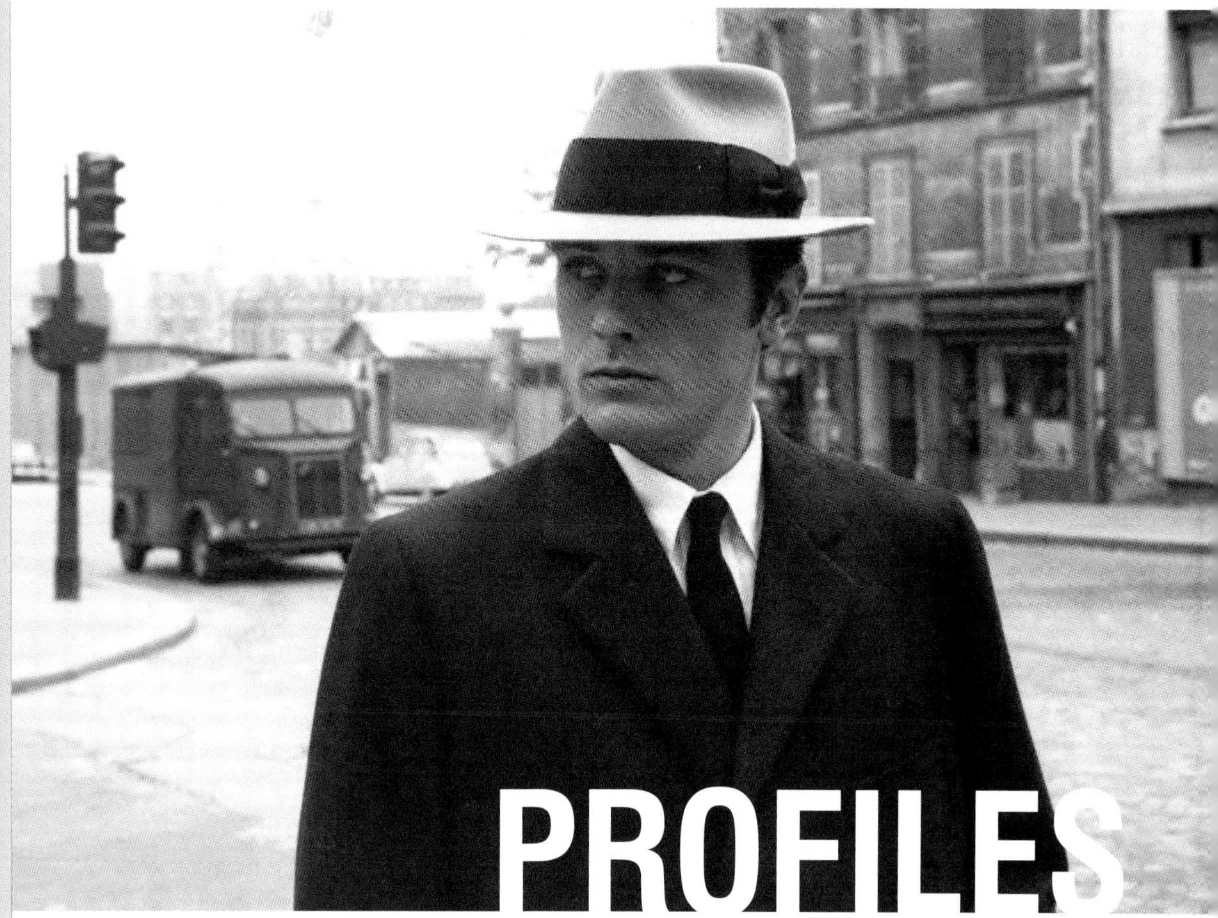

PROFILES

SECTION TWO

Pearl's pushing paid off—at least for her. In November 1937, 20th Century-Fox talent scout Ivan Kahn visited Dallas in search of new faces. Pearl Darnell brought her 14-year-old daughter to him, and Kahn was immediately struck by the girl's exquisite beauty. Fox studio chief Darryl F. Zanuck initially thought her too young for a contract, but at age 15, Monetta Darnell (with the help of the Stage Mother from Hell) inked a deal with Zanuck, who changed her name to Linda Darnell. She promptly made her screen debut in 1939's *Hotel for Women*. Her loveliness, innate charm and nascent talent captivated audiences and critics. Writer John Rosenfeld gushed: "Handed the greatest movie break since Clara Bow's time, the 15-year-old Dallasite grabbed it, hugged it to her and made one of the most successful starts in the history of talking pictures." Whether she liked it or not, Linda Darnell had become a star. A year later, Darnell literally played herself in *Star Dust*, a semi-biopic loosely based on her own meteoric rise to fame. Her youthful glow and exotic beauty cast a seductive spell in *The Mark of Zorro* (1940) and *Blood and Sand* (1941). Both films featured Darnell opposite her real-life screen idol Tyrone Power, but the luster of celebrity was soon replaced by boredom and typecasting: "People got tired of seeing the sweet young things I was playing and I landed at the bottom of the roller coaster." Darnell repeatedly refused to share the casting couch with Zanuck, resulting in spiteful rejections for choice roles and loan-outs to "B" studios for unwatchable tripe. Darnell continued to suffocate under her mother's consumptive presence. Depressed and tearful, she turned to Fox cameraman J. Peverell "Pev" Marley for solace and advice. Marley, who worked with Darnell on her first two films, befriended her, fell in love with her, and eventually eloped with her. It was the first in a series of failed marriages for the actress.

BY 1944, Darnell's career was crumbling. Stardom stultified her. She despised Darryl Zanuck, who gave her no opportunity to broaden her acting skills. When she was sent the script for United Artists' *Summer Storm*, she convinced Zanuck to loan her out for the role of Olga Urbenin, a peasant girl whose beauty and greed drive three men to destruction. The *Storm* shoot was itself stormy. When Darnell broke down after being forced to do several takes for a scene, director Douglas Sirk took her over his knee and spanked her. The shocked actress returned to the set and nailed the scene cold. Based on Anton Chekhov's "The Shooting Party," *Summer Storm* provided Darnell with her first truly mature role. "I was told that such a violent change of type might ruin my career," she later said. "But I insisted on taking the chance." Darnell had chosen wisely. Her dark side had finally emerged. She returned to Fox and notched her niche in noir with *Hangover Square* (1945), playing opposite the formidable Laird Cregar. Darnell poured herself into the role of Netta Longdon, a stunning-but-tawdry dance hall singer seeking the big time. Cregar's George Harvey Bone, an accomplished composer with a homicidal streak, takes one look at the sultry songbird and falls hard. Unfortunately, Netta is bad to the Bone. Darnell plays the wannabe diva as a cocksure teaser, feigning affection for the naïve musician, conniving him into writing the songs she needs to become a star. Bone becomes putty in the hands of the coy coquette. "All for you," she coos in his ear. "There's nothing I wouldn't or that I couldn't do." With a sigh and a smile, the sly seductress soothes Bone's bouts of jealousy, cuddling and cajoling him in a voice dripping with honey: "George, you're cross with me. Make me comfortable." Netta wraps her fingers around Bone's heart and snaps it like a twig. Yet, who can blame the blustery Bone for his infatuation? Netta is irresistible.

The film is a showcase for Darnell's dark, distinctive beauty. Fox's ace lensman Joseph LaShelle lights her in subtle chiaroscuro, focusing on her flawless profile, bee-stung lips, and bedroom eyes. The camera loves her, and so do we. Netta's a merciless minx. She coldly dumps Bone when he's no longer useful to her, sending him into a murderous rage. Her sweetness turns sour as she glares at the heartbroken composer with eyes of ice: "George, sometimes you can be such a bore." Yet, Darnell makes Netta likeable, infusing her with a girlish glow, a radiance that barely conceals her desperation for attention and admiration. Darnell understood Netta's neediness. Sharing a sad vulnerability, the actress and her character were kindred spirits.

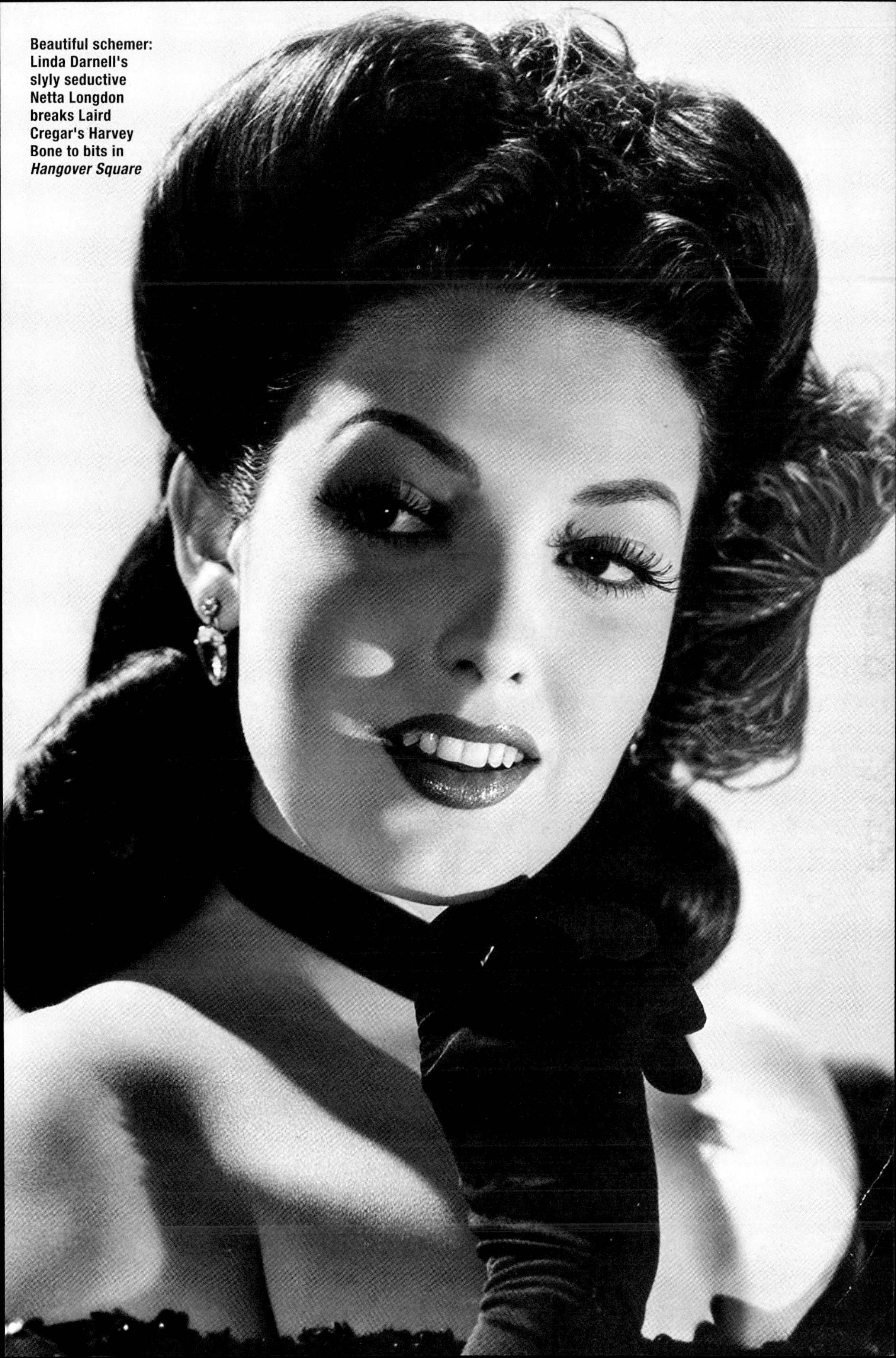

Beautiful schemer: Linda Darnell's slyly seductive Netta Longdon breaks Laird Cregar's Harvey Bone to bits in *Hangover Square*

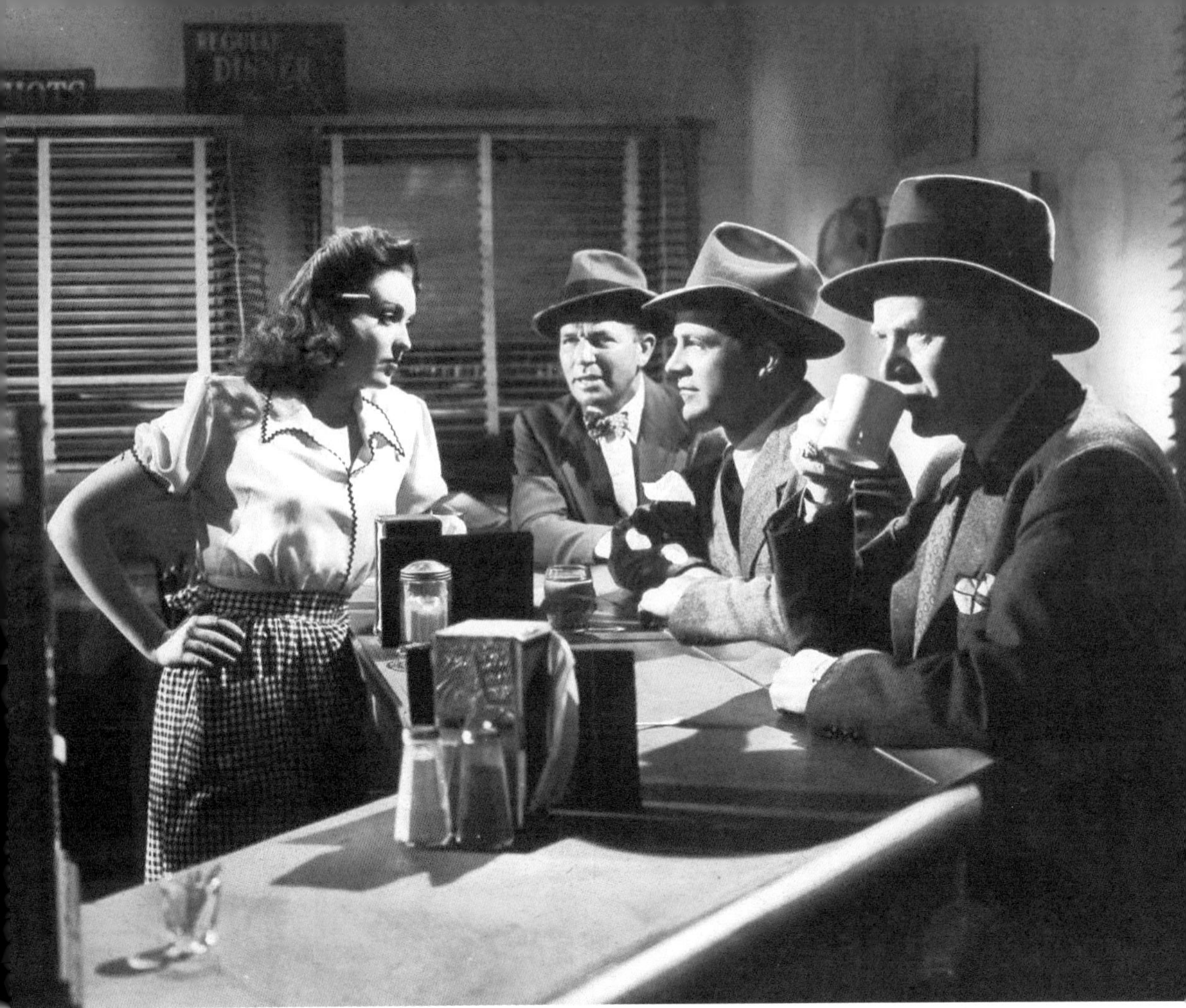

The Bored and the Beautiful: Linda Darnell laconically looks over obsessed admirers Bruce Cabot, Dana Andrews, and Charles Bickford in *Fallen Angel*

Hangover Square holds a pivotal place in Darnell's filmography. Her acclaimed performance prompted Zanuck to extend her Fox contract for another year. *Time* magazine labeled her "Hollywood's most rousing portrayer of unhousebroken sex." The flattery encouraged the actress. "They've never paid much attention to me before," she asserted. "I've had to act, appear and behave older than I was ever since I came to pictures. The main difference is that now I'm old enough to know how." Despite the plaudits, Darnell was always unimpressed with Hollywood's *hauteur*. Her *Hangover Square* co-star Faye Marlowe described her as "a sweet, wonderful person. . . unpretentious." During World War II, Darnell ignored the trappings of Hollywood. She preferred entertaining servicemen and volunteering for the American Red Cross.

In late January 1945, Darnell learned that her next studio assignment would be *Fallen Angel*, a moody, masterful noir helmed by the tyrannical Otto Preminger. She understandably detested the director. Still, under his supervision, she delivers a definitive performance as Stella, a stunning-but-cynical waitress working in a small-town diner (to prepare for the role, Darnell actually waited tables at the Fox commissary). Eric Stanton (Dana Andrews), a penniless itinerant, steps off a bus, steps into Pop's Diner, and is immediately smitten by the sexy, sultry Stella. He's not alone. Pop (Percy Kilbride) and local cop Mark Judd (Charles Bickford) are equally obsessed with her. Stanton wants Stella. Stella wants security, so Stanton woos and weds the town's wealthy spinster June Mills (Alice Faye). After he grabs June's fortune, he'll grab Stella. The scheme goes south when Stella turns up murdered. Suspects are everywhere.

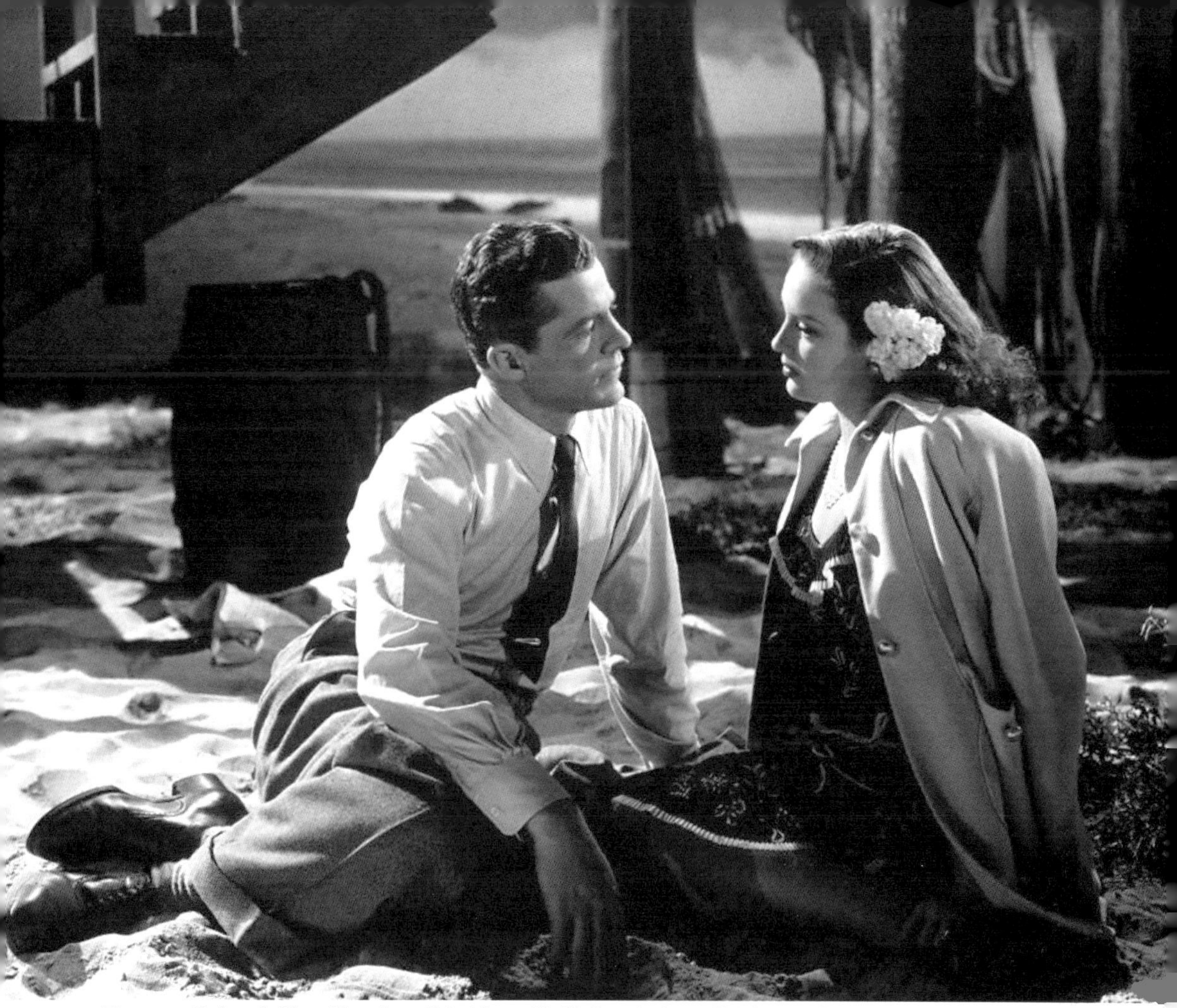

The romantic beachside setting doesn't fool Darnell's Stella, who immediately pegs Dana Andrews' Eric Stanton as a loser in *Fallen Angel*

Fallen Angel belongs exclusively to Darnell. Her canny, carnal exterior doesn't belie a bitter disillusionment with the cheap losers who've used and abused her. Men slaver over her, but she repays their attention with an insouciant scowl, casually brushing back her hair as she languidly munches a hamburger and steals cash from under Pop's nose. Her smoldering chemistry with Andrews lingers in the air, but she's too smart to fall for his character's sweet talk. Instead, she spits spitefulness at him: "You talk different, sure, but you drive just like the rest. You got into town with one dollar in your pocket. You're a fake." Stanton's sexual advances leave her cold. Stella may be flirty, but she's not dirty: "That's for kids, but not for me. Not anymore." Darnell blends Stella's icy cynicism with an innate sadness. She mournfully recalls her impoverished childhood: "My old man came from a long line of drunks. My mother ran a boarding house." The despair is reflected in her eyes, in the way she stares at the bare walls of Pop's Diner like a prisoner awaiting parole. She's trapped in a tank town and she knows it.

Darnell's smoky, sensual Stella was a cinematic sensation. Darryl Zanuck, still captivated by her, ordered Preminger and Joseph LaShelle to highlight Darnell's distinctive eroticism (bruising the ego of co-star Alice Faye, who promptly quit Fox and abandoned the film industry for 17 years). Dana Andrews hailed Darnell's world-weary performance as "the best thing in the picture." Even cranky critic Bosley Crowther was impressed, applauding the actress as ". . . beautiful and perfectly cast as the sultry and single-minded siren." In his commentary on Fox's *Fallen Angel* DVD, Eddie Muller notes that Darnell's Stella became a paradigm for such noir vamps as Rita Hayworth, Joan Bennett, and Ava Gardner.

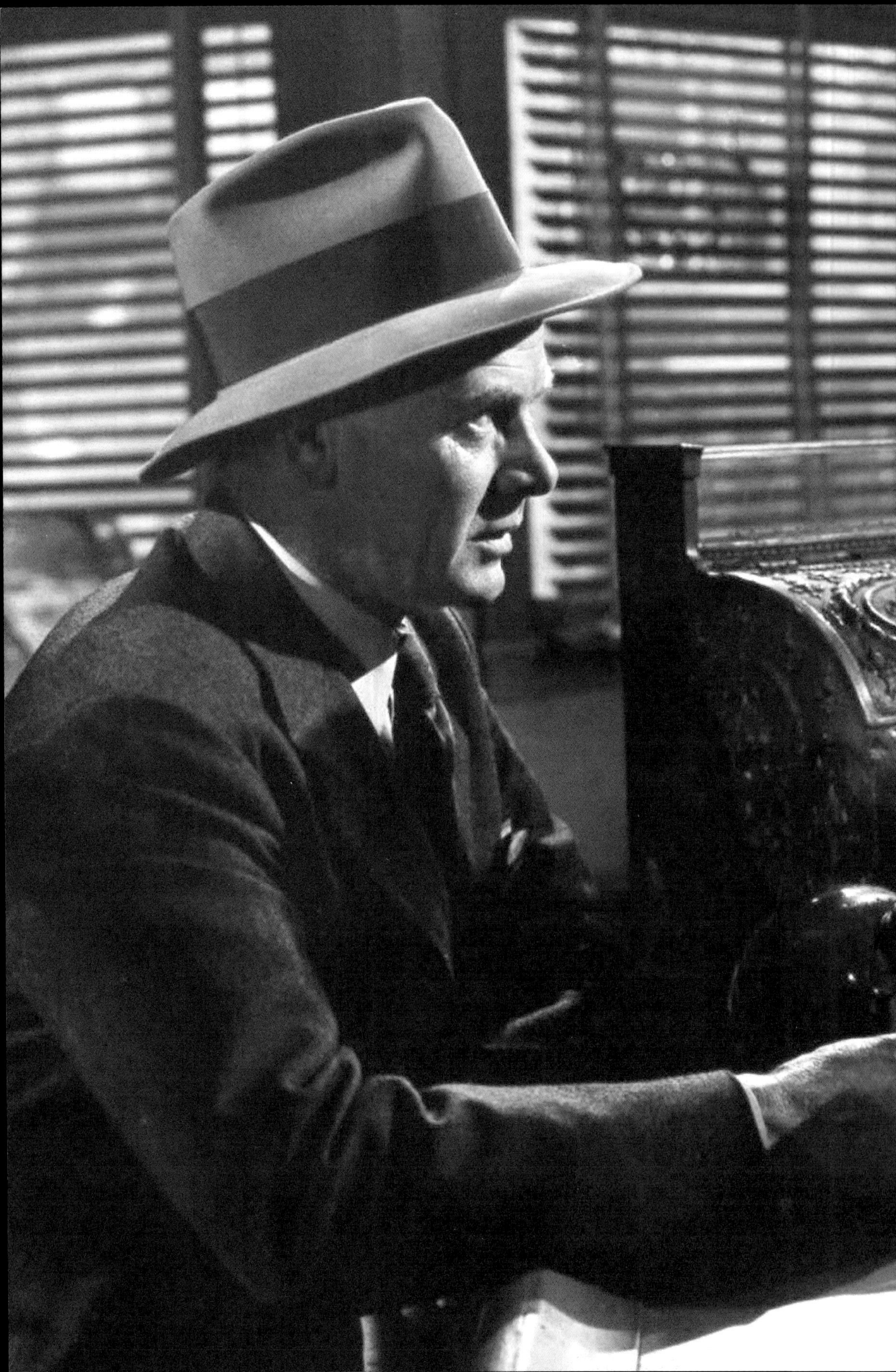

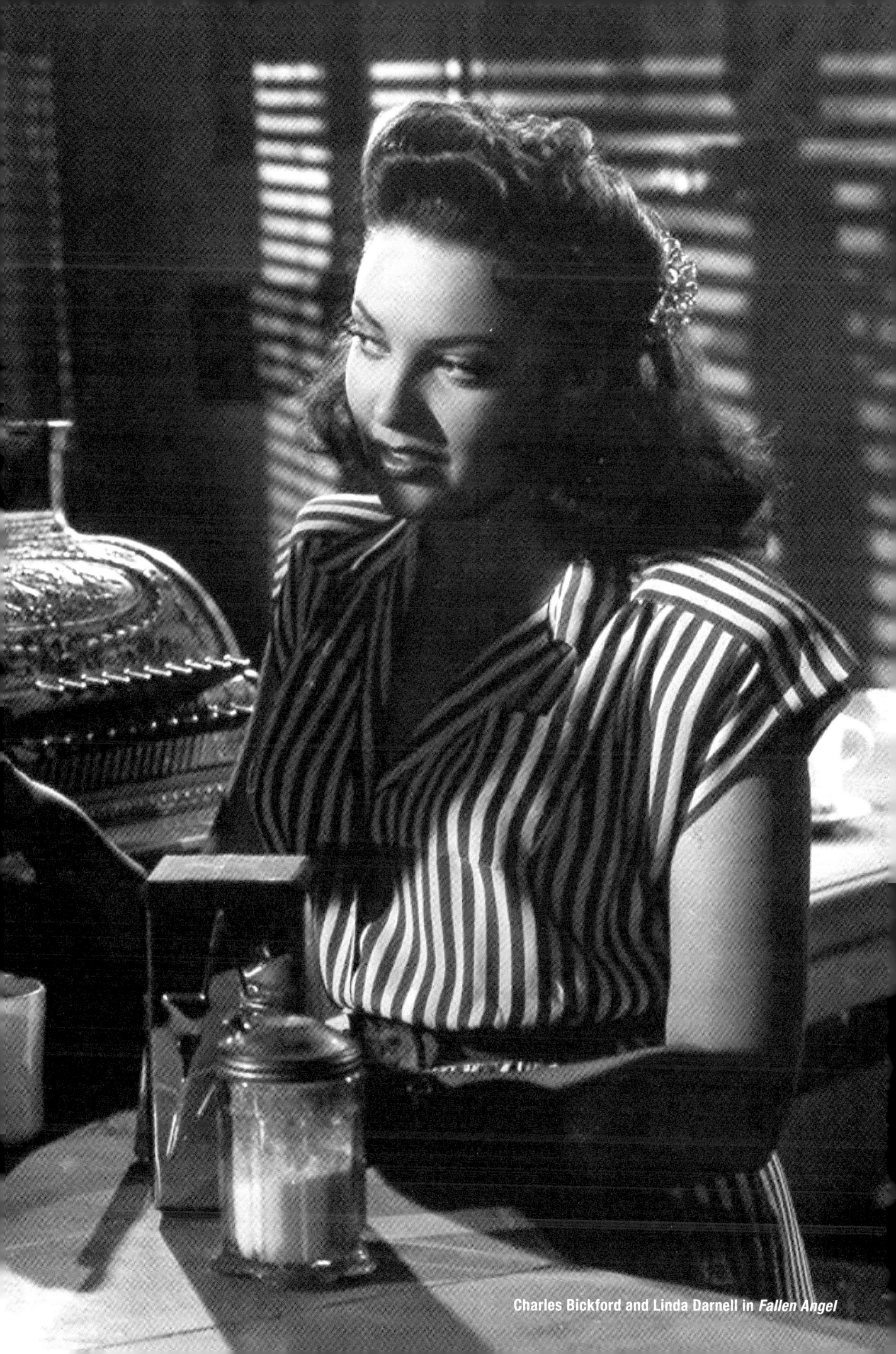

Charles Bickford and Linda Darnell in *Fallen Angel*

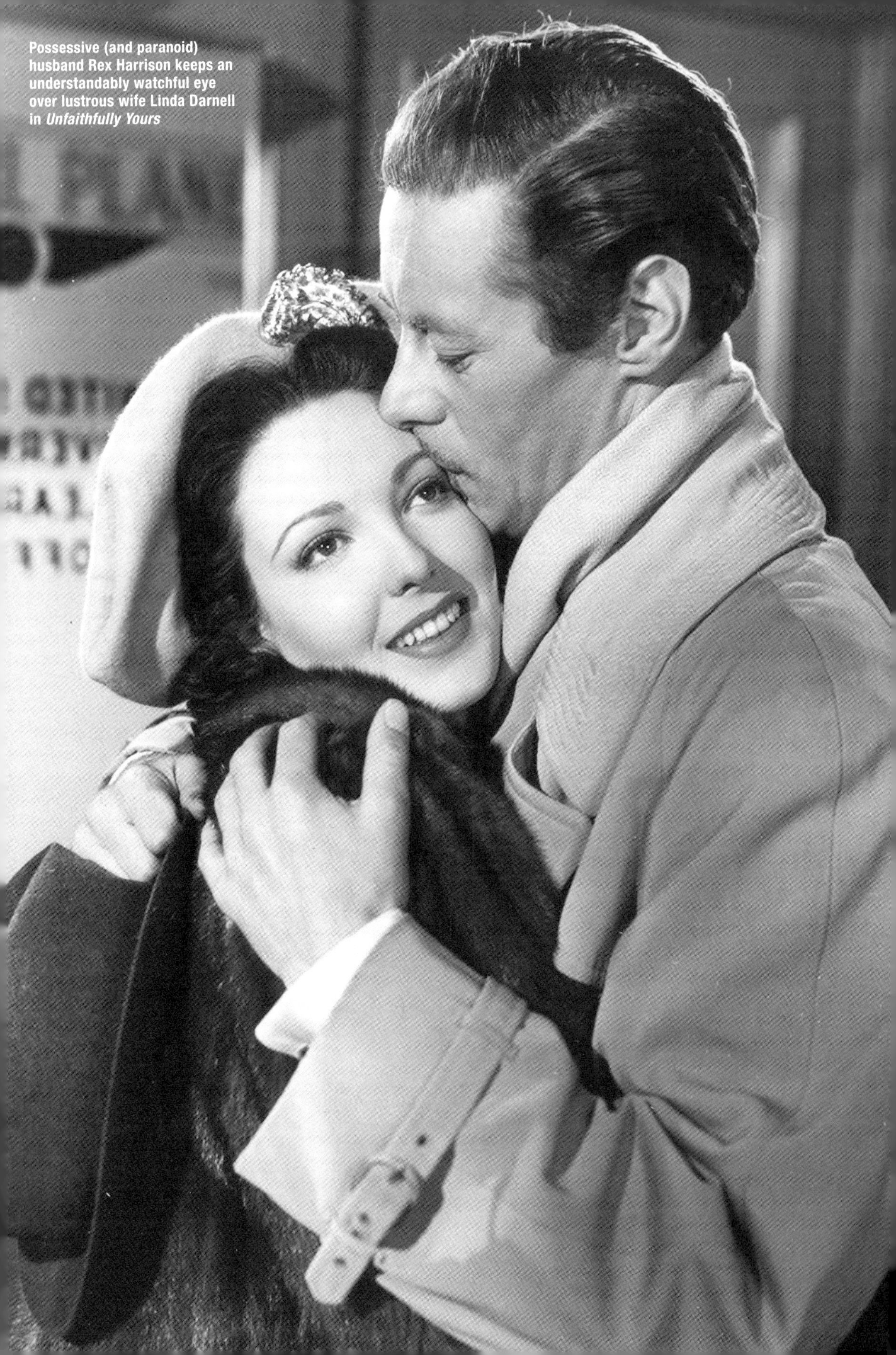

Possessive (and paranoid) husband Rex Harrison keeps an understandably watchful eye over lustrous wife Linda Darnell in *Unfaithfully Yours*

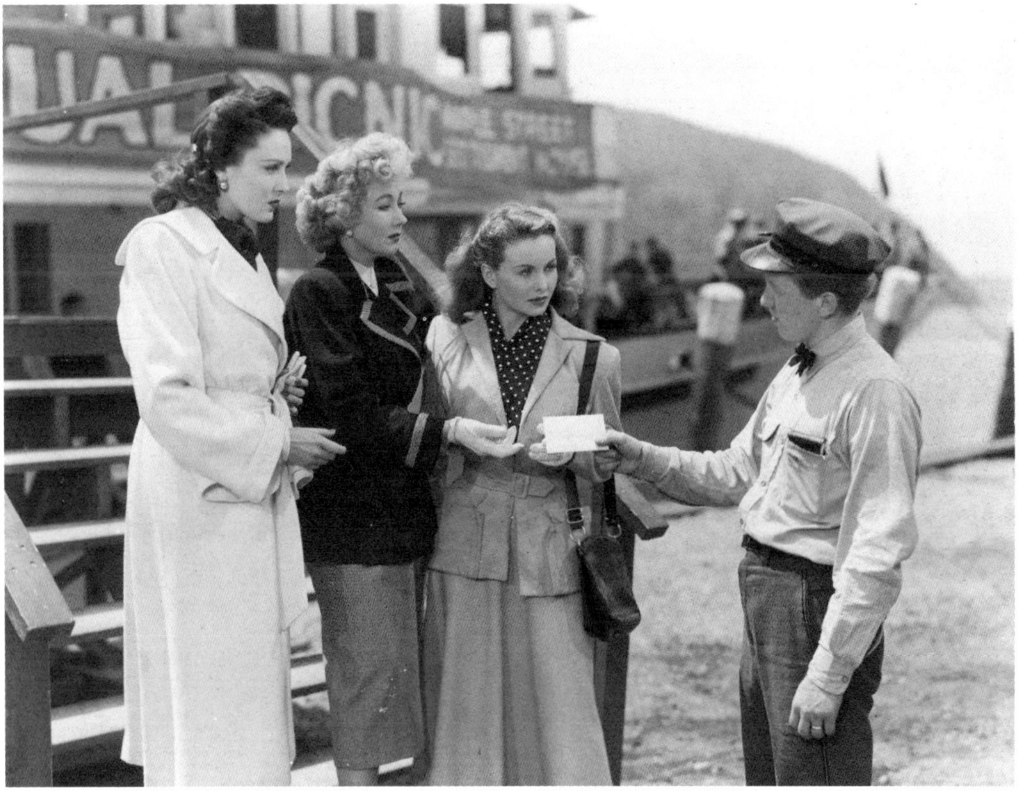

A bad day awaits Linda Darnell, Ann Sothern, and Jeanne Crain when they're handed *A Letter to Three Wives*

FALLEN ANGEL may have rejuvenated Darnell's career, but her personal life plummeted. Her unhappy marriage to "Pev" Marley resulted in renewed depression and a dangerous dependence on alcohol. She had a brief fling with Howard Hughes before returning to the Fox lot to replace a too-young Peggy Cummins in the florid romantic drama *Forever Amber* (1947). The movie was a box office hit, but Darnell hated the picture, hated her role in it, and hated her forced reunion with the despicable Otto Preminger. Darnell's despondency was compounded by her inability to bear children. In January 1948, she and Marley adopted a baby daughter, Lola. The joy of adoption was lost on Darnell, and her demanding work schedule made her ill-suited for motherhood. That same year, she co-starred in Preston Sturges' *Unfaithfully Yours*. Bejeweled and beautifully attired, Darnell never looked lovelier. It's understandable that her allure would drive jealous husband Rex Harrison to contemplate a series of methodically planned murders, each of which dissolves into mirthful mayhem. Though the film depicts Darnell as little more than a gorgeous confection, Sturges captures her warmth, elegance, and charm in a role that veered radically from her work in *Fallen Angel*.

It took Joseph L. Mankiewicz to reinvigorate Darnell's range as a comedic and dramatic actress. In *A Letter to Three Wives* (1949), her character, Lora Mae Hollingsway, struts the sets with style and panache delivering Mankiewicz' scorching dialogue with near-demonic delight: "Anybody wants me can come and get me. This ain't a drive-in." When a radio advertiser offers to put her husband, a wealthy department store magnate (Paul Douglas), into millions of homes for half-an-hour a day, Lora Mae quips: "He doesn't spend that much time in his *own* home!" Brassy, sassy, and subtly salacious, Lora Mae is *Fallen Angel*'s Stella with a polished veneer—worldly, but not world-weary. She knows how to live large, but she hasn't forgotten her poverty-stricken roots. Darnell owns *Letter*, deftly juggling comedy and pathos, easily outshining a wholesome Jeanne Crain and a wry Ann Sothern. The artistic rapport between Mankiewicz and Darnell was unmistakable (when the director needed to elicit a

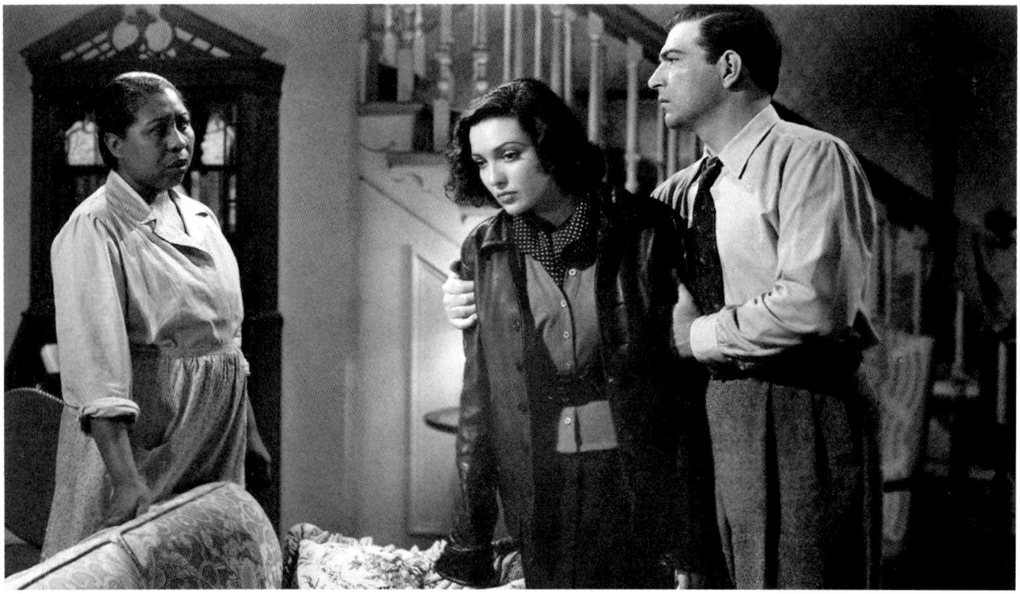

An embittered Linda Darnell learns some important life lessons from Amanda Randolph and Stephen McNally in *No Way Out*

look of disgust from the actress, he astutely showed her a photo of Otto Preminger in a Nazi uniform). *Letter* vaulted Mankiewicz to Hollywood's top tier and rewarded Darnell with renewed confidence in her artistry. By the time the film wrapped, Mankiewicz and Darnell were wrapped in each other's arms. The actress and her director had fallen in love, and the two began a six-year relationship. Their romance was no secret, though Mankiewicz would only speak of Darnell as "a marvelous girl with very terrifying personal problems."

Mankiewicz' searing *No Way Out* (1950) is marked by Darnell's last great film performance. The movie is a bold hybrid of noir and social commentary, and Darnell provides the picture's heartbeat with her nuanced portrayal of Edie Johnson, a callous racist whose redemption becomes crucial to the film's finale. Edie's moral fiber is tested when she's caught between two polar opposites: her bigoted brother-in-law Ray Biddle (Richard Widmark), shot while attempting a robbery, and Luther Brooks (Sidney Poitier), the doctor assigned to save Biddle's life. Neither actor is required to stretch much. Poitier's Brooks is a tightly wired picture of moral rectitude, ethically obligated to spare a vicious racist who spits slurs at him. Widmark's psychotic Biddle recalls *Kiss of Death*: he's Tommy Udo with a KKK card. *No Way Out* is truly Linda Darnell's film. Stripped of glamour, she plays Edie Johnson as slatternly and trashy. She's a perfect fit for the messy dump she lives in and the backwater town she comes from. Her face is lined with rancor. Yet, Darnell imbues Edie with pride and dignity. We see it in her poised body language, her confident walk, her defiant attitude. She tosses off Mankiewicz' corrosive dialogue with remarkable aplomb: "I'm a carhop at a drive-in. *Anything wrong with that?*" When Brooks tells her she's better than the bigots she grew up with, she retorts: "Yeah, I've come up in the world. I used to live in a sewer. Now I live in a swamp." As Biddle begs Brooks to save him from bleeding to death, Edie spews venom: "Let it bleed," she tells Brooks. "Tear it some more. Let it bleed fast." It's Darnell who pushes and prods the picture into noir's outer edges. She digs deeply beyond her surface beauty, revealing a woman burdened by bitterness, bad men, and bad luck. "I'm a female bum in *No Way Out*," she told reporters. "It's a good role. I do everything—get drunk, go on a couple of crying jags, and get slapped by Richard Widmark." She marveled at Mankiewicz' writing and direction, calling *No Way Out* "the only good picture I ever made." It also represented her last inspired performance, her last notable noir, and her final collaboration with Mankiewicz.

DARNELL'S AFFAIR with Mankiewicz continued, despite his refusal to leave his wife for her. Her fragile ego went into freefall. An acrimonious and expensive divorce from "Pev" Marley left her nearly broke. Two more luckless marriages followed. Forced to maintain a brutal work schedule, Darnell became an absentee mother to her daughter. "Mother and I were never really close until I was older," recalled Lola Marley. "We missed all the fifteen years before, and I think that's sad." Her final forays into film noir were undistinguished and unworthy of her. In *Night Without Sleep* (1952), she effortlessly exudes charm, but the script spirals into mediocrity. In 1952, the persistent onslaught of television forced Fox to cancel Darnell's contract, and her depression festered into bitterness. As a free agent, she allowed Howard Hughes to personally cast her in Republic's *Second Chance* (1953), uniting her with noir alumni Robert Mitchum, Jack Palance, and director Rudolph Maté. Unfortunately, she's given little to do but cuddle with Mitchum and cower from Palance. As film work dried up, Darnell moved into television and even formed a nightclub act—but alcoholism, depression, and bankruptcy continued to plague her. She was devastated when Joseph Mankiewicz selected Ava Gardner for the lead in 1954's *The Barefoot Contessa.* Darnell was convinced that Mankiewicz had written the script for her. She severed all ties with him, but her self-esteem was destroyed. Failed marriages and a thieving business manager had drained her finances. Her exquisite face and figure became marred by alcohol and junk food. She was only 32 when she mournfully reflected on her life and career: "I am told that when surface beauty is gone, the real woman emerges. My only regret will be that I could not have begun it earlier—that so many years have been ruined because I was considered beautiful."

Near the end of both *Hangover Square* and *Anna and the King of Siam* (1946), Darnell's characters are consumed by fire. These scenes were eerily prescient. Darnell had a lifelong fear of fire, and harbored a premonition that she would die in flames. On April 8, 1965, she was staying at the Glenview, Illinois, home of her best friend Jeanne Curtis. Around 5:00 a.m. on April 9, a fire quickly spread through the house. Darnell helped Curtis and her daughter escape through an upstairs window before inexplicably bolting downstairs toward the front door. Firefighters found her wrapped in a blanket in Curtis' living room. Ninety per cent of her body was covered with second- and third-degree burns. One of Hollywood's most beautiful faces was disfigured beyond recognition. Frantic efforts to save her life were unsuccessful. Darnell's final words were whispered to a priest who asked her if she wanted to receive the last rites of the church: "You're goddamn right I do!" She died on April 10, 1965 at the age of 41. The cause of the fire was never determined, but speculation is the fire started from a cigarette. That evening, before the fire, Darnell and Curtis had finished watching *Star Dust* on television.

Neither her tragic life nor her cruelly ironic death could erase Darnell's legacy as an actress. In her best films, she etched indelible, incisive portraits of shrewd, tough women who knew that physical beauty was ephemeral, providing no protection against the hard knocks of everyday life. Linda Darnell left this world with one certainty: she was much more than just another pretty face. ■

For more information on Darnell's life and legacy, read Ronald L. Davis' book Hollywood Beauty: Linda Darnell and the American Dream (University of Oklahoma Press, 1991).

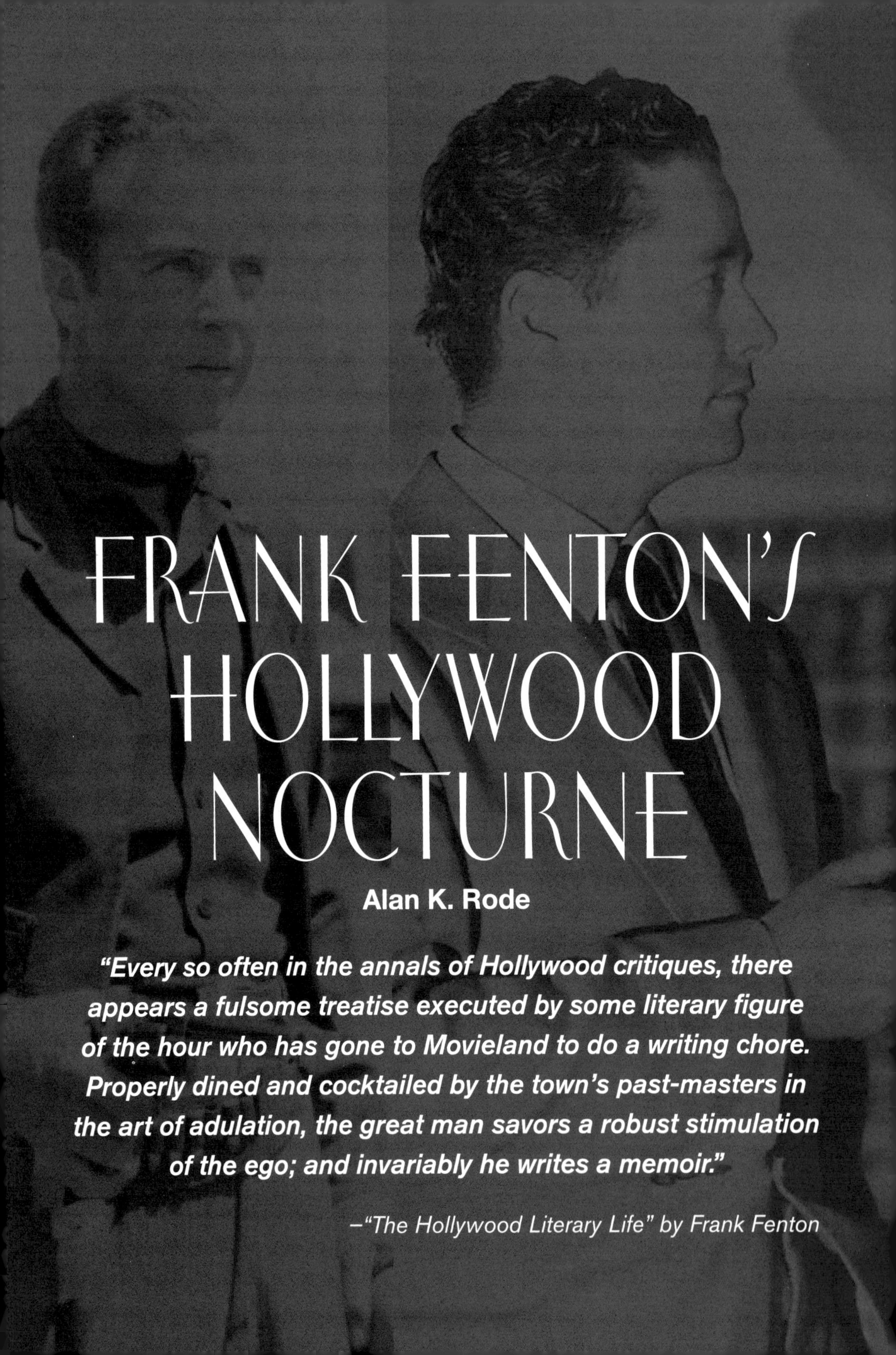

FRANK FENTON'S HOLLYWOOD NOCTURNE

Alan K. Rode

"Every so often in the annals of Hollywood critiques, there appears a fulsome treatise executed by some literary figure of the hour who has gone to Movieland to do a writing chore. Properly dined and cocktailed by the town's past-masters in the art of adulation, the great man savors a robust stimulation of the ego; and invariably he writes a memoir."

–"The Hollywood Literary Life" by Frank Fenton

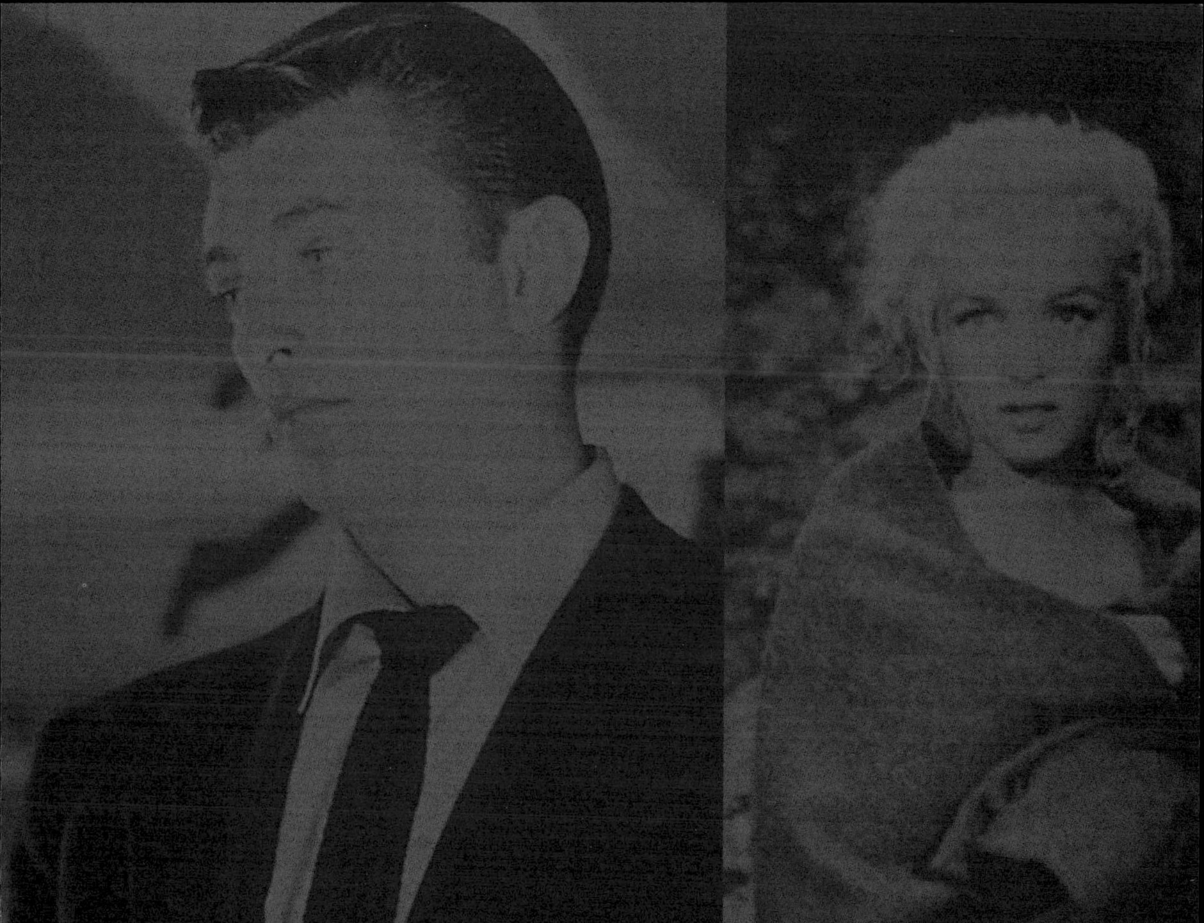

Frank Fenton never got around to writing a memoir. With a resume of over 60 feature films and television shows (and a profusion of uncredited and unproduced work) over a 40-year career, he was too busy for self-reflection.

Fenton was establishing himself as a proficient scenarist of B-films when the above-quoted article appeared in the November 1938 issue of *The American Mercury*. He would pen several other fictional short stories about the Hollywood movie scene whose posturing he mocked. Another Fenton piece, "Boy Meets Gorilla," was published in *Collier's* the following month. His story of a Hamilton, Ohio, hick who is transformed into an acclaimed Hollywood writer-producer after saving a movie star from a gorilla on the set of a South Seas potboiler was a spot-on satire of Tinseltown pretentiousness.

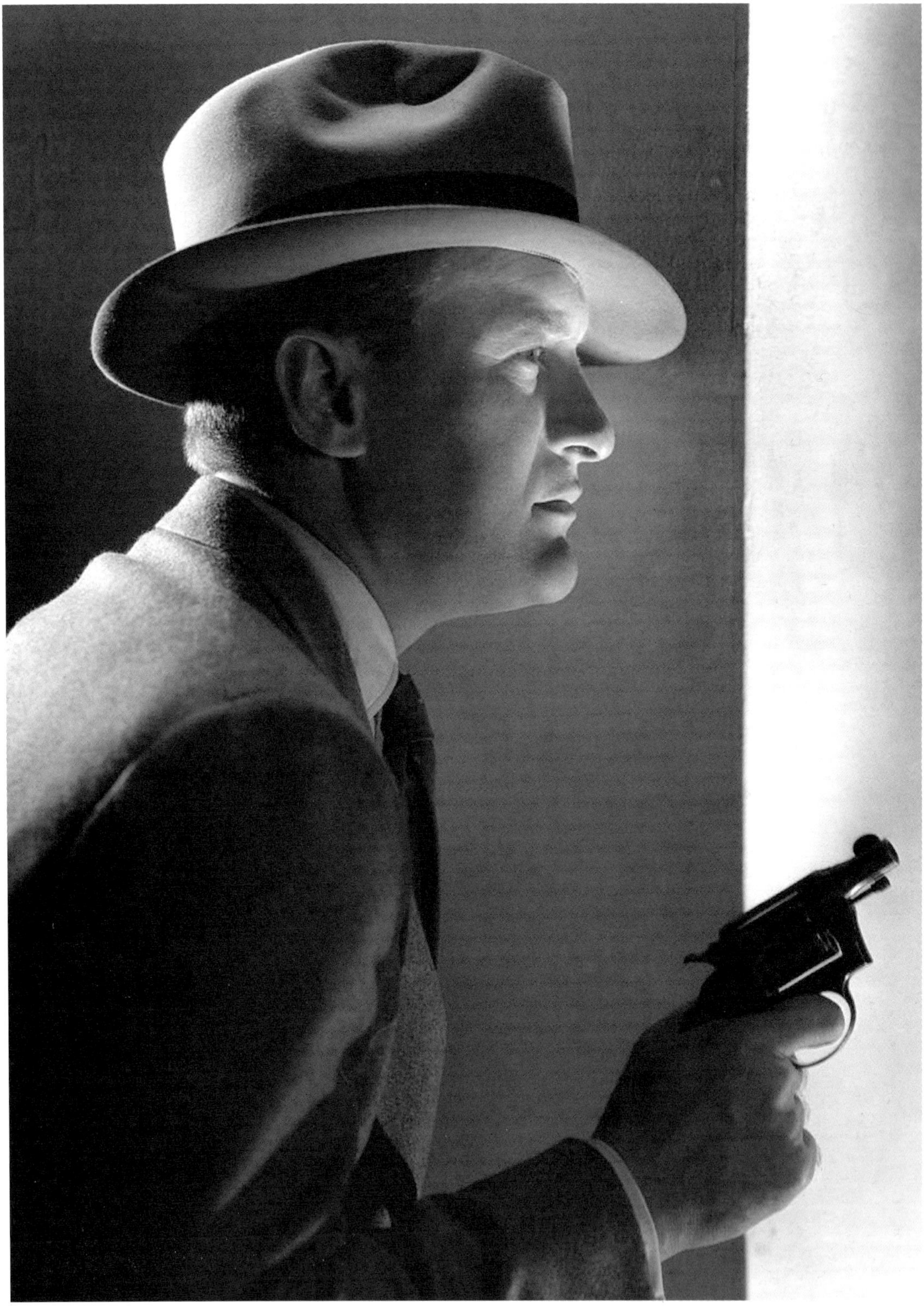

Fenton began to find his rhythm as a writer with the RKO-produced Falcon film series, starring George Sanders as the titular crime solver

Fenton's professional outlook (along with a fondness for booze) resembled that of Robert Mitchum, for whom he wrote some of the actor's most memorable dialogue. Like the laconic movie star, Fenton never hesitated to mock the suits that signed his checks—even as he cashed them.

Much of Fenton's work has become overlooked, forgotten, or unavailable. Some of his best writings were uncredited script rewrites, extensive polish jobs, or original stories that were adapted by others. Fenton established an emblematic standard for cynical dialogue and innovative plotting in some of the best film noirs and Westerns, despite few people remembering who actually crafted the words. He is frequently confused with another Frank Fenton, a character actor who enjoyed an overlapping career in film and television.

Frank Edgington Fenton was born in Liverpool, England, on February 3, 1903. He arrived in America with his family at the age of three and was raised in the Ohio heartland. Despite erroneous claims on the internet (and a similar Ohio immigrant lineage), Fenton was not the brother of Leslie Fenton, a British actor who incurred the wrath of Jack L. Warner after he eloped with Ann Dvorak in 1932.

Fenton was American-bred, but he never abandoned his British roots. His son Mark Fenton remembered, "Dad never became an American citizen—he always carried a green card." The younger Fenton said his father would "toast the Queen every evening with a glass of Cutty Sark."

His father, John Fenton, was listed in the 1920 census as a shoe manufacturer. In addition to Frank and his two sisters, the Fenton household included a 36-year-old female servant and Fenton's maternal grandmother, Mary Edgington. The elder Fenton was apparently well off enough for son Frank to attend college. After graduating from Ohio State University, Fenton journeyed to Los Angeles and remained there for the rest of his life. A film buff as well as a student of classical literature, he dreamed of writing for the movies and was drawn to Hollywood like the proverbial moth to the flame.

Fenton's earliest film credit was an original story for the 63-minute programmer *Behind Jury Doors* (1932). He co-wrote *Dinky* (1935) with his pal John Fante, which the pair sold to Warner Bros. Fante would become renowned for his 1939 semi-autobiographical novel *Ask the Dust*, about a struggling Depression-era writer–Arturo Bandini, and considered to be the definitive Los Angeles novel. His "Bandini quartet" of stories, along with screenplays for *Full of Life* (1956, based on his novel), *Jeanne Eagels* (1957), and *Walk on the Wild Side* (1962) earned Fante a great deal of late-career and posthumous acclaim. During the Depression, he and Fenton were just another pair of hungry writers attempting to scratch out a living in the City of Angels.

Fenton and Fante remained lifelong friends even after the former began working with Lynn Root. Root was a Broadway actor who ditched treading the boards to take up writing. He would eventually hit it big with his play *Cabin in the Sky*, adapted into a major 1943 MGM production with an all-star African-American cast. Fenton and Root began with a couple of flop plays. They sold one of them, *Stork Mad*, to 20th Century–Fox, which turned it into a Jane Withers comedy. The pair gained a professional toehold by cranking out three more Withers features for Fox.

From 1937 to 1946, Fenton and Root collaborated on over 20 original stories and screenplays. Many of their scripts became leanly produced RKO programmers, usually for The Saint or The Falcon series.

A prototypical entry was *The Falcon Takes Over* (1942). Shot in 20 days for $140,000, it was the first screen adaptation of Raymond Chandler's work. Based on *Farewell, My Lovely*, the not-yet-famous author received $2,012.70 from RKO for the rights.

Fenton and Root shifted the locale from Los Angeles to Manhattan and compressed Chandler's mystery into a 65-minute feature starring George Sanders as The Falcon and a padded Ward Bond as Moose Malloy. Although much of Chandler's story and characterizations had to be tossed in order to streamline the plot (while also getting the script by the censor's office), the film was permeated with the amusing dialogue that became a Fenton trademark. RKO appreciated the results and remade Chandler's yarn two years later to greater acclaim as *Murder, My Sweet* (1944) starring a repurposed Dick Powell.

Even as Fenton ascended to scripting major productions like *The Sky's the Limit* (1943), he aspired to be more than a screenwriter. For most writers of his era, the path to Hollywood usually began after a stint with newspapers, writing for the "slicks," or authoring a successful novel. Fenton stood this formula on its head by authoring a pair of novels just as his screenwriting career gained significant traction.

The New York Times praised Fenton's debut novel *A Place in the Sun*, which was published by Random House in July 1942:

> "Fenton's [book] is notable for its sensitive portrayal of a young man who lived with the inferiority of a physical handicap. [He] does a masterly job of balancing the forces which molded the character of Rob Andrews...[and] he succeeds in giving the story the glow of human fulfillment."

The respected California writer-historian Carey McWilliams believed *A Place in the Sun* was one of only four novels (including Nathanael West's *The Day of the Locust* and John Fante's *Ask the Dust*) "that suggest what Southern California is really like." Fenton's depiction of pre-war Los Angeles in *A Place in the Sun* remains poetically descriptive:

> *Down the foothills into the city the air changed. The lingering mist of morning fog was rising and in the fog there was the salt flavor of the sea. Then the shreds of fog melted and the great yellow and white city lay at the mercy of the sun.*
>
> *He drove down one street after another. It was all beautiful. A million bungalows and mansions of all conceivable architectures; flowers he could not name, and trees he had never seen before. Strange races on the sidewalks: Mexicans, Filipinos, Japanese, Chinese.*
>
> *A strange and wonderful city.*
>
> *It was not like some Middle-Western city that sinks down roots into some strategic area of earth and goes to work there. This was a lovely makeshift city. Even the trees and plants, he knew, did not belong there. They came, like the people, from far places, some familiar, some exotic, all wanderers of one sort or another, seeking peace or fortune or the last frontier, or a thousand dreams of escape. And all these malcontents had joined in a dreamy effort to create a city of their dreams...*

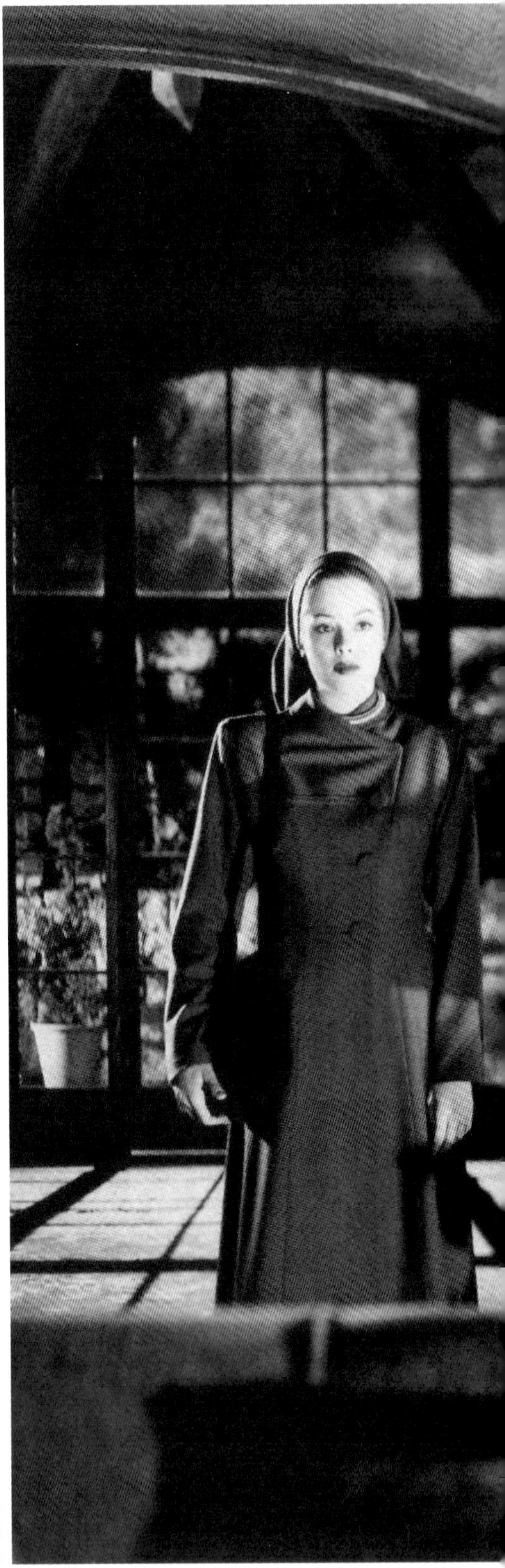

Fenton did the final drafts of *Out of the Past*, perhaps the quintessential noir; he provided most of the most quotable lines delivered by co-stars Jane Greer and Robert Mitchum

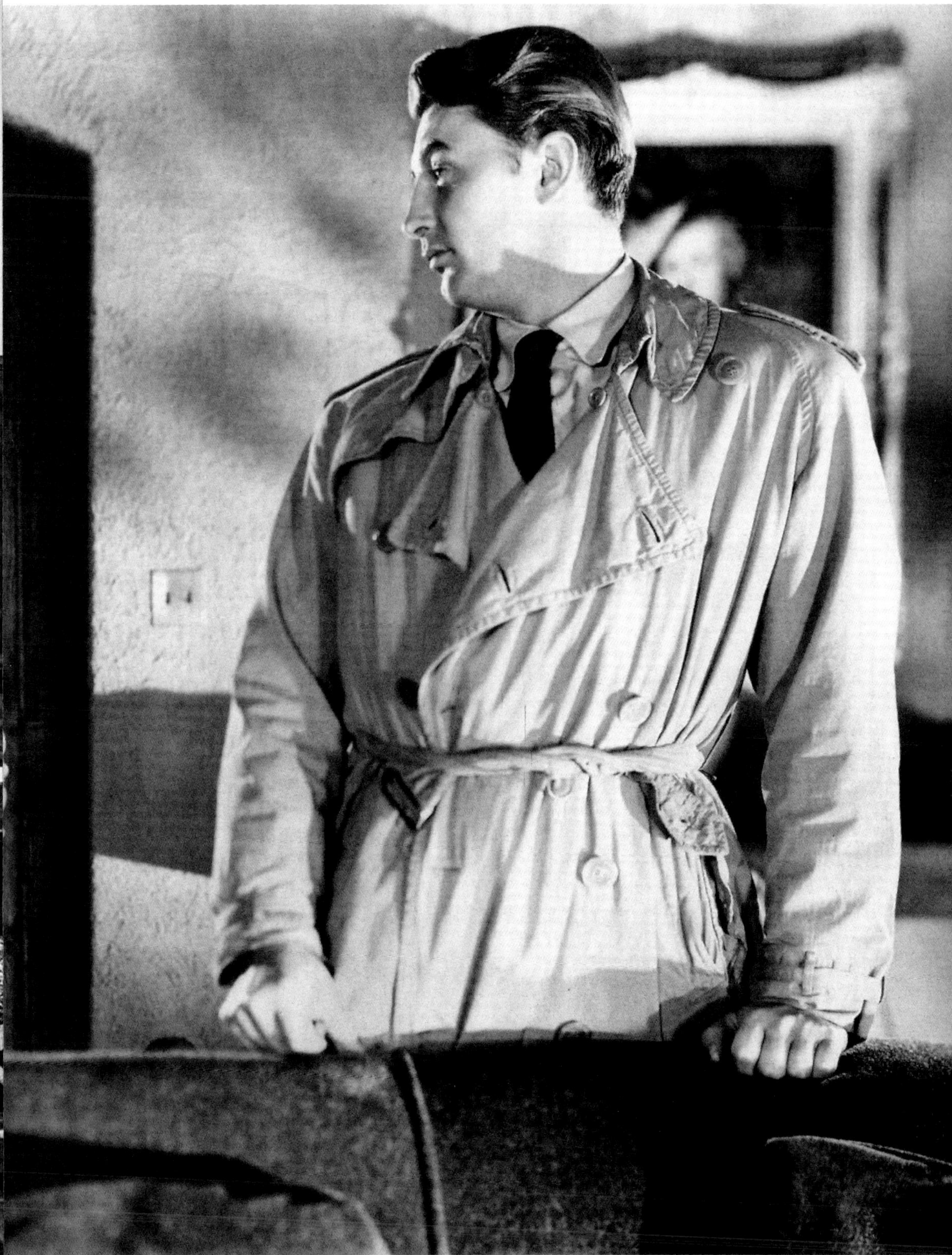

Jack Leonard expanded the yarn into a screenplay titled "Smiler with a Gun." The plotline was shifted away from Hughes' obsession of foiling domestic communism to Mitchum being inveigled to arrive at the resort so a deported mob boss modeled on Lucky Luciano (played by a sinister Raymond Burr) could assume his identity and re-enter the country.

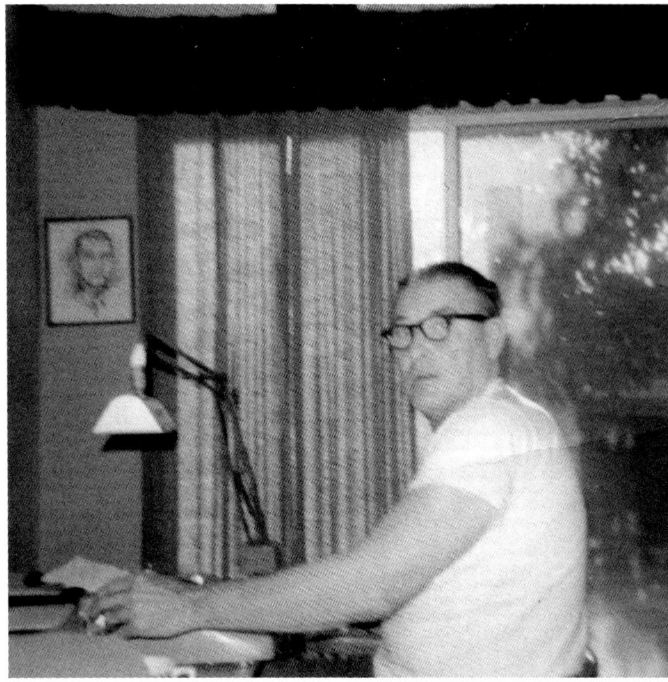

Photo courtesy of Mark Fenton

Frank Fenton at work... Grinding out TV scripts was never as much fun as writing for the movies

A rewrite by Roy Huggins made few discernable changes to the original script. Fenton and Jack Leonard received sole screen credit. Nearly everything they wrote remained in the final cut including an over-the-top movie star memorably portrayed by Vincent Price. But Howard Hughes wanted much more of a slam-bang ending.

After John Farrow finished directing the picture, Hughes assigned director Richard Fleischer and his writing partner Earl Felton to add more pizzazz with a wild fight scene on a yacht (that Hughes had purchased) and a prolonged gunfight between Price and Charles McGraw, along with a large number of retakes. Twenty-five additions or changes to the shooting script (from April 10, 1950 to April 26, 1951) took place after the picture first wrapped. The retitled picture, *His Kind of Woman,* lost $850,000—almost exactly the amount of money Hughes put into a year's worth of retakes. The film remains eminently watchable due to the excellent cast, a delightfully ridiculous plot, and Fenton's crisp dialogue[1].

Fenton moved on from RKO to write for studios that treated moviemaking as a business more than a form of personal amusement. The 1950s became a decade of Westerns, and Fenton cashed in big-time with *The Wild North* (1952), *Ride, Vaquero!*, *Escape from Fort Bravo* (both 1953) and *Garden of Evil* (1954).

He was reunited with Robert Mitchum when he wrote the screenplay for *River of No Return* (1954). It was a troubled production whose problems began when Fox mogul Darryl F. Zanuck forced director Otto Preminger on producer Stanley Rubin. "Preminger was totally wrong for this kind of picture," said Rubin. "I wanted Raoul Walsh or Henry King, but Zanuck wasn't having it because Otto had a "pay-or-play" contract." Rubin spent the balance of the production attempting to maintain a semblance of comity between the mercurial Preminger, a terribly insecure Marilyn Monroe, and an imbibing Mitchum. Fenton became irritated when Preminger preemptively decided to drop a scene that had Mitchum attempting to maul Monroe. When the screenwriter objected, Preminger banished him from the set.

Fenton's life underwent a major change by the middle of the decade. After a brief marriage to diminutive actress June Martel had flamed out in 1942, he wed actress-stuntwoman Mary Jane Hodge in 1945. Hodge could be as spirited as her husband. Mark Fenton recalled a family story about his

1 For a more detailed description of the *His Kind of Woman* debacle, please refer to Richard Fleischer's memoir *Just Tell Me When to Cry* and the author's *Charles McGraw: Film Noir Tough Guy* biography.

mother being terminated by RKO during the filming of *Folies Bergère de Paris* (1935) for playing a practical joke on star Maurice Chevalier that backfired. The Fentons would have two children, Mark and Joyce, and they resided comfortably in the Cheviot Hills area of Los Angeles near Fenton's other home, the California Country Club. According to Mark Fenton: "My father loved golfing and the cocktail hour."

The marriage eventually fell apart. Both Fenton and his wife drank. At the time, he could handle it. She couldn't. After the 1957 divorce, Fenton ended up with custody of seven-year-old son Mark, with his ex-wife raising their daughter. Fenton moved to a small house off Olympic Boulevard. "I had kind of a weird childhood with my father," said Mark Fenton. "We had a housekeeper and I was a latchkey kid." The ups and downs included being taught how to swim by Tarzan—Johnny Weissmuller was a chum of his Dad's—and having his father fend him off when he was busy with a screenplay. "He was a very intense, driven man when it came to his writing," recalled Mark. "I think it was very difficult for him to stop and become immersed all over again in what he had been doing."

According to Mark Fenton, his father's movie work dried up after Barbara Stanwyck accused Fenton of being a communist during the filming of *These Wilder Years* (1956). The younger Fenton vividly remembers a high school teacher humiliating him publicly in class over his father being listed as a communist or suspected subversive in a press report. Whether Fenton was actually blacklisted or graylisted remains unknown. I could not locate his name on any source or archival material denoting the era's blacklisted artists. Nevertheless, he managed only two more screenplay credits. His final feature film, *The Jayhawkers!*, was released in 1959.

After a lean period of spec work, Fenton caught on again with television. He did a lot of work for famed television writer-producer and HUAC-friendly witness Roy Huggins, but it was a far cry from writing for Mitchum and Monroe. Mark Fenton surmised: "I think my father had trouble adjusting to the changing tastes of the public. He loved writing stories about tough guys and men of action. I think he found it difficult to write love scenes."

The drinking continued. His son remembered occasions when his father "came home from the Cock 'n Bull pub late or the next morning, with a black eye or a missing tooth." He continued his irreverence toward a new generation of TV suits. Mark chuckled at the memory: "He always dressed nicely, but would wear dirty white tennis shoes whenever he had a meeting at the studio."

The younger Fenton concluded: "I liked my father. I always felt protected by him."

Frank Fenton's last hurrah was *Something for a Lonely Man*, a 1968 Western TV movie he co-wrote with his friend John Fante. He suffered a stroke and died on August 23, 1971. He left behind an unpublished poem that was an ode to his career and the lost Hollywood night.

I did not love you greatly, I only lied.
I loved all things and none. I merely tried.
Never forgive me love, I was not true.
To anything I loved but love, not even you. ■

Thanks to Mark Fenton for his candor and family photos, Craig Hodgkins' blog, the late Joseph Pevney, the late Stanley Rubin, and the Charles E. Young Research Library Special Collections.

ONE HUNDRED YEARS OF JEAN-PIERRE MELVILLE

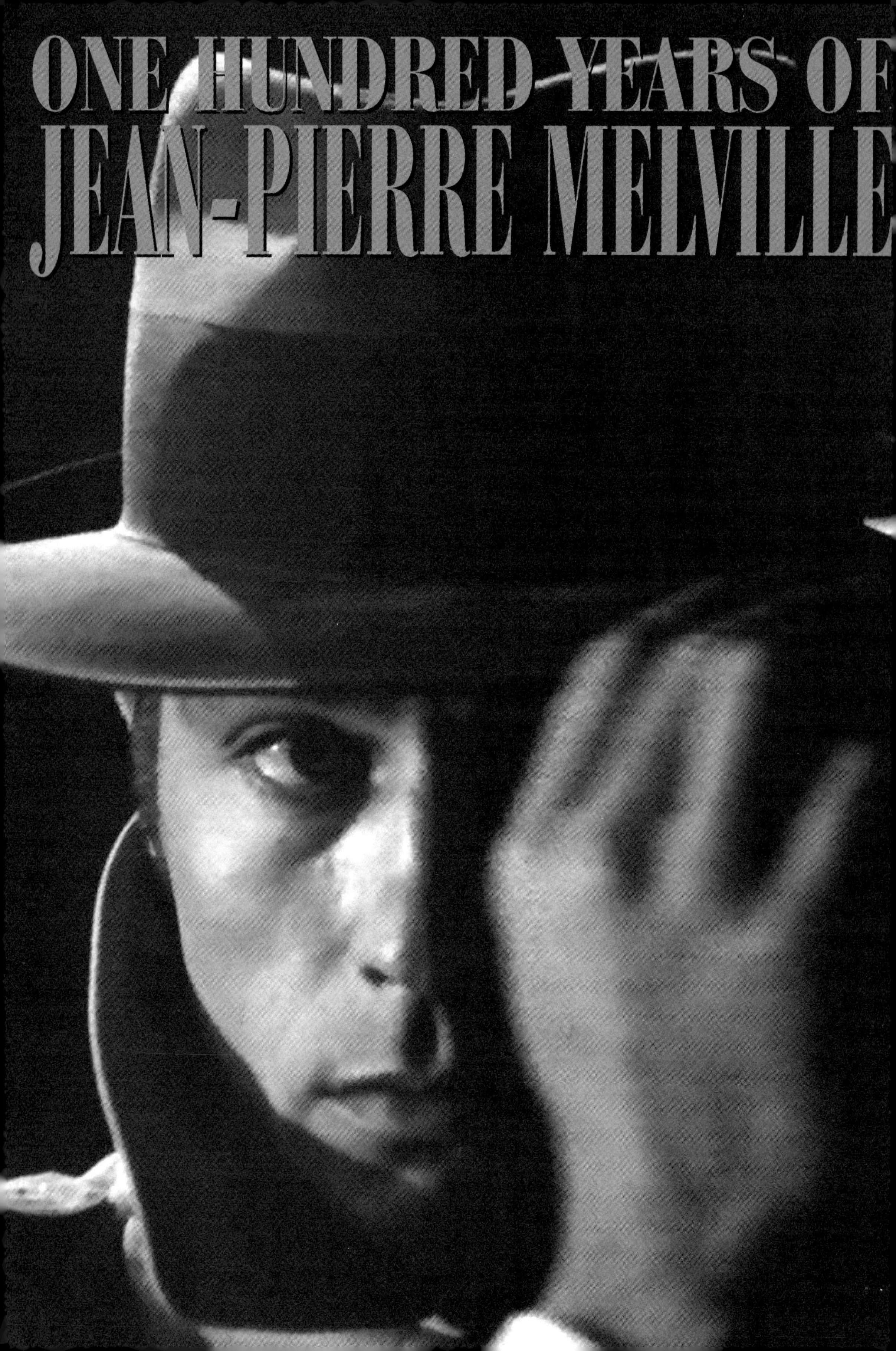

NO GREATER SOLITUDE

Imogen Sara Smith

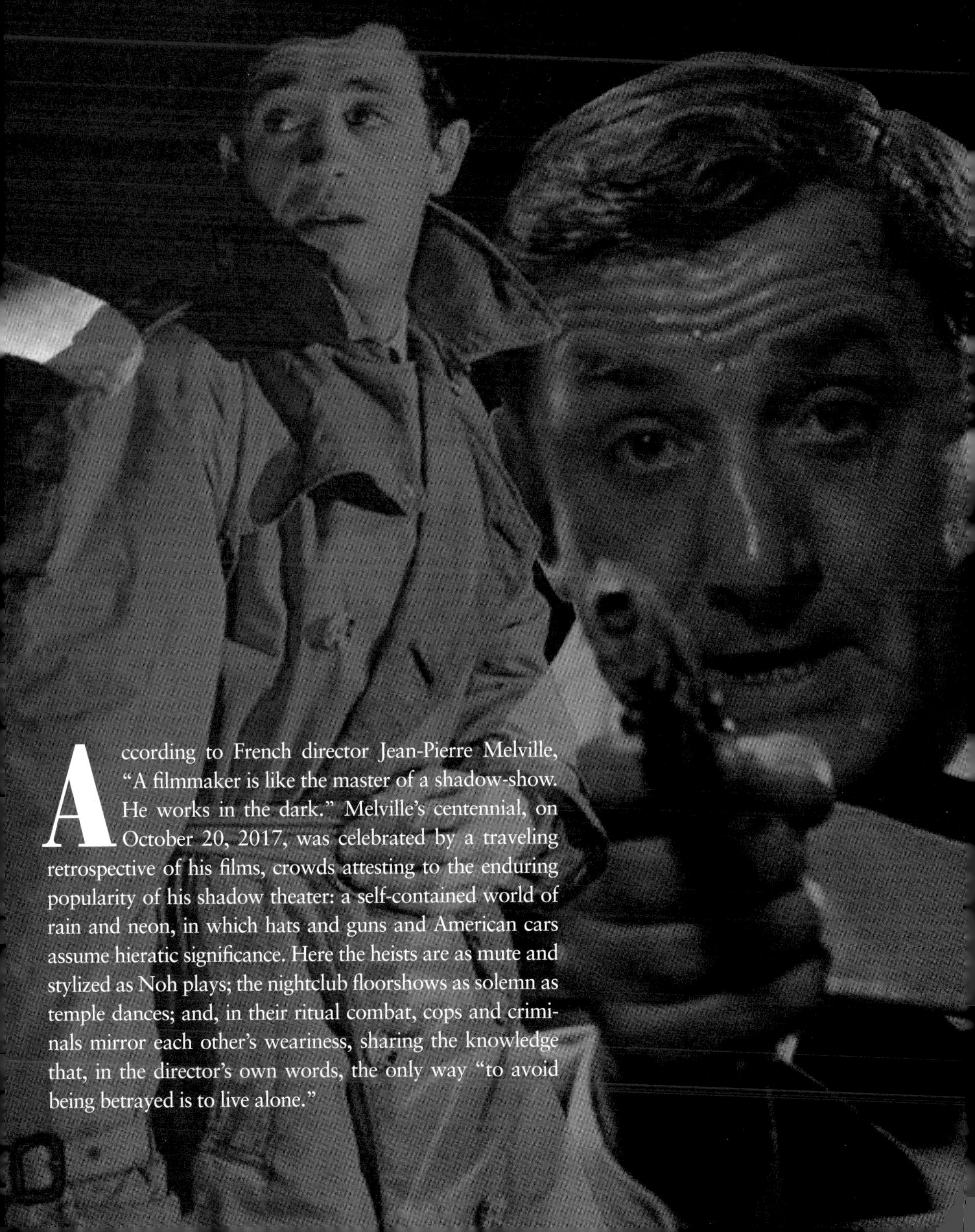

According to French director Jean-Pierre Melville, "A filmmaker is like the master of a shadow-show. He works in the dark." Melville's centennial, on October 20, 2017, was celebrated by a traveling retrospective of his films, crowds attesting to the enduring popularity of his shadow theater: a self-contained world of rain and neon, in which hats and guns and American cars assume hieratic significance. Here the heists are as mute and stylized as Noh plays; the nightclub floorshows as solemn as temple dances; and, in their ritual combat, cops and criminals mirror each other's weariness, sharing the knowledge that, in the director's own words, the only way "to avoid being betrayed is to live alone."

Cinema's great loner, Melville even recalled falling in love with movies not in the communal darkness of a theater but on his own, compulsively watching films he rented and played at home on a Pathé Baby projector. The original cinephile director, he believed it was necessary not only to "be madly in love with cinema" in order to make films, but also to possess a "huge cinematic baggage." This baggage shows up on-screen when he dresses Alain Delon in *Le Samouraï* (1967) like Alan Ladd's hit man in *This Gun for Hire* (1942), or recreates a set from Rouben Mamoulian's gangster drama *City Streets* (1931) or a police detective's office in *Le Doulos* (1963). But Melville transmuted all of his influences into his own unmistakable cinematic language, which has become the baggage of later filmmakers enamored of his flawlessly cool style.

One of his actors, François Périer, said Melville "was so crazy about cinema that basically he could only live in the atmosphere of a movie, like a darkened movie theater." He came as close as possible, living in an apartment above his own movie studio on the rue Jenner in a semi-industrial neighborhood of Paris. (The bleak alley behind the studio shows up as a location in several of his films.) In the most collaborative of art forms, he was notoriously intransigent, insisting he could only work by himself. He survived for decades largely outside the film industry, even as he came to direct France's biggest stars in huge box-office hits. Fiercely independent, he also believed it was the duty of movies to be commercial; a classicist whose touchstone was 1930s Hollywood, he was also claimed as a godfather of the New Wave for his location shooting and do-it-yourself freedom. He wrote or co-wrote almost all of his 13 feature films, and designed some of the sets with fanatical attention to detail.

Though Melville maintained that every one of his original scripts "without exception" was a transposed Western, open spaces are rare in his films. It is a cinema of interiors. Melville's solitary, taciturn men kill a lot of time in hideouts, such as the spare, sepia-brown room where *Le Samouraï* opens. Light, entering the darkened chamber through two symmetrical windows, fans across the ceiling like beams from projectors. The eye is drawn first to a domed, silver-wire birdcage, a delicate miniature prison. It takes longer to notice the man in a dark suit stretched out on a daybed; the smoke curling up from his cigarette is the only sign of life in this exquisite tableau. Alain Delon, the man on the bed, first appears in *Le cercle rouge* (1970) once again in repose, lying in a clean prison cell with walls painted half white and half battleship-gray. Lino Ventura's escaped convict in *Le deuxième souffle* (1966) spends New Year's Eve alone in the whitewashed kitchen of a rustic safe house, eating a mutely stoic meal accompanied only by the ticking of a mantel clock. These criminals have the patience and self-control of monks—but while rooms may be whitewashed, men are not. The austerity and precision of Melville's films is a counterpoint to the inevitability of violence, betrayal, and moral corruption.

Much of Melville's first film, *Le silence de la mer* (1949), based on a celebrated underground novel about resistance to the German occupation of France, is confined to the small, fire-lit living room of a farmhouse. What might be a cozy space is instead charged with tension as an old man and his niece tacitly resist by refusing to speak to the civilized, conflicted Nazi officer billeted with them. The director's next film, an adaptation of Jean Cocteau's *Les enfants terribles* (1950), is even more claustrophobic, burrowing into the bizarre, ingrown, incestuous dramas enacted by a brother and sister in a series of cluttered, windowless rooms they rarely leave. (Truffaut said the film had "the odor of children's sickrooms.") The hideaways of Melville's characters are replete with private rituals: the hit man in *Le Samouraï* feeds his caged songbird, the police inspector in *Le cercle rouge* pampers his three cats (played by the director's own beloved pets), the eponymous *Bob le flambeur* (1956) routinely tries his luck at a slot machine hidden in a closet in his apartment. The peculiarly hermetic, sealed-off and self-reflexive world of Melville's films is expressed by interiors that grow increasingly surreal: the odd, cramped lair where an alcoholic former police detective played by Yves Montand suffers the DTs in *Le cercle rouge*, with its dizzying striped walls and framed pictures of guns; or the glittering, mirror-lined apartment where Delon's cop in *Un Flic* (1972) kisses a double-crossing woman.

In these films, people's lives are as circumscribed as their rooms, whether by the strict codes of cops and robbers, the deadly rules of the Occupation and the Resistance, or the narrowness of private fixa-

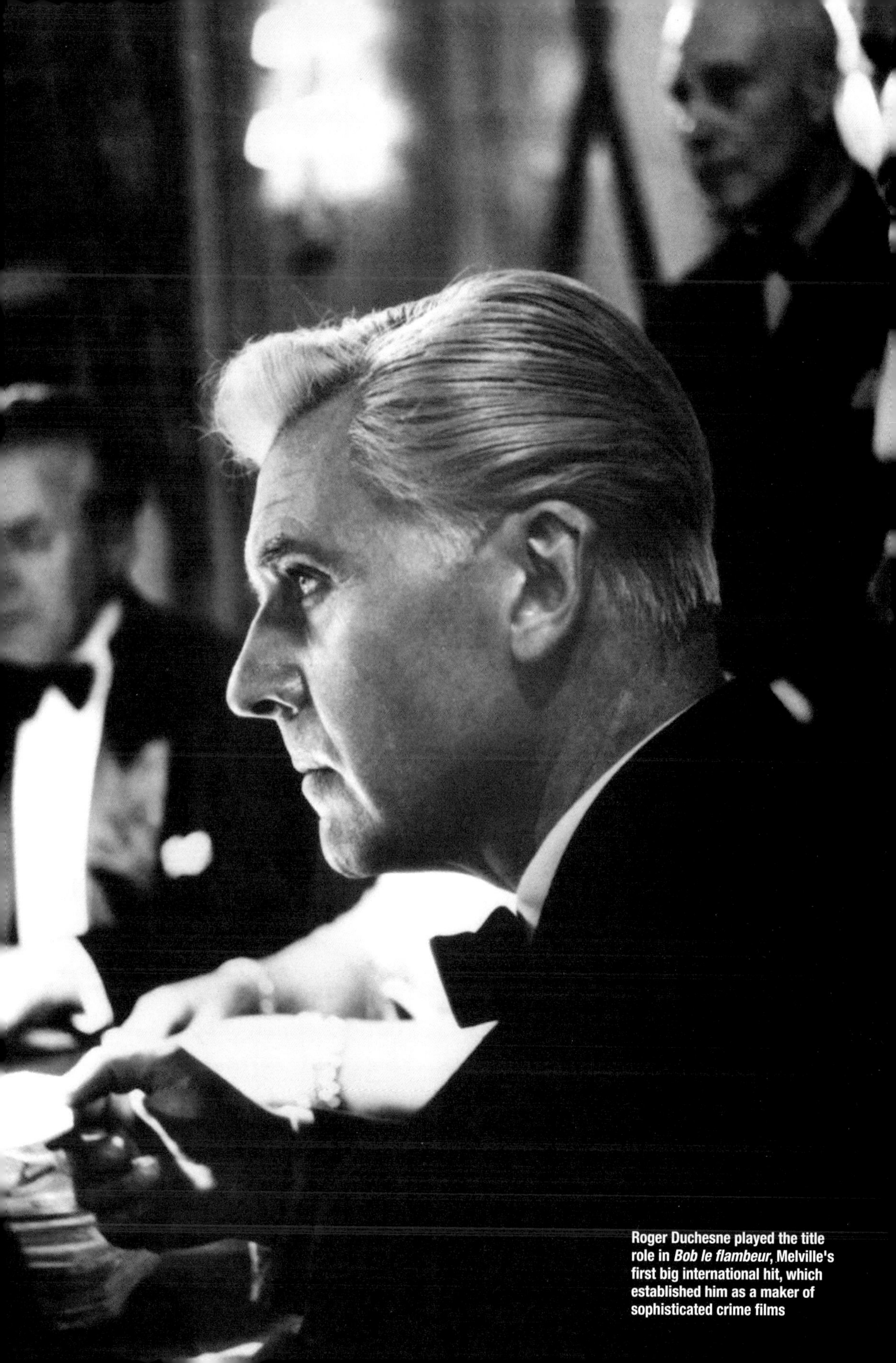

Roger Duchesne played the title role in *Bob le flambeur*, Melville's first big international hit, which established him as a maker of sophisticated crime films tions. Unlike the men and women in American film noir, Melville's characters scarcely seem to struggle against these restrictions. Maybe they are trapped by the sheer beauty of their prisons: the enameled patterns of rain on car windshields, the glittering caves of nightclubs and casinos. For all the stylistic flourishes that the Stetson-sporting Melville imported from Hollywood movies—he famously filled the streets of Paris with *American* cars, and he made two films set in the U.S., *Two Men in Manhattan* (1959) and *L'Aîné des Ferchaux* (1963)—his deeply fatalistic, unchanging, death-haunted worldview feels closer to that of Japanese cinema, with its tragic feudalism and obsession with honor. (He made up his own Japanese influences, penning the alleged quote from the "Book of Bushido" in *Le Samouraï* and the Buddhist parable in *Le cercle rouge.*) In American noir, the belief in individual freedom is ruthlessly crushed; in Melville's grim yet formally elegant visions, men know from the start that there is no such thing.

Breaking Out and Breaking In

Capers and jailbreaks, which mirror each other in their procedural rigor and long-shot defiance, are two of Melville's favorite subjects. He revered Jacques Becker's *Le trou* (*The Hole*, 1960), a stripped-down, minutely observed, and subtly devastating prison-break movie filmed at his own Studios Jenner. But when he adapted another book by *Le trou*'s author, ex-con José Giovanni, Melville eschewed the realistic, durational detail of Becker's film in favor of a compressed, ravishingly abstract distillation of an escape. The opening of *Le deuxième souffle* (*The Second Wind*) is a minimalist rhapsody: the stark planes and angles of prison walls are framed with the compositional authority of Mondrian. Yet, as three escapees run for a freight train in the leafless woods, small details also ratchet up suspense and reveal the vulnerability of the aging, worn-out gangster Gustave Minda (Lino Ventura).

Very different is the escape of Vogel (Gian-Maria Volontè) in *Le cercle rouge*, while he is being transported to jail in handcuffs, sharing a train compartment with a police inspector (André Bourvil). In this small, dim space, we watch patiently in extreme close-up as the prisoner manages to pick the lock of his handcuffs with a safety pin and gracefully slip out his hands before suddenly crashing through the train

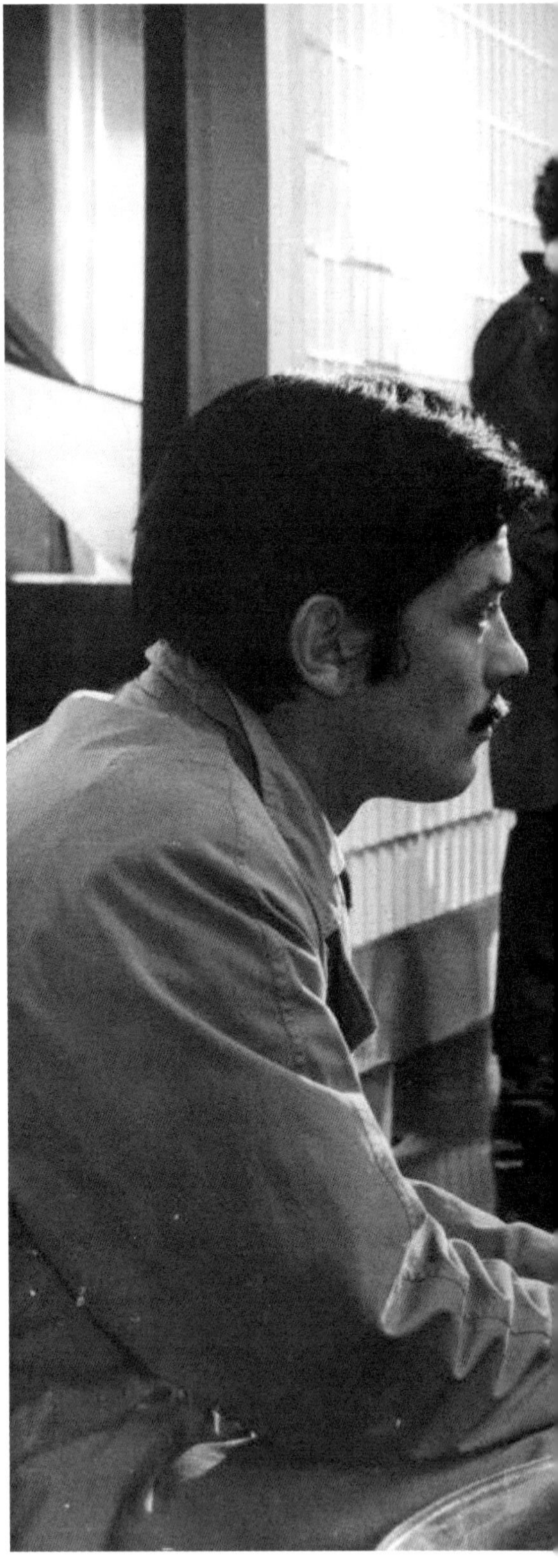

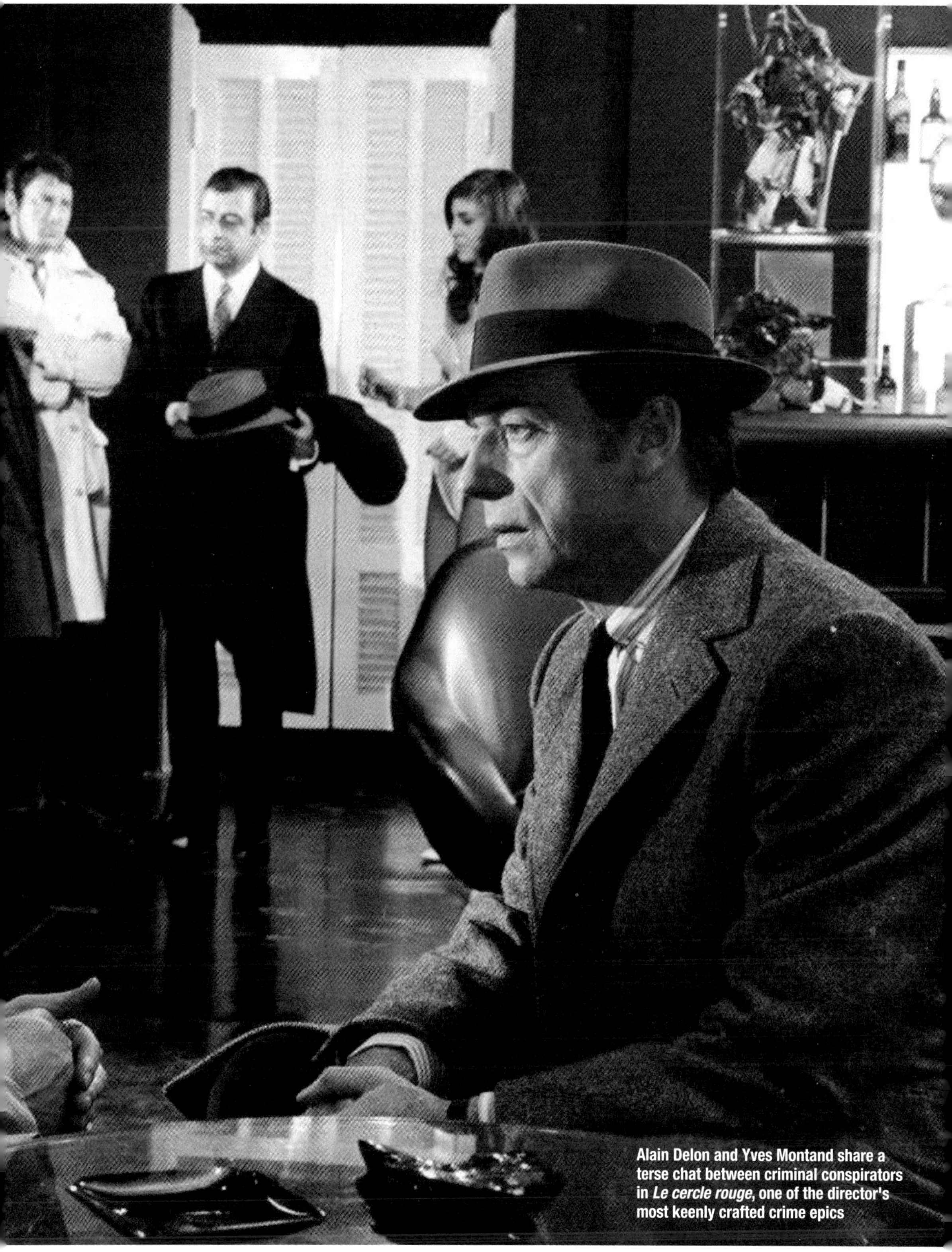

Alain Delon and Yves Montand share a terse chat between criminal conspirators in *Le cercle rouge*, one of the director's most keenly crafted crime epics window and fleeing, again, into the wintry woods. (In Melville's films, it always seems to be winter.) Both of these long sequences unfold without any dialogue, a common feature of the director's later films. There is even a joke about this laconic quality later in *Le cercle rouge*, when a detective watching a surveillance video of masked robbers in a jewelry store comments, "They're not much for talk."

This 30-minute silent heist is a vision of perfection, from Delon and Volontè's long, stealthy journey over rooftops and through a maze of stairs and passageways, to their balletic leaps over electronic eye alarms, to Montand's supreme triumph in nailing the wall key with a single rifle-shot causing all the glass cases to smoothly open and disgorge their treasure. If this is the most suave, *Le deuxième souffle*'s heist is the most thrilling, as Ventura and three other men rob an armored truck in the dry hills overlooking the ocean high above Marseille. The sequence is a masterpiece of pacing, with an agonizing wait giving way to a sudden, jolting rush of action: crisply efficient, ruthless, and reaching a spectacular climax when they push the truck off a cliff for a long swan-dive into the sea.

By his last film, *Un Flic*, the heists are downright languid. The first, in a desolate, sleekly modern seaside town in the pouring rain, has the beauty of abstract art, but the second, an endlessly protracted, MacGyver-ish job on a train, lacks enough tension to hold our interest. Since even successful heists nearly always lead to ultimate loss and defeat, they have to seduce us into hoping this time will be different. In Melville's first caper film, *Bob le flambeur*, which he called "a comedy of manners," he pulled off a priceless twist by having the casino heist not merely foiled but rendered moot, as the gang's leader indulges his gambling addiction and wins more money than he had hoped to steal. "I like futility of effort," Melville said, "the uphill road to failure is a very human thing."

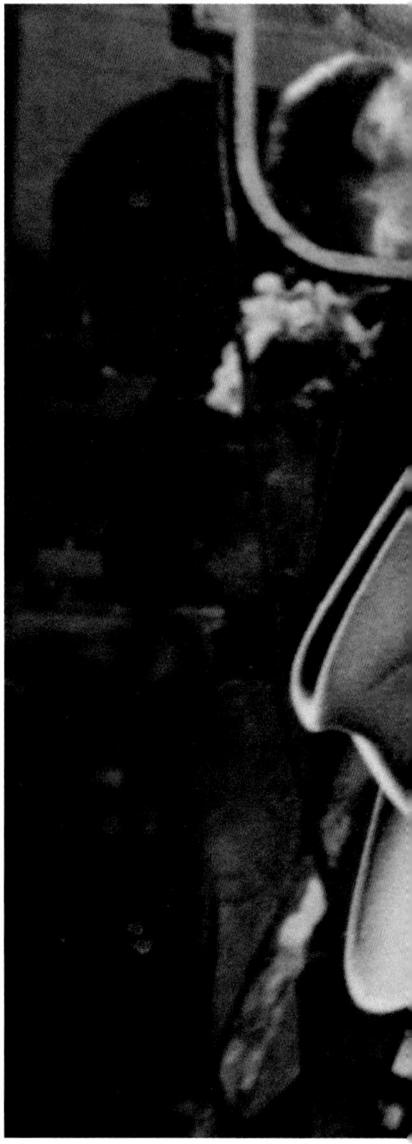

Hot Shadows, Cool Colors

This principle applies to more than heists. Even the heroics of the Resistance come off largely as doomed gestures in *Army of Shadows* (1969)—as only a Frenchman who had actually been a *résistant* and served in the Free French forces could present them, no doubt. And what could be more futile than the forbidden yearning of the widowed Barny (Emmanuelle Riva) for the celibate Léon Morin (Jean-Paul Belmondo), as she climbs the stairs to his monastic chambers again and again to grapple with his slippery, teasing ambivalence in *Léon Morin, Priest* (1961)? A self-proclaimed atheist and "right-wing anarchist," Melville professed a dim view of human nature, but the drama of his films comes from the bright shafts of passion, fierce loyalty, or conviction that slice through the shadows.

It is well known that the director, born Jean-Pierre Grumbach in Paris to a family of Alsatian Jews, adopted Melville as his *nom de guerre* to honor a favorite American author, Herman Melville. The novel he cited as marking him forever was not *Moby-Dick* but the controversial, obscure *Pierre; or, The Ambiguities*. His embrace of this strange melodrama, with its themes of incest, desperation, and suicide, its hero living in a fraught ménage of women, seems surprising in light of the cool, hardboiled crime movies for which he is best known. But both it and *Les enfants terribles* foreground motifs that

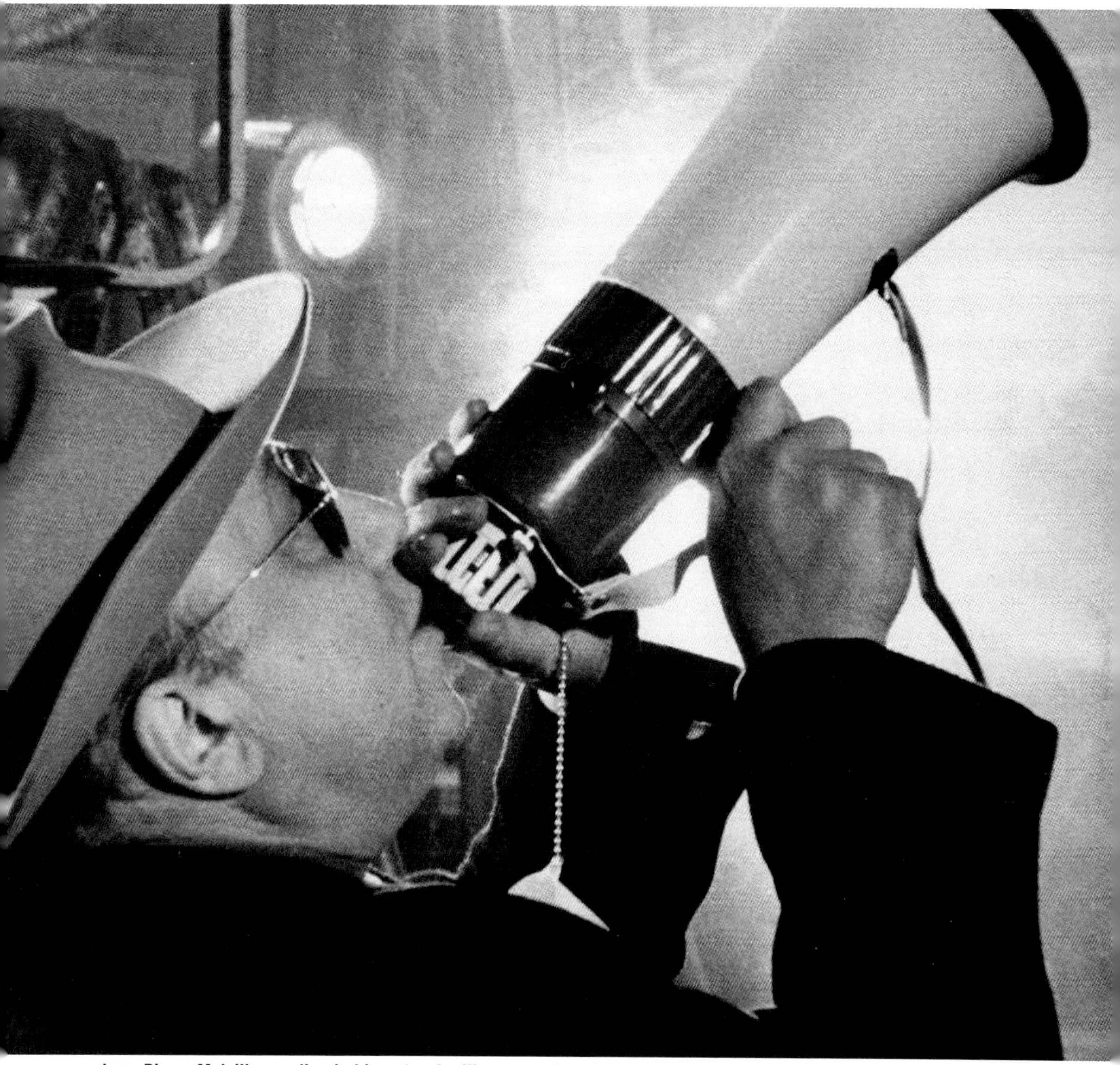

Jean-Pierre Melville reveling in his natural milieu, a movie set

run throughout his work. Cocteau's story, filled with queasy eroticism and emotional violence, was a departure from Melville's debut, *Le silence de la mer*, with its snowy landscapes and intense quietude, but the films (both starring Nicole Stéphane, an actress of striking intensity and androgynous beauty) share that insular, shut-in quality that pervades his whole body of work. The fever of melodrama continued to rage in Melville's third feature, *When You Read This Letter* (1953). He later dismissed this—the only film he directed which he had no hand in writing—as an impersonal commercial project, which he undertook largely to earn money to set up his studio, but his description of it as "a very conventional, sensible film" is truly baffling.

Set in a decadent Cannes splashed with hot sun and inky shadows, it follows the exploits of a sleazy antihero and *homme fatal* (Philippe Lemaire) who starts as a mechanic and nightclub boxer before graduating to chauffeur/gigolo, dabbling in robbery, rape, and murder before meeting his match in a

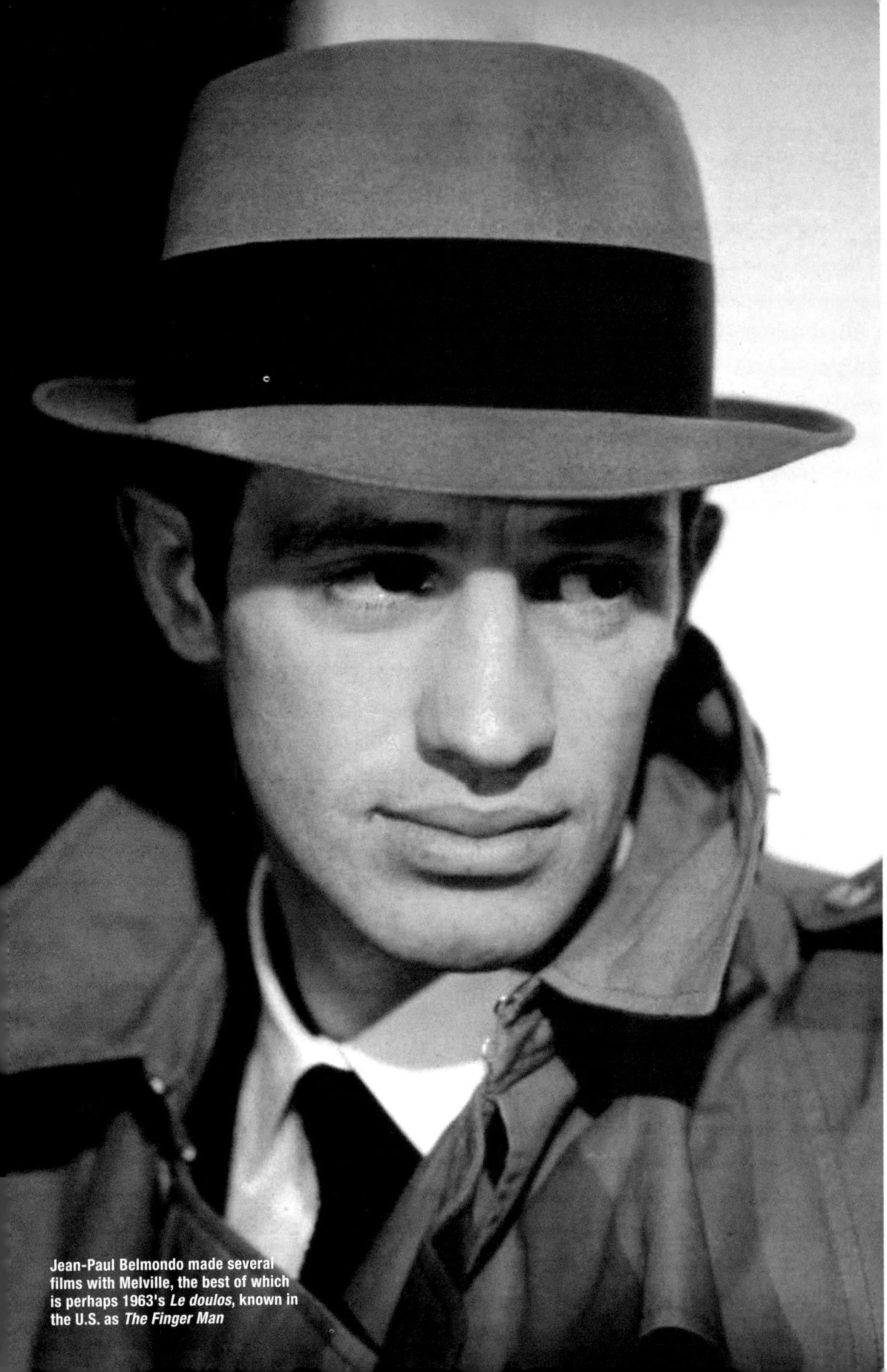

Jean-Paul Belmondo made several films with Melville, the best of which is perhaps 1963's *Le doulos*, known in the U.S. as *The Finger Man*

smolderingly severe ex-postulant played by chanteuse Juliette Gréco. The film grows weirder and more superheated on its way to a highly ambiguous ending, feeding off the torrid chemistry between real-life lovers Lemaire and Gréco. In a black raincoat and beret, she is every inch the existentialist icon, and, as is often the case in Melville's films, consummation comes in the form of death rather than romantic union. The couple's tortured relationship escalates into deep noir territory of lust, guilt, temptation, and masochism, garnished with Catholic imagery—at one point there is a shot of Gréco disrobing next to a huge crucifix. Apparently, the film never opened in America, and no wonder: it would have made censor Joe Breen's head explode.

This taboo blend of religion and sexuality recurs, of course, in *Léon Morin, Priest*, though Melville was drawn to Béatrix Beck's source novel chiefly by its portrait of the Occupation. (In 2017, a new cut of the film was released, restoring eleven minutes of scenes dealing with the moral dilemmas and compromises of life under the Nazis.) *Léon Morin, Priest* proves that Melville was quite capable of making a film with a complex, fully realized female protagonist. Indeed, Emmanuelle Riva's Barny is perhaps the most richly human character in any of his films: intelligent, flawed, self-contradictory, confronting us with both her physicality and her inner life. Yet, after this, women begin to disappear from his films, and sexuality is reduced to floorshow leg art. (From the topless bubble dancers of *When You Read This Letter* to the plumed, Vegas-style showgirls of *Un Flic*, nightclub acts are a Melville staple.) At the furthest extreme, *Le cercle rouge* has exactly one brief line spoken by a woman, and she is gratuitously naked. Melville knew he would be accused of misogyny and denied the charge, though his claim that he was instead reacting against the excessive explicit sex in films of the time is hard to credit when women are still present as barely clad decor, but not as characters. He was, to be sure, a chauvinist who once confidently asserted that "there are no lady film artists," and whose self-presentation as a loner overlooked the fact that he lived for thirty years with a woman who also helped run his studio.

To be fair, even men become more mannequin-like in Melville's later, hyper-stylized films, as the messiness he embraced in earlier works gives way to a nearly paralyzing perfectionism that increasingly inhibited his output. The director had famously difficult relations with his crews and actors—he admitted to being "impossible" at times, and he worked on a number of aborted or unrealized projects, including a spy thriller that he abandoned on impulse because of "a silly argument about the brim of a hat." Nonetheless, he did have fruitful partnerships, above all with the great cinematographer Henri Decaë, and his films were strongly imprinted with the personalities of certain actors, even as mutual loathing usually defined these working relationships. He explained, "Though it often happens that my stars and I aren't on very good terms during shooting, the sacrament of our relationship still persists, because one can marry and hate and still retain the complicity of mutual understanding."

Thus, the three late films with Alain Delon are just like Delon: hypnotically beautiful but chilly, more notable for surface than depth. The color in these films is much cooler than the black-and-white of earlier works: dusky blue-gray, the beige of wintry beaches, smoky brown and milky pallor. In *Le cercle rouge* the muted mise-en-scene is dotted with ominous "red circles": a traffic light, a single billiard ball, the garters on nightclub dancers. Melville declared that he was "careful never to be realistic," but in the Delon films he went furthest into realms of fantasy. The earlier *Bob le flambeur*, which he called a love letter to pre-war Paris, was suffused with the nostalgia of an aging hero, but by the late '60s Melville made nostalgia redundant by constructing a world that never changed, where men still wore trench coats and fedoras, where jazz still played in every nightspot and rock-and-roll was unheard.

While the Delon films reflect their star's cat-like impassivity, three with Belmondo play on the capacity for deceit and manipulation in his smiling seductiveness. (Melville claimed that the star himself didn't figure out until he saw the finished film whether or not his character was really the titular stoolie in the impenetrably dark and convoluted *Le doulos*.) The director's two films with Lino Ventura are weighted by the actor's monumental gravity and rugged, obdurate, bluntly honest presence. *Le deux-*

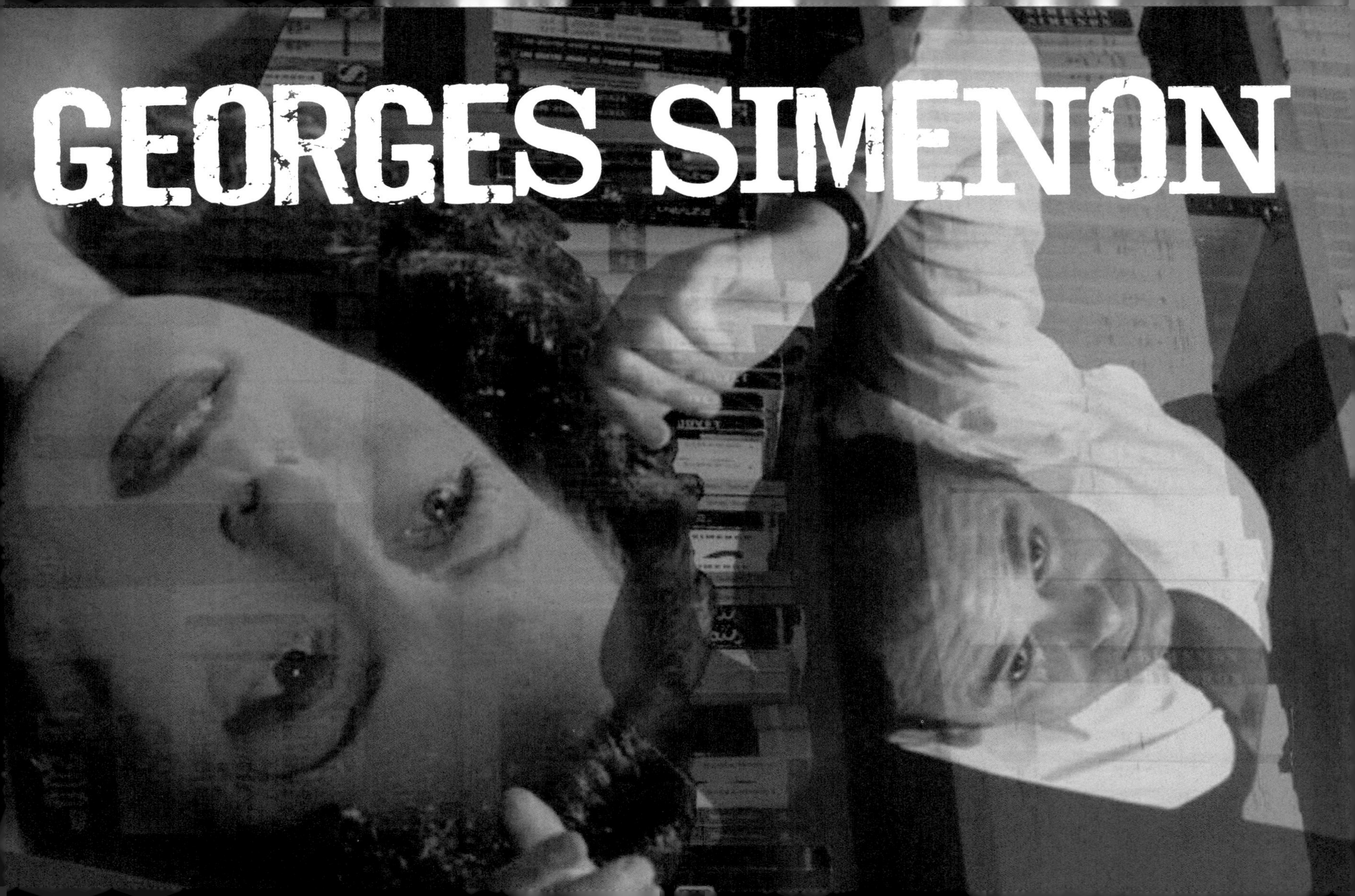
GEORGES SIMENON

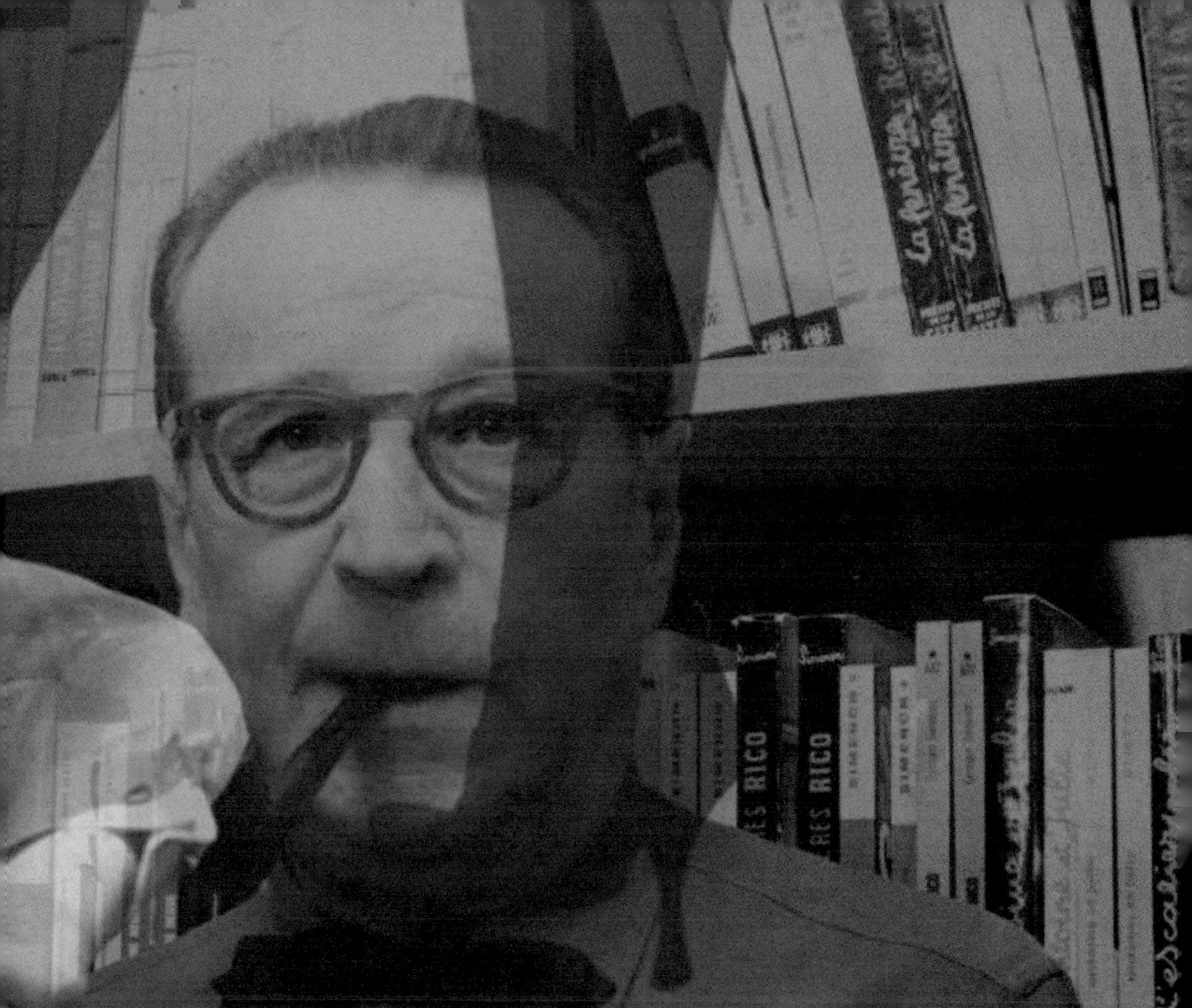

THE FATHER OF EUROPEAN NOIR

Jake Hinkson

The ongoing debate over Belgian author Georges Simenon goes something like this: was he a prolific hack or an existential genius? Although he wrote hundreds of novels and sold millions of copies, earning praise from literary heavyweights like William Faulkner and André Gide in the process, his sheer prolificacy and success is often used as the strongest evidence against him. Simenon himself couldn't seem to decide what his final legacy was, arguing bitterly that he should have won the Nobel Prize for Literature and then declaring years later that he had "nothing to say."

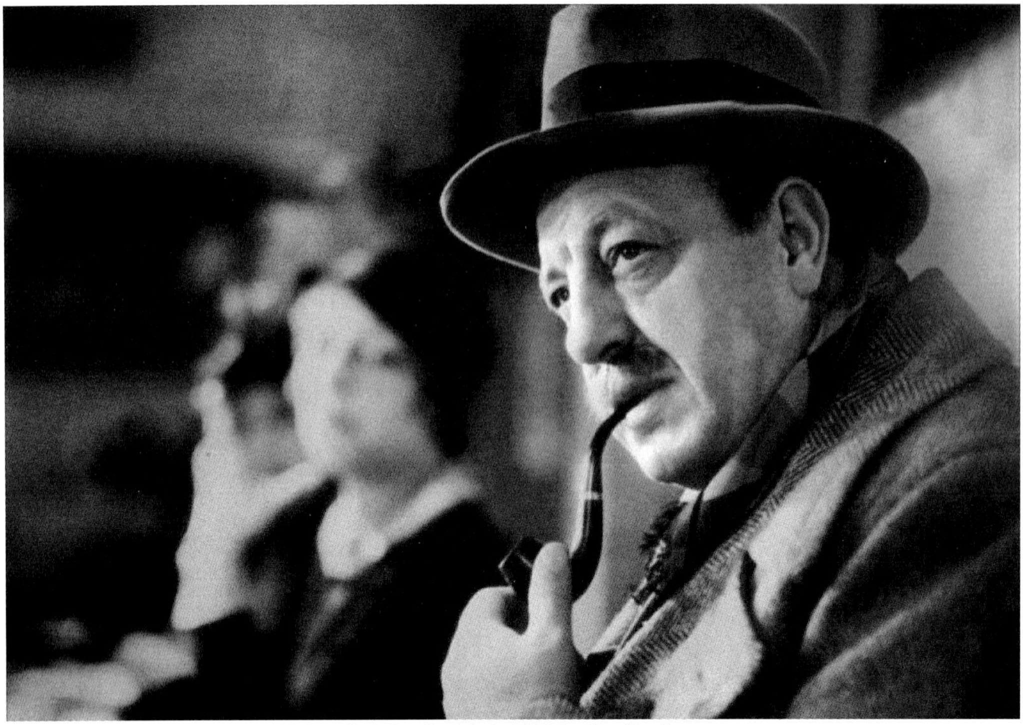

Harry Baur as the good Inspector Maigret in Julien Duvivier's 1933 *La tête d'un homme*

The matter of quality control aside—while no one writes hundreds of novels without producing some duds, Simenon wrote more good books than most other authors—the real question about his work is how to define it. In his lifetime, he was seen as a mystery writer who also wrote "psychological novels" on the side. The truth of the matter, however, is that Simenon is best understood today as one of the fathers of noir. Human weakness, emotional isolation, and violent obsession were the themes he returned to again and again; and, in writing about these things, he usually eschewed easy answers or comforting conclusions. Simenon was writing noir before it was called noir.

One of his greatest legacies is his ongoing influence on film noir. Adaptations of his work outnumber those of either Cornell Woolrich or Raymond Chandler, and he's been adapted more times than Dashiell Hammett, Evan Hunter, Erle Stanley Gardner, and Mickey Spillane *combined*. Among all mystery writers, only Arthur Conan Doyle and Dame Agatha Christie have made it to the screen more often.

Why this outsized impact on cinema? Part of it is that Simenon is a naturally cinematic writer. His plots have catchy set-ups, his characters are starkly drawn, and he prizes exterior action over interior monologues. The average length of his books is 150 pages, easily manageable for would-be adaptors. Simenon was made for the screen.

His most famous creation, of course, was the French Inspector Maigret, about whom Simenon would write 75 novels and 28 short stories. Although Maigret is the kind of master detective one finds mentioned alongside the likes of Hercule Poirot and Sherlock Holmes, next to those cold-eyed scientists of murder, he is a philosophical humanist, usually solving cases with some insight into human psychology rather than the principles of detection. While Maigret has a long history of film and television adaptations, however, his adventures have rarely received the noir treatment. Simenon's influence on film noir derives, instead, from his psychological suspense novels, which he called his *romans durs* (or "hard novels"). These are stories of ordinary men and women caught up in the destructive undertow of their passions. This is the stuff of real film noir.

PROTO-NOIR

Although most adaptations of the Inspector Maigret books have been conventional mysteries, two early films were the first to interpret Simenon through an essentially noir lens: Jean Renoir's *La Nuit du carrefour (Night at the Crossroads*, 1932) and Julien Duvivier's *La tête d'un homme* (*A Man's Neck*, 1933).

Renoir was the first director to bring Simenon to the screen. The story, based on Simenon's 1931 novel, finds Maigret investigating the murder of a Jewish diamond merchant in a small town outside of Paris. Maigret pursues the truth, dueling wits with a one-eyed Dane, a snooty insurance salesman, and a sexy young woman who may or may not hold the key to the mystery.

Together with his cinematographers Georges Asselin and Marcel Lucien, Renoir gives the film a vibrant visual sense that is pure proto-noir, a world of smoke and shadows, representative of the small community's web of lies and simmering mistrust. As Maigret, Renoir cast his brother, Pierre Renoir, who gives the detective an air of cool intelligence. While the plot is famously hard to follow (Renoir himself would call it "rather incoherent"), the film finds its meaning in its mood, in the pervasive sense of uncertainty and dread, as well as the hovering threat of bigotry and anti-Semitism. In a horror movie of the time, dread would usually come from the supernatural, but here the fear is about what lurks inside seemingly ordinary people. Few films from this era *feel* more *noir* than this one.

Duvivier's *La tête d'un homme*, based on another 1931 Simenon novel, begins in a crowded pub where a rake named Willy Ferriére tells his girlfriend he wants to get rid of his rich aunt. Unnoticed, someone slips him a note proposing a murder-for-hire arrangement, and, sure enough, the next day the aunt is murdered. Soon the murder is pinned on a poor sucker named Joseph Heurtin. Enter Inspector Maigret (Harry Baur), who knows something is wrong and eventually unmasks the scheme's mastermind, an insane medical student named Radek (Valéry Inkijinoff).

La tête d'un homme combines a story that some critics have called "Dostoyevsky meets Fritz Lang" with a visual flair that rivals Renoir.[1] The central set piece—Radek's framing of Heurtin for the murder—is a *tour de force* of shadow play, canted angles, and editing that creates an air of insanity and random menace overhanging the rest of the film. It is Inkijinoff's demonic (yet strangely sympathetic) portrayal of the tubercular Radek that moves the film along, rather than Baur's stolid turn as Maigret.

Tellingly, both Renoir and Duvivier present Maigret himself as incorruptible, and perhaps this helps explain why, despite these early experiments, Maigret novels are not usually noir. Most adaptations place the famous detective at the center of their stories, and there's nothing noir about the decent, avuncular inspector.

THE ROMANS DURS

As noir coalesced as a film movement in the 1940s, Simenon began to have his first real impact. Nothing had changed in terms of the author's work, but world cinema, and world events, seemed to be catching up to his dark vision.

Filmed versions of his novels popped up throughout the decade. In 1942, for instance, Henri Decoin adapted the suspense novel *L'Inconnu dans la maison* (*Stranger in the House*), which Simenon had published two years before, while Georges Lacombe filmed the early Simenon novel *Monsieur La Souris* as *Midnight in Paris*, starring Raimu.[2] More movies followed by a range of different filmmakers (including another film by Decoin, 1943's *The London Man*, as well as the excellent 1947 British noir *Temptation Harbour* by director Lance Comfort), but the best Simenon noir of the 1940s was

1 *La tête d'un homme* was adapted again in 1949, to lesser effect, as *The Man on the Eiffel Tower*. A clunky color spectacular starring Charles Laughton as Maigret, it is mostly notable for its location shooting in Paris, and for being directed by co-star Burgess Meredith, who took over after Laughton had the original director fired.

2 *L'Inconnu dans la maison* was remade as *Cop-Out* (1967) with James Mason, and *L'Inconnu dans la maison* (1992) with Jean-Paul Belmondo. Gordon Parry re-made *Monsieur La Souris* in the UK as *Midnight Episode* (1950), starring Stanley Holloway.

by one of his earliest adaptors.

In 1946, ready to take on Simenon again, Julien Duvivier adapted the 1933 novel *The Engagement of Mr. Hire*. The book was an early breakthrough for Simenon, putting some distance between the author and his pulpier early days, earning the designation of "hard novel" by placing the reader in a bleak world that has no heroes, not even the sad, misunderstood man at its center. Duvivier's film, retitled *Panique* (1946), is faithful in the broad outlines: a woman has been murdered and the investigating inspector suspects the killer is a quiet man named Mr. Hire (Michel Simon). Mr. Hire is something of a recluse who stays in his room, except for secret excursions with his camera and trips to the butcher to get extra bloody meat, but his real consuming passion is spying on his attractive young neighbor Alice. The girl catches him peeping, but instead of getting mad, she's intrigued. She's mixed up with a hood named Alfred who treats her like garbage, and Mr. Hire, for all his reclusive weirdness, is kind to her.

The story of Mr. Hire in Simenon's novel is rougher around the edges than Duvivier was allowed to make it in 1946. (For instance, in the novel the murder victim is a prostitute, while in the film she's an old maid.) Yet what remains intact is the slow rolling tragedy of the curious Mr. Hire himself. He misjudges Alice, and he misjudges her badly. In a Simenon story, everyone is driven by their own solitary passions, and Alice's attachment to the loathsome Alfred is as much a mystery as is Hire's attraction to Alice.

The end of the film is a masterful set piece in which Mr. Hire, framed for the murder, attempts to escape the police. The chase is suspenseful, but not in the usual manner of a thriller. After all, we're watching a man attempt to outrun fate, and this being film noir, we all know how successful he will be. These scenes of bystanders watching an innocent man hunted to his death by stone-faced cops and wild-eyed rabble-rousers also have a disturbing resonance given the postwar setting. As with something like the anti-lynching noir *The Sound of Fury*, aka *Try and Get Me!* (1951), *Panique* sees the fascism at the heart of mob justice.

An interesting way to mark Simenon's adaptability in different eras is to compare *Panique* to a later adaptation of the same book, director Patrice Leconte's 1989 *Monsieur Hire*. While following the same broad outlines, *Monsieur Hire* swerves away from Duvivier in terms of tone and theme. Part of the shift has to do with the presentation of Mr. Hire himself. Duvivier cast Michel Simon, best remembered as the burly ship's mate in Jean Vigo's *L'Atalante*, as Mr. Hire, and the actor couldn't help but bring his earthiness to the role. His Hire is grumpy but also warm, and his fateful courtship of Alice can't help but be sweet. Leconte, on the other hand, cast Michel Blanc, who plays Hire with icy intensity. He's self-contained—unflappable when taunting children throw chalk at him, yet given to sudden bursts of anger, always with women, and usually around the subject of sex. He's the opposite of earthy; in fact, he seems deeply resentful of every sexual urge he experiences. The exploration of sexual obsession can be found in Simenon's novel, but Leconte makes it the driving force of the story. Gone are almost all of the subplots about the spying neighbors, and Duvivier's postwar subtext about mob justice is subsumed by Hire's sexual obsession for Alice. Fittingly, Sandrine Bonnaire's turn as Alice is the fullest realization of the character, improving on both Simenon and Duvivier. She is as swept up as Hire is in their relationship.

SIMENON IN ENGLISH

As the 1940s came to an end, there had already been over two dozen Simenon adaptations in Europe (mostly in France, with additional films in Spain, Portugal, and the UK), but the '50s would be the decade filmmakers in the English-speaking world fully embraced the author. From this point on, with the world's largest markets open to adaptations of his work, the pace of Simenon films proliferated. Those two-dozen movies in the '30s and '40s, it turned out, were only the overture.

It didn't always go smoothly. *The Man Who Watched Trains Go By* is widely considered to be

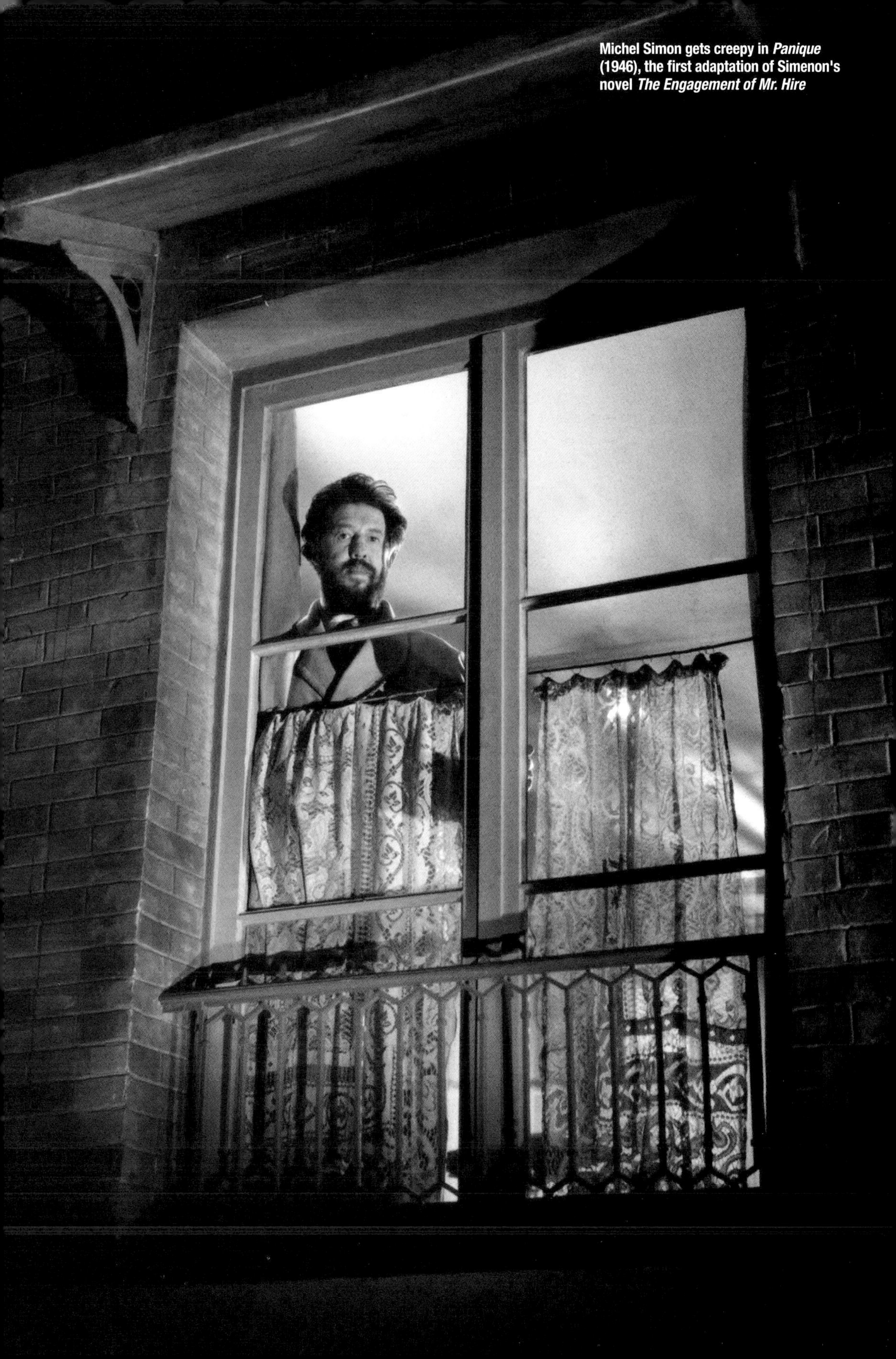

Michel Simon gets creepy in *Panique* (1946), the first adaptation of Simenon's novel *The Engagement of Mr. Hire*

one of Simenon's greatest novels, but, unfortunately, its 1952 English adaptation by writer-director Harold French and producer Raymond Stross is an overly self-conscious stab at making an important film. Retitled *The Paris Express* for its U.S. release, the film stars Claude Rains as Kees Popinga, a mild-mannered Dutch bookkeeper who discovers that his boss has bankrupted the firm and faked a suicide in order to run away to his mistress in Paris with a bag of money. Popinga is enraged at this betrayal and in an ensuing fight, the boss dies. On the spur of the moment, knowing that everyone will think that his employer committed suicide, Popinga takes the money and heads to Paris. Claude Rains makes Popinga quietly clueless in the early scenes, unable to recognize that deep down he regards his orderly life, with his good reputation and his happy family, as ultimately empty and futile. When he runs off to Paris to find his boss' mistress, Michele (Märta Torén), the demure little clerk undergoes a shift. In a sense, Popinga wants to take the dead man's place.

The Man Who Watched Trains Go By is a telling example of how many filmmakers in England and America would misinterpret Simenon, mistaking his sweaty tales of lust and murder for something that should smack of transcontinental class. The film has the uncomely scent of importance about it, and it's stuffy and respectable just when it should be rolling in the grime. Harold French's uninspired staging is overly restrained, even in big set pieces like Popinga's transformation from thief to murderer. While Rains delivers a solid central performance, the film as a whole is a missed opportunity.

If *The Man Who Watched Trains Go By* feels like a would-be "prestige film" misfire, one finds far more interesting interpretations of Simenon's work further down the economic food chain. In 1955, his short story "A Matter of Life and Death" was adapted by producer Leonard Goldstein as *A Life in the Balance*, a U.S./Mexico production that was co-directed by Harry Horner and Rafael Portillo. The plot follows a fanatically religious serial killer (Lee Marvin) who is murdering "sinners" in Mexico City. When widower Antonio Gómez (Ricardo Montalban) is falsely accused of one of the murders, his young son Paco (José Pérez) sets out to prove his innocence. Largely unseen since its release, this tiny low-budget gem is a gonzo blend of serial-killer story and child-in-danger noir (think *Follow Me Quietly* meets *The Window*). The film has its deficiencies, to be sure: the script by Robert Presnell Jr. and Leo Townsend gets too talky, especially after the climax, and the filmmakers can't find much for Montalban to do except look handsome, but José Pérez, more scrappy than cute, gives a winning performance as Paco, and a young-and-hungry Lee Marvin sinks his teeth into the role of the fanatical murderer. ("I'm punishing people," he tells Paco. "God punishes people...and I'm helping him.") Best of all, master cinematographer Manuel Gómez Urquiza, shooting on location, paints the film in gorgeous shadows and light, making *A Life in the Balance* the rare English-speaking film of the era to turn the streets of Mexico City into a noir landscape on par with New York or Los Angeles.

In 1957, director Phil Karlson adapted one of Simenon's rare excursions into the realm of organized crime, *The Brothers Rico*. With a script secretly worked on by the blacklisted Dalton Trumbo, *The Brothers Rico* stars Richard Conte as Eddie Rico, a Florida businessman with longstanding ties to a New York crime lord named Sid Kubic. Eddie's bound to Kubic because his two younger brothers, Gino and Johnny, are still back in New York working for the gangster. When Kubic orders a hit on a rival hoodlum, the younger Rico brothers help carry out the killing, but then they drop out of sight. Now fearing that Gino and Johnny might be talking to the cops, Eddie starts looking for them, one step ahead of Kubic's enforcers.

The Brothers Rico is neither typical Simenon nor typical Karlson, but it's well worth seeing on its own merits. Karlson keeps his actors on edge without pushing them to the bloodlust that was his calling card. Conte, so often the gangster in noirs, makes for a nicely anguished leading man, and the third act of the film springs two wonderful supporting performances by Harry Bellaver and Rudy Bond as a couple of laidback California gangsters. Bellaver, in particular, gets some great lines as the enforcer Mike Lamotta. Informing Eddie that Johnny is as good as dead, he says, "So he's your brother. We're all brothers, aren't we? Did that ever stop anything?"[3]

3 In 1972, *The Brothers Rico* was adapted for television as *The Family Rico*, directed by Paul Wendkos and starring Ben Gazzara.

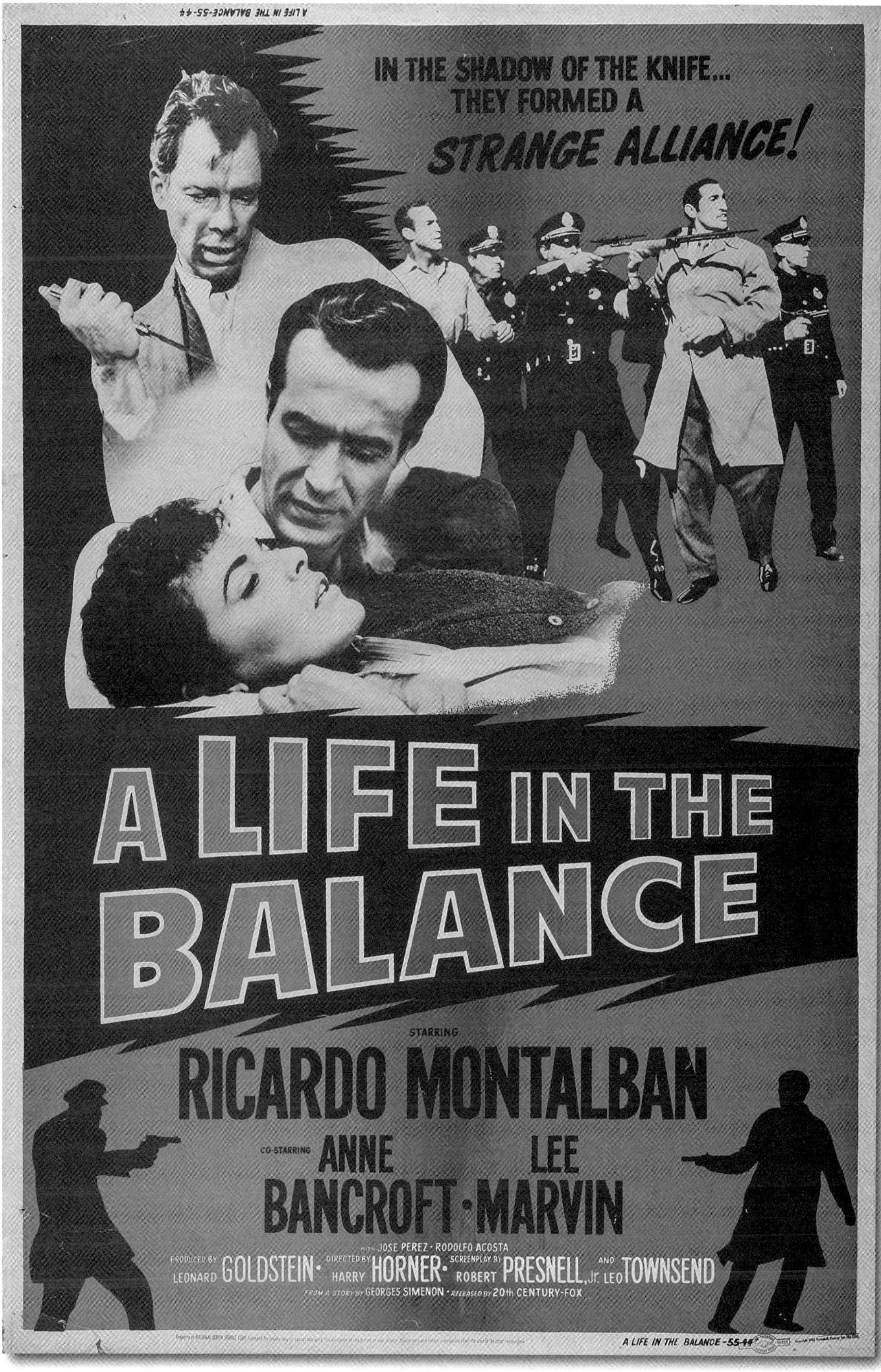
IN THE SHADOW OF THE KNIFE...
THEY FORMED A
STRANGE ALLIANCE!
A LIFE IN THE BALANCE
STARRING
RICARDO MONTALBAN
CO-STARRING ANNE BANCROFT · LEE MARVIN
WITH JOSE PEREZ · RODOLFO ACOSTA
PRODUCED BY LEONARD GOLDSTEIN · DIRECTED BY HARRY HORNER · SCREENPLAY BY ROBERT PRESNELL, Jr. AND LEO TOWNSEND
FROM A STORY BY GEORGES SIMENON · RELEASED BY 20th CENTURY-FOX
A LIFE IN THE BALANCE -55-44

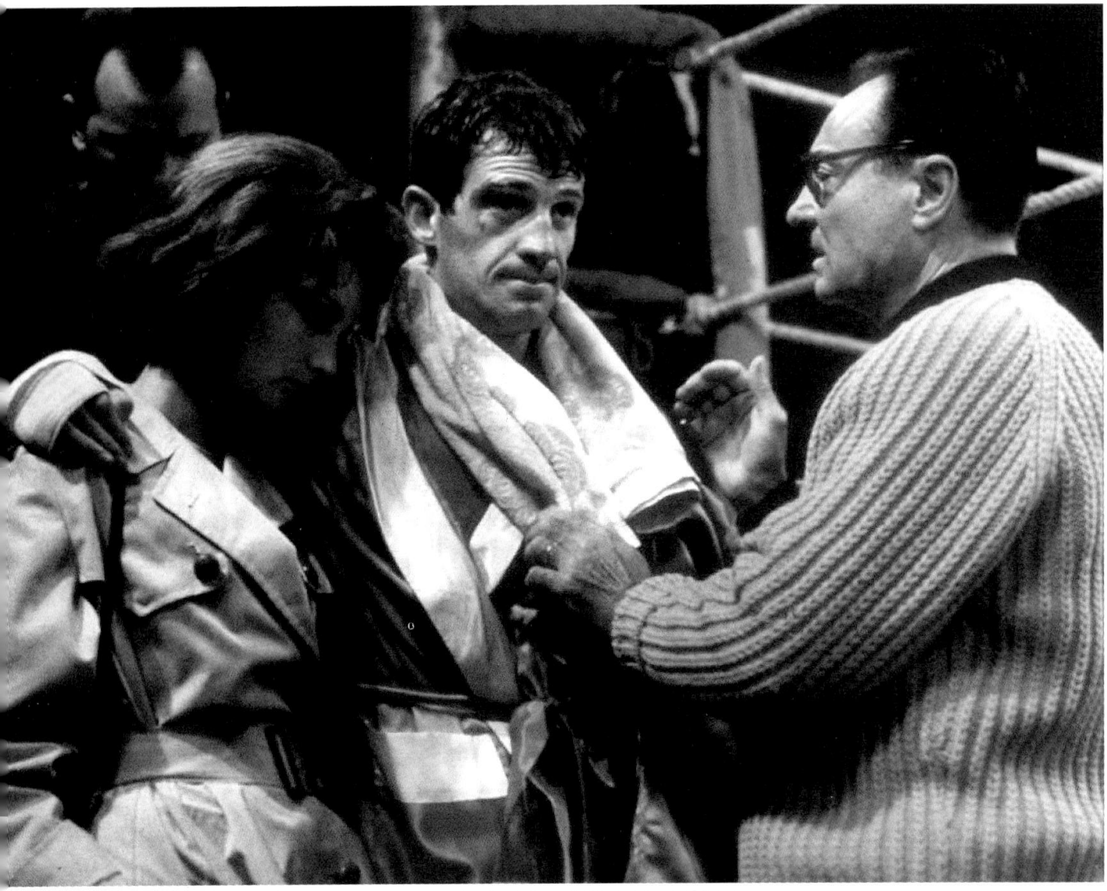

Malvina Silberberg and Jean-Paul Belmondo in Melville's 1963 *Magnet of Doom*

OLD STORIES AND NEW WAVES

Although Simenon would never really become one of the muses of the French *Nouvelle Vague*, throughout the sixties and seventies he continued to supply rich source material to filmmakers. His book *Magnet of Doom* was the basis of director Jean-Pierre Melville's strangest film of the era. The film, released in 1963, begins with the look and feel of a Melville gangster flick, as an overhyped boxer named Michel Maudet (Jean-Paul Belmondo) loses his first big fight and gets canned by his promoters. Desperate for cash, he takes a job as a bodyguard for Dieudonné Ferchaux (Charles Vanel), a sleazy old banker on the run from the authorities. Together, they go to America so Ferchaux can retrieve millions of dollars in New York, only to find that the money has been seized by authorities. Escaping with a huge bundle of cash from a safety deposit box, they drive down to New Orleans to shack up until Ferchaux can find a way to get to the rest of his money.

Magnet of Doom has a killer set-up, but it's really a chamber piece, a study of two men trapped in cars and cheap hotels together. Even more than most of the director's crime films, it's a deconstruction of the crime film. As they wait for something to change, they argue. The old man gets sick. The young man gets bored. He has an affair with the dancer at a local club, and he gets too chummy with flinty-eyed rednecks who wonder why two seemingly well-to-do Frenchmen are cooling their heels in a rundown dump in The Big Easy. The film observes these events, but it isn't about plot twists—it's about betrayal of a deeper sort. It's about how human beings keep creating worlds for themselves that they can't really inhabit.

As the boxer and the banker drive across America, it's also Melville's most pointed commentary on a country that fascinated him. If not exactly a love letter to America—at one point, Michel asks the old man, "Couldn't we have escaped to a country less rotten?"—the film is fascinated by the country's disparities, its largeness, its friendliness, its unacknowledged failures. Following Simenon's lead, Melville presents America as a land of dislocation.

Undoubtedly, the most devoted interpreter of the works of Simenon was director Pierre Granier-Deferre, who adapted *Le Chat* (*The Cat*, 1971), *La Veuve Couderc* (*The Widow Couderc*, 1971), *Le Train* (*The Last Train*, 1973), and *L'Étoile du Nord* (*The Northern Star*, 1982), as well as writing 15 episodes of a long-running *Maigret* television series starring Bruno Cremer. "What interests me in Simenon," he explained, "is the ambiguity and ordinary madness of his characters which manifests itself at the least disturbance. I don't despise action, but I have a penchant for psychology. I'm a director of chamber works." This is especially true of the two works he directed in 1971 that each starred Simone Signoret.

In *La Veuve Couderc*, Signoret stars as Tati Couderc, a French widow in 1934 who meets a handsome drifter named Jean Lavigne (Alain Delon) when he offers to lug a heavy incubator home for her. He stays on to help around the house, and the two begin a relationship that gets her little village talking. Tati eventually learns that Jean is an escaped convict, but she allows him to hide away with her, perhaps because they're already falling in love. Their romance, however, doesn't stop him from sneaking across the canal to have sex with Félicie (Ottavia Piccolo), Tati's unwed niece whose fatherless baby is another local scandal. With the cops closing in on Jean, the triangle between Jean, Tati, and Félicie reaches a breaking point.

Until its violent climax, which tries too hard to tap into the annihilating nihilism of *Bonnie and Clyde*, *La Veuve Couderc* is a superior chamber piece drama—a Simenon specialty—focusing on a few characters in one or two locations, with sex as the main point of conflict. Jean, with time running out, is drawn to two women who promise starkly different futures. He and Tati are outsiders who together create a little world made up of work and intimacy, rejoicing in the incubator that will allow them to hatch dozens of chickens. They have passion together, but he's drawn to Félicie because of her youth. The girl constantly has her baby with her (in fact, her big move is to breastfeed in front of Jean), and his attraction to her isn't just sexual, it's procreative. Around this sexual gamesmanship is the rising anti-Semitism of France in the '30s and the hypocrisy it bred in the population, perfectly captured in a scene where the scandalous Tati and Jean walk past a parade of pious worshipers going into a cathedral that sports a handmade sign reading: "The House Of God Is Not For Jews."

Le Chat deals with quite a different love triangle. Here, Signoret co-stars with Jean Gabin as Clémence and Julien Bouin, an elderly couple whose marriage long ago sank into mutual animosity and quiet resentment. Granier-Deferre begins the film by showing Clémence and Julien at the store. They don't speak and barely make eye contact, and it's not until they separately return to the same dilapidated house that we realize they even know each other. They each cook for themselves in the same kitchen and then sit at different tables to eat. While Julien slips away to visit his mistress at a bordello, their relationship seems to consist entirely of him complaining about his wife. The only real affection he feels is for a cat he takes in and names Greffier. After years of living in stony silence, Clémence resents Julien's gentle fondling of the cat. When her jealousy boils over, things take a violent turn.

Gabin is perfect as the rumpled Julien. By 1971, he was one of the few giants of Golden Age cinema still alive, much less working, and he brings a hard-won world-weariness to the role that no one else could have rivaled.[4] Long gone is the gangster dash of Pépé le Moko or the cool intelligence of Inspector Maigret. His Julien is a small man made smaller by the limits of his moral imagination. He loves his wife, after a fashion, but he'll never understand his own mind, much less hers. Signoret

4 By 1971, in fact, Jean Gabin was the consummate Simenon actor, having previously starred in *La Marie du port* (1950), *The Truth of Our Marriage* (1952), *Blood to the Head* (1956), *Love is My Profession* (1958), *The Baron of the Locks* (1960), and *The President* (1961), as well as a trio of Maigret films: *Inspector Maigret* (1958), *Maigret and the St. Fiacre Case* (1959), and *Maigret Sees Red* (1963).

matches Gabin beat for beat. Though Signoret was substantially younger than Gabin (he was 67, she was 50), Clémence seems to have aged prematurely, to have begun the process of dying years earlier when she began to turn into someone she didn't want to be. Signoret's performance here makes a fascinating counterpoint to her work in *La Veuve Couderc* (the bitter old wife and the romantic middle-aged widow couldn't be more different), and together they help to show that Simenon's famous real-life misogyny (coolly documented by the author himself in interviews and memoirs) did not prevent him, in his fiction, from making his women as layered and interesting as his men.

Melville and Granier-Deferre, freed from old constraints, showed how Simenon's work, around since the '30s, could still be strikingly fresh in the '60s and '70s. Other filmmakers would take it further still.

LATER ADAPTATIONS

In truth, Simenon benefitted more than most writers by the passage of time, at least when it came to the presentation of his work on-screen. Even by the standards of crime fiction, Simenon's vision was dark and bleak, given over to ruminations on sex and violence and various forms of self-destruction. For many years, film adaptations of his novels were diluted by censorship or mainstream sensibilities. It speaks well of his work, to its continuing power and its prospects in the future, that many of the best adaptions of his *romans durs* have been in recent years.

Simenon's 1961 novel *Betty* was one of the few books the author wrote which focused on a female protagonist. In *Betty* (1992), writer-director Claude Chabrol (who had previously adapted a Simenon serial killer story, "Le petit tailleur et le chapelier," as *The Hatter's Ghost* in 1982) follows the titular heroine (Marie Trintignant) as she attempts to endure the worst period of her life. "Heroine" is probably too strong a word, though. Betty mostly drinks. In the first scenes of the film, she meets a gentlemanly doctor at a bar, gets smashed with him, and allows him to take her to another club called The Hole. Turns out, the doctor is a junkie who wants to cut open Betty's arms to dig out the worms he thinks are crawling under her skin. She's rescued from this fate by the intercession of Laure (Stéphane Audran), the well-to-do widow of a renowned professor, who scoops up Betty and puts her up in a room at the Trianon in Versailles. We learn that Betty is going through a divorce and that her children have been taken away from her. As we recoil into the past in elliptical flashbacks, we realize that she is neither all victim nor all villain. At the end, there is a final, brutal betrayal. *Betty* is not a crime film and belongs, instead, in the great tradition of noirish adultery dramas like Fritz Lang's *Human Desire* (1954) or Richard Quine's *Strangers When We Meet* (1960). The story locates sources for Betty's particular problems—specifically, the alcoholism and clinical nymphomania that are the result of childhood scars—but the power of the piece as a whole derives from the truth at the center of most of Simenon's work, the truth that people are condemned to be themselves. Betty herself is a walking disaster, but every other character in the story is trapped in their own particular version of helplessness.

Red Lights (2004) is a superb thriller based on the 1953 Simenon novel *Feux rouges*. The book takes place in America, but director Cédric Kahn and his screenwriters Laurence Ferreira Barbosa and Gilles Marchand move the action to France. Jean-Pierre Darroussin plays Antoine, a middle-aged insurance agent who's going on holiday with his wife Hélène (Carole Bouquet) to pick up their children at a camp in the Basque country. As the trip commences, Antoine is quietly annoyed at his wife for staying too late at the law firm where she works, so he has a few drinks before they leave. Once they're on the road, they get stuck in traffic. Along the way, he stops a couple of times and has a few more drinks. He's a double whiskey man, and the booze makes him irritable. A little further down the road, they get lost when Antoine misses his turn. They fight. When he pulls into the parking lot of yet another bar, Hélène warns him that she'll drive away and he'll be stuck taking the train. Instead, he just takes the car keys with him. When he gets back, she's gone.

Red Lights is one of those "Long Dark Night of the Soul" noirs where a seemingly ordinary man

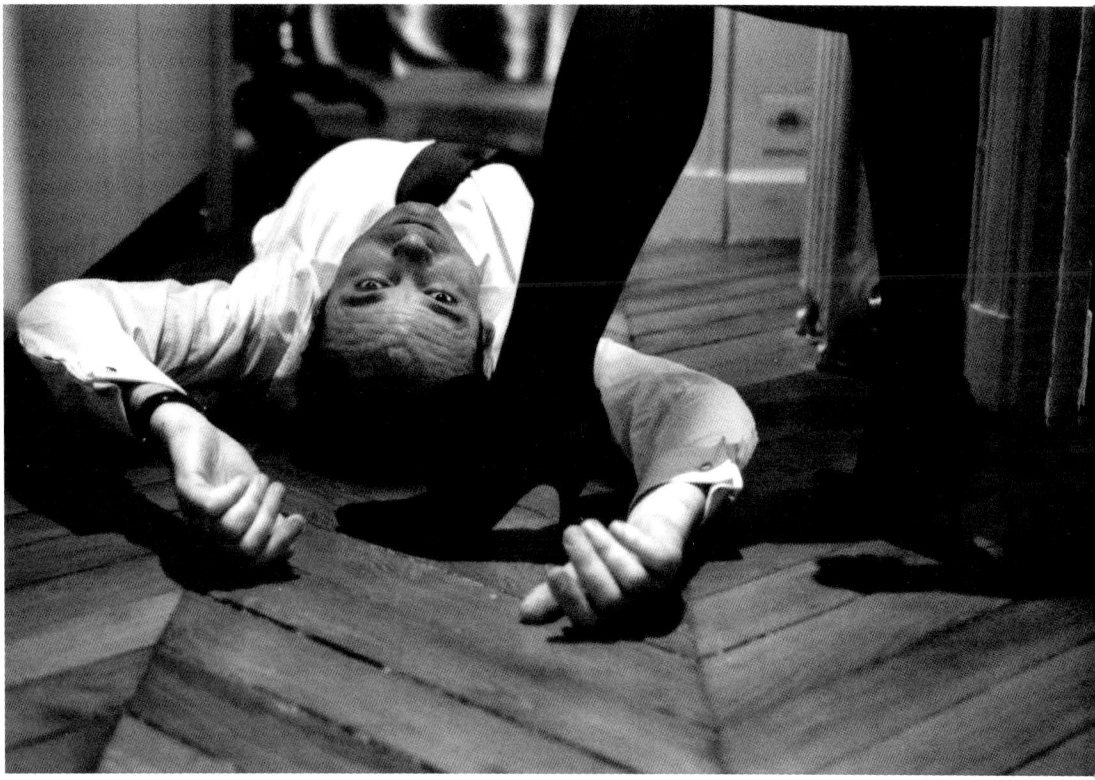

Jean-Pierre Darroussin portrays a man whose holiday trip runs off the rails when his wife goes missing in 2004's *Red Lights*, adapted from Simenon's 1953 novel *Feux rouges*

slips over the line one night and plummets into hell. Kahn and his screenwriters escalate the tension beautifully, following Simenon's lead, but also improving on it. For instance, in the opening moments, the filmmakers add a quick scene of Antoine sending his wife an email telling her that he's excited for their trip. She doesn't reply. He goes to meet her, but she's late. He tries not to drink, but he's irritated and bored and stuck waiting. We don't realize he has a serious drinking problem until it's too late.

The film goes into nail-biting mode when Hélène disappears. Assuming that she has taken the train to meet their children, Antoine says to hell with it and keeps drinking, but soon he's face to face with a man (Vincent Deniard) who may or may not be the fugitive he vaguely remembers hearing about on the radio. (Although, isn't it a pretty good bet, especially in a film noir, that the stranger in the parking lot is the escaped convict on the radio?) The best part about the meeting between Antoine and this man is the way the filmmakers play around with what Antoine knows, or thinks he knows, about the situation he is in. While these scenes are where the film gets its biggest thriller moments, the most suspenseful scenes come later when Antoine discovers that his wife never picked up their children. In one long scene of Antoine working the phone, Kahn finds the emotional apex of the film.

Alas, the story keeps going a little too long after its climax and stumbles a bit in the final stretch. Like so much of Simenon's work, the story is about the male ego in crisis. Does the violent stranger represent some id-unleashed version of Antoine himself? The darkness embedded in that question is one step beyond where the film is willing to go, and so, after a riveting hundred minutes, we end on a fairly pat note. Still, for most of its running time, the film equals Simenon at his best. Jean-Pierre Darroussin and Carole Bouquet create a real marriage in their scenes together, filling their silences with old suspicions and nursed resentments, and as a result, *Red Lights* ranks among the best adaptations of the author's work.

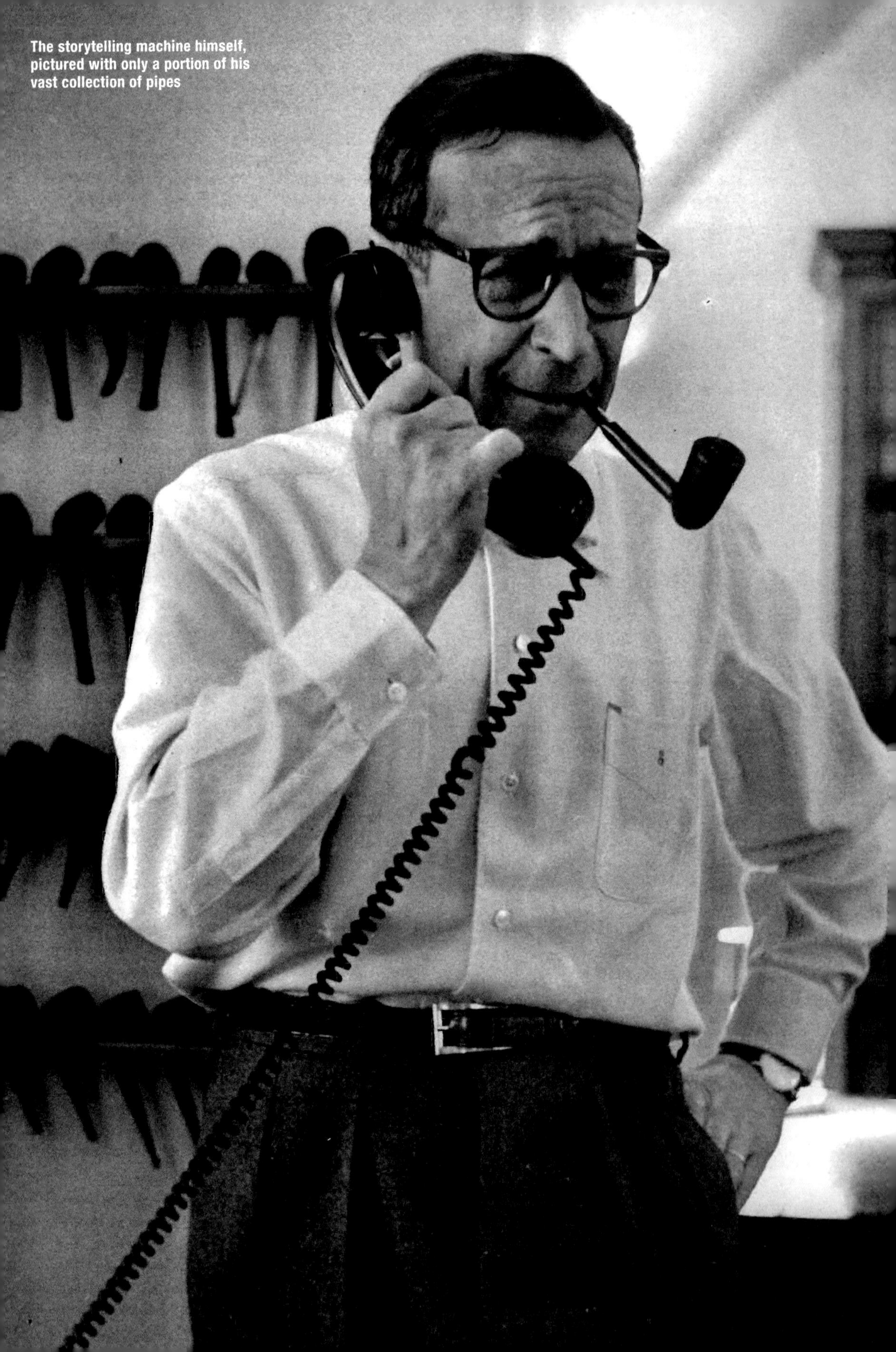

The storytelling machine himself, pictured with only a portion of his vast collection of pipes

The latest film to tap Simenon for the big screen was *La chambre bleue* (*The Blue Room*, 2014)[5]. Directed by Mathieu Amalric, it stars Amalric as a family man named Julien Gahyde. As the film begins, we see Julien having rough sex with his mistress Esther Despierre (Stéphanie Cléau) in a quiet little hotel room not far from the pharmacy owned by her husband. She bites him. He bleeds. The film jumps into the future where Julien is being questioned by police officers. The rest of the story unfolds this way, alternating between the consuming passion of the blue hotel room and forceful interrogations by cops, lawyers, a prison shrink, and an examining magistrate.

La chambre bleue is about as *Simenon* as a Simenon adaptation can be. It's compact (75 minutes), emotionally restrained, and rooted in the physical. The hotel room sex scenes map the pleasures of the flesh in skin and sweat and hair. Amalric and Stéphanie Cléau allow the camera to linger on their nakedness as Julien and Esther try to lose themselves in sexual oblivion. She asks him if he could love her for the rest of their lives. He says yes, but he and the audience both wonder if this affair could survive the light of day. Later, as we learn of their subsequent crimes, the story moves to another blue room, the imposing courtroom where their sins are exposed to the world and their love is rendered tawdry and monstrous. As Julien tells one of his interrogators, "Life is different when you live it and when you go back over it." The film doesn't try to justify them. In true Simenon fashion, in true *noir* fashion, it simply observes the bewildering disconnect between the public and the private selves, and dispassionately notes the way passion destroys human beings.[6]

Writing about the author in the afterword of a reissue of *The Engagement of Mr. Hire*, the philosopher John Gray argued, "The absence of meaning is the subject of Simenon's novels. Throughout his *romans durs* he shows the meaning of any human life to be a matter of habit, easily destroyed and soon forgotten." More than any other author, Simenon imbedded this existential idea into the DNA of noir, both in literature and in film. ■

5 Simenon's novel, released in 1964, was previously adapted in Mexico as the film *La habitación azul* (2002) by director Walter Doehner.

6 Because his body of work is so vast, any single overview of Simenon films is doomed by the constraints of space and time. Further films to explore should include Lance Comfort's *Temptation Harbour* (1947), Bertrand Tavernier's *The Clockmaker of St. Paul* (1974), and *The Man from London* (2007) by Béla Tarr and Ágnes Hranitzky.

Tarpé Mills & Miss Fury

"IT'S ALL DONE WITH MIRRORS"

Trina Robbins

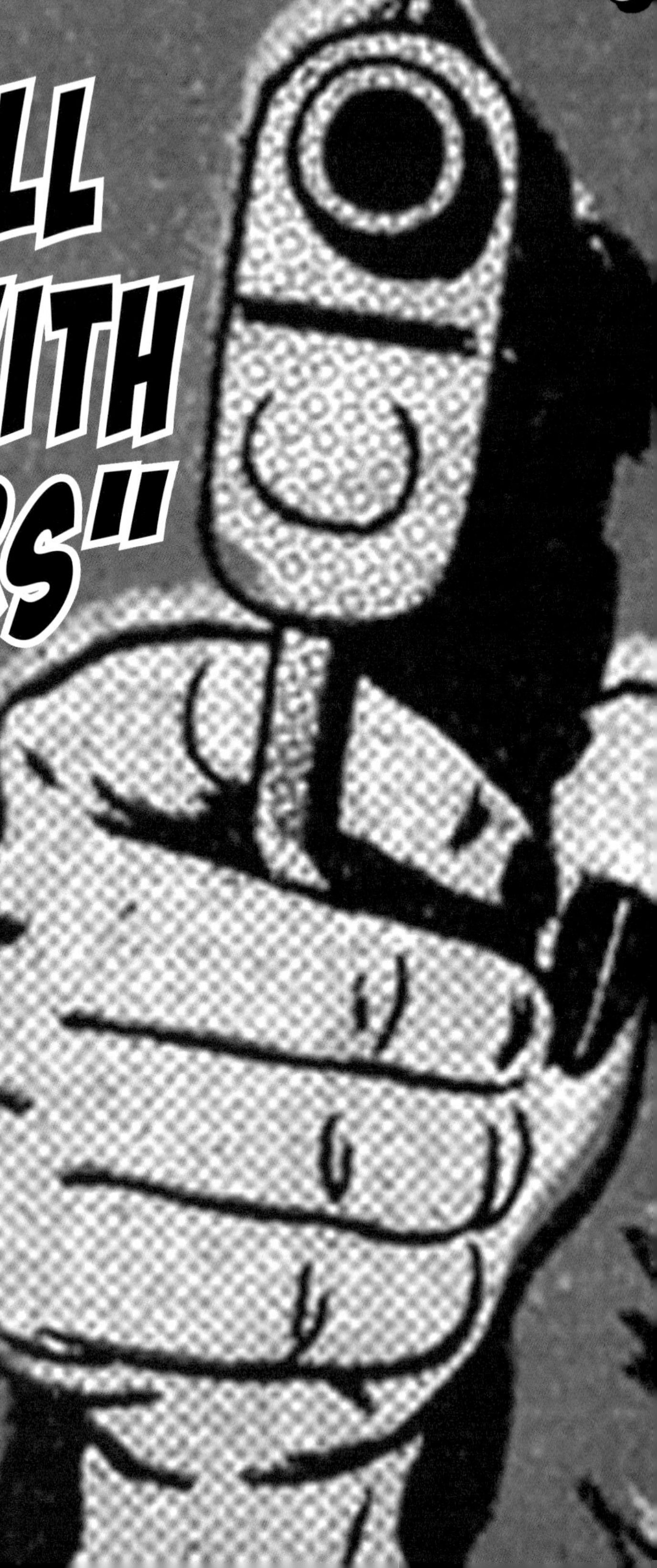

In 1941, a beautiful socialite follows her handsome-but-spineless fiancé to Brazil after a misunderstanding threatens their engagement—and she arrives too late to prevent him from marrying a platinum-blonde German adventuress. She saves a man from being lynched by an angry mob, but winds up the prisoner of bald German General Bruno, held in an underground fortress hidden in a hollowed-out hill. Escaping, she joins a band of anti-Nazi guerillas led by a Carmen Miranda look-alike named Era. She and Era parachute from a crippled airplane only to be recaptured by the Germans—but they're rescued by a platoon of American marines! And all of this takes place in *Brazil*.

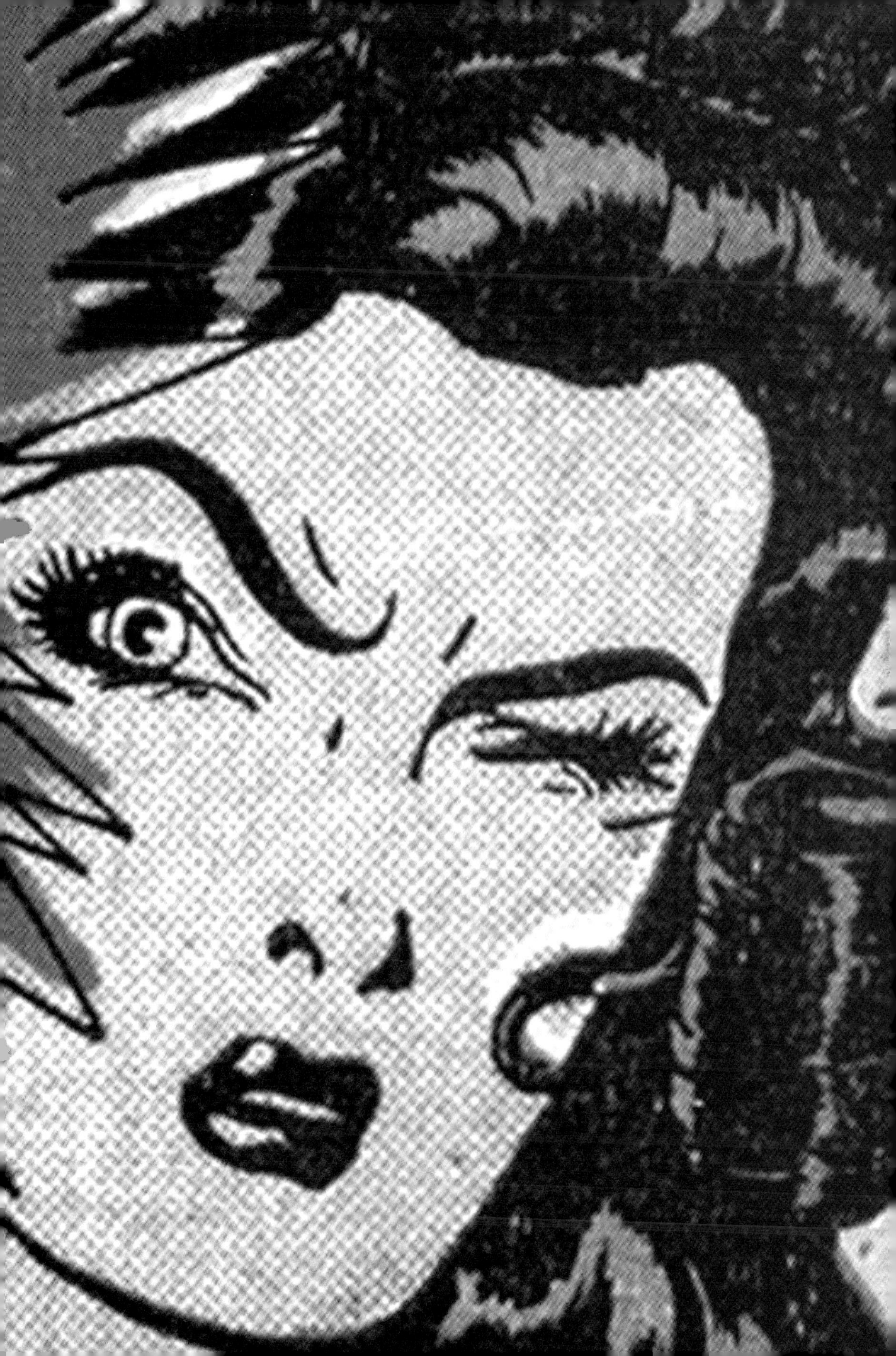

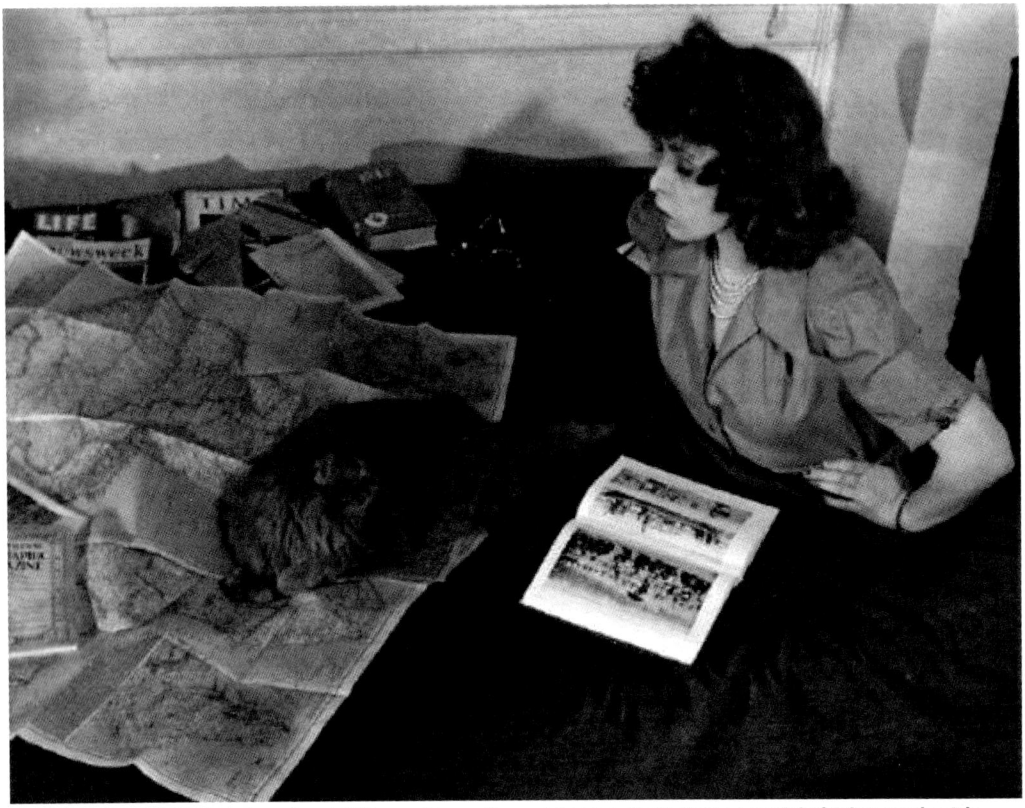

Stylish and sophisticated, June Tarpé Mills used herself—and her cat, Perri-Purr, as models for her comic strip

This is not a movie. It's a comic strip.

Hard to believe if all you know of newspaper comics is *Peanuts*, *Garfield*, and *Dennis the Menace*, but, once upon a time, America's "funny pages" were filled with amazing adventure strips featuring tough guys with cigarettes dangling from their lips and beautiful women in slinky evening gowns, all prowling the most exotic locales.

The adventure strip that started it all, Milton Caniff's *Terry and the Pirates*, set in China and points east, debuted in 1934. Similar strips by Roy Crane, Noel Sickles, Frank Robbins, and others followed throughout the 1930s and '40s. Their heroes, typically snappy-talking flyboys attired in leather jackets, had slangy names like Buz Sawyer, Captain Easy, Scorchy Smith, and Johnny Hazard.

Only one of these adventure strips starred a woman, as well as being written and drawn by a woman. *Miss Fury* was the creation of June Tarpé Mills, aka Tarpé Mills. Mills had already dispensed with "June" in favor of the sexually ambiguous "Tarpé" when her first comics, among them *Daredevil Barry Finn* and *Mann of India*, appeared in comic books in 1939. In an interview, Mills once explained, "It would have been a major letdown to the kids if they found out that the author of such virile and awesome characters was a gal." But by the time Miss Fury graced the Sunday comics pages, it was well known that the creator was a woman and that she based the look of her brunette heroine on none other than herself. The strip had been running for only a year when a newspaper article announced: MEET THE REAL MISS FURY — IT'S ALL DONE WITH MIRRORS.

You can do that in comics. If you want a kid to acquire super powers after being bitten by a radioactive spider, all you have to do is draw the story. And because Tarpé Mills wanted to fly to Brazil and have romantic adventures with handsome men, and battle Nazis while wearing frilly lingerie and stylish shoulder-padded dresses she could never afford in real life, she drew it—and it was real.

In case anyone thought Mills' resemblance to Marla Drake, the socialite who dons a panther skin to become Miss Fury, was mere coincidence, the artist put her own cat into the strip, too. Why be a lone heroine when you can fight Nazis and bad guys alongside your beautiful white Persian, Perri-Purr? Yes, Miss Fury's cat had the same name as Mills' cat. And along with his owner, Perri-Purr made newspaper headlines, too, when in 1945, in what one hopes was only a publicity stunt, Mills donated him to the war effort by lending him to a battleship to be its mascot. "Cartoon Strip Cat Goes Off to War," wrote the *Miami Daily News*, subtitling its story, "It's Sir Admiral Purr Now." Since the war was winding down, one assumes Mills got Perri-Purr back safe and sound.

About those exotic locales: air travel in the 1930s was pretty much unattainable unless you were very rich and had a lot of time to kill (a flight from London to Australia would typically take about 11 days and set you back as much as $20,000 when adjusted for inflation). And during wartime, air travel was severely restricted, so those adventure strip artists relied on the silver screen for anything vaguely resembling authenticity. Milton Caniff never got to China in his entire life ... but that didn't stop him. Movies like *Red Dust* (1932) and *China Seas* (1935) were all the research he needed for

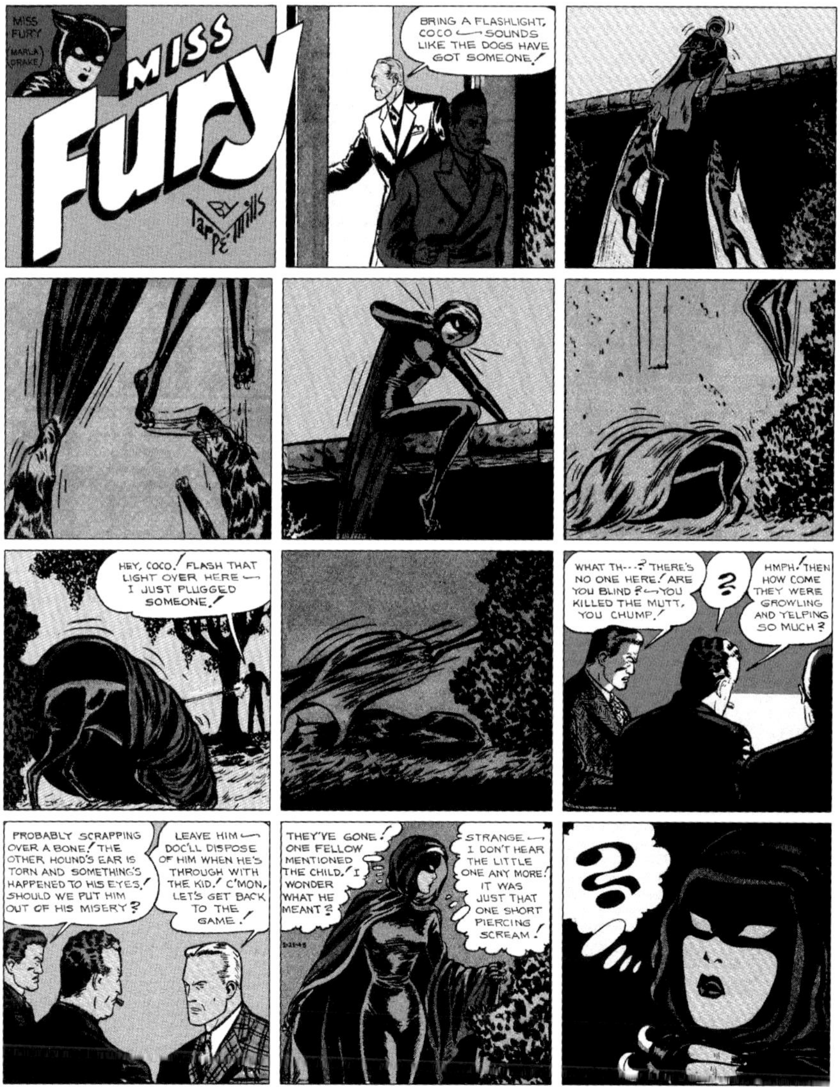

Like cats and dogs: an example of Miss Fury, in her sleek catsuit, executing some derring-do under the noses of her male antagonists

his iconic adventure strip *Terry and the Pirates*; his vampy heroine, Burma, is a dead ringer for Jean Harlow. Will Eisner, whose comic *The Spirit*, was always informed by film, based his vamp, P'Gell, on Hedy Lamarr in *Algiers* (1938).

From 1941 to 1945, Tarpé Mills' strip took place in Brazil. By way of research on Latin America, there were a number of Hollywood movies she could watch, most featuring Carmen Miranda: *Down Argentine Way* (1940), *That Night in Rio* (1941), *Week-End in Havana* (1941), and others of that ilk, none of them particularly authentic. So her colorful characters emerged from a combination of Technicolor musicals and Mills' own fertile imagination: Era, the Miranda look-alike Nazi fighter; dashing gaucho Don Chico, the pride of the pampas; Albino Jo, the white-haired, dark-skinned Harvard-educated albino Brazilian Indian. (It's a safe bet Mills had never seen a real albino.) Equally memorable are her villains: one-armed General Bruno, who lost the limb in a failed assassination attempt, is a Rommel-esque anti-hero who hates Hitler but is nevertheless a German patriot, commanding a secret platoon of soldiers hidden in a mountain. Marla Drake's nemesis, who is sometimes also Bruno's nemesis, is the platinum blonde adventuress Baroness Erica von Kampf, a character who, according to one newspaper report, received more fan mail than Marla herself.

Wartime readers didn't know or care any more than Mills did about authenticity, and they ate up Miss Fury's adventures. The strip was cut and pasted and reprinted in comic books, which sold a million issues each. The heroine was painted on the nosecones of warplanes, and Mills mailed out sexy pin-ups of Marla to GIs who sent her fan mail. About those sexy pin-ups: if "Miss Fury" was cinematic, it was pre-code cinema. Mills drew her heroine and the other female characters in pretty risqué poses. One sequence consisted of panels showing Baroness von Kampf doffing her nightgown and slipping into a bath, her back coyly turned to the reader but obviously stark naked. Mills was also the queen of the comic strip catfight, and her heroine managed to routinely get her clothes prettily rearranged when she fought (and won) battles with babes who tried to shoot her or push her off penthouse ledges. Mills didn't always get away with it. The Catholic church condemned the strip and declared it suitable for burning. In 1947, Era returned to the strip as a nightclub dancer wearing the equivalent of a bikini—so shocking many papers canceled that week's strip, while others opted to cover Era's body with a blob of red ink.

One way to tell if a comic is drawn by a woman is the attention paid to fashion. While male cartoonists of the '40s were content to put female characters in simple knee-length red dresses, or red strapless evening gowns, Mills' women wore drape-shape outfits and peplum-trimmed suits with matching hats, fox stoles draped over their shoulders. According to the artist's contemporaries, Mills herself was no slouch in the fashion department, although she couldn't afford the leopard skin coats she gave her heroine. A female colleague of Mills' recalled the artist's penchant for ankle-strap heels, and her nephew, Bill Finn, remembers his aunt attending a funeral dressed to kill in a suit with matching wide-brimmed picture hat and open-toed pumps.

It's hard to resist a casting call for the leads in *Miss Fury*. Let's pretend I have a time machine: The Baroness Erica von Kampf, her blonde bangs cut into a V to hide the swastika branded on her forehead, can only be Marlene Dietrich. Carmen Miranda never did any serious acting, and it's doubtful she could, so my choice for Era, the beautiful Latin guerilla queen, would be Dolores del Río. Gary Hale, Marla Drake's handsome-but-weak-willed fiancé could only be Farley Granger, fresh from his role as the handsome-but-weak-willed Guy Haines in *Strangers on a Train* (1951), while Dan Carey, the cop who loves Marla, is either Sterling Hayden or Dan Duryea. Our heroine, lovely brunette Marla Drake, is played by Jane Greer (or any other of Howard Hughes' stable of brunette beauties). General Bruno is a problem. Erich von Stroheim would be fine if Bruno were a really *bad* bad guy, but, though bald and German, he's nonetheless an anti-Nazi and kinda sexy, involved in a love-hate relationship with the Baroness. The only solution is to take my time machine to 1960, yank Yul Brynner from the set of *The Magnificent Seven*, and ship him back about 18 years.

According to Bill Finn, in her later years, Mills became somewhat eccentric and reclusive, living alone with her cat, a successor to Perri-Purr, and seldom leaving her house. She continued to dress in the shoulder-padded dresses and platform shoes of her glory days. She died of emphysema in 1988 without ever seeing Brazil. Her movie has yet to be made.

Legendary cartoonist Trina Robbins has written and drawn comics for more than 50 years, from the early days of underground comix in the 1960s to her feminist take on *Wonder Woman* in the late 1990s and right up to today. She has written numerous books on the role on women in the history of comics. In 2013, she was inducted into the Will Eisner Hall of Fame. Her recent books, *Miss Fury: Sensational Sundays 1944–1949* (2011), as well as *Miss Fury: Sensational Sundays 1941 – 1944* (2013), are available from the Library of American Comics.

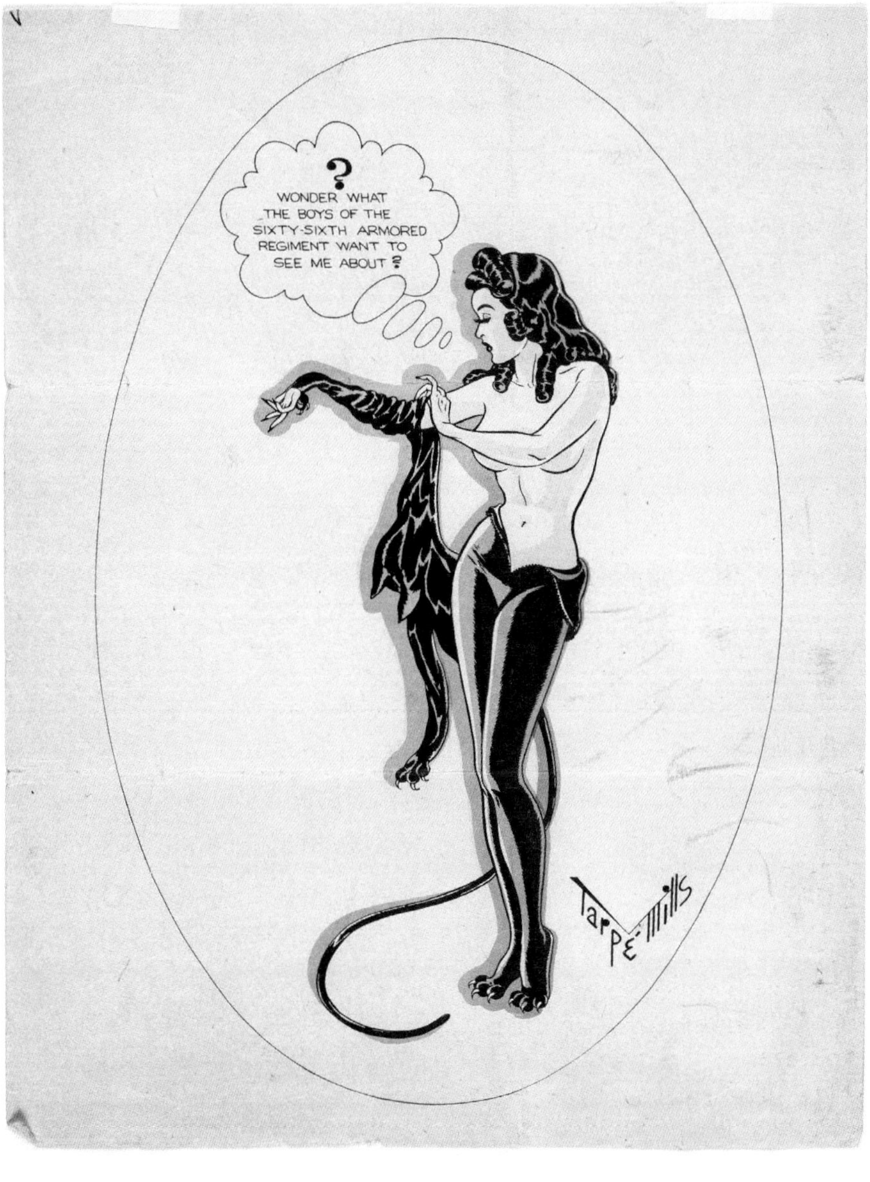

Milton Caniff had nothing on Tarpé Mills when it came to illustrating sexy cheesecake pin-ups for the troops

Susan Shaw, Brit Noir's Tragic Sweetheart

Gary Deane

Her mother told friends and neighbors that she thought her daughter was daft. The girl seemed "movie mad," living only for the pleasures of the pictures and latest movie magazines, but young Patsy Sloots—blonde, petite, and uncommonly pretty—had thoughts of her own. At age 17, Patsy Sloots was signed by the J. Arthur Rank Organization, tagged with the stage name "Susan Shaw," and hustled off to the studio's charm school to be made a proper lady.

Soon after, Patsy-now-Susan was given her first screen assignments—uncredited minor supporting parts in a series of sombre melodramas, most of them now part of the British film noir canon. These included *The Upturned Glass* (1947), a macabre tale of a doctor driven to avenge the death of his lover; *Jassy* (1947), an elegant period thriller in which murder and the sins of the flesh richly thicken the plot; *It Always Rains on Sunday* (1947), a grimly poetic depiction of backstreet life in postwar London; and *To the Public Danger* (1948), a cautionary psychodrama based on a radio play by Patrick Hamilton, playwright of *Gaslight* and *Rope* and *Hangover Square* novelist.Though the roles were small, Shaw brightened the screen corner-to-corner. It was clear there was more to her than girlish good looks and a buoyant personality. Unselfconscious and matter-of-fact, Shaw was suited to play strong-willed young women. Growing up in West Norwood, a working-class district of South London, she'd come by her candor and forthrightness honestly, deciding early to be more than an office clerk, the vocation waiting for most girls graduating school at 16. Like the characters she'd play—be it daughter, sister, girlfriend, fiancée, wife, confidante, or companion—she would always resist expectations.

Shaw's breezy impudence would next find her cast in a trio of light-hearted comedies charting the exploits of a working-class London family, the Huggetts. Starring Jack Warner and Kathleen Harrison as the clan's good-hearted parents, and Jane Hylton, Petula Clark, and Shaw as their spirited young daughters, the movies—*Here Come the Huggetts* (1948), *Vote for Huggett* (1949), and *The Huggetts Abroad* (1949)—charmed audiences and were hits at the box office. They also showcased Shaw's maturing talents; months later she'd be seen in Ealing Studio's poignant *portmanteau* production *Train of Events* (1949). The film recounted a railroad disaster told through four short stores; "The Engine Drive" segment teamed Shaw with audience favorite Jack Warner as her father. Though only a middling success, the film cemented her relationship with the general public and its sense that the actress was 'one of us'—as opposed to the snobbish 'well-bred.'

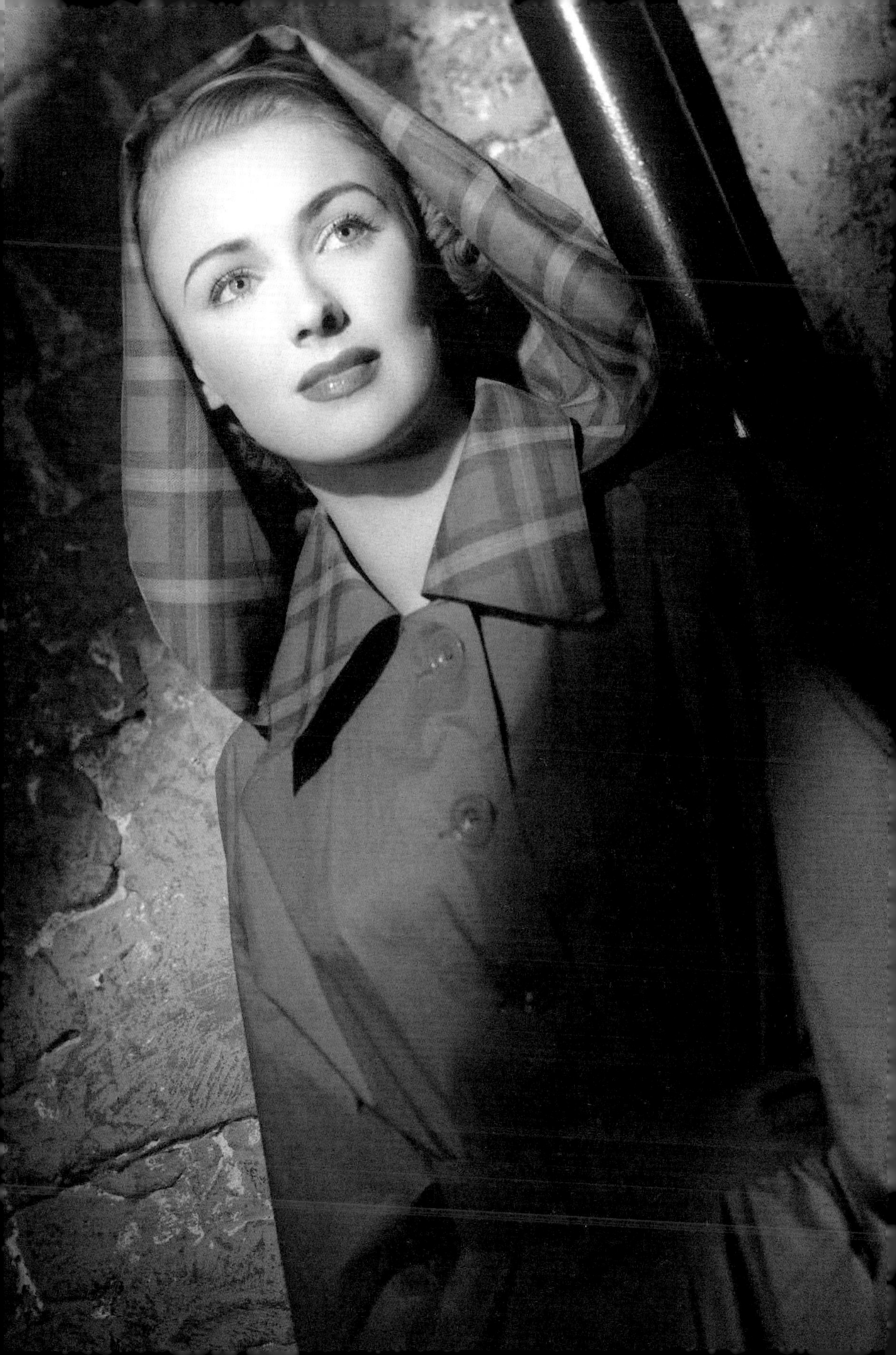

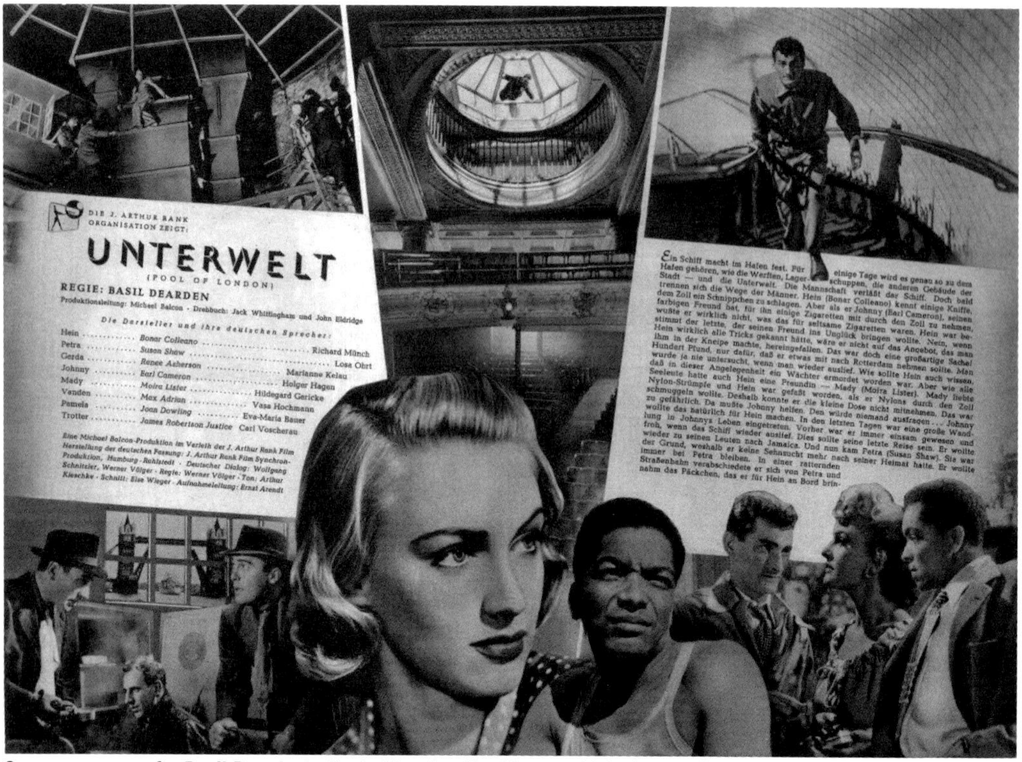

German program for Basil Dearden's *Pool of London*, the film on which she met future husband Bonar Colleano

Shaw looked to be on her way. She was given higher billing in 1950's *The Woman in Question* (released in the U.S. as *Five Angles on Murder*), directed by Anthony Asquith and headlining Jean Kent and Dirk Bogarde. Shaw was featured as Catherine Taylor, the self-centered younger sister of Kent's character, Astra, who is mysteriously murdered. The police interview five of those closest to Astra, each of whom offer dramatically different views of the dead woman. Catherine recalls Astra as a cheap tramp, though she's no angel herself. Catherine's flinty insolence showed Shaw in yet another light—on-screen she was becoming unpredictable, more vivid, and much more interesting.

The Woman in Question was Susan Shaw's full entrée into film noir. It was a world she'd soon make her home, as nearly all the films in which she'd next feature would be unconditional noir dramas and thrillers. One of the first and best was Basil Dearden's groundbreaking *Pool of London* (1951). The film tells of a merchant seaman, Dan (Bonar Colleano) who gets in over his head with a smuggling racket. He recruits a black shipmate, Johnny (Earl Cameron) to help pull him out, but fails to tell Johnny what's really going on. Shaw gives an emotionally uncluttered and touching performance as an empathetic cinema cashier drawn to Johnny as she witnesses his wounding encounters with racial prejudice. She begins to share his vagrant hopes.

It was on the set on *Pool of London* that Susan Shaw first met Bonar Colleano, a charismatic American actor who'd been featured in the Hollywood productions *Stairway to Heaven* (1946) and *Sleeping Car to Trieste* (1948). Colleano was now working in the UK and had become the go-to actor for roles requiring a brash, voluble New Yorker. He starred in films such as *Good-Time Girl* (1948), *Give Us This Day* (1949)—released in the U.S. as *Christ in Concrete*, *Escape by Night* (1953), and *Joe MacBeth* (1955). Shaw was married at the time to German actor Albert Lieven, but their marriage ended in divorce in 1953. She and Colleano wed in January 1954.

Their union grabbed the attention of the daily press and it wasn't long before Shaw and Colleano had been anointed as British filmdom's Golden Couple. Their celebrity was transcendent and strikingly

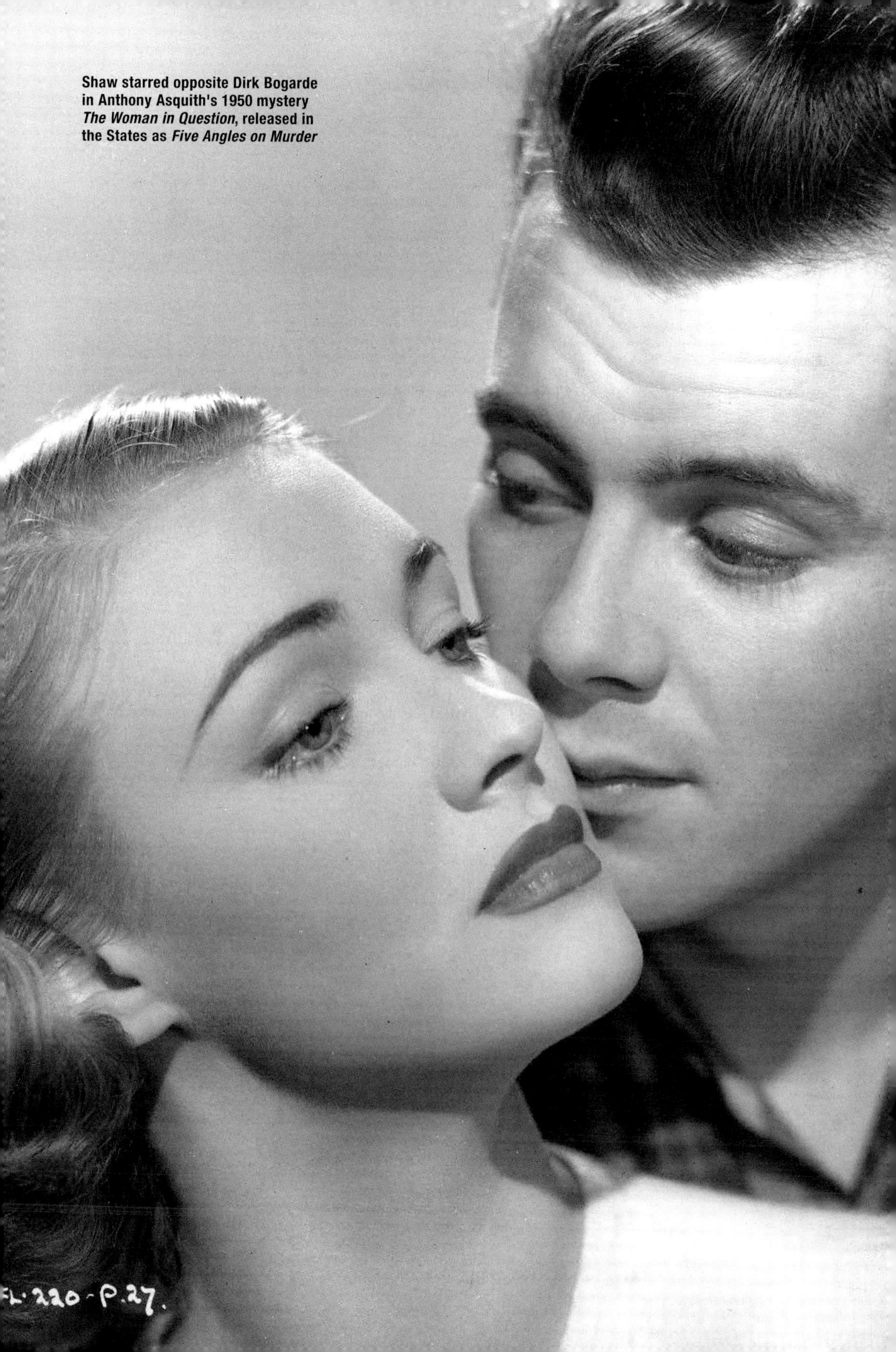

Shaw starred opposite Dirk Bogarde in Anthony Asquith's 1950 mystery *The Woman in Question*, released in the States as *Five Angles on Murder*

modern. She was coveted by both movie and women's magazines, and interest in her began to eclipse that of more established and critically appointed actresses like Deborah Kerr, Valerie Hobson, Kathleen Byron, and Ann Todd. Shaw's attraction crossed class and generational divides. Among her fans were older moviegoers who had watched her come of age on-screen, as well as younger women and teenage girls infatuated by her persona on- and off-screen. Her trademark blondeness was embraced as fashionable and acceptably glamorous—unlike that of brassier sexpots Diana Dors, Greta Gynt, or Christine Norden who were seen as 'common.'

The couple's storybook life came to a devastating end in 1958 when Colleano, returning to London from Liverpool after a stage performance of *Will Success Spoil Rock Hunter?*, crashed his sports car and was killed. Shaw was distraught—and destitute. Colleano was a reckless spender who owed thousands in back taxes. Friends, including James Mason and Stanley Baker, volunteered to sponsor a charity football match to cover funeral expenses and raise funds toward the support of the couple's three-year-old son, Marc, who would be taken in and raised by Colleano's mother. Shaw struggled to keep working, but heavy drinking finished her acting career by 1963. She survived on menial office jobs and waitressing in bars, but fell deeper and deeper into alcoholism and depression. Eventually, she was banned even from London's seediest clubs and, in 1978 at 49 years old, cirrhosis of the liver killed her. She died penniless, her burial costs covered by the Rank Organization. No former co-stars or colleagues came to her funeral, though Jack Warner and Kathleen Harrison, then respectively 83- and 86-years old, sent flowers.

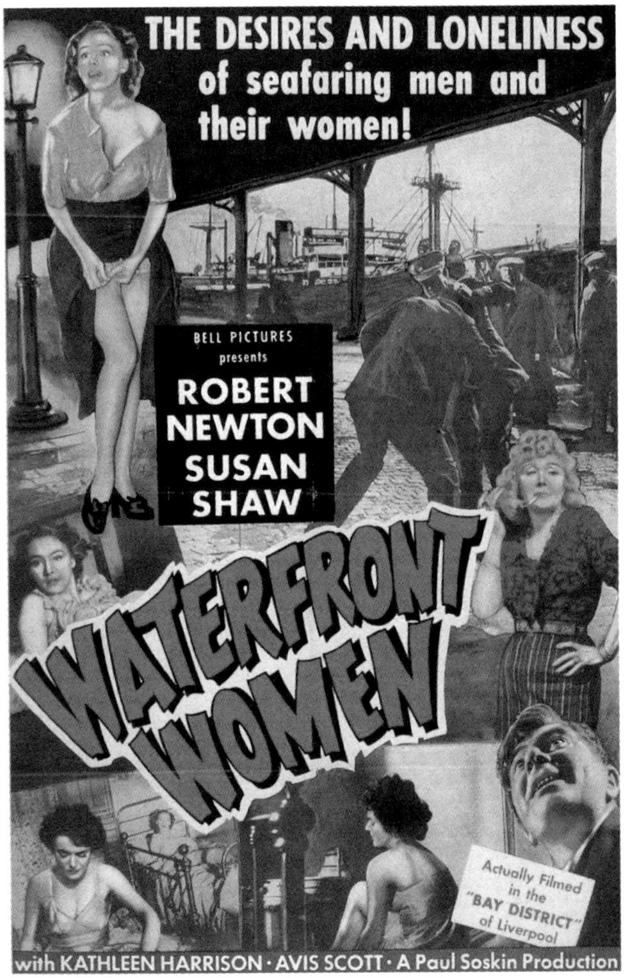

Celebrity deaths are often attended by infamy. Examples are plentiful and sadly familiar, such as Barbara Payton living out her days addicted and selling herself on Sunset Strip, or the beautiful Gail Russell who medicated herself to death with alcohol initially attempting to overcome crippling stage fright. Susan Shaw's premature death, like Russell's, was all the more tragic because of the shining promise of her early life and career. Fortunately, Shaw left behind an array of memorable, full-of-life performances, a testament to a lovely and vibrant actress who appeared more than any other actress in classic-period British noir. Following are the 'best of the rest' of Susan Shaw, the uncontested Sweetheart of British Noir.

1. *Waterfront Women* (1950)
Robert Newton, Kathleen Harrison, Richard Burton, Kenneth Griffith, Avis Scott

A bleak postwar noir about a family long abandoned by its father (Newton) who went to sea years earlier. Newton suddenly returns home and ends up jailed for murder while the youngest daughter (Shaw) is pursued by a wealthy scoundrel (Griffith) who wants only to bed her. She resists, holding out for more and determined to get it. This was Shaw's first casting in an adult part. Just 19, she seems years beyond her age as the hardened little social climber.

2. *Wall of Death* (1951)
Laurence Harvey, Maxwell Reed

Reed, a motorcycle stunt rider and low-life, convinces his boxing buddy (Harvey) to help him rob the carnival office. Reed is lusting for a new bike so he can rejoin the racing circuit after recklessly killing a fellow racer. Shaw, once Reed's girlfriend and now Harvey's, begs Harvey not to get involved with the thick-eared Reed, but is left only to pick up the pieces when everything goes 'pear-shaped.' Shaw's performance in *Wall of Death* is one of her most sympathetic and affecting.

3. *Wide Boy* (1952)
Sydney Tafler, Ronald Howard

Tafler is a street hustler with big ambitions and no prospects. His girlfriend (Shaw) despairs of him, but enjoys his patter and his favors. One evening, Tafler dips into a woman's purse and comes up with a letter showing this same woman is having an affair with a well-to-do married gent (Howard). Tafler tries blackmail, but ends up on the run for murder. *Wide Boy* was Shaw's coming-out film: her transformation from a pretty young slip-of-a-thing to a self-assured beauty.

4. *A Killer Walks* (1952)
Laurence Harvey, Trader Faulkner

Laurence Harvey plays a farm worker existing on subsistence wages paid to him by his grandmother who owns the farm. Shaw is his glammed-up girlfriend who's looking for money in a marriage. They both know where they can get it, but granny has to die first. Shaw's made it plain that she's just a city girl who wants to open a beauty parlor. Bible-thumping granny makes it plain she thinks Shaw's just a floozy. She is, and a thumping good one at that.

5. *The Intruder* (1953)
Jack Hawkins, Michael Medwin, Dennis Price

Jack Hawkins returns home to find a burglar (Medwin), a former member of his wartime regiment. Medwin makes a dash for it and Hawkins, hoping to help him, goes on a country-wide search. Shaw is Medwin's girlfriend from before the war who'd promised to marry him but now has other plans. Shaw's natural believability was a large part of her appeal. In *The Intruder,* that truthfulness of character is heart-rending.

6. *Small Town Story* (1953)
Kent Walton, Donald Houston, Alan Wheatley

A Canadian ex-serviceman (Walton) returns to the English town where he'd been posted during the war, hoping to find the girl (Shaw) with whom he'd fallen in love. Walton, a promising footballer, hears that the local club stands to inherit £25,000 from a recently deceased supporter if it places high in the league. The supporter's nephew (Wheatley) wants the money and enlists Shaw's help to make sure that Walton never plays. This was one of Shaw's few parts as an all-out bad girl. Would that there had been more...

7. *The Good Die Young* (1954)
Laurence Harvey, Stanley Baker, Richard Basehart, John Ireland, Joan Collins, Gloria Grahame

Three good men are desperate to redeem themselves: a broken boxer (Baker); a U.S. veteran (Basehart) attempting to win back his wife (Collins); and an air force sergeant (Ireland) married to a faithless actress (Grahame). The trio are persuaded by an amoral layabout (Harvey) to hijack a postal

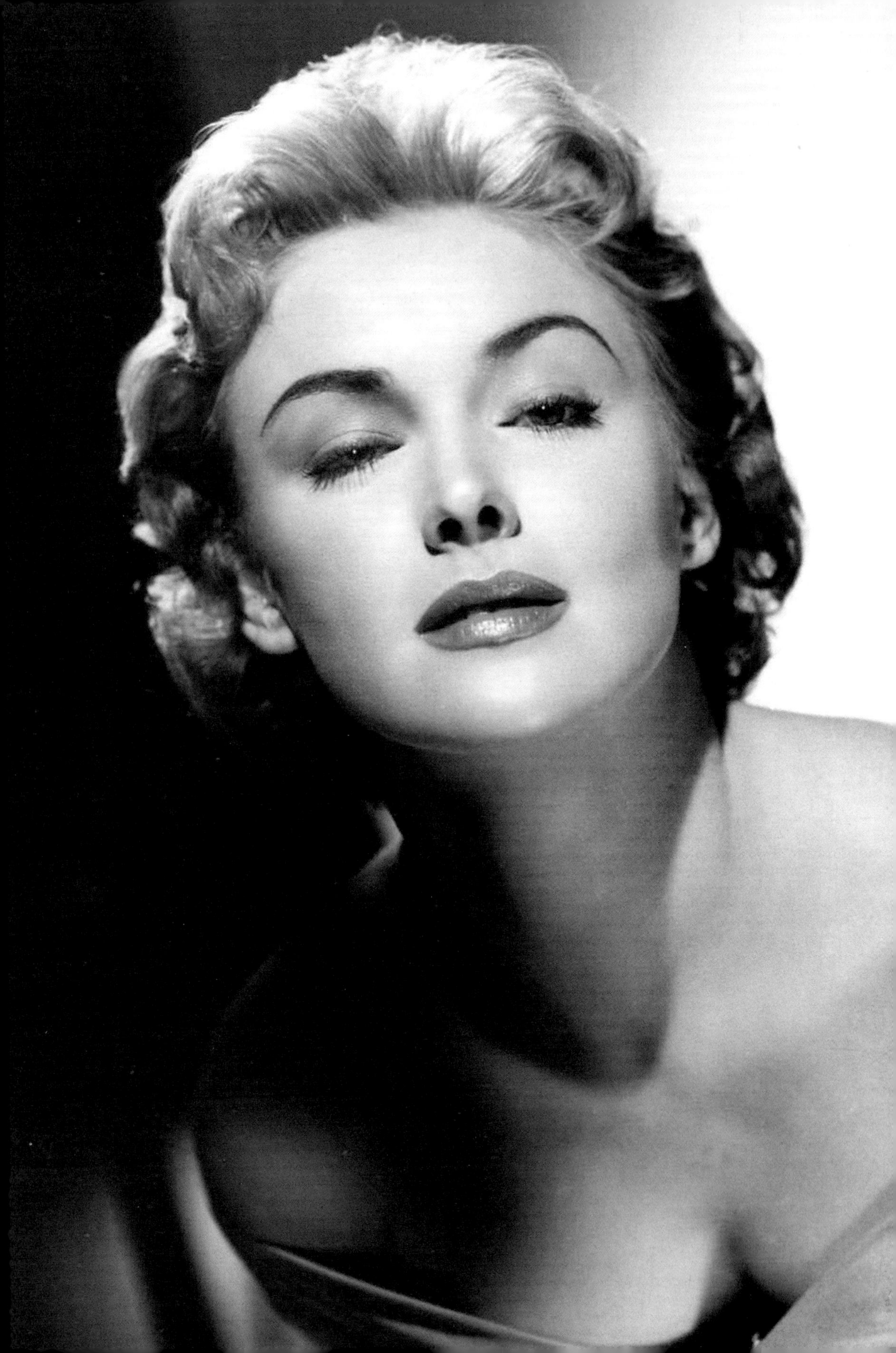

van. Shaw has a small part but owns the moment. As Ireland tries to chat her up in a pub, she asks, "Are you married?" When he asks her why she cares, she says, "Oh, I just like to know what the weather's like before I put out to sea." The last word often went to Shaw, who was always ready to deliver it.

8. *Blonde Blackmailer* (1955)
Richard Arlen, Constance Leigh

After serving seven years for a murder he didn't commit, Arlen is determined to clear his name. Evidence at the trial showed the murdered girl to be a known blackmailer. Arlen and his fiancée Leigh track down Shaw, a model who had been a close friend of the murdered girl. However, she turns out to be something worse. Shaw relished the part and makes a meal of it, the film's tag line being, "Man Bait! By Day, the Fashion Model! By Night, the Racket Girl!" Three full courses, no waiting.

9. *The Diplomatic Corpse* (1958)
Robin Bailey, Liam Redmond

Reporter Bailey is investigating the murder of an employee of a Middle Eastern embassy. Clues lead to the ambassador himself, and Bailey's fiancée/gossip columnist (Shaw) finds her way into the embassy as a fill-in receptionist. It's a risky play. Her predecessor had been killed in an untimely "accident." Despite the serious subject matter (drug smuggling under diplomatic cover), things are agreeably lighthearted at times thanks to the playful script which allows Shaw free reign.

10. *Chain of Events* (1958)
Kenneth Griffith, Dermot Walsh

A taut noir melodrama, *Chain of Events* features Griffith as a bank clerk who boards a bus and deliberately neglects to pay his fare. Caught by an inspector, Griffith foolishly gives the name and address of one of the bank's clients, setting in motion an ugly chain of events involving blackmail, robbery, and murder. Walsh plays a reporter following the story. Shaw glows as the newspaper owner's secretary, who also happens to be Walsh's girlfriend and partner in crime-busting. The show is there for the stealing and Shaw walks away without anyone laying a hand on her, as she most always did. ■

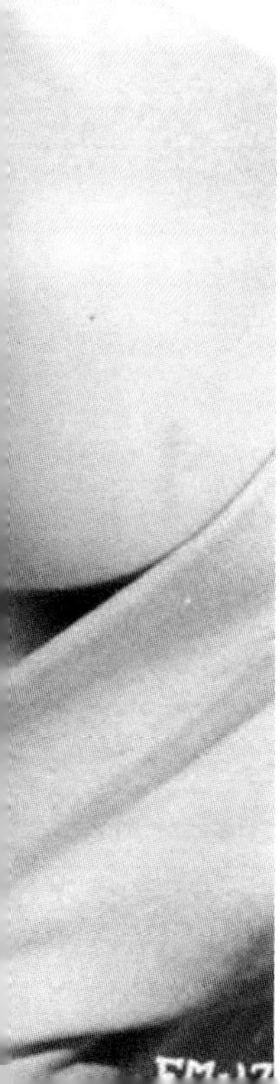

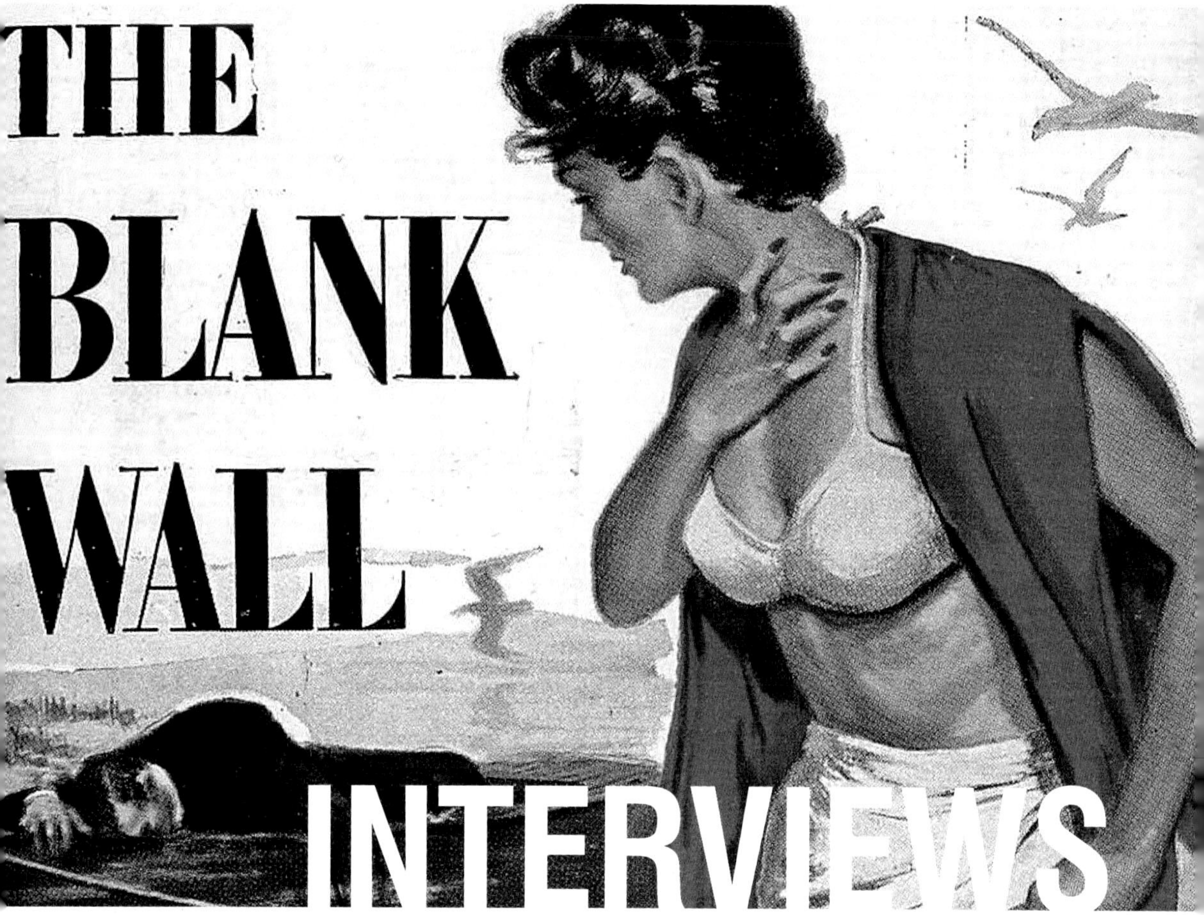

INTERVIEWS

SECTION THREE

LAURA LIPPMAN

Dreamers become Schemers

NOIR CITY Interview by Vince Keenan

"In her black dress, black gloves, and retro heels, she looks like Joan Crawford or Bette Davis. She feels like them, too. Tough, yet brittle. That's the thing about being really hard. When you do break, you shatter." — from Sunburn

Twenty years as a newspaper reporter, most of them in Baltimore, gave Laura Lippman a keen observer's eye and the ability to write fast. She has parlayed both gifts into an impressive career as a crime novelist. Lippman has been nominated for every award in the field, and won most of them. Her Tess Monaghan series stands at 12 entries and counting, and her standalone novels are critically acclaimed; 2016's *Wilde Lake* reimagines *To Kill a Mockingbird* in a contemporary suburb. Her latest, *Sunburn* (February 2018), draws on dark sources to tell an intimate tale.

"The summer of 1985, the film series was all black-and-white films from the 1940s. Double Indemnity. Mildred Pierce. The Postman Always Rings Twice. *Polly didn't understand at first how they were all linked, why the series was called Raising Cain, but then someone explained they were all based on books by a Maryland man who had lived in Baltimore and Annapolis, grown up on the Eastern Shore."*

It's a summer afternoon on a Delaware beach in 1995 when Polly leaves her husband and daughter without warning. Before she can start her life anew, though, she attracts the attention of Adam. Only Adam has no idea what Polly is really running from—or toward. And Polly doesn't suspect that Adam may not be the stranger he appears to be.

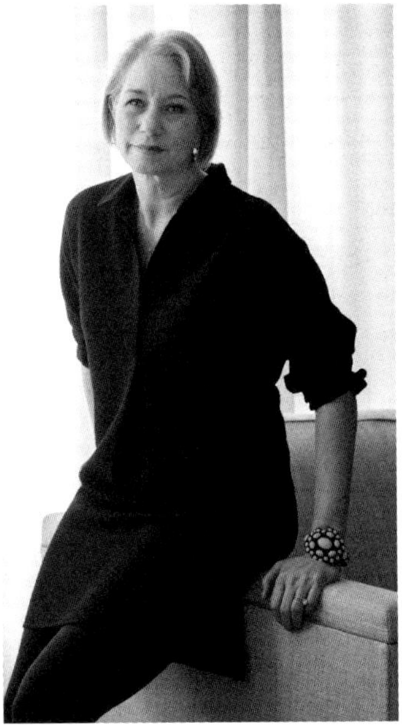

"In cartoons, devils and angels argue it out on a guy's shoulder, but he's long past a fight between right and wrong. There's work to be done."

A story of two people either desperately in love or determined to use each other, *Sunburn* harks back to classic pulp fiction in a wholly modern way. It's both indisputably noir and unmistakably Lippman. *NOIR CITY* interviewed the writer via email about her newest effort.

NOIR CITY: Your standalone novels in particular have never shied away from darkness, but Sunburn *is pure noir from start to finish. Secrets, betrayals, characters who can't get out of their own way. Was this an itch you'd longed to scratch, or simply the story that came to you?*

LAURA LIPPMAN: I had pretty much given up on my ability to write true noir. It's what I wanted to do, what I intended to do, but when I started writing novels I think I had this very female desire to be liked—so I made little jokes and softened the edges and then assumed that was my natural range. I often described my series character, Tess Monaghan, as having a rueful optimism about the human condition. I do, too. And in *Wilde Lake*, I had allowed myself to write in the first person at great length for the first time, and that was a very talky, brooding voice.

But I've long been fascinated by how Anne Tyler took a potentially dark idea—woman abandons family while on beach vacation—and found in it this wonderful story of reinvention and compassion. That was *Ladder of Years*, published in 1995. And for years, I kept circling a story I wanted to write, inspired by a Steve Earle song, "The Week of Living Dangerously." *I threw the car seat in the dumpster and I headed out into the night.* I wanted to write about a woman with a baby in the hospital who just keeps driving past the hospital, onto the interstate, destination unknown, incapable of dealing with what's happening. It's dark enough when a man leaves his family. When a woman does it—well, as everyone in the novel keeps reminding us, Polly is "unnatural."

NC: For all the recognition and occasional cachet that "noir" has, is it a dirty word in publishing circles?
LL: It's a misunderstood word, that's for sure. By my count, we have had at least 1,372 panels at mystery cons on "What is noir?" and we still don't seem to know. I think Eddie Muller is the one who says that a PI novel begins with a client trying to hire a PI, whereas a noir novel is one where the client and the PI end up having sex. My own preferred definition is "dreamers become schemers." And now that I think about it, it's often two people sparking off one another, an explosive little chemistry experiment where two benign things become dangerous upon contact. We all want the same things—good lord, I think I just quoted the musical *City of Angels* right there—but it's the main characters in a noir novel or film who decide they will pursue them, no matter the costs.

NC: Noir all too often conjures images of the femme fatale. *Does fiction with that label create new opportunities for women's stories?*
LL: I think so. I hope so. When it comes to women's stories, I'll cheer for anything that opens up mainstream opportunities.

NC: Polly is an instantly compelling figure, a woman who walks away from married life and motherhood to go after what she wants. A male character could do likewise and have his actions dispensed with in a line or two. Here, it feels transgressive. Do you think women face a different standard when it comes to judging their behavior? Are female characters in fiction also judged differently, and did you have to take that into account when writing?
LL: Women in life and fiction absolutely face different standards when it comes to their behavior *vis a vis* family. It is what it is. In the past year, I've read two profiles of famous men in the *New Yorker*, divorced men who emphasize how great their relationships are with their kids—even if they don't see them a lot. Can you imagine a woman trying to assert that her relationship with her children improved when she stopped living under the same roof with them?

NC: Did any particular noir films influence the book? How about noir fiction? After all, in this very magazine Sarah Weinman called you "our generation's Margaret Millar."
LL: The work of James M. Cain and some of the films based on that work were big influences. But, in the film world, I've tried to pay close attention to some less successful modern noirs. Examining something that doesn't work is a good way to try to figure out what *does* work.

A couple of years ago, I had the bizarre good fortune to review Jules Feiffer's first noir graphic novel and it was simply grand. And, in all seriousness, as I was writing *Sunburn* I often said to myself, "I think I've found my inner [Duane] Swierczynski."

NC: Polly talks about feeling like Joan Crawford or Bette Davis. What is it about the characters played by such actresses that still resonates today?
LL: What's the line from *Sunset Boulevard*? "We had faces then." It's so interesting to me—the best actresses working now have distinctive, unusual faces—Streep, Witherspoon, Gyllenhaal—but plastic surgery factories keep churning out these bizarre look-alikes. Anyway, I was definitely channeling Stanwyck for this book. It became a bit of a joke on Twitter, my obsession with *The Big Valley*. Linda Evans, one of the most beautiful women in the world, appears on screen next to Stanwyck, then in her 60s, and you don't even look at Evans. You can't take your eyes off of Stanwyck. (Okay, technically Stanwyck is only 59 when *The Big Valley* debuts.)

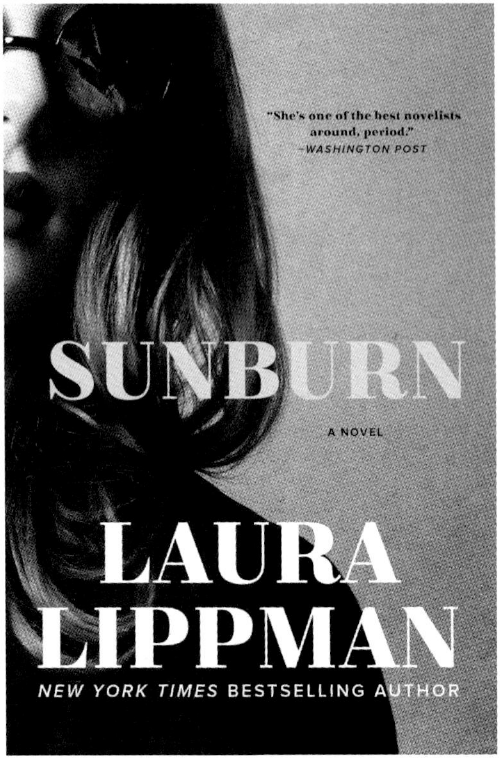

NC: Given the societal changes since those films were made, what makes a character, particularly a woman, a noir protagonist now? Or, say, in 1995?
LL: I think any woman who sees people in her life as stepping stones to what she wants is pretty noir. In the book, Polly makes it clear early on that money matters to her. She's not heard and she thinks, "Pay attention. I just told you who I am."

NC: You've said, "I feel like 1995 was one of the last good years to disappear." Why?
LL: Almost no one had cell phones, it was pre-Google and there just wasn't that expectation that you would be available 24/7.

NC: Sunburn *is scrupulously researched. What was your biggest surprise about looking back at a period only 20-some years ago? What if anything did you misremember?*
LL: It was hard to get the clothes right! Thank God Polly liked to wear vintage finds from the Purple Heart.

NC: Maryland's own James M. Cain is called out by name more than once. How is he viewed there? Is he seen as a favorite son? Did you want to reclaim him for your fellow Marylanders?
LL: I don't think most people even know how deep Cain's Maryland roots go, that he was born here—and came back here to die. I once read that Cain, who was scared to take advances lest he fail to produce the work, often celebrated in grand fashion when he turned the work in and finally got paid. One time, he bought a snowball machine like the one he remembered from an Annapolis market as a child; he used it to make mint juleps. I think there should be a plaque highlighting this somewhere in Maryland. (And almost everything I know about Cain is from Roy Hoopes' biography, so full credit to him.)

NC: Polly is an idiosyncratic but fiercely loyal mother. What fed this portrait? Was Cain's own depiction of maternal love in Mildred Pierce *an inspiration?*
LL: It's a different shade of the rainbow. Mildred believes herself to be a great mother and she's horrible. Polly sees herself as a failure as a mother, but I could make a strong argument in her favor.

NC: Time to talk about grilled cheeses. You offer a lot of fascinating detail about the evolution of the High-Ho, the restaurant where Polly and Adam find themselves working. That also called to mind Mildred Pierce, *which the writer Benjamin Schwarz has called "the greatest work of American fiction about small business." What led you to concentrate on this nuts-and-bolts aspect of the story, and to trust that readers would find it interesting?*
LL: I think everybody's job is interesting. The details, the patois. I decided early on that Adam had this background as a chef because, well, I love *Top Chef*! I'm a total chef groupie. And it happened that in the year I was working on *Sunburn*, I got to know Michael Ruhlman, a Culinary Institute of America trained chef and writer (and now the husband of one of my best friends, Ann Hood). He read all the parts about Adam's work and the High-Ho and made invaluable contributions.

NC: Seriously, about the grilled cheeses. They sound amazing. Any extra pointers you can give?
LL: Yes. Michael and I have now made the grilled cheese and we were very faithful in terms of using ingredients that would be available in a place like the High-Ho in 1995. He showed me how to cook bacon in water (it's genius, I wish I had known that detail for the book). We buttered the inside of the bread and used grated cheddar, but the outside of the bread had a light coating of mayo, which keeps it from browning too quickly. They're divine.

NC: Your novel Every Secret Thing *was brought to the screen by an all-woman production team. Did that have any impact on your experience?*
LL: I was just so happy and honored to see my work translated to the screen with respect. It was a great experience. I don't know if that was a by-product of the all-female team, but I know it didn't hurt.

NC: Now that Sunburn *has outed you as a noir writer, any plans to keep working this side of the street?*
LL: The next book, which is about halfway done, doesn't feel so noir. I thought it was going to be kind of Ellroy-esque, but it's fighting me on that. I know I want to go back to noir, though. I liked my year of living dangerously.

THE DARK PAGE

Finding Noir in Crime Fiction

Eric Beetner

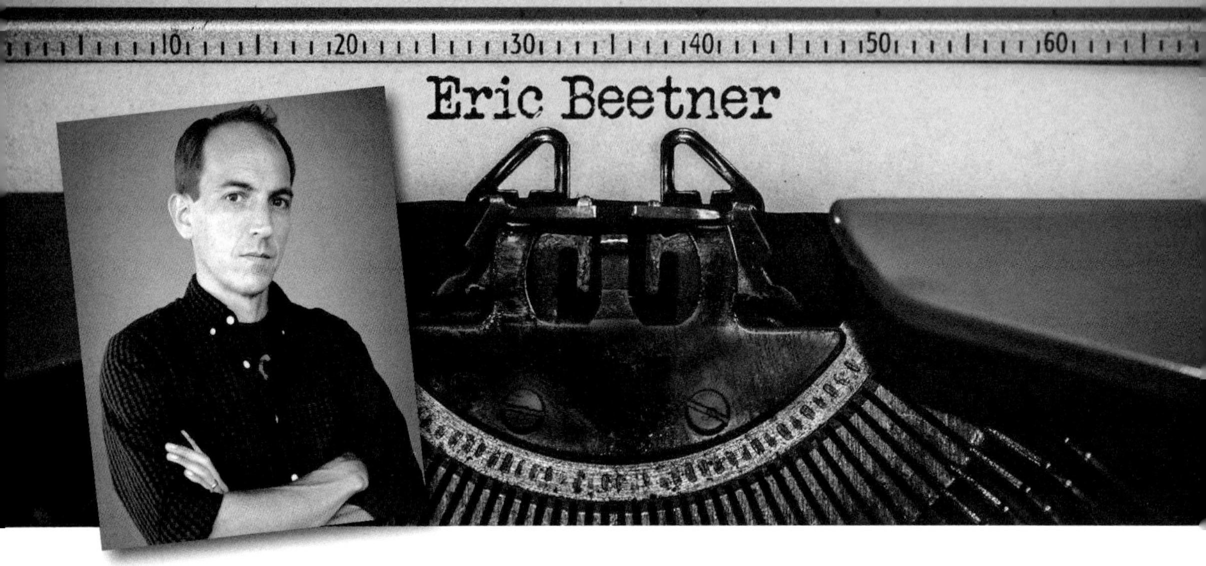

When talking noir fiction, it's best to engage with someone who knows his stuff—and I could think of no one better than Bill Crider. An Anthony Award-winning author of over 50 mysteries and Westerns, Bill earned his PhD writing a dissertation on hardboiled fiction. Also an avid book collector, Bill was the perfect person to sit a spell and discuss noir writers while the sun sank and darkness set upon us.

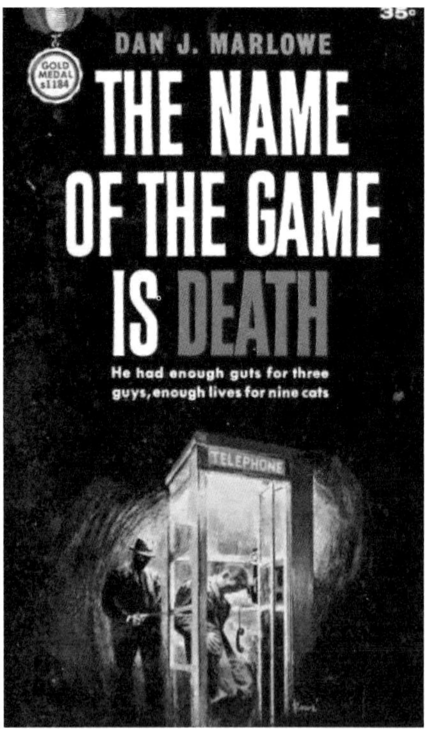

Eric Beetner: *I know you are a big fan of Gold Medal paperbacks which published a certain type of hardboiled and noir fiction starting in 1950. While that is well past the inception of noir fiction, what is it that appealed to you about stories that pushed the crime, and often the criminals, front and center, frequently skipping the whole "crime does not pay" ending where justice prevails?*

Bill Crider: The Gold Medal books that got me hooked on the line weren't noir. I was reading the Matt Helm series, Philip Atlee's earliest Joe Gall books, and John D. MacDonald. The style was terse and colloquial. The books were short, most of them around 144 pages. Just what I liked.

So I started looking around for used copies of other Gold Medals and also buying the new ones as they came out. This is what resulted in my finding some great noir fiction, like Dan J. Marlowe's *The Name of the Game is Death* and *The Vengeance Man*. Then one day, I plucked Jim Thompson's *The Killer Inside Me* off the spinner rack. What a great discovery *that* was, just what you mentioned—crime and criminals front and center. Eventually, I stumbled across *Black Wings Has My Angel*, another one that really knocked me out. It should be said, though, that in most of these the outsider, the criminal, doesn't get away with it. The punishment isn't the conventional kind, but it's just as bad, if not worse.

Why did these books appeal to me? I guess because I could see that the real world didn't always work out the way it did in most mystery novels, with order restored and things back the way they were before the murder or crimes occurred. In these books, the world is pretty much changed; nobody's life is going to be safe and sane again after the protagonists of these books have touched them. That seemed real to me.

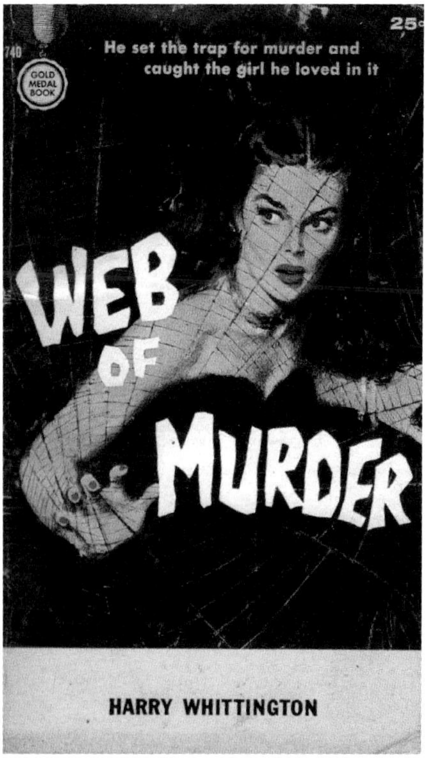

EB: *I think you got to the heart of noir there—characters punished by something other than the justice system. Quite often by their own hubris in thinking they could get away with whatever crime they were attempting. Caught in a web of their own making and many times not making it out alive. It's a twist on crime doesn't pay, I suppose, but in more traditional mysteries a cop or Sherlock Holmes brings the culprit to justice by arresting them. Like you say, order is restored. Does that make us pessimists or curmudgeons for liking a story where the world is exposed as a cynical place?*

BC: I should say that I like having order restored, and I write books in which that (nearly) always happens, but I don't think the world works that way all the time. We could probably give examples of times when things didn't work out well for all concerned, or even for anybody concerned, and when there was really nothing anybody could do to set everything right. I don't think that makes us cynical or pessimistic, just realistic. Or maybe we're just curmudgeons!

In my definition of noir, the characters bring their problems on themselves, and often get just what they deserve. It's a form of justice, just not the traditional kind approved by society. I like your use of the phrase *web of their own making* because one of my favorite Harry Whittington noirs is *Web of Murder*, in which there's certainly a form of justice, though nothing is set right, and the last line of the book is a killer.

EB: *Okay, I just had to go to my shelf and check out that last line of* Web of Murder *and yes, that is a doozy. Whittington is a writer who is highly regarded among pulp aficionados, but somehow didn't get the Hollywood treatment like so many of his contemporaries, which surprises me.* Web of Murder *got one tepid TV adaptation in the 1990s and a select few of his Westerns were adapted for film and TV, but given his output of more than 200 novels, his lack of success in Hollywood is shocking.*

Do you see any reason why his particular brand of noir wasn't put on film the way someone like William

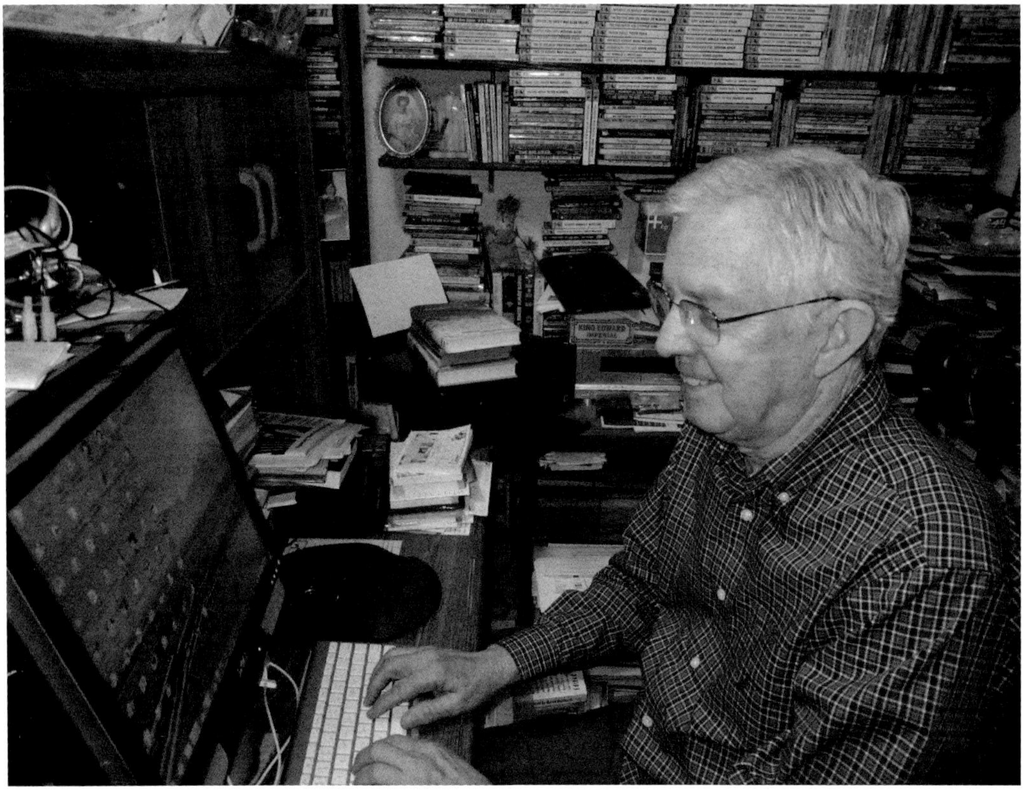

Bill Crider at home, in the confines of his historicially hardboiled lair

*P. McGivern (*The Big Heat, Shield for Murder, Odds Against Tomorrow*) or W. R. Burnett (*Little Caesar, The Asphalt Jungle*) or James M. Cain (*Double Indemnity, The Postman Always Rings Twice*) was?*

BC: Whittington deserved better from Hollywood, for sure. He had a bad experience with a movie he wrote and produced, *Face of the Phantom*. I'd like to know the story of that one. I've never seen it, and I don't know anyone who has. Success in Hollywood has a lot to do with luck, I think, and Whittington just didn't have it. The writers you mention had more mainstream success with their books than Whittington did, too, and they had more prestigious publishers, which helps. Writing for Gold Medal paid well, but it wasn't like writing for Knopf.

EB: Given that noir fiction can really be said to have started in the late '20s with Hammett, Burnett and others—I'm thinking of something like Criss-Cross *by Don Tracy which is fabulously noirish and much more rough and tough than I expected of a novel from the '30s—it took Hollywood a while to catch up.* The Maltese Falcon *we all think of, directed by John Huston and starring Humphrey Bogart, was not the first adaptation, but the "noir" treatment of it didn't hit until the 1940s. By the late '40s and '50s, do you see fiction as being dominated by hardboiled? Film noir really flourished during the mid-to-late '40s and by the time someone like Spillane rolled in, Hollywood seemed much quicker to respond to his type of hardboiled fiction.*

But then there are still some outliers like Jim Thompson and Charles Williams, two of my favorites, who had to wait decades for their novels to get picked up by Hollywood in any meaningful way.

BC: I agree with you about *Criss-Cross*. I haven't seen the movie version, but it has a good cast.

The crime fiction that I like from the late '40s through the early '60s is dominated by hardboiled, but I'm not sure that's generally the case. I do know that radio ran a full slate of hardboiled, or at least semi-boiled, detective shows in the late '40s and early '50s, with *Sam Spade* and *Philip Marlowe* being two of them. And radio was running plenty of full-on noir shows, too, like *The Whistler*, *The Mysterious Traveller*, *Inner Sanctum*, and on and on.

A good many neo-noir films have come along in the decades after the '50s, too. I'm surprised that no one picked up on Charles Williams and Jim Thompson sooner. Those two were top-of-the-heap noir guys.

EB: *I'll let it pass that you haven't seen the film version of* Criss Cross (1949)*—except to say that you should [see it] immediately. It's a true classic. I wasn't such a fan of Steven Soderberg's remake,* The Underneath *(1995), so if anyone is going to seek out one adaptation of Tracy's novel, I'd say stick with Burt Lancaster. Good advice in life, really. When in doubt, go with Burt Lancaster.*

It seems like once the books were in the reading public, noir fiction was here to stay and still enjoys a robust slate of writers carrying on the tradition today. What do you see as the biggest differences in today's noir and hardboiled versus the Gold Medal period?

BC: I agree about Burt Lancaster, and I know I should see the movie ... One of these days. This is just me, but I think the noir fiction of the early years was mostly written by blue-collar guys, for blue-collar guys. Not that there aren't obvious exceptions. Later on, a lot of white-collar guys discovered the books, and some of them started writing books like the ones they admired. So there's a difference in tone. Remember, this is just me. I don't know of anybody else who thinks this or who has said it. I also don't think the themes are quite the same. Often in the neo-noir books, the characters survive and there's no real justice for them. There are plenty of exceptions, so maybe I'd better not try to carry this too far. I'll bet you'll have some readers with vigorous opinions about this.

EB: *Many of my favorite neo-noir novels feel like they could be throwbacks, maybe not to '30s noir, but the '40s or '50s, for sure. Books like* The Cleanup *by Sean Doolittle is a version of the innocent man who lets his obsession with a woman lead him down an immoral path.* The Cold Kiss *by John Rector is a classic found-money/money corrupts story.* No Tomorrow *by Jake Hinkson explores how far someone will compromise their morals for love. It's another tale with no real good guys or girls.*

Any of those themes could, and were, explored in classic noir fiction. I love the "found a bag of money" story and I wonder when the first example of that occurred? Too Late for Tears *(1949) is the earliest I recall, but I'm sure it probably popped up before that.*

You've mentioned some great titles, what would be on your list of essential noir novels?

BC: I've read a couple of those books you mentioned, and they're very good. I like *The Ice Harvest* a lot. I like the "I've found a bag of money" books, too, but have no idea what the first one was.

When it comes to my favorite noir books, I'm pretty much a classicist. *The Postman Always Rings Twice* and *Double Indemnity* are right there at the top of the list. The Gold Medal titles I mentioned are up there, too. Several Jim Thompson novels are favorites: *Pop. 1280, The Getaway, Savage Night.* It's a long list. I mentioned Charles Williams, and you can't go wrong with him. So many books, so little time.

EB: *Yeah, Charles Williams'* Hell Hath No Fury *(filmed as* The Hot Spot *in 1990) is one of my favorites; I think that needs to be on any Top 10 list.*

BC: Charles Williams is so good that I've never understood why he's not as well known as a lot of lesser writers are. He could flat-out write, and *Hell Hath No Fury* should be known as a classic.

EB: *To close out, I'll ask my favorite noir-head question: The ending of* Double Indemnity *is different in the book and film. I'm assuming the NOIR CITY crowd is one we can't spoil on this one, since everyone has seen the film and, hopefully, has read the book—if not, rectify that immediately (and skip this question): Which do you think is more tragically noir: them murdering each other in the film or them running off together in the book, but knowing they can never trust each other?*

BC: I prefer the ending of the book to the movie version. That may be because I read the novel first, or it may be because the ending of the book is so great. I think it's pretty clear what's going to become of Walter and Phyllis. They're going to get what they deserve, but it's the way it's told that knocks me out. Powerful stuff. Just thinking about it makes me want to read the book again. Not that the ending of the movie is weak, but the one in the novel *really* gets me. ■

In Conversation with Sarah Weinman

Sarah Weinman knows her noir. Specifically, she has championed the female writers of noir and mystery fiction from the golden age until now in the books she has edited: *Troubled Daughters, Twisted Wives: Stories from the Trailblazers of Domestic Suspense* and the two-volume set *Women Crime Writers of the 1940s and 1950s*. We sat down to talk *noir* and ended up adding a whole lot of titles to my must-read list.

Eric: *I know entire books have been written about this, but is there a short answer to why readers are so fascinated with the* femme fatale*? If there is one character in all of noir that is the most popular, certainly it has to be the evil spider-woman who lacks any moral compass and is driven by greed or lust.*

Sarah: The short answer is in the phrase itself—"death woman," literally translated, but essentially, the woman who brings about doom and the man knows this and goes along with it anyway. Like a compulsion. Of course, it's also about fantasy, and mythmaking, and the *femme* isn't much of a human being. Which is why the contemporaneous noir novels by women remain so fascinating to me because of how they try to assert humanity, and autonomy, to that archetype. Look at Laura Hunt (from the novel-turned-film *Laura* by Vera Caspary): the way Caspary writes her, she's a career woman who resists all attempts by the men in her life—Lydecker, McPherson, Carpenter—to be whom they want her to be. She can only be who *she* wants herself to be. It's different in the movie because Preminger willfully changed things, but the embers are still there.

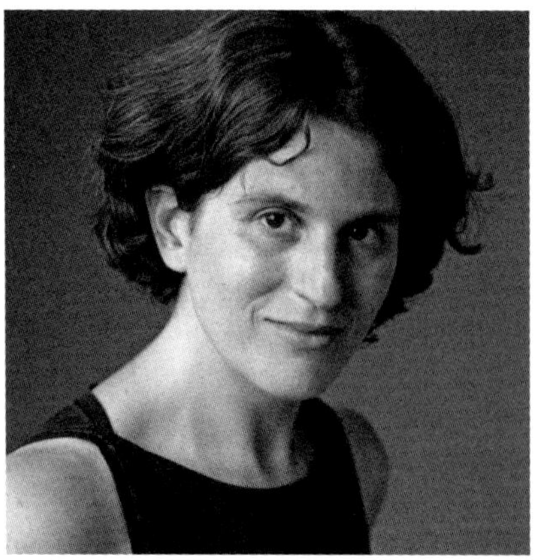

What would be your answer to the question, and who do you think best subverted this trope once it was established?

Eric: *I think it stems in part from losing or lacking control of something the men thought they were in control of. Given that the classic period of novels were written at a time when men could reasonably count on the women in their lives being subservient, when one defied that expectation it comes as a disruption of the world in the same way as a cop going crooked does. It is antithetical to the established system.*

As much as I love the classics like Phyllis Dietrichson from Double Indemnity *or Cora Smith from* The Postman

Always Rings Twice, I do love it when a female character starts in the subservient role and then breaks out of that. Something like Too Late for Tears *where Jane breaks out of her housewife role in spectacular fashion. Or even* Sudden Fear, *adapted from a novel written by Edna Sherry, where Myra Hudson, played by Joan Crawford, discovers her lover is up to no good so she turns the tables on him. She doesn't start out as a manipulator, but she doesn't roll over in the face of deception from her man, either.*

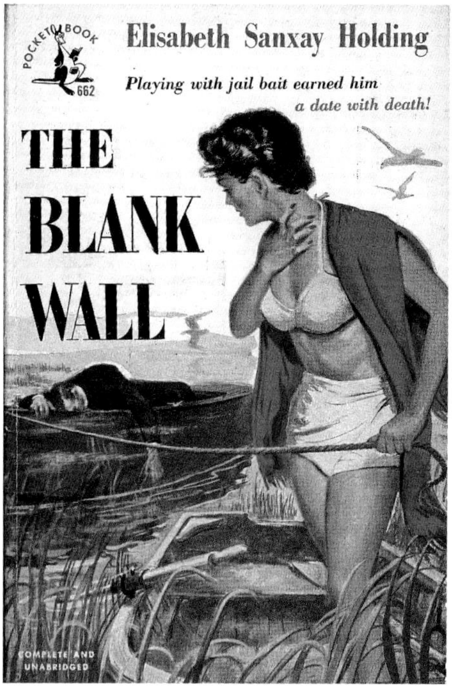

Sarah: I need to read that Edna Sherry story! Or Sherry in general. I know she is on a par with Elisabeth Sanxay Holding, whose novel *The Blank Wall* (made as *The Reckless Moment*) is so key to domestic suspense and female-driven noir stories. Lucia Holley is stuck between generations and roles and the very idea of covering up for her daughter, who may well have murdered someone, forces her to be someone she never thought she would be and do things she never thought she would do.

Eric: *Are there male authors in that classic noir period who you think gave their female characters their three-dimensional due, or was it predominantly a sexist time and there was no getting around that?*

Sarah: In terms of the male authors of that period, sexism was a key thing, for sure. Or a general lack of awareness—from a personal or a commercial standpoint—that there was any other way to depict women than as a trope, defined in relation to a man, that sort of thing. Or maybe when the doom is shared more or less equally, thinking of Horace McCoy's *They Shoot Horses, Don't They?*, it rings more true from a character standpoint.

Let's talk about setting and sense of place. I feel like my own favorite crime novel, *In a Lonely Place*, is so strong on post-World War II Los Angeles. Which noir novels really evoke that for you?

Eric: *Immediately my mind went to a rural setting.* They Don't Dance Much *by James Ross was recommended to me by Joe R. Lansdale and he knows his rural settings. Jim Thompson really nailed small-town noir. A contemporary author who I love for his sense of place is Jake Hinkson. His country noir is very retro—many of his novels are set in the '40s and '50s—and all couldn't be set anywhere else but in the country.*

Most people think of the urban jungle when they think of noir, but when you really drill down it's not dominated by city settings at all. Think of the noir on the high seas of Charles Williams in books like Dead Calm, Aground, *and* Scorpion Reef.

Do you have a preference for your noir in the city or in the suburbs?

Sarah: I don't have a preference. But we can't possibly talk about rural noir without bringing up Daniel Woodrell, who would fill me with envy if I didn't revere his writing and evocation of the Ozarks so damn much. *Tomato Red, The Death of Sweet Mister*—I mean those are stone masterpieces. Also Vicki Hendricks, who took the bones of *Postman* and made it all her own in *Miami Purity*, which is a blackened love letter to the entire state.

There is something about suburban ennui, though. Megan Abbott obviously gets to this very well.

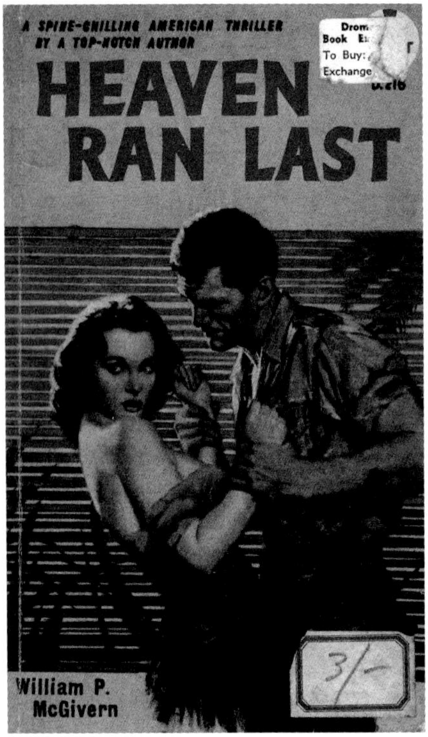

And way back, so did Dolores Hitchens. A reason her *Fools' Gold* holds up so well is that it is as much about the plot and the sense of doom of these godforsaken kids as it is about the suburban California malaise they are trying, and failing, to get away from. Whether Hitchens intended the *Rebel Without a Cause* vibe is still not clear, but I like to think she did.

Eric: *Yes, Vicki Hendricks nails it. I've not read Hitchen's* Fools' Gold. *I'll need to check that one out.*

Sarah: How about this meaty point of discussion, then: noir is a subgenre that, in the wrong hands, can go spectacularly awry. What is it, in your view, that attracts people to writing it, and what should they understand that sometimes is missing?

Eric: *If I let myself, I can be quite a purist, so I think too many people label fiction as noir when it lacks so many elements. I think people get drawn to the darkness of a story and pushing the criminals forward, but that can end in bleakness and a lack of an emotional center for a story. If it starts down in the gutter then there is no place to fall.*

The best noir makes you think, "What would I do?" It doesn't matter what the situation is or how far out of your world experience it is. If it makes you wonder how you would react in those situations, then it is an involving story.

Whether it's being asked to kill someone's husband to get the girl, or if it's how fully I understood the mind of a 13-year-old girl in Megan Abbott's The End of Everything, *putting myself in the story is key.*

And to have a central character that is flawed, but not amoral. For the same reason, I don't find much to like in serial killer fiction because psychopaths don't make me feel anything; when writers go full dark for the sake of being "edgy" or "hardboiled", then it loses me.

Ordinary guys and gals in novels from Sean Doolittle, Jason Starr, Laura McHugh, Urban Waite, John Rector, and many more are what draw me in.

What did you think? Are too many writers reaching for noir and only hitting dark crime fiction with no emotional center or are they afraid of rehashing tired storylines?

Sarah: I love how you describe noir, which is also how I would describe domestic suspense. I think they are twinned subgenres, it is a matter of whether one hurtles headlong into doom (noir) or overcomes in some way that also alters you permanently (domestic suspense). And I think the sense of being grounded in reality as things go very, very bad is what makes noir work so well, but also why it is altogether easy to cross the line into a place where the reader doesn't care anymore. Serial killer novels are kind of camp. Real serial killers are terrifying because they are so boring and random in their surface.

I think part of what vexes me about what I would call "bad thrillers" whether they are noir or not, is the sense of whether I care about whom I'm reading. If the plot takes me away from actual emotion, then I don't care and my disbelief takes over. But when I do care—and boy, do I with most of the writers you mention, also Christa Faust, Dreda Say Mitchell, Sara Gran, Cathi Unsworth, to add some more names—I am with them all the way.

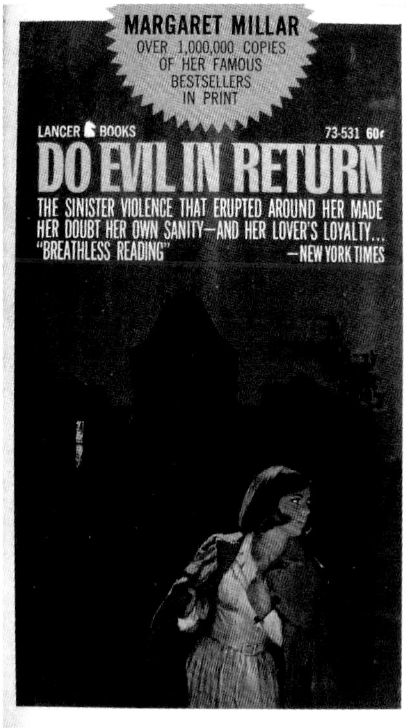

Eric: *Okay, to wrap up—what are your hidden gems of noir fiction that more people should know about?*

I think William P. McGivern's Heaven Ran Last *is as good as any James M. Cain. Also Margaret Millar's* Do Evil In Return *is a lost noir masterpiece dying for rediscovery.*

Sarah: I am happy to report that Margaret Millar is less of a hidden gem then she used to be, and I hope this persists and grows because she is amazing. I'd like to see more attention to Dolores Hitchens beyond *Fools' Gold* (*Sleep with Slander* is such a great PI novel, *The Watcher* is a strong suspense thriller, etc.) My current vote is for *Death of an Intruder* by Nedra Tyre, a passive aggressive war of wills between two aging, lonely, single women. You know one of them is going to lose, the question is how badly she is doomed. Tyre was a Southern writer with a nasty streak who also managed to be warm. Her short stories are even more amazing.

And more recently, one of my favorite writers who is almost never discussed in a noir context is Eoin McNamee; from *Resurrection Man* onward, but especially *The Blue Tango*—the mood, the rendering of Ireland then and now, it's all excellent. ■

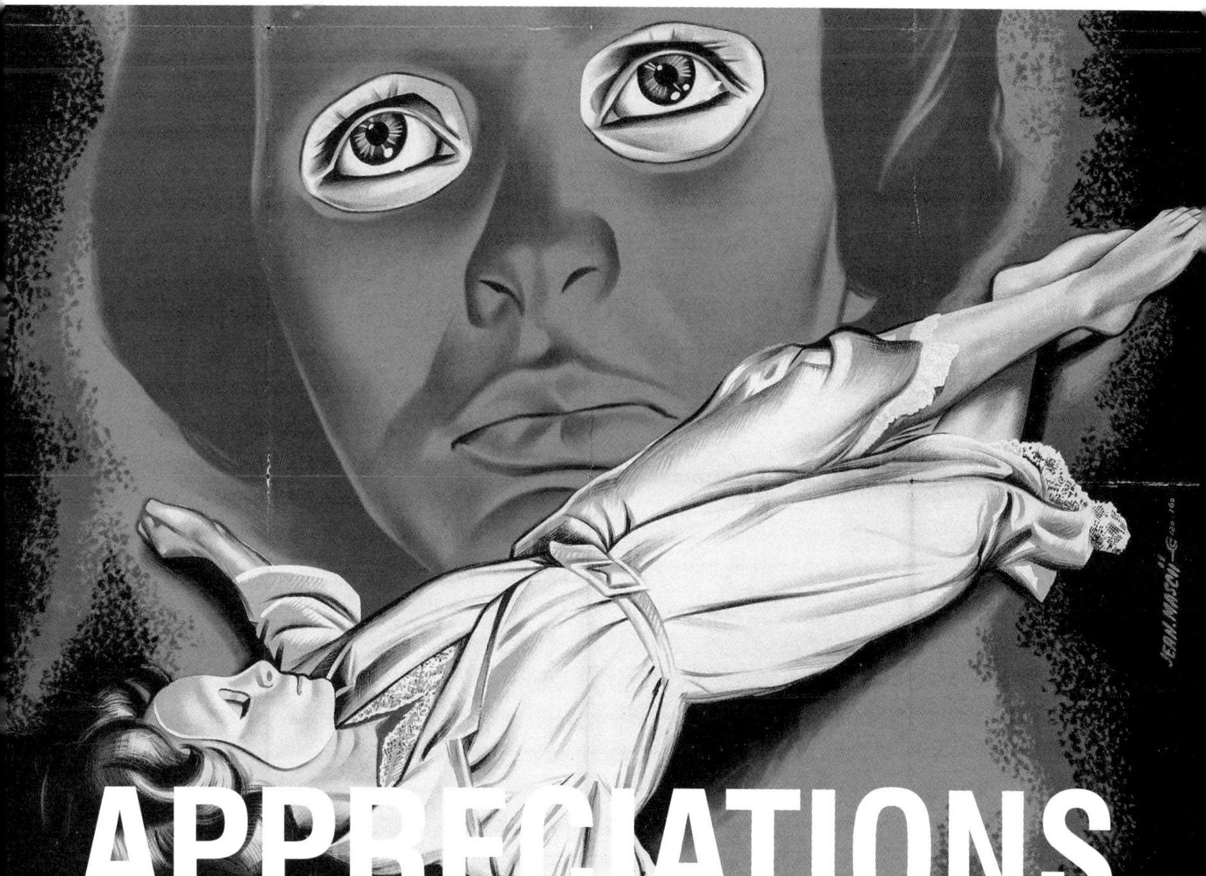

APPRECIATIONS

SECTION FOUR

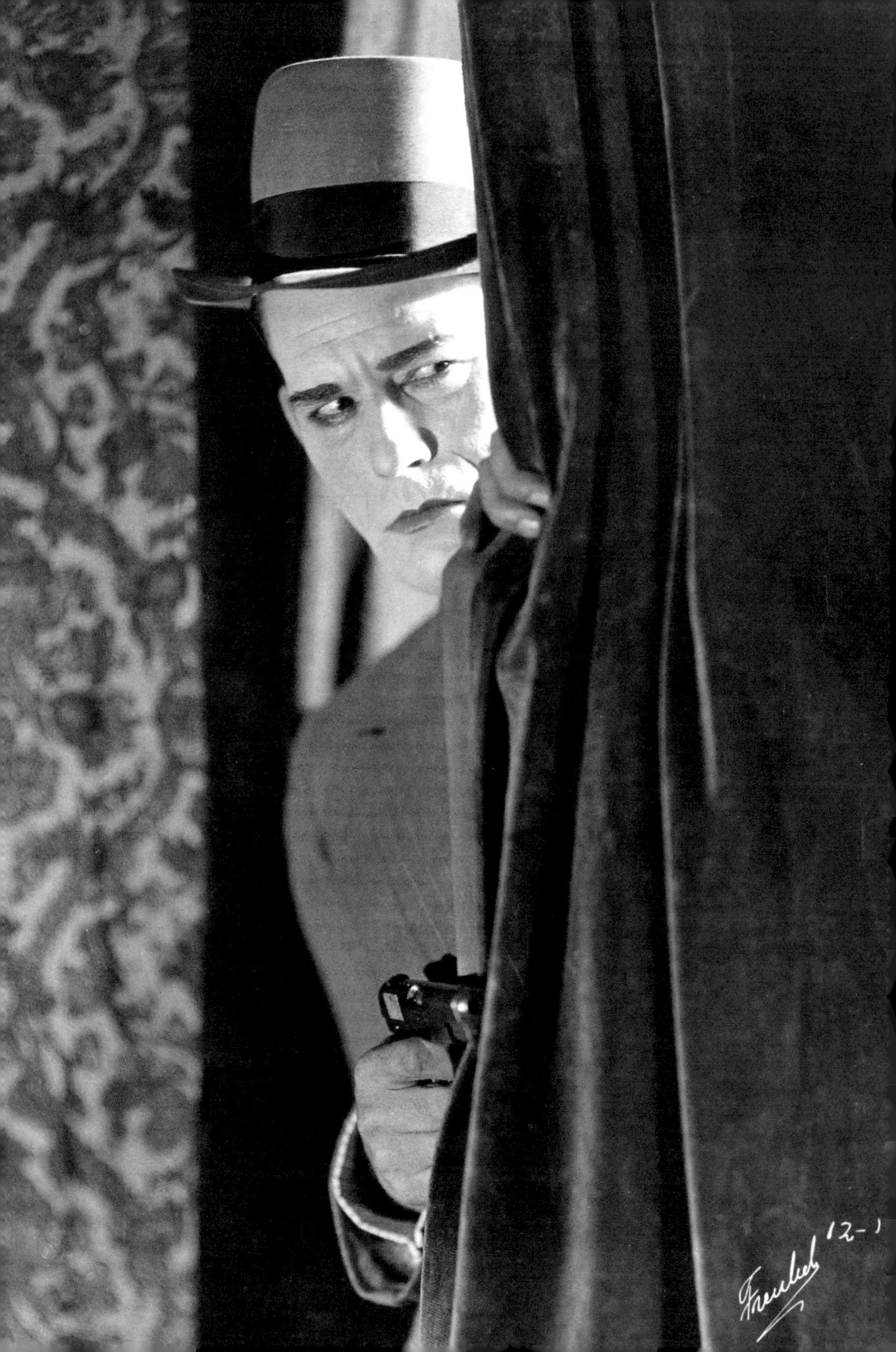
12-1

SILENT NOIR

Outside the Law (1920)

Eddie Muller

Outside the Law stars the legendary "Phantom of the Opera" and is written and directed by the creator of *Dracula* and *Freaks*—but don't expect a horror film.

This movie has more in common with the pioneering crime fiction of Dashiell Hammett, who'd become synonymous with stories set in the San Francisco underworld—which is the *demimonde* director Tod Browning brings to vivid life in this 1920 drama released two years before Hammett's first short story was published. In fact, so many elements of *Outside the Law* later appear in Hammett's "Continental Op" stories, I wonder if the one-time Pinkerton detective didn't see Browning's film at a local San Francisco movie house.

Oddly, the only thing missing from *Outside the Law* is a detective. And some competent cops. One of the most striking aspects of this film is, in fact, its lawlessness. Vestiges of the infamous Barbary Coast remain in streets and alleyways rife with Irish gangsters and prowling tongs. The local cops are gullible pawns in a scheme by Black Mike Sylva (Lon Chaney) to railroad gang boss Silent Madden (Ralph Lewis) into jail, so Mike will get a crack at becoming the town's new vice lord. Browning

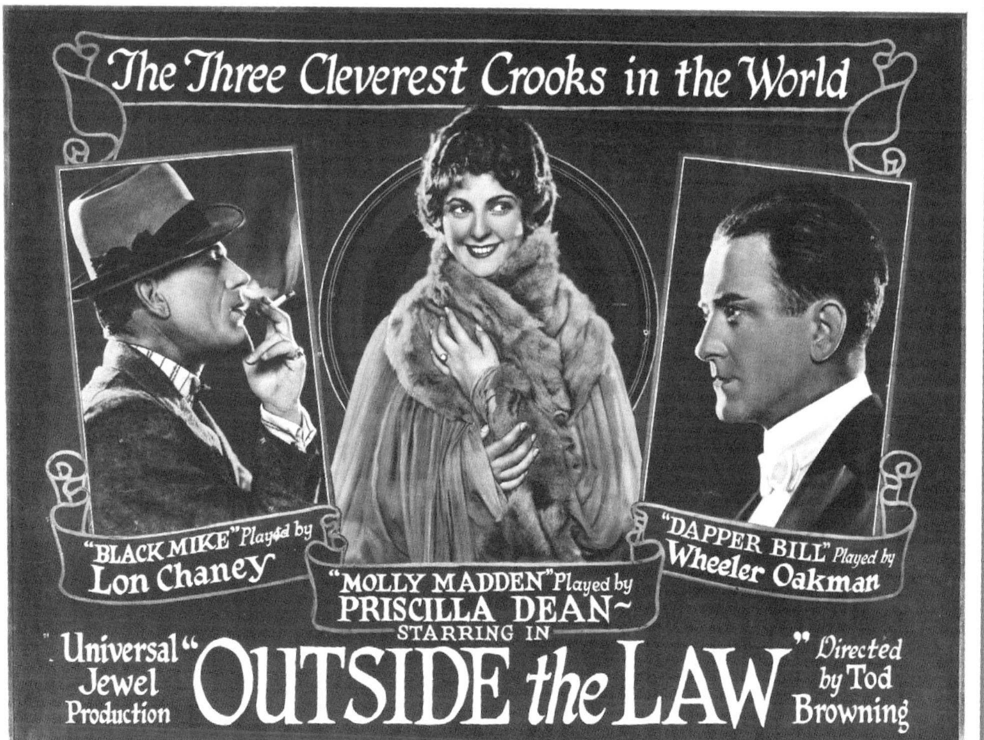

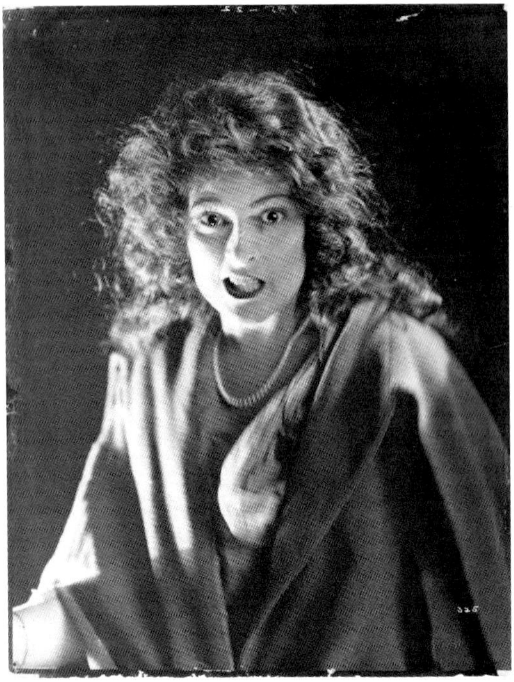

Fierceness was a major part of Priscilla Dean's on-screen persona in Westerns, adventure yarns, and crime sagas

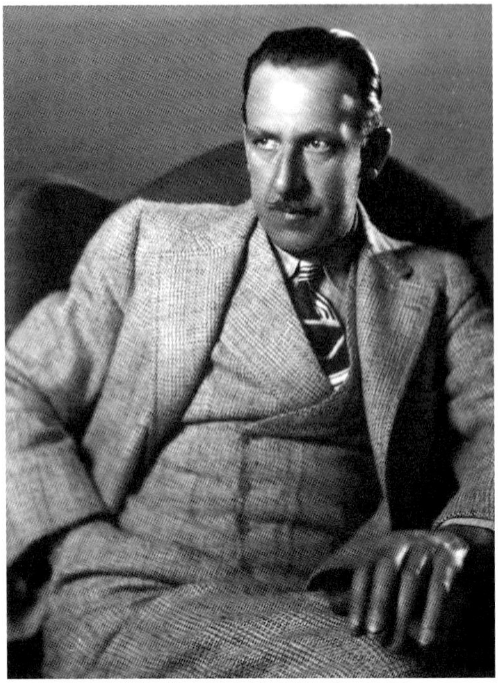

Before horror, crime was Tod Browning's specialty

renders this nefarious terrain with the pungent exotica that was his specialty, from the sawdust-strewn saloons, to the mysterious maze-like corridors of Chinatown, to the opulence of a Pacific Heights society gala.

But this isn't just standard underworld stuff. Browning has a few surprises up his sleeve. Before you cringe at white actors playing all the main Asian roles[1] (Chaney's makeup as the omniscient "Ah Wing" is, of course, monstrously grotesque), consider that the story posits the Chinese as the stabilizing force in this wide-open seaport town. It's the sagacious Chang Lo (E. Alyn Warren, white as rice) who convinces Silent Madden to cease his criminal ways and go straight; it's Chang Lo from whom the police seek inside "dope" and guidance; it's Ah Wing who susses out the motives of the crazy white men.

Most surprising of all, however, is that the story revolves around Madden's daughter, Molly—known in the underworld as "Silky Moll." As portrayed by Priscilla Dean, Moll is the feisty flipside to silent cinema's many shrinking violets. She may swan around in a bustle skirt and favor flamboyantly feathered hats, but nothing shows off Moll to better advantage than a gun gripped in her fist. Once her father gets sent up, she scuttles all talk of reform and leaps at a plan to steal jewels from some high-society swells. Her partner in this daring caper, Dapper Bill Ballard (Wheeler Oakman), has one-tenth her tenacity—and once they're on the lam, Moll proves herself the brains *and* the brawn of this chaste (chased?) pair. Moll's disdain toward Bill's attempts at intimacy is even more amusing when you know Dean and Oakman were married in real life, a union that only lasted the few years they were atop the movie business. At times, Oakman flashes the buoyant charm of Jimmy Cagney, minus the piss-and-vinegar panache. By the late '30s, however, the once debonair actor was dissipated, reduced to playing lechers in "Adults Only" sleaze like *Gambling with Souls* (1936), *Slaves in Bondage* (1937) and *Escort Girl* (1941).

Hiding out in a "Knob" Hill walk-up (a glaring goof by title writer Gardner Bradford), Bill fights off cabin fever while Moll staves off Bill's growing ardor. A scene-stealing little boy (Stanley Goethals, credited merely as "That Kid") makes a habit of barging into the apartment and trying, with all his mini-might, to melt Moll's hardened heart. Dean plays it so frostily you expect her to pitch him out a second-story window.

1 Only the women are allowed to actually be Chinese; look for an all-too-brief appearance by 15-year-old Anna May Wong.

For modern viewers, the most shocking (and suspenseful) aspect of *Outside the Law* may be the uproariously unsafe ways "that kid" amuses himself—with axes and loaded guns. Interestingly, all this cutesy domestic stuff was retained in Browning's 1931 sound version of *Outside the Law*, in which Mary Nolan took the Moll role, and Edward G. Robinson—warming up for *Little Caesar*—filled Lon Chaney's shoes. In 1946, Universal realized it still owned Browning's original story, and remade it again as *Inside Job*, a goofy B-movie that again got good mileage from the pesky punk across the hall.

So what of Lon Chaney? As Black Mike, he's a sinister presence, but the role is tame compared to the physically deformed and psychically scarred characters that would soon make him a legend. By some accounts, there was more of Chaney as Ah Wing in the film's initial release, but much of the Chinatown subplot was cut prior to the film's 1926 reissue. This later version is the only one that remains, thanks to it being discovered in a Minnesota barn in the 1970s, left there sometime in the 1920s by a traveling roadshowman. Sections of the film, even after restoration, were degraded beyond repair; fortunately, these patches occur when it's easy to imagine the characters being licked by the flames of eternal damnation, not just nitrate decomposition.

Priscilla Dean is virtually forgotten today, which is shameful—she was a feminist icon before such a label ever existed. After appearing in a slew of one-reel comedies in her teens, she broke out in 1917 as "Morn Light," a comic opera star battling male villains in the 16-chapter crime serial *The Gray Ghost* (now lost). She starred the same year in the extraordinary Lois Weber-directed *The Hand That Rocks the Cradle*, a pro-birth control tale in which she played Mrs. Graham, "a young wife whose frail strength is overtaxed by a repetition of motherhood." Dean, it seems, took the film's message to heart; she never had children.

The actress developed her mature screen persona for Universal-Jewel, the studio's premier production unit. In the late 'teens, Dean radiated from American screens as a beautiful, formidable, and undomesticated woman who proved herself equal, if not superior, to men. She would ride, shoot, and even brawl with her male co-stars. Studio publicity mavens bolstered her indomitable image by dutifully reporting that the actress performed all her own stunts. Grace Kingsley, film editor of the *Los Angeles Times*, called Dean "The wild girl of the films, 1920 model," and more than one reviewer noted her propensity for portraying "dominating females." The public loved the power she wielded on-screen; especially the skeptical sneer that became the actress' trademark, alerting audiences that there soon would be hell to pay and Miss Dean would be cashing the checks.

Kiss or Kill (1917), *The Wildcat of Paris* (1918), *The Silk-Lined Burglar* (1919), *Pretty Smooth* (1919) were all Priscilla Dean crime pictures, but it was her flinty performances for Tod Browning that earned her the title "The Queen of Crookdom." Between 1918 and 1923, they made nine pictures together: *The Brazen Beauty* (1918), *Which Woman?* (1918), *The Wicked Darling* (1919), *The Exquisite Thief* (1919), *Outside the Law* (1920), *The Virgin of Stamboul* (1920), *Under Two Flags* (1922), *White Tiger* (1923), and *Drifting* (1923).

In all these films, Dean demonstrated what contemporary critics call "female agency." Her talent agency had great savvy, as well: with the expiration of her Universal contract in 1924, Dean became the prize in a bidding war between the major studios. Eventually signing an exclusive pact with producer Hunt Stromberg worth $3,000,000, she'd never work with Tod Browning again. He'd find his next muse in the twisted and maniacal persona of Lon Chaney, with whom he'd make the string of perverse and memorable melodramas for which they are both remembered.

But this is Priscilla Dean's picture, and what a pleasure it is to see her back on a movie screen. One hopes that her other films will be rediscovered and that her underappreciated role in Hollywood history will be redeemed. ■

This essay originally appeared in the program of the 2017 San Francisco Silent Film Festival, and is reprinted here with the festival's permission.

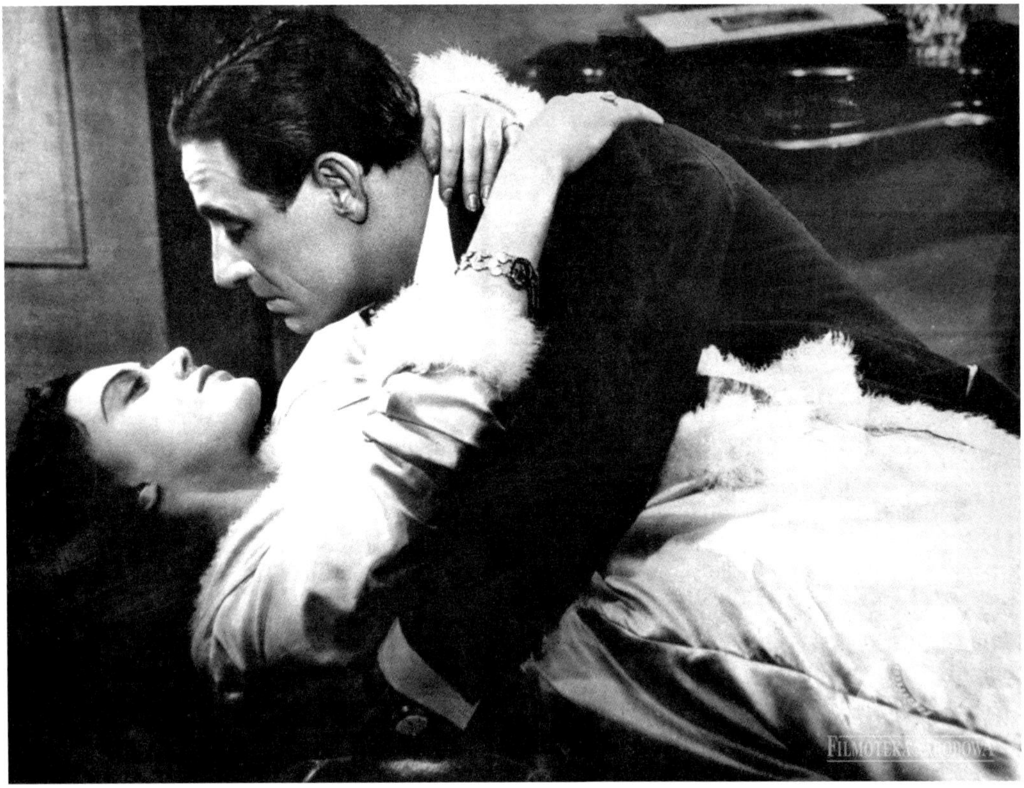

Grigorij Chmara and Maria Majdrowicz in a scene steamier than anything coming out of Hollywood in 1929

in the 1930s with actress Lila Kedrova; and made his final appearance in a French TV adaptation of *Crime and Punishment* in 1970, the year he died. He has the fierce gaze of a bird of prey and the furrowed brow of a habitual malcontent.

The first time Bielecki smiles in the film is when, with calculating malice, he tells his tubercular friend Górski (Artur Socha) that his just-finished novel is "mediocre," driving the poor man to suicidal despair. The sordid scenes of his morphine overdose and Bielecki's subsequent theft of the manuscript are submerged in grubby-looking, noirish shadows, complete with an electric sign blinking fitfully outside the window. We never know much about the stolen novel, though its title—*A Strong Man*—invokes Nietzsche's übermensch, a concept obviously appealing to the arrogant, self-absorbed Bielecki, who feels entitled to grab whatever he wants and eliminate anyone who gets in his way—even by means of murder. The individual set apart from society by his genius or his demons was a fixation of Przybyszewski, whose scandalous writings, filled with lurid decadence and extreme psychological states, belonged to the innovative, modernist Young Poland movement that flourished around the turn of the 20th century.

Introducing a screening of *A Strong Man* at the San Francisco Silent Film Festival in 2017, Film Noir Foundation president Eddie Muller pointed out intriguing parallels between the film's plot and the life of Przybyszewski, a womanizer who was accused (and acquitted) of murdering his common-law wife, and who worked for a time on the magazine *Zycie* for an editor named—like the author of the stolen manuscript—Artur Górski. This bleeding between truth and fiction adds to the film's argument that artistic creation is far murkier and less pure a process than we usually think. Unlike the talentless Bielecki, however, Przybyszewski was a prolific and influential thinker who became a champion of Poland's nationhood after World War I, and received a hero's burial when he died in 1927, two years before his novel was adapted by Henryk Szaro.

It is easy to imagine that the film's purloined book, which becomes a sensation, shares the provocative elements that made Przybyszewski's work so controversial; the one excerpt that makes its way into an intertitle suggests that the book's popularity is due to its titillating steaminess. Indeed, once Bielecki moves from brooding in smoky cafes to hobnobbing at the racetrack in a sea of summer hats, sex takes the place of ambition as the plot's driving force. Tired of his live-in lover, the loyal but sullenly reproachful Łucja (Agnes Kuck), Bielecki is instantly smitten with the sensual, dark-eyed Nina (Maria Majdrowicz), his friend's neglected wife.

With Nina's entrance, the film opens out from its cramped urban settings and takes on a more fluid, organic naturalism. A stroll to a ruined fortress in the country is thrillingly animated by wind that shakes the wheat fields and ripples through the leaves, snatches at Nina's scarf and flattens her diaphanous white skirt against her legs. The cinematography by Giovanni Vitrotti makes each image seem at once freighted with meaning and quivering with life. Like Chmara, Vitrotti exemplified the internationalism of silent cinema: starting in Italy, where he was known for his pioneering use of traveling shots, he worked on German films throughout the 1920s, including the 1924 Italian co-production *Quo Vadis?*, starring Emil Jannings. Vitrotti also shot movies in Russia and Poland.

A Strong Man shuttles between city and country, sometimes distilling familiar visions of the two and sometimes playing against expectations. The metropolis is a kaleidoscopic whirl of nightclub signs, champagne bottles, leggy chorus lines, and twitchy jazz bands—all the classic symbols of sin—but it is in the countryside that lust and violence break loose. In a memorable set piece, Bielecki takes Nina to a large, gloomy mansion where the furniture and chandeliers are swaddled in white dust-cloths, and an old, forbidding housekeeper comes to the door with a candelabra. Suddenly we are in the realm of gothic romance, presided over by a sinister, Munch-like painting of lovers that hangs above the fireplace. The torrid love scene accompanied by a raging thunderstorm must have been a cliché even then, but this instance is so superbly crafted that it feels fresh. A rapid, rhythmic montage of wind tearing at trees, clouds boiling, curtains billowing, and rain hammering the street is intercut with images of Bielecki feverishly kissing Nina's leg, their embrace lit by strobe-like spasms of lightning. A sharp cut reveals the abandoned Łucja sitting at home, waiting, with the pendulum of a clock slicing the foreground of the shot.

The last part of the film brilliantly uses such bold juxtapositions and counterpoint to illustrate the way everything falls apart for Bielecki. The betrayal of the woman who knows his secret and threatens to expose him crowns his self-destructive hubris. His final unraveling coincides with the premiere of a play adapted from the stolen novel. Szaro's theater background is evident in his richly detailed presentation of the backstage world. Early in his career, Szaro had studied in Moscow with the groundbreaking theater artist Vsevolod Meyerhold, whose influence is evident in the boldly experimental stage production, with its stylized makeup and costumes, constructivist sets, and masked dancers with faces on both sides of their heads. The successful premiere, which should be his ultimate triumph, is ruined for Bielecki, who can't take his eyes off a single empty seat in the audience. The contrast between the elaborate spectacle on stage and his anxious fixation on Nina's absence beautifully illustrates how false glamour crumbles at the touch of real feeling. Posters for the play multiply, its title taunting the man whose weakness is now laid bare.

The film's jagged, bitter depiction of a society that has lost its moral bearings feels even more consequential given the horrors that would consume this part of the world within the next decade. Vsevolod Meyerhold, a mentor to Sergei Eisenstein, would be tortured and killed in the Great Purge of 1940, his theater productions already suppressed by Stalin. Henryk Szaro, who was born Henoch Szapiro, would be interned and then killed in the Warsaw Ghetto in 1942. World War II decimated Polish cinema—the industry had been heavily Jewish—and *A Strong Man* was believed to be lost until a print turned up in the Royal Film Archive of Belgium in 1997. The rediscovery of this film, with its heat-lightning energy, emotional resonance, and Art Deco swank, resurrects a lost world. Its message, that in the end liars will unmask themselves, has not lost its relevance. ■

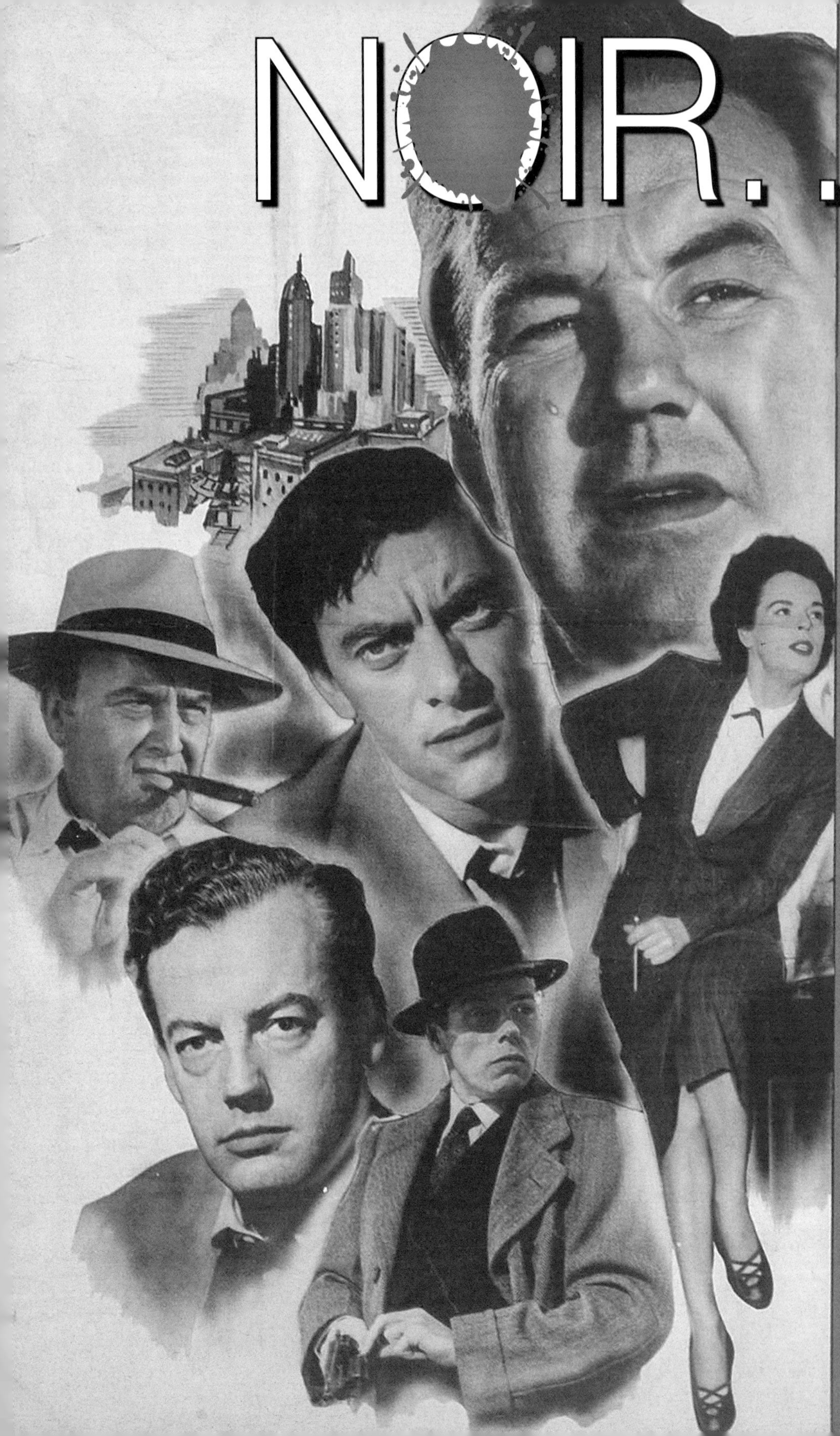
NOIR. .

OR NOT?

Jake Hinkson

ALL THE KING'S MEN

HOMEGROWN FASCISM

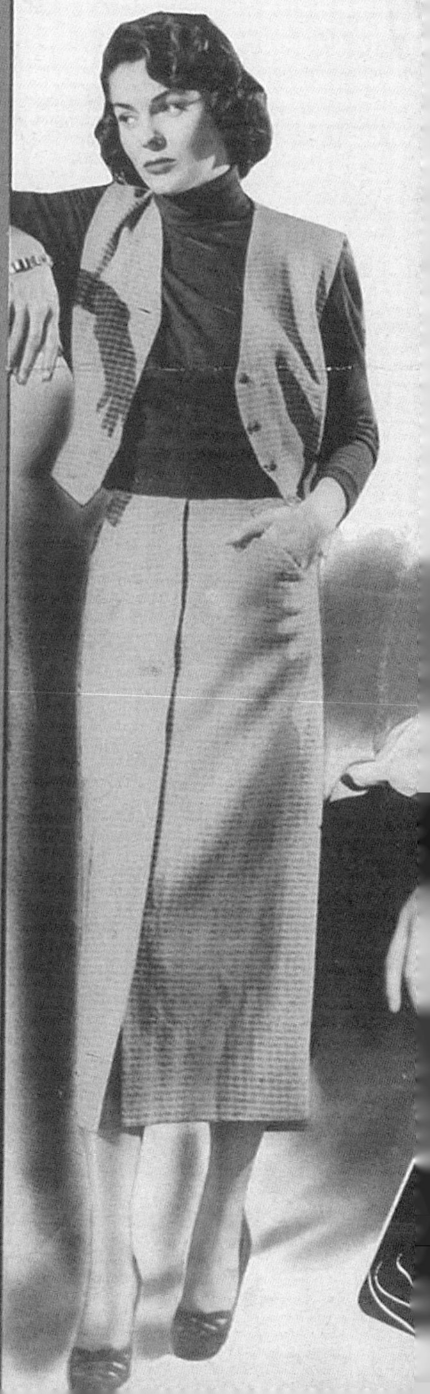

**There's no god but Willie Stark.
I'm his prophet."**

–Jack Burden, *All the King's Men*

At this point in history, Robert Penn Warren's novel *All the King's Men* might well be one of those classics more discussed than read. Although it won the Pulitzer Prize in 1947 and inspired two movie adaptations, Warren's book is a densely written epic, an attempt to tell a sprawling story in the lyrical, winding prose tradition of Faulkner. And yet, many people who have never read the book know, or think they know, its central story: the rise and fall of the political opportunist and burgeoning fascist Willie Stark, a figure patterned after Louisiana's notorious governor Huey Long. Never mind that the central character of the book is actually its narrator Jack Burden or that the central story of the book is his relationship with his childhood crush Anne Stanton. Time has a way of dictating what matters, even in great works of literature, and in the decades since the book's release the popular imagination has threshed the raw materials of *All the King's Men* and shaken loose the story of Willie Stark.

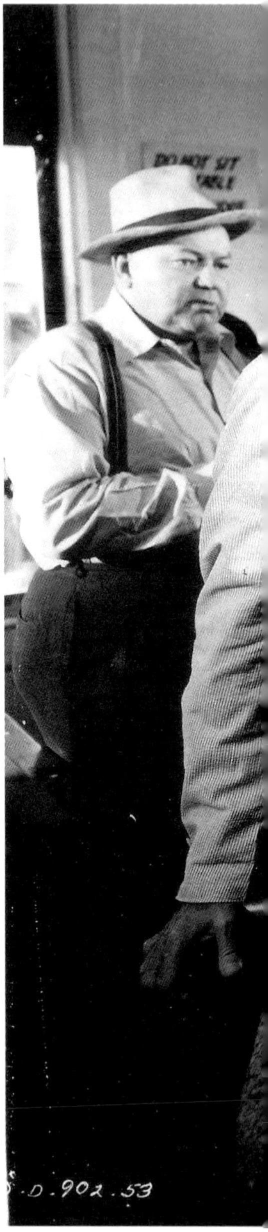

The main factor in this threshing was, of course, Robert Rossen's 1949 adaptation of the novel. When he made *All the King's Men*, Rossen was a politically conscious writer-director coming off two successful 1947 noirs, the entertaining *Johnny O'Clock* with Dick Powell and Evelyn Keyes, and (working from a script by Abraham Polonsky) the masterpiece *Body and Soul*. Rossen's crime film bona fides actually extended further back, however, to screenwriting credits on *Marked Woman* (1937), *The Roaring Twenties* (1939), and *The Strange Love of Martha Ivers* (1946), so perhaps it's not surprising that in adapting Warren's expansive novel, he zeroed in on the story of the corrupt Stark's rise and fall. The story of Jack Burden became the entry point to the film rather than the central point of the film itself.

The narrative reshaping of *All the King's Men* came about through consultations with Columbia, the studio producing the film, as Rossen hammered out the script in story conferences overseen by studio chief Harry Cohn. In post-production, Rossen and editor Al Clark further restructured the film, and the final edit, substantially different from Clark's, was assembled by an uncredited Robert Parrish. Cohn never loved the results. Even after the film's runaway success (it was Columbia's second highest grosser of 1949 and brought home three Oscars®), he said that he couldn't tell "who or what" the audience was supposed to be rooting for.

No one familiar with the dictatorial Cohn, an early and enthusiastic admirer of Benito Mussolini, could be shocked to discover that he missed the point of *All the King's Men*. In the end, Rossen hadn't shaped the story of an admirable hero or even a rakish antihero. He was telling the story of a homegrown American fascist.

Rossen's *All the King's Men* tells the tale of Willie Stark (Broderick Crawford) through the eyes of Jack Burden (John Ireland). When they meet, Burden is an old-money scion slumming as a reporter and Stark is a self-described "hick" running for office in the dry and dusty (and fictional) Kanoma County. Stark loses this first fight against the state's political machine, but Burden, inspired by Stark's fierce intelligence and flame-throwing honesty, begins writing articles casting him as a champion of the people. Jack follows Stark's rapid ascent up the political ladder every step of the way, becoming an advisor and foot solider, and even introducing the politician to his well-connected family friends, the Stantons. Judge Stanton (Raymond Greenleaf), the patriarch of the family, and his nephew Adam (Shepperd Strudwick) are both suspicious of Stark, but Adam's sister Anne (Joanne Dru) is immediately taken in by the rising political star. Burden, who is closer to the Stantons than his own dysfunctional family, is torn in his loyalties, a conflict complicated by the fact that he's been in love with Anne since they were children. The only person who seems to see both Stark and Burden with real clarity is Sadie Burke (Mercedes McCambridge), Stark's jaded campaign manager. Once Stark becomes governor, he begins accruing power at an alarming rate. His appetites, controlled at first, become ever more expansive. He drinks, and he chases women. He begins an affair with Anne that pushes Burden to the side. His main appetite, however, is for power, and soon it brings him into direct, and fatal, conflict with the Stantons.

Rossen's narrative focus on the story of Stark made *All the King's Men* a parable of power with unmistakable resonance in the postwar era. Warren didn't care for the changes, telling author William Kennedy in 1973, "About two-thirds through [Rossen] left my character entirely and made a total

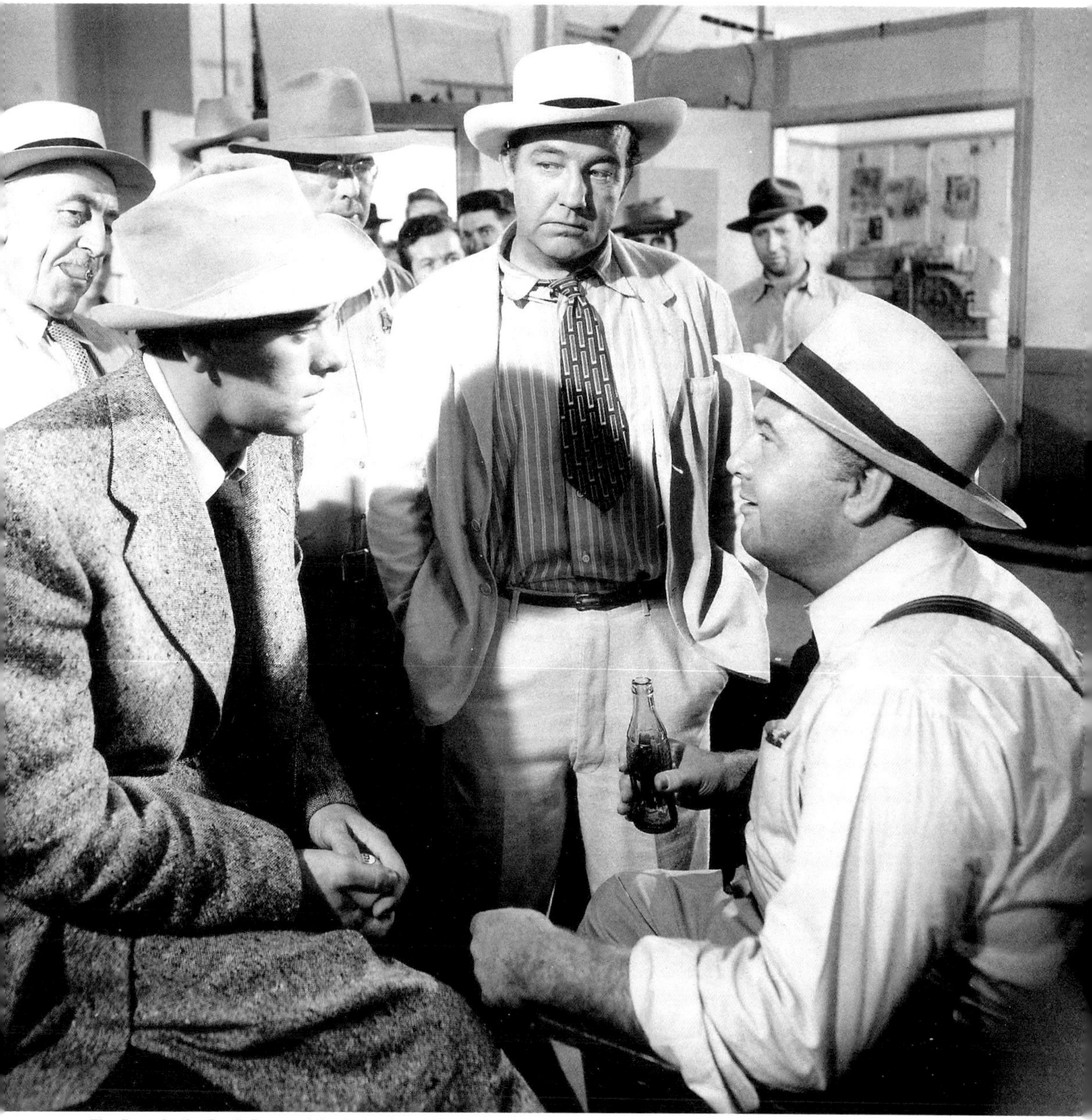

The Boys in the Back Room: John Ireland and Broderick Crawford confront corrupt Kanoma County councilmen Will Wright and Ralph Dumke in *All the King's Men*

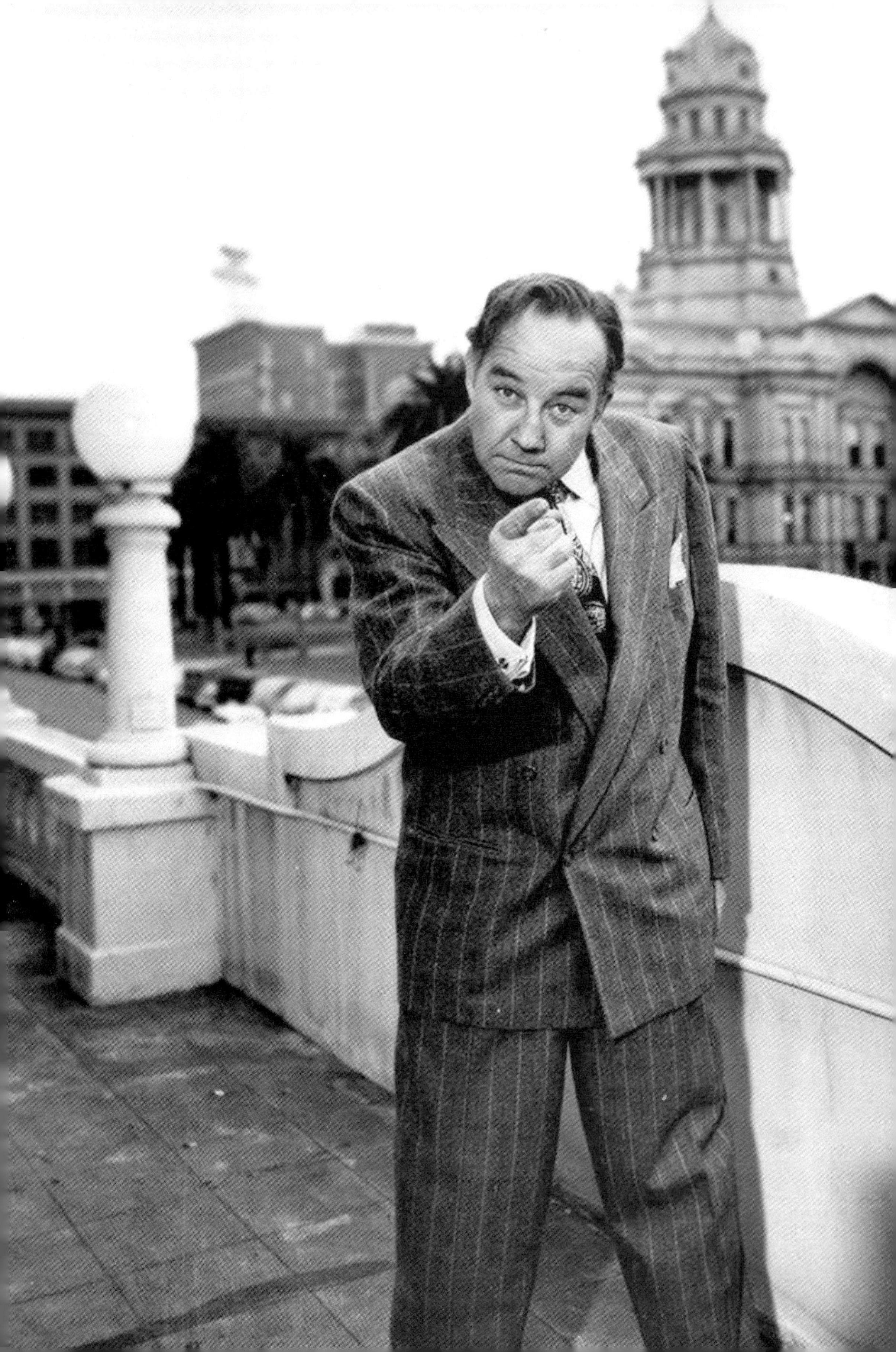

villain out of Stark: the fascist brute. My man, you see, gets some redemption out of the novel..." When Warren complained to Rossen about this all-important shift, the director told him, "Son, when you come to Hollywood you've got to learn one thing—there's not going to be anything called irony in the end of an American picture." Like many an author before and since, Warren concluded that he had to let the filmmaker make his film. "It's his movie," he told Kennedy, "not mine."

So what, then, is Rossen's movie saying about Willie Stark?

In many ways, the continuing power of *All the King's Men* rests less in its story than in the raw effectiveness of its images and set pieces. If the political specifics of the story are muted and indistinct, what still resonates today is the blunt force imagery of Willie Stark, sweaty and disheveled, coming to power by stoking the resentments of white rural voters:

> *Now, listen to me, you hicks. Yeah, you're hicks too, and they fooled you a thousand times, just like they fooled me. But this time, I'm gonna fool somebody. I'm gonna stay in this race. I'm on my own, and I'm out for blood. Now listen to me, you hicks! Listen to me, and lift up your eyes and look at God's blessed and unfly-blown truth. And this is the truth. You're a hick, and nobody ever helped a hick but a hick himself!*

Stark's rallies grow in size and furor the more he follows Burden's advice at the outset of the campaign: "Willie, make 'em cry, make 'em laugh, make 'em mad... Stir them up, and they'll love it and come back for more. But heaven's sakes, don't try to improve their minds." In a sense, the film can eschew specifics because Stark isn't playing to the minds of his audience, he's playing to their inherited grievances, to the (correct) suspicion that the powers-that-be look down on them. "He roared across the state," Burden tells us, "making speech after speech all adding up to the same thing: it's not me they're after, it's you. [...] He knew if you hollered long enough, hard enough, and loud enough, people begin to believe you."

What this emphasis on style means is that, at its core, the film isn't a political allegory for anything specific as much as it is a warning about the manipulations intrinsic to base populism. Over footage of Stark supporters carrying placards reading *Willie's Law Is Our Law,* we hear a radio announcer blaring, "From all over the state, they're streaming in. From the hill country and farms, the lumber camps, by boat, by train, by horse and by foot, Willie Stark's army." Cinematographer Burnett Guffey creates striking images to match this feeling of a rising mob, such as a shot of Stark thundering away on the stump, his back to us, surrounded by torches—a shot that resembles nothing more than a Klan rally.

Despite all of this, an important point to make about *All the King's Men* is that it's less political than it first appears. Although still clearly based on Huey Long—the consummate Southern politician whose meteoric rise was cut short by an assassin's bullet in 1935—this Willie Stark isn't a Southerner. The film takes place in an unnamed state and region, with the Philadelphia-born and Harvard-educated Broderick Crawford playing Stark without an accent. Unlike Karlson's *The Phenix City Story* (1955), the film doesn't touch on racial violence (even obliquely), nor is it an extended critique of the system of political patronage like the Dalton Trumbo-scripted *The Boss* (1956).

Instead, stripped of politics, Rossen's *All the King's Men* is more of a character study. It doesn't find the roots of Stark's downfall in a fading capitalist system or in the specific hypocrisies of any particular place or people. It's a personal tragedy, about a man brought low by his own greed, lust, and ambition. In a sense, Rossen made the story into a film noir.

As a character piece, the film owes a lot to the actor at its center. Broderick Crawford would go on to issue impressive performances in excellent noirs like *Scandal Sheet* (1952) and *Human Desire* (1954),

Broderick Crawford's Willie Stark stares, glares, and blares his way to the top in *All the King's Men*

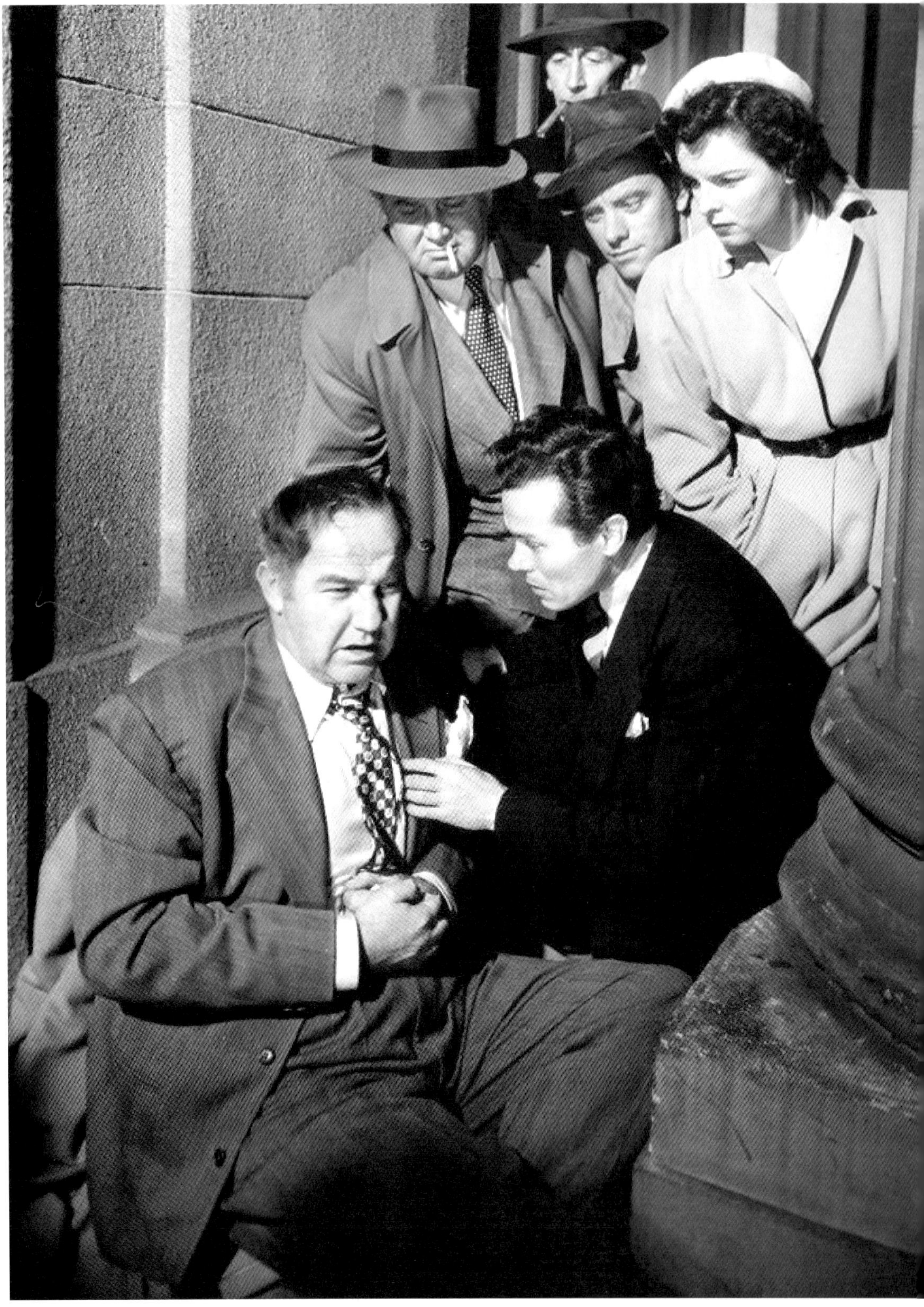

and he would enjoy a successful television run on *Highway Patrol* in the late 50s, but he will always be defined by Willie Stark. He's charming and scary, selling lines like "Jack, there's something on everybody. Man is conceived in sin and born in corruption," by delivering them more as a statement of faith than as an attempt at persuasion.

Broderick's matched in his power by Mercedes McCambridge as the smart-mouthed political operative Sadie Burke. First assigned the job of molding Stark into a candidate who can "split the hick vote" for the benefit of the state's political machine, she's the first to realize that Stark can consolidate that vote, instead. More than anyone else in the cast, McCambridge creates the air of permeant corruption that hovers over the film. She's the one who gives the viewer a sense that Stark's antics are nothing new. He's just better at the game than most people.

While Crawford and McCambridge create the tarnished soul of the film (they would both win Oscars), John Ireland, never a particularly riveting actor, makes for a bland Jack Burden. Is he supposed to be the tortured soul of the film? If so, the film doesn't have a tortured soul. In a sense, Harry Cohn was right. We know we're rooting *against* Stark, but what are we rooting for? With the void created by the rewrites, editorial restructuring, and Ireland's rather affectless performance, the answer is that we're also rooting *for* Stark. He and Sadie (the most noir characters in the film, it must be said) become the film's true center.

Though Rossen and Guffey were both experienced hands on film noir (they had worked together on *Johnny O'Clock*), stylistically *All the King's Men* makes no claim to being a noir, opting instead for a visual palette of crisp straightforward images. As a harbinger of the politics of cultural resentment as the ladder to American fascism, the film finds its noir voice in its hero-free center and its bleak view of human motivation. Or to quote Willie Stark—part preacher, part populist—"Man is conceived in sin and born in corruption." ■

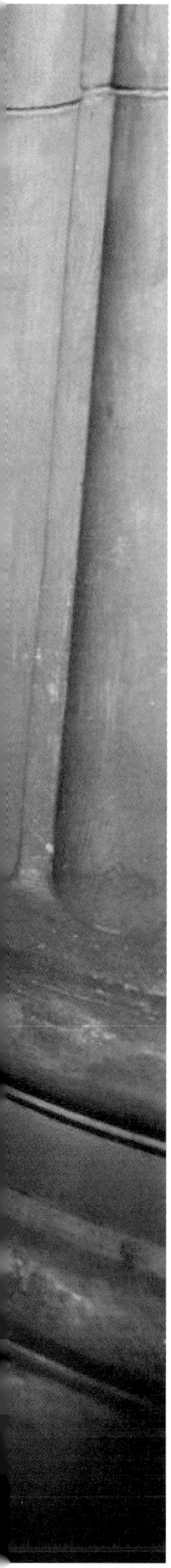

Fallen king Broderick Crawford bids farewell to his court: (counterclockwise from lower right): Walter Burke, Mercedes McCambridge, John Ireland, Will Wright, and Ralph Dumke

NOIR... OR NOT?

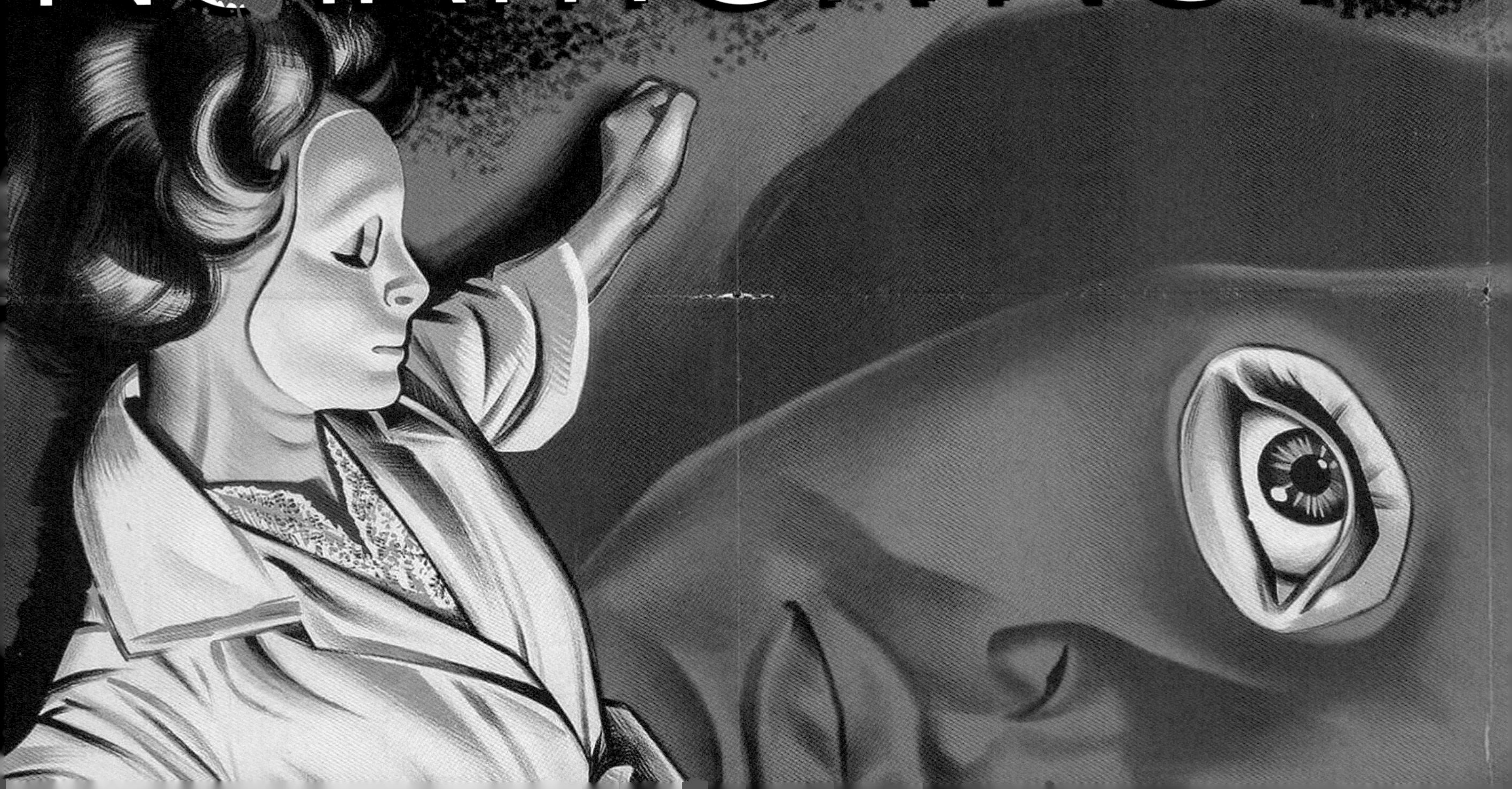

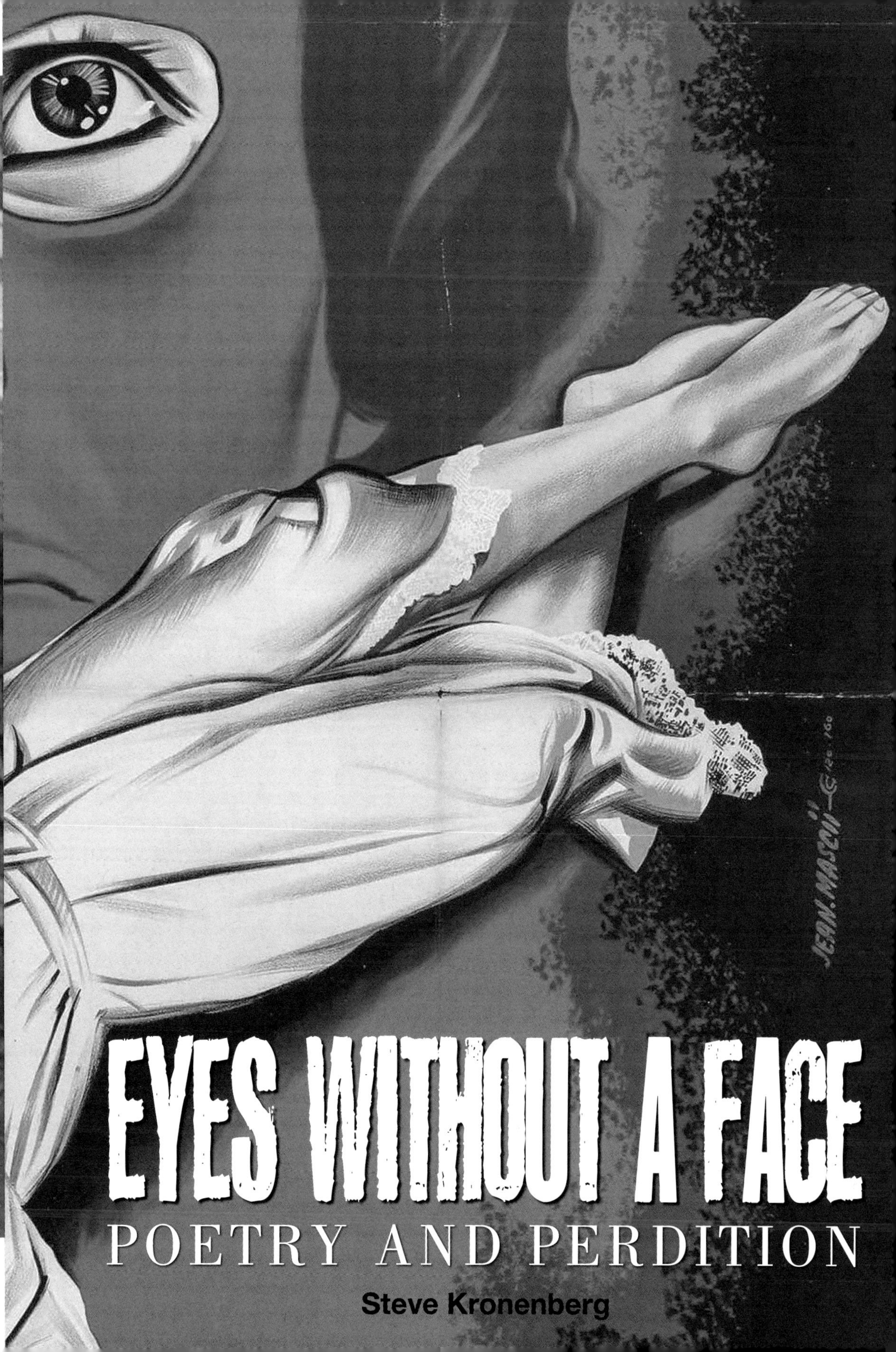

EYES WITHOUT A FACE

POETRY AND PERDITION

Steve Kronenberg

PETER GUNN

Sean Axmaker

Peter Gunn is not the most famous private investigator to hang his shingle on the small screen, not with the likes of James Rockford and Thomas Magnum having left their mark on the genre. He's certainly not the toughest; for that, I'd give the nod to Mike Connors' Joe Mannix. He may very well be the coolest, though fans of *77 Sunset Strip* and *Honey West* may beg to differ. And while he's plenty resourceful, he's not necessarily the smartest nor even the street-smartest. He is, however, the only TV detective who operates entirely within a carefully constructed small-screen recreation of a big-screen film noir. *Peter Gunn*—the series and the shamus—has style, from Craig Stevens' portrayal of the gentleman PI plying the rough underworld to the shadowy imagery of abstracted mean streets to the growling brass of Henry Mancini's iconic cool jazz score.

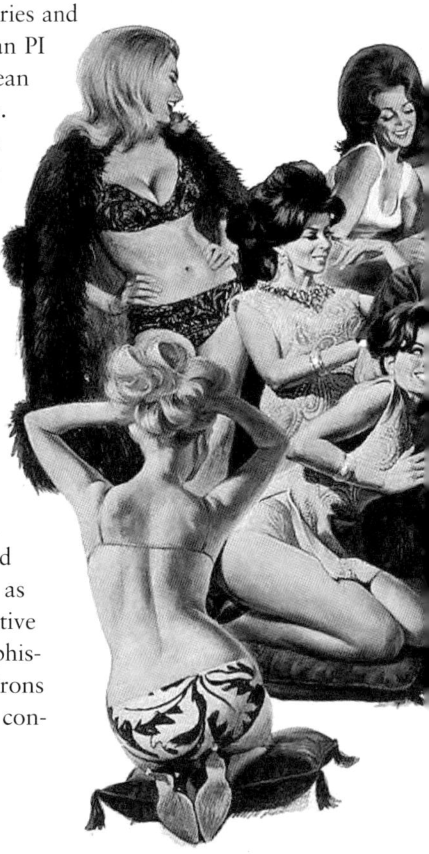

The half-hour *Peter Gunn* debuted in the fall of 1958 on NBC with "The Kill," written and directed by its creator, Blake Edwards. Not exactly a name we associate with the hardboiled attitude of film noir, sure, but the prolific Edwards wrote for TV and radio, as well as film, and he was no stranger to the private-eye genre. He created the radio series *Richard Diamond, Private Detective* for Dick Powell (David Janssen played the character in the later TV version, which Powell produced) and Willie Dante, a shamus who worked out of a bar and gambling house called Dante's Inferno, for Powell's TV anthology series *Four Star Playhouse*.

Edwards clearly had a thing for private detectives and *Peter Gunn* was his ultimate take on the genre. He modeled the character on Cary Grant, and Stevens, up to then a studio contract player and occasional B-movie lead with A-minus charisma, brings the debonair charm and suave manner of a small-screen Grant to the part; maybe not quite as worldly, but plenty continental for this crowd. He's a high-priced detective (he rarely speaks of fees, but wealthy clients pony up a grand) and a sophisticate equally at home in the shadowy underworld and the sleek environs of high society that co-exist in this generic city of night. He drives a con-

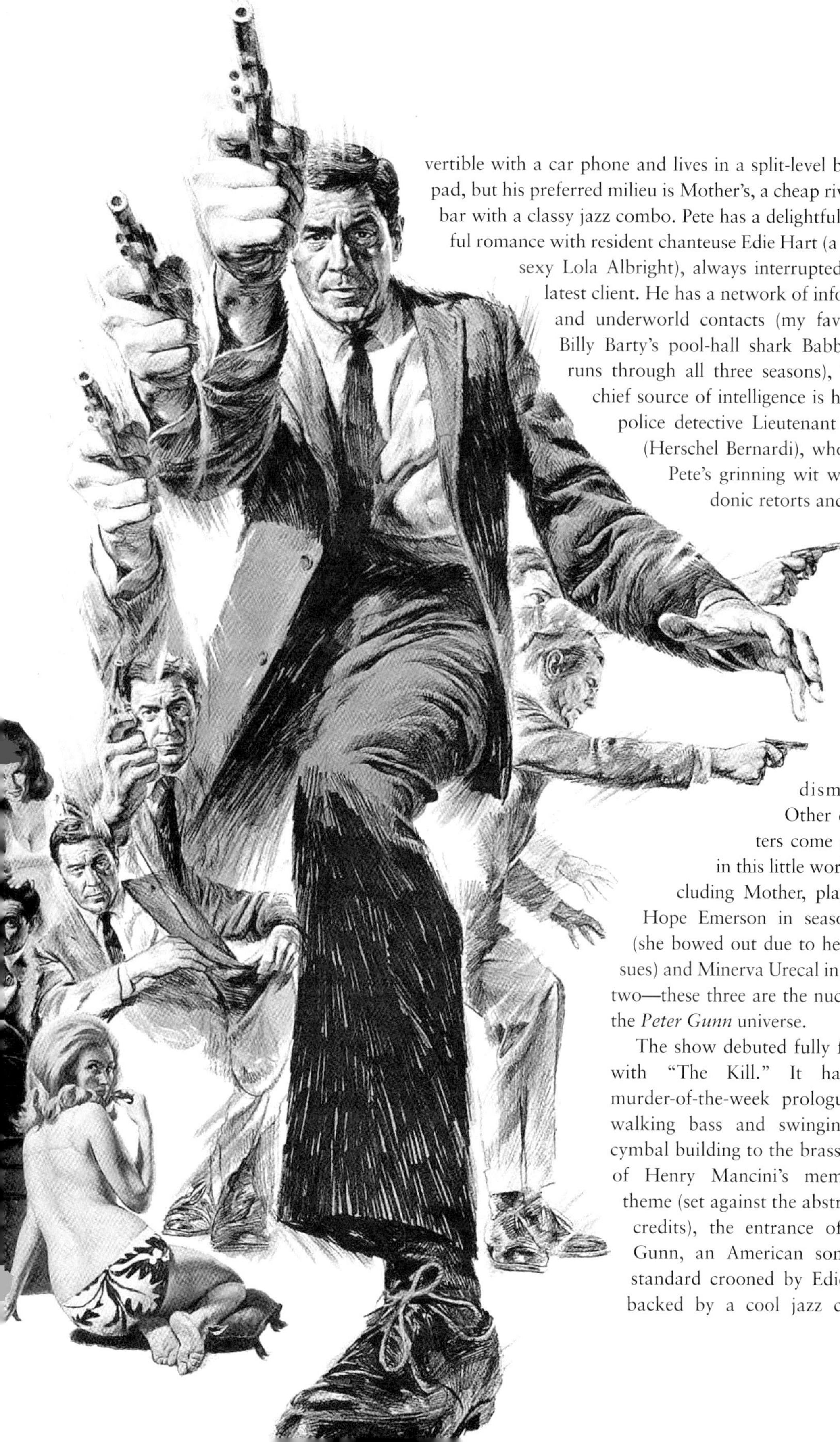

vertible with a car phone and lives in a split-level bachelor pad, but his preferred milieu is Mother's, a cheap riverfront bar with a classy jazz combo. Pete has a delightfully playful romance with resident chanteuse Edie Hart (a sweetly sexy Lola Albright), always interrupted by his latest client. He has a network of informants and underworld contacts (my favorite is Billy Barty's pool-hall shark Babby, who runs through all three seasons), but his chief source of intelligence is hangdog police detective Lieutenant Jacoby (Herschel Bernardi), who greets Pete's grinning wit with sardonic retorts and weary dismissals.

Other characters come and go in this little world—including Mother, played by Hope Emerson in season one (she bowed out due to health issues) and Minerva Urecal in season two—these three are the nucleus of the *Peter Gunn* universe.

The show debuted fully formed with "The Kill." It had the murder-of-the-week prologue, the walking bass and swinging ride cymbal building to the brassy blast of Henry Mancini's memorable theme (set against the abstract art credits), the entrance of Peter Gunn, an American songbook standard crooned by Edie Hart backed by a cool jazz combo, then enter a client, and a case. Gavin MacLeod played an out-of-town mobster moving in with a crew of thugs who execute rivals in the guise of patrol cops. That first prologue ends with a gun barrel firing into the camera, a classic but effective visual gimmick; the blast of the gunshot jumps directly into the trumpet blast of the theme. It set the style for the show and, with a few minor refinements and variations, it would remain a constant through all three seasons.

At 24 minutes (minus commercials), the show's length doesn't lend itself to fully developed short stories, not like the hour-long *The Naked City* or the anthology classic *The Twilight Zone*. But the show could sketch an instant archetype in a couple of scenes and the best episodes distill the aesthetics of film noir with a jazzy lilt and a distinctive look, stripped down and stylized for the low fidelity of late-1950s black-and-white broadcast TV. The unnamed city is a collection of sparsely populated streets filled with generic storefronts and dive bars and flop apartments, with the occasional high-end restaurant or posh manse tossed in for the well-to-do client. Mother's, Peter's *de facto* office, opens onto a studio street set out front and the river out back, a minimalist setting sketched out of light dancing off gently lapping water and a cut-out skyline suggesting the city behind. This ain't *Johnny Staccato*, which would actually take the cameras onto the New York streets and inject the busy city life into the show with a nervous energy. *Peter Gunn* never leaves the studio, or at least not the studio lot (season one was at Universal Studios, the second and third seasons at MGM). Gunn may leave the city for a case, but the real world never intrudes on the pulp fantasy.

That wasn't unusual for a late-1950s show—American TV preferred the control of studio shooting—but *Peter Gunn* turned it into the defining aesthetic. This wasn't a soundstage posing as reality. This was the American city reduced to stylized cinematic shorthand and stripped to the essentials: a shadowy fiction of pulp visions. Edwards directed six of the first eight shows and, working with cinematographers Arthur Arling, Oscar® winner for *The Yearling* and nominee for *I'll Cry Tomorrow*, and future Oscar®- and Emmy-winner Philip Lathrop, he crafted the shows with clear focus. And not just the overtly stylized chiaroscuro sequences of lonely streets, mist-shrouded nights, and slashes and pools of light picking furtive figures out of the darkness. American TV—drama and comedy—had a tendency to rely on middle-distance full shots with scenes staged flatly against the stage set, camera movement restricted to simple follow-pans across the stage keeping the characters in frame, and rhythm and visual drama was a matter of cutting in to close-ups of the characters: the basic grammar codified by D.W. Griffith decades before. Edwards and his team developed a style of long takes with scenes staged in depth and images built on dynamic visual contrasts. Many of Gunn's visits to Jacoby's office open with Herschel Bernardi in close-up and Craig Stevens entering in the background, an intruder into his space. Banter aside (and some of those asides are quite entertaining), these are largely expositional scenes with details on the crime and the suspects, but the camera plays them as visual as well as verbal jousts, Peter intruding with a request and Jacoby putting him off until he's worn to submission. The staging and camerawork reflects that as Stevens becomes more prominent, Bernardi is eased out of the foreground, and they end up on equal visual footing. Not every episode, mind you, but the show offers variations on this theme with remarkable regularity.

Cinematographer Philip Lathrop, who shot 60-some episodes over the first two seasons, was particularly well suited to help Edwards carve out this visual aesthetic. Though relatively fresh as a DP before joining *Peter Gunn*, he was a camera operator on (among other things) Orson Welles' *Touch of Evil*. He surely picked up tricks on shooting long takes, deep focus, and choreographed camerawork. *Touch of Evil* was also the first major score by Henry Mancini, who was given creative freedom by Welles to incorporate a variety of influences into the music. The brassy *Touch of Evil* opening theme, with its build from gentle percussion to big band blast, could be the template for the *Peter Gunn* theme. I can't claim direct influence with any authority, but it sure feels like there's a Welles connection.

It even offers a little continuity along the way. Executive producer Byron Kane took no screen credit as Barney, Mother's loyal bartender and bouncer, but was reliably behind the bar while Emmett (Bill Chadney), the combo's piano player, was on stage backing Edie in those first two seasons.

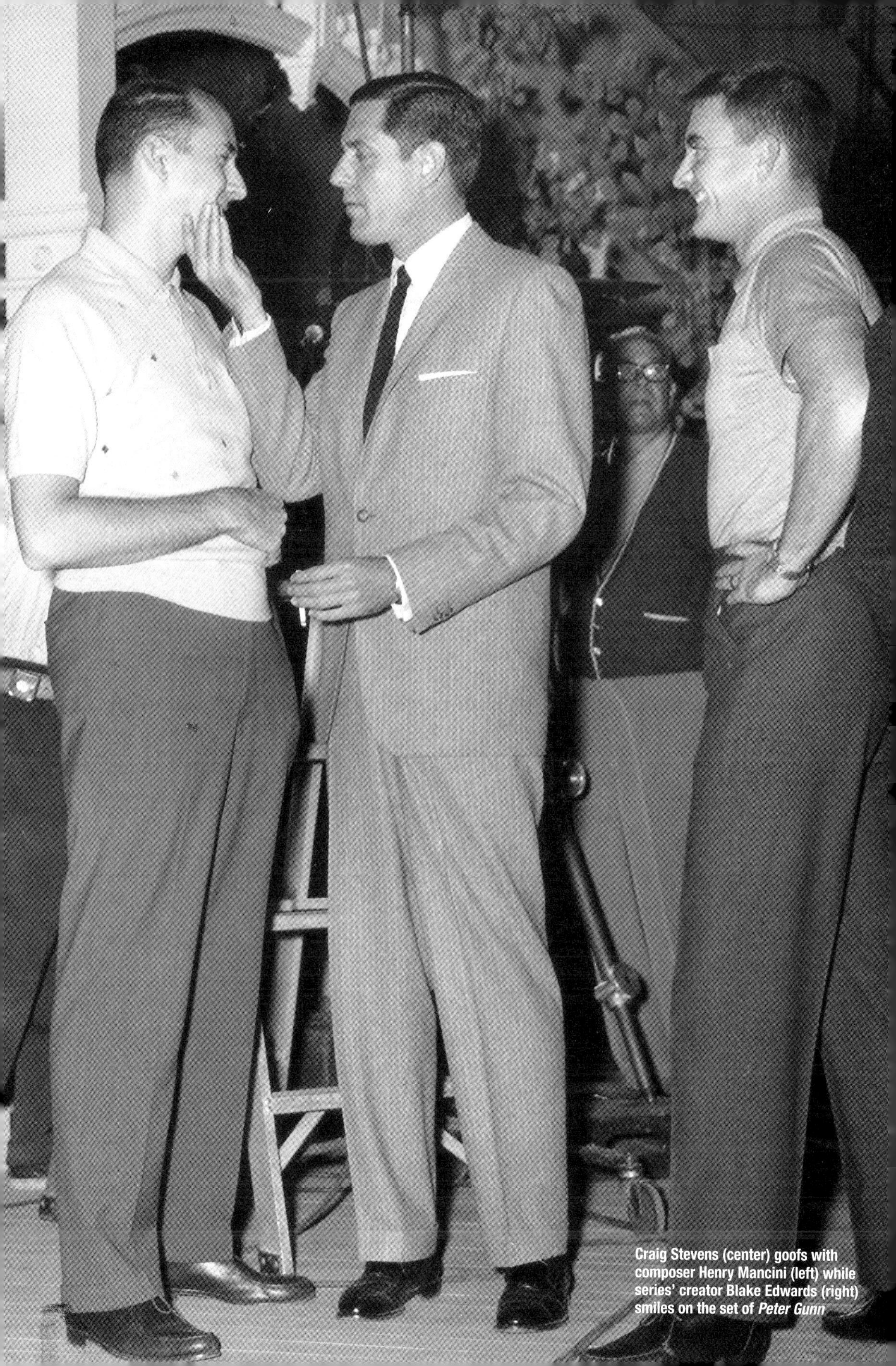

Craig Stevens (center) goofs with composer Henry Mancini (left) while series' creator Blake Edwards (right) smiles on the set of *Peter Gunn*

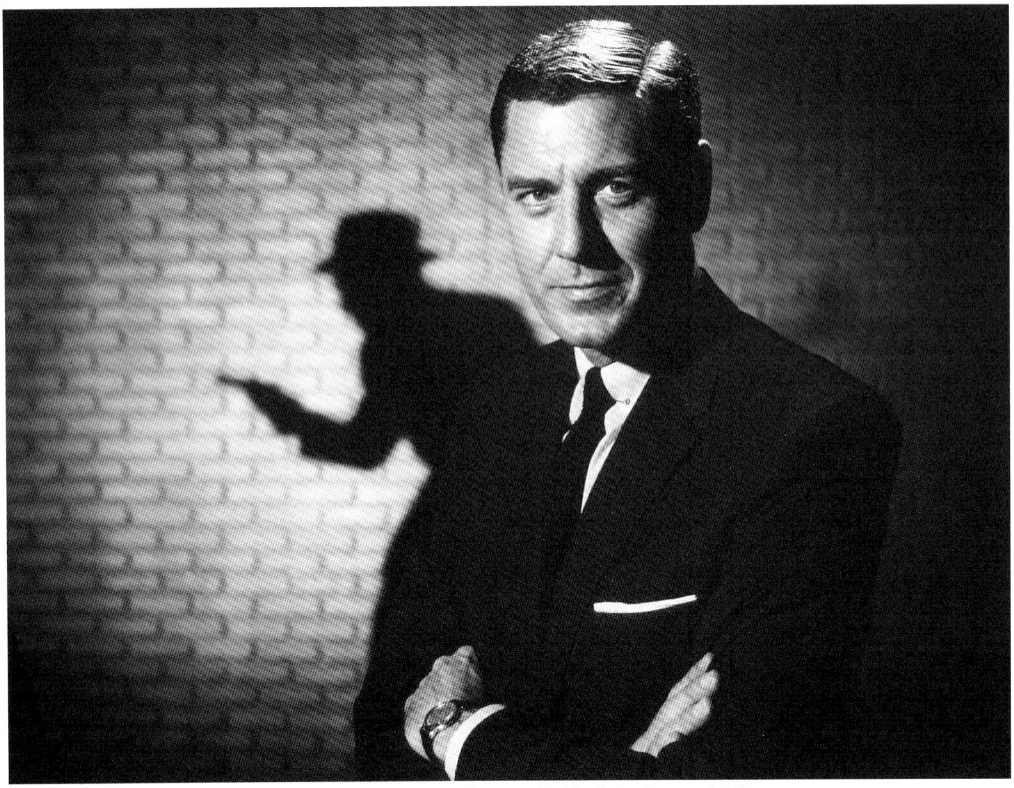

That shadowy gunman won't faze the unflappable Craig Stevens in this *Peter Gunn* publicity pose

When Jacobi is ambushed in "Bullet for a Badge" (S1 Ep34) and sent to the hospital (Berry Kroeger, the corrupt lawyer from *Cry of the City* and carnival boss in *Gun Crazy*, is the sleazy mobster behind the plot), his recuperation stretches out through the next few episodes, a reminder that not everything resets at the end of an episode. Mother's is trashed by thugs in the season two opener and Mother rebuilds and remakes the riverfront dive into a somewhat more upscale joint with a patio (or a lanai, as Mother prefers calls it) and a nautical theme. In season three, Edie opens her own, classier place and hires Leslie (James Lanphier) as her maître d', a restaurateur in his own right with both *Le Cordon Bleu* credentials and a brown belt in judo. Handy skills when one of your regulars is Peter Gunn. Yet it all feels like home when you step out back into the same dark riverfront loading dock.

The first season was a hit, registering as one of the top twenty most-watched shows of the 1959-1960 season and earning eight Emmy nominations, with nods for actors Stevens, Bernardi, Albright, and Emerson, Mancini's theme, and Edwards for the script and direction of "The Kill" and as producer for Best Dramatic Series (under an hour). Edwards personally helmed eight episodes that first season (most of which he scripted) and they feature some of the most complicated narratives and entertaining clients and suspects. Some even echo big-screen noir classics. "The Chinese Hangman" (S1, Ep6) sends Gunn out of country to track down the runaway lover (and the money she ostensibly absconded with) of a religious cult guru, and his south of the border odyssey evokes the first act of *Out of the Past*. In "Death House Testament" (S1 Ep11), Pete is knocked out and drugged in a head-swimming ordeal that recalls *Murder, My Sweet* and *Kiss Me Deadly*. He only directed two more installments, but those season two episodes are among the show's best: "The Comic" (S2, Ep4), a tight little psychodrama with Shelley Berman in a jittery, unsettling turn as a paranoid comedian convinced his wife is out to murder him, and the tangled and marvelously entertaining "The Briefcase" (S2 Ep12), an energetic free-for-all that reworks the basic premise of *The Maltese Falcon* in a criminal scramble for a missing prize. The former is intimate and uneasy, while the latter wrangles a busy plot of colorful characters with competing interests double-crossing Pete and each other. Edwards juggles humor and danger and gives each character a distinctive personality, including a *femme fatale* with screwball energy.

As Edwards shifted focus to other projects, he handed the show over to a team that continued, and sometimes refined, the style. Boris Sagal took over as the show's house director over the course of the first season (the roster includes Lamont Johnson, Jack Arnold, and one episode helmed by Orson Welles alumnus Paul Stewart). In the second season, Tony Barrett and Lewis Reed took over scripting duties, writing or co-writing the vast majority of the season's episodes, while Alan Crosland, Jr. (son of *The Jazz Singer* director Alan Crosland) joined Sagal and Johnson as the show's go-to helmers.

The signature prologue sequences generally fall into two styles: stylized set pieces of abstracted acts of violence (these could be audition pieces for the school of noir—all images, no words spoken) or dialogue scenes that set up dramatic personae and defining conflicts. Jack Arnold directed one of the best of the former in "Love Me to Death" (S1 Ep31), an elaborate booby-trap staged with a riveting efficiency that ends with a gruesome shock. As the veteran in a stable of mostly young directors, Arnold was handed the most ambitious episodes and striking set pieces, like the beautifully choreographed and startlingly brutal fight on a spinning merry-go-round in "Vendetta" (S1 Ep36). Philip Lathrop's lighting and imagery gives it a nightmarish intensity and Mancini matches it with a distorted calliope, like a bare knuckle B-movie version of the *Strangers on a Train* climax.

For my money, however, Boris Sagal best embodied the chiaroscuro style of the classic noir. His best work is dramatically sculpted in light and shadow and often staged in long takes with deep-focus compositions. Season two opener "Protection" fine-tunes the pre-credits prologue to a wordless, multi-layered long take where thugs loom darkly in the foreground and a civilian toils away in the bright light of a storefront shop, oblivious to the violence about to be unleashed. The climactic scene, a bruising fistfight in a novelty warehouse, is all pools of light on an inky labyrinth of crates as the fighters slip in and out of the shadows. Even more baroque is "The Price of Murder" (S2 Ep11), where every shot takes on an urgency after thugs kidnap Edie to get to Pete; a ringing telephone looms so insistently in the foreground that it could be a character in its own right. Sagal guides guest star John McIntire through one of the show's rare character portraits as an alcoholic shuffling through the streets begging money for a drink in "Fill the Cup" (S2 Ep18) and he enhances McIntire's raw spiral into degradation with expressionist distortions and visions. In a TV business where the producer reigned, these episodes are unmistakably *directed*.

Over the course of three seasons, *Peter Gunn* played variations on almost every classic noir trope, but they abandoned the most familiar—the hardboiled voice-over—after the first episode. The voice-over was brought back, though, for the series finale, "Murder on the Line" (S3 Ep38), directed by series stalwart Robert Gist from a story penned by Edwards. This one takes Gunn out of the mean streets and shadowy dives to wade through the moral swamp of the rich, eccentric, and corrupt. That final episode also features director Gist in a central role and executive producer Kane in an uncredited bit part: one last fling before the finish.

Peter Gunn is the great small-screen incarnation of film noir. It doesn't necessarily have the dark heart of the classics, but the scripts straddle both desperate innocents and the corrupt souls who receive poetic justice before the credits roll—all packaged with romantic repartee, buddy-movie banter, and a dash of hardboiled dialogue. More uniquely, it embraces the shadowy lighting and seedy characters of the genre and makes a virtue of long takes and deep-focus photography, a rarity for 1950s television. The style and attitude may be pastiche, but it is loving mimicry, celebrating the conventions with affection rather than ridicule and, every once in a while, the show delivers set pieces that triumph over its modest resources through creative lighting and compositions, ominous low-angle shots, and cameras that soar on cranes and creep through scenes on dollies. It's a near-perfect distillation of the classic noir detective story delivered with hardboiled visuals and cool style—in 24-minute bursts. ■

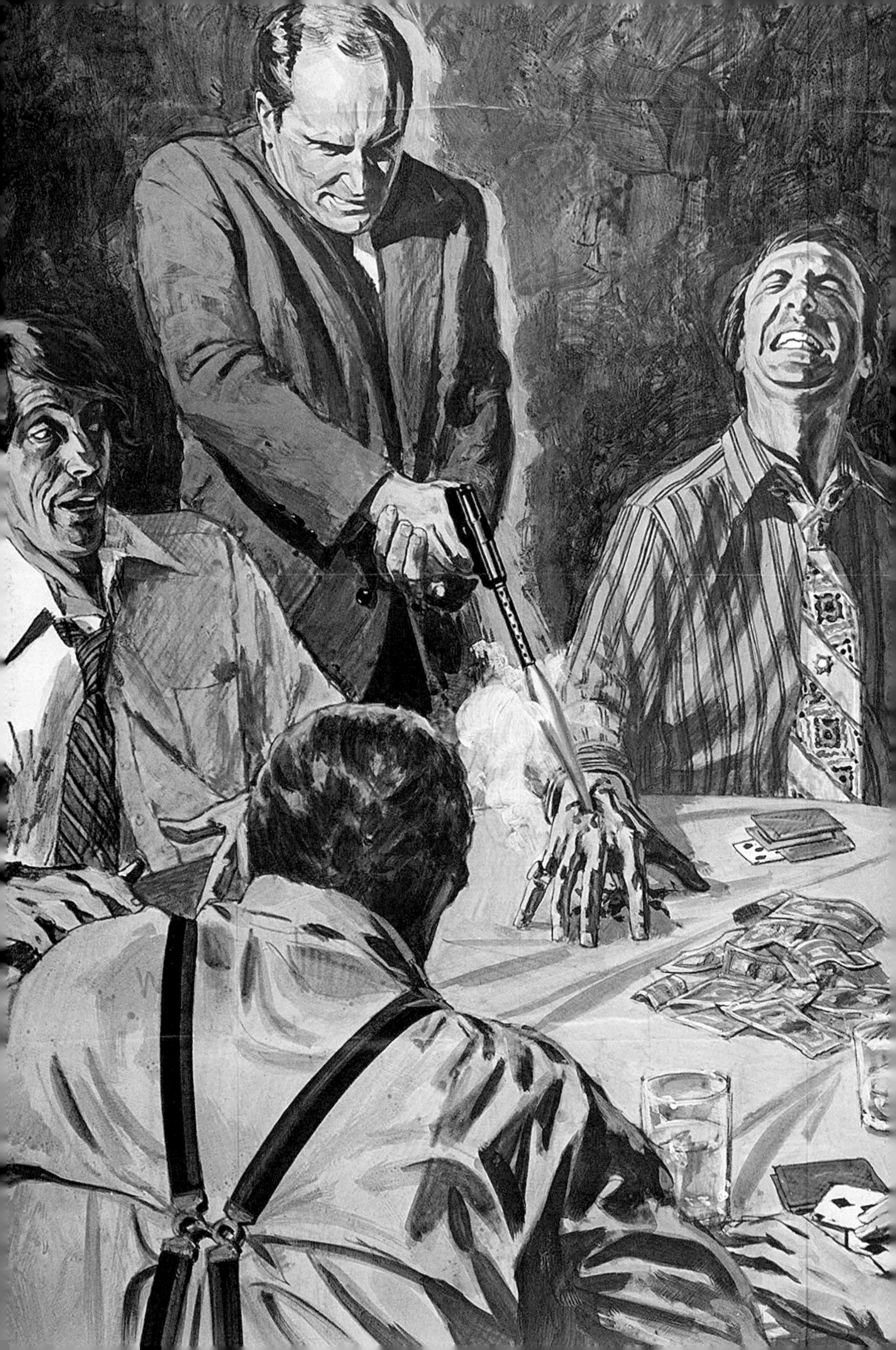

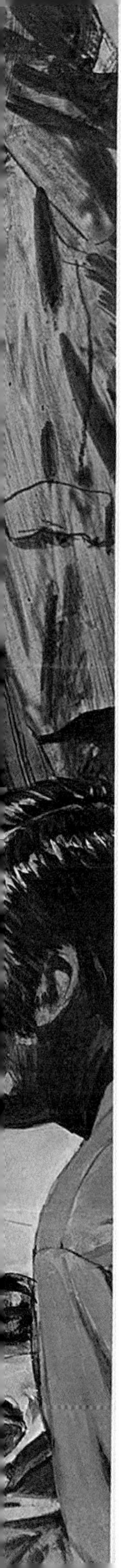

PRIME CUTS

MY FAVORITE NEO-NOIR

THE OUTFIT

Danny Gardner

The most curious aspect of movies based on Donald Westlake's Parker is that none of them wound up Parker. The character serves, at best, as a template for exciting, if not altogether faithful, film incarnations. Lee Marvin's incarnation, renamed "Walker" in *Point Blank* (1967), may match Westlake's physical description of the man, but that's where it stops. It's rather obvious the ways Jim Brown's "McClane" (*The Split*, 1968) isn't Parker. When Jean-Luc Godard turned Parker into "Paula" (*Made in USA*, 1966), Westlake joked it all off. "A friend of mine said, 'So far, Parker's been played by a white guy, a black guy and a woman. I think the character lacks definition.'" Yet, that also could be precisely what the character has going for it when he's taken from the page to the silver screen.

According to Westlake, Parker in print was a bad guy meant to meet justice at the end of his first outing, but Bucklin Moon of Pocket Books offered him a series, so long as the bad guy got away—and kept getting away—with everything. Moon sensed male readers would lap up stories about a mononymous arch-criminal who lacked all regard for rules and laws. Men of the 1960s had developed deep resentment toward the strictures of social propriety. Through Parker, they could experience what they so desperately craved: to cut loose. *Mad Men*'s Don Draper would have kept *The Hunter* on his nightstand.

Which brings me to *The Outfit* (1973). Westlake is on record that this was his favorite adaptation of Parker. Of Robert Duvall's performance as Parker stand-in Earl Macklin, he's known to have remarked, "That's the guy I wrote." I wonder if he preferred this version because it gave his creation the outcome he was originally denied: a long, stiff bid in the slam. Parker was only locked up twice, and never longer than it took for him to escape. Macklin is a guy changed by prison, and while not reformed from his criminal ways, he has learned to hold on to the people who are loyal to him Perhaps Donald Westlake wouldn't—or couldn't—have written Parker that way, but

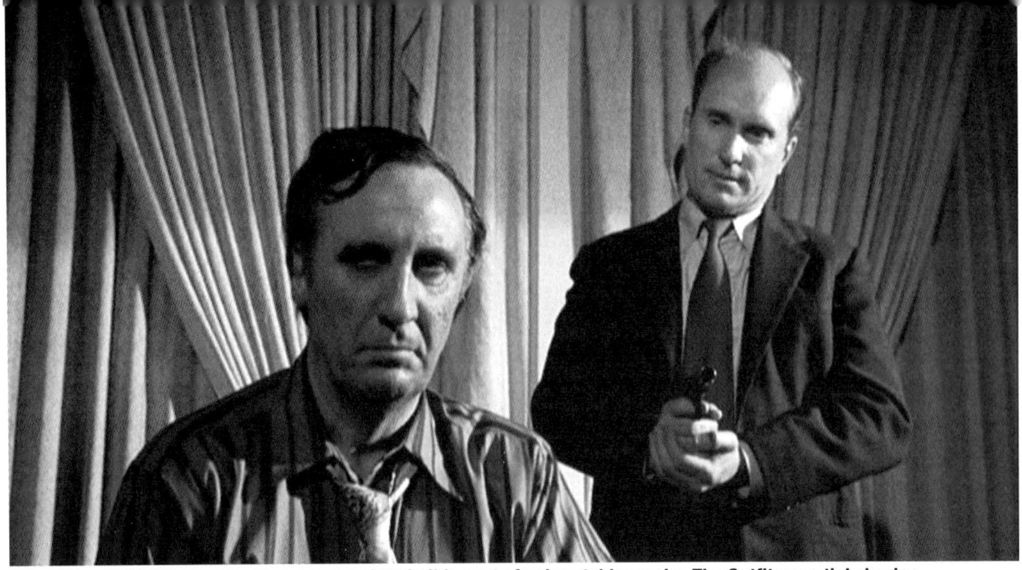

Robert Duvall (right), Timothy Carey, and an irresistible cast of noir notables make *The Outfit* essential viewing

it's revealing that he enjoyed this iteration most of all.

Director John Flynn's screenplay, drawn from Stark's 1963 novel of the same title, opens with Macklin's release from the penitentiary after 27 months of hard time, during which he mourned the death of his brother Eddie. Although Parker on the page has the emotional capacity of a Greenland shark, in Duvall's portrayal you can see purpose quivering in Earl's eyes. The Macklins knocked over Midwest National Bank, an Outfit operation, and in the words of Timothy Carey's mobster Jake Menner, "You hit us. We hit you." They got Eddie while Earl was in stir. Now out, Earl knows he's next—except vendetta is this Parker's first order of business. Earl got Eddie killed, and guilt and grief do funny things to a man's heart and mind. As he hurts, so must the Outfit.

Macklin starts by boosting the purse at a mobbed-up high-stakes poker game, the score punctuated with a bullet through Menner's card-dealing, contract-issuing, cigarette-extinguishing hand. Here, Carey *(*1956's *The Killing)* grimly adds counterweight to Duvall's limber footwork and speedy verbal jabs. He is but one of many sublime casting choices that reference classic noir films, including Jane Greer *(*1947's *Out of the Past),* Marie Windsor *(The Killing),* Elisha Cook Jr. *(*1941's *The Maltese Falcon)* and screen legend Robert Ryan, here in his next-to-final performance as the Outfit heavy, Mailer. Flynn denied that *The Outfit* was intended as an homage to classic noir, and if he is to be believed, I wonder if the filmmakers dipped into the pool of brilliant noir actors for their aged faces and collective weighty presence. Macklin moves fast, and hits faster, yet when confronted by one of these legends, Duvall pauses, almost in reflection, and then states exactly how it's gonna be—no more, no less. Duvall seems to be telling the old hands he's the new guy come for what's his, no different than Parker striding into New York's underworld, or Westlake into publishing. Take Macklin's face-to-face meeting with Mailer. Is this a conversation between a rogue and a big boss whose young wife and idiot henchmen weary him? Or are we seeing a rising star being put through his paces by an old hand at the game? The performances are delicious. "You've got confidence," Ryan says. "I like that." Duvall's smirk in response is barely perceptible. You sense the two of them could've had this same toe-down at a Screen Actors Guild mixer.

While some scenes are lifted directly from the source, the film makes a hemispheric divergence with the character of Bett. In the novel, Elizabeth Ruth Harrow Conway—four names implying the complexity of her means and motives—is a body upon which Parker can work out his satyric cravings; his jones after successful scores is so strong, he can't get to the business of planning the next one until he's sated. She is granted a sliver of Parker's truth in order to maintain her sexual utility. It turns her on to watch him work over the Outfit's hit-man for answers, and that turns on Parker. He gives her a token so that she sticks around, just in case he isn't finished. Westlake describes her as "a good animal" with "a panther craving for brutality," rather detailed imagery with which to illustrate a sadist. She's the blunt instrument of a blunt instrument, and while she adjusts the hem of this garment a few times, nothing in the narrative suggests wearing it makes her uncomfortable.

Bett in the film, however, has a core of goodness that even collusion with the likes of Macklin can't erode. She admits to setting Earl up for the hit and you believe along with him that she's contrite. Her confession and countenance are threadbare as she describes the pressure the Outfit applied. Once she reveals where Menner put out his cigarettes, she earns Earl's sympathy as well as his protection. Macklin accepts responsibility for her once it's clear the Outfit will add her to his death warrant. He even appoints her getaway driver so he can keep an eye on her, since right next to him is the safest place she could be. Elizabeth is in it for kicks, and to be useful to a man who uses her. Bett of the movie seems locked in a desperate gamble to save Macklin from himself, and when it costs her dearly, it's her sacrifice that moves Earl to go for broke and settle matters once and for all. Elizabeth is never trusted by Parker, but John Flynn's Bett is so much a ride-or-die chick, she actually rode and died. Earl breaks from his planned retribution only long enough to ensure she receives a proper burial.

Some writers and reviewers contend that Karen Black was miscast, but I suspect this may be because they are enamored with the Bett of the novel, a go-along-to-get-along betty who came complete with her own kinks. No sliver of the original character can be found in Black's well-crafted performance. When Earl is about to dispatch a button-man with his own silenced target pistol, Bett serves as the voice of restraint.

"Earl...don't hurt him anymore."

Here you see why she was given the role. An actress like Faye Dunaway would have looked like she could give a toss. Parker knows exactly what he wants Bett for, and he only does enough to make sure she doesn't mind sitting on the bench. Aside from smacking her around after she tries to relieve him of his gun—to relieve him of the burden of revenge—Earl Macklin seems to not desire Bett's body beyond an oddly staged pillow fight. When Karen Black is on-screen, *The Outfit* seems like the closest thing to a chick flick we'd get in 1973.

The relationship between Parker and Handy McKay, transformed here into Joe Don Baker's charismatic and ingratiating Jack Cody, finally pulls this version of Parker completely out of the stark masculinity of the novels. In the scene where Cody meets Bett, he doesn't respond to her acknowledgment, deliberately rendering her invisible. It's like an uncomfortable encounter between a man's old used-to-be and his new main squeeze. As the two men catch up, Black sits to the left, putting her man at the center of a tug of war between his two love interests. Cody looks at Earl with affection and deep concern. Bett swivels her barstool to look at Cody. The scene shows Macklin in a whole new light; smiling, relaxed, optimistic, grateful. No wonder Bett stares daggers at them. All Earl has for her is smacks upside the head and taciturn responses for any appeal to his better angels. Only Cody inspires Macklin to ponder a life beyond criminality. He won't run away with Bett and drop the whole thing, but somehow another country feller can make this vengeful raptor wonder about the snowfalls in rural Oregon. When it all comes to a head at the Outfit's front door, the one thing worth more to Macklin than his revenge is the survival of his good ol' boy. If it were released today, *The Outfit* would be ranked among the great Hollywood bromances.

Westlake's refusal to allow the name "Parker" to be used in the adaptations of his Richard Stark novels has been ascribed to everything from creative control to financial holdouts to a desire for an integrated series of films, à la James Bond. Whatever Westlake's reasons, I've always found Parker to be a stronger character in film than in print. A funny thing happens when you take a leanly drawn character and put him in the skin of a human being. You get a heartbeat, and a soul, and a purpose—even if you don't particularly want any of that. For us to enjoy an Earl Macklin, we need to leave Parker where he best exists—in the minds of his loyal readers. Perhaps Donald Westlake knew this, or maybe he didn't care. Regardless, we as lovers of film noir are left better for it. ■

UNDER SURVEILLANCE

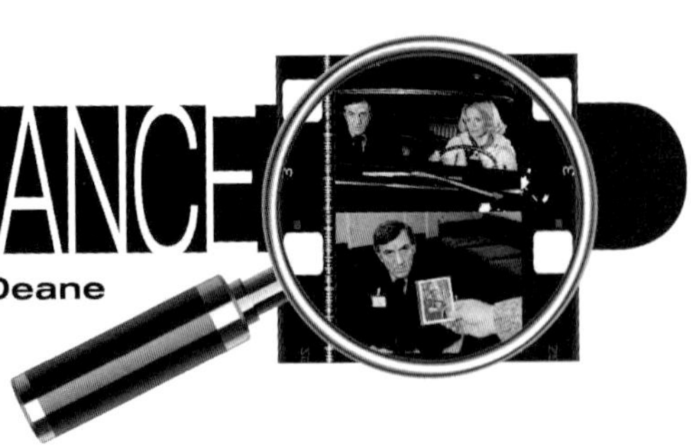

A Closer Look at Forgotten Film Noir | **Gary Deane**

L'Homme en colère (The Last Angry Man)

In 1974, Canada's government passed legislation allowing all investment in Canadian feature film production to be deducted from a citizen's taxes. The intent of the Capital Cost Allowance (CCA) was straightforward: American dominance of the movie marketplace had made it impossible for Canadian-made features to turn a profit or even find a booking at the local bijou. This tax shelter was designed to move Canadian films beyond parochialism toward commercial sustainability. The CCA also was structured to open up projects to foreign participation. Productions needed only a single Canadian producer and limited 'above the line' Canadian participation to qualify. As a result, caravans of Hollywood producers and stars hightailed it north, and many ended up making out like bandits.

As anticipated, introduction of the CCA spurred a production boom as well as the hoped-for boost in box-office sales. In 1974, only three home-grown Canadian films were produced; by 1979, the program's peak, the number had increased to 77. Admittedly, some were stinkers, such as *City on Fire* (1979) starring Henry Fonda and Ava Gardner; *Running* (1979) with Michael Douglas and Susan Anspach; and *Circle of Two* (1981) directed by Jules Dassin, who'd been dragged out of retirement to salvage the laughable love story of a womanizing artist, Richard Burton, and a much younger Tatum O'Neal.

More than a few CCA-produced films were successful, both critically and commercially, including: *Murder by Decree* (1979), *The Changeling* (1980), *Atlantic City* (1980), *Quest for Fire* (1980), and two of the highest-earning Canadian movies of all time, the amiably wacko *Meatballs* (1979) and the progenitor of all teen gross-out comedies, *Porky's* (1981). Also among the winners was Canadian director Daryl Duke's adrenaline-fueled thriller *The Silent Partner* (1978), filmed (and set) in Toronto, starring Christopher Plummer, Elliott Gould, and Susannah York, with a spellbinding script by Curtis Hanson (1997's *L.A. Confidential*) and an uncharacteristically edgy score by jazz great Oscar Peterson. The movie gave English-Canadian movie audiences, long inured to drab tales of rural, small-town hardship, something to get excited about.

In French-speaking Quebec, things happened differently. Quebec cinema was firmly rooted in the province's Francophone culture and audiences welcomed their heritage and everyday stories being reflected on-screen. It was also possible for Quebec-made films to be successful without being distributed beyond the province, but maverick producer Denis Héroux (*Atlantic City, Quest for Fire*) had bigger ambitions. The first was a Canadian/French co-production, *L'Homme en colère*, an atmospheric noir thriller set in Montréal featuring an international cast, including Lino Ventura, Angie Dickinson, and Donald Pleasence.

Ventura, the gravel-voiced French actor who specialized in stoic tough guys on either side of the

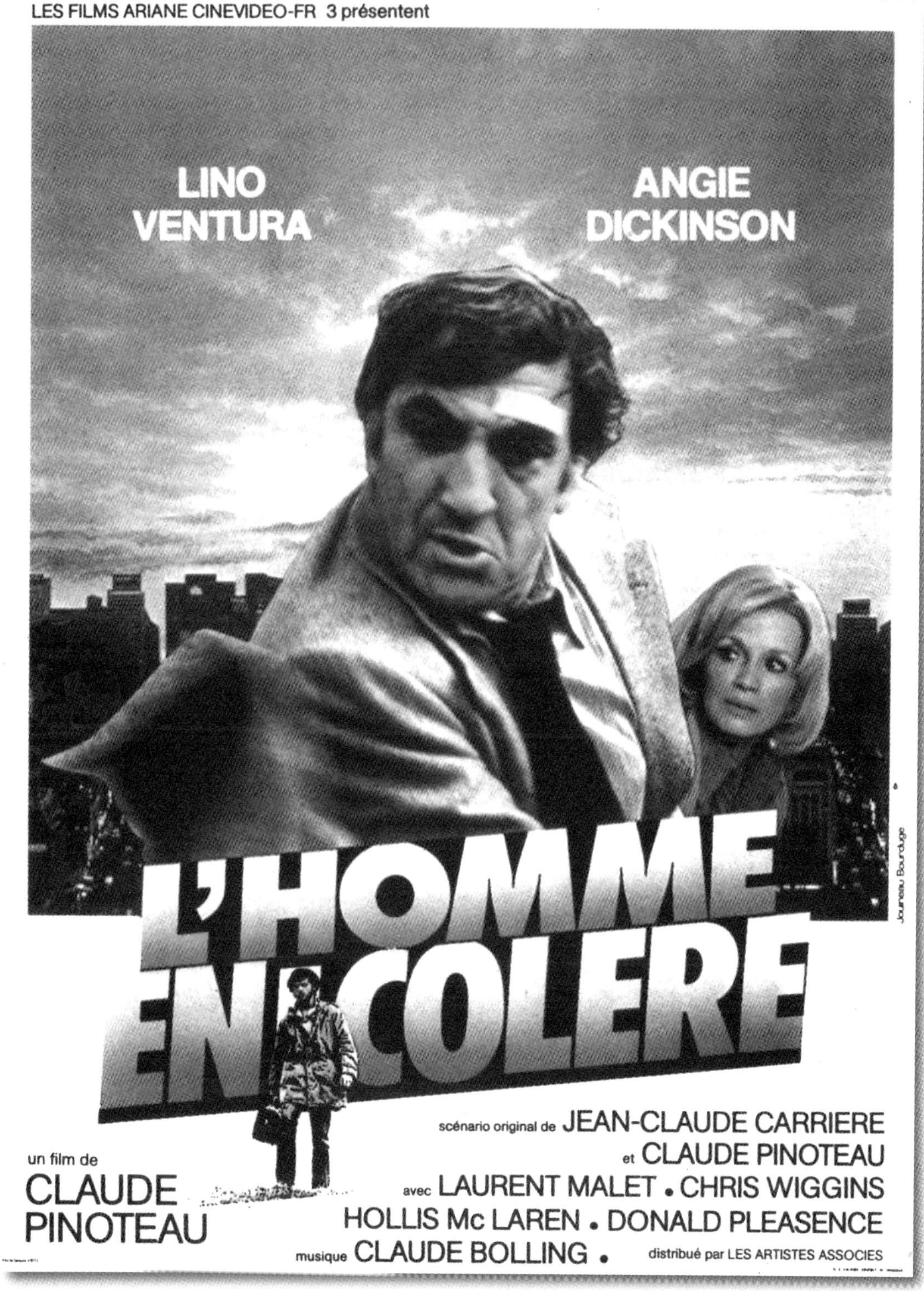
LES FILMS ARIANE CINEVIDEO-FR 3 présentent
LINO VENTURA
ANGIE DICKINSON
L'HOMME EN COLERE
scénario original de JEAN-CLAUDE CARRIERE
et CLAUDE PINOTEAU
un film de
CLAUDE PINOTEAU
avec LAURENT MALET • CHRIS WIGGINS
HOLLIS Mc LAREN • DONALD PLEASENCE
musique CLAUDE BOLLING •
distribué par LES ARTISTES ASSOCIES

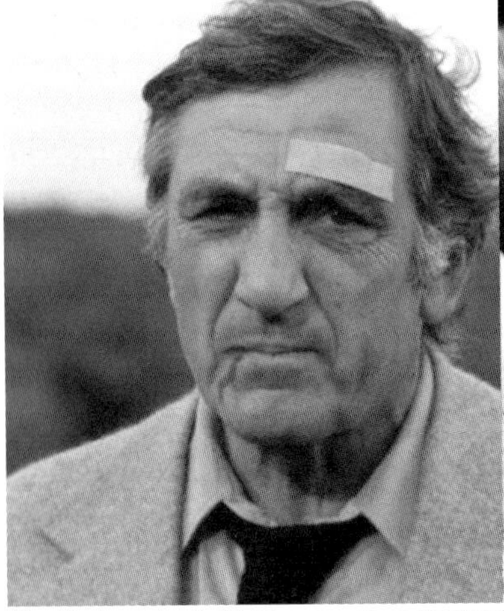

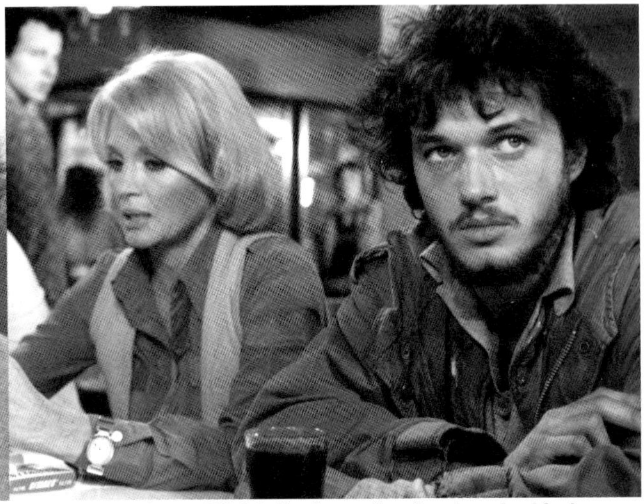

Lino Ventura, Angie Dickinson, and, as Ventura's wayward son, Laurent Malet all get more than they bargained for in *L'Homme en colère*

law, plays an Air France pilot, Romain Dupré, whose wife dies in a forest fire which his young son, Julien, manages to escape. Years later, father and son have become estranged, and Julien immigrates to Montréal where he becomes involved in dope peddling and smuggling illegals across the U.S./Canadian border. Notified that Julien has been killed in a shootout with police, Dupré flies to Montréal to identify the corpse—which turns out to be an imposter who's lifted the son's passport and assumed Julien's identity. Committed to finding his on-the-lam son, Dupré runs afoul of the Quebec mob with whom Julien had been involved. He meets Karen (Dickinson), an ex-pat American working as a waitress, and draws her into the hunt. Donald Pleasence is a creepy go-between looking for both Julien and a suitcase full of mob money that had disappeared.

Director Claude Pinoteau and the venerated Ventura made four films together, three of them noirish *policiers*: *Le Silencieux* (1973), *L'Homme en colère* (1979), and *La 7ème cible* (1984). *L'Homme en colère* flaunts its mixed parentage, being an amalgam of Euro-crime splashiness, bare-bones Canadian realism, and the unsparing violence of American crime dramas of the period such as *Across 110th Street* (1972) and *The Nickel Ride* (1974). In *L'Homme en colère*, a roused Dupré makes his way through a sleazy world of mob-controlled clubs and discos, seedy boxing gyms, drug arcades, shooting galleries, and fleabag walk-ups. Interestingly, Montréal can't help being Montréal, long the most style-conscious city in North America, its streets filled with boho-hippy fashionistas and mod bistros done up in beads and burnished Naugahyde. It's the '70s—no way around it!

There also is no way around Angie Dickinson, who at 48 is as attractive and sexual a presence as ever. Though her virtues as an actress maybe were not world class, she was an assured performer who was featured for over five decades in film and television. In the '50s, she was memorable as 'Feathers,' a flirtatious saloon girl in the classic *Rio Bravo* (1959); in the '60s, she was in full bloom as Frank Sinatra's wife in *Oceans 11* (1960); and then was cast alongside Lee Marvin in *The Killers* (1964), a role that anticipated the remote and brittle *femme fatale* she'd play in the existential 1967 thriller *Point Blank*. In the '70s, she broke the age barrier as a libidinous teacher in *Pretty Maids All in a Row* (1971), a lusty bank robber in *Big Bad Mama* (1974), and as sexy undercover cop Sergeant "Pepper" Anderson in the TV series *Police Woman*, which ran from 1974 to 1978. Dickinson became a household name by eschewing the sex kitten compliancy of Monroe and Mansfield in favor of parts more in keeping with her real-life, one-of-the-guys persona. As she said in a 2010 interview, "If you're only trading on your looks and your body, that's only going to go so far. But that was never me. I was always about the whole package."

No one understood this better than the French. *The Killers* and *Point Blank* were far more lauded in France than at home—as was Dickinson, who always received expansive coverage and praise for performances which all too often were underrated in America. French director Roger Vadim insisted on her for *Pretty Maids*, ignoring the list of actresses proffered by the studio and choosing Dickinson because she "was someone who looks like she likes men." In *L'Homme en colère,* Dickinson definitely likes Lino Ventura, though their relationship takes time to develop. For the first half of the film, it's unclear what her relationship is to Ventura or to the story itself. They meet (and re-meet) coincidentally, and she eventually admits that nearly everything she's revealed about herself is a lie; she's really an ex-con who's spent two years in prison. She asked Dupré if he wants to know why—"No," he replies. He knows little about her, nor do we. Karen disappears from the film as Dupré resumes the search for his son, but we know she'll return and we're ready. Karen is a noir heroine, worn down but not out, holding onto cautious hope. Dupré finds her after he's beaten by mob thugs and, suddenly, he and Karen are sharing too much.

That said, Dupré struggles with the intimacy. As he boards a train, Karen says, "I don't think you're the type to kiss a woman on a platform before a train leaves." He may say "No," but now Dupré embraces and kisses her with passion. The scene was difficult for Ventura, a profoundly moral man who had never before kissed a woman on-screen, both out of personal modesty and respect for his wife and children. This time, he made an exception. Dickinson said that on the first take he grabbed and kissed her to the point of near asphyxiation. It took several more tries before Ventura relaxed enough to offer a more gradually tender and sensual kiss with his co-star's willing participation.

Ventura is his usual dominating persona in *L'Homme en colère,* though it's more dependent on physicality than acting skills. As with Robert Mitchum, Ventura only had to show up to give an indelible performance. His peasant strength provides an anchoring counterpoint to Dickinson's troubled vulnerability and need.

L'Homme en colère is a harsh and hectic crime thriller, but one with a beating heart. Though it refers to American crime dramas of the early '70s, it also evokes French *policiers* and Italian *poliziotteschi* of the time, due in part to the distinctive international milieu. Only French jazz composer Claude Bolling's mawkish score and the film's fabricated ending bring it down a notch.

The CCA came to an end in 1982. Too many of the films it beget failed to find distribution, being derivative efforts indistinguishable from U. S. productions just as badly made. However, like the British quota system of the 1930s, which resulted in sub-standard output but also nurtured Alfred Hitchcock and Alexander Korda, the CCA gave rise to the beginnings of a dynamic Canadian film and television industry. It also gave us *L'Homme en colère* and *The Silent Partner,* two certifiable Canadian film noirs—something one might reasonably have thought to be an oxymoron. *Vive le film noir, vive le Canada.* ■

Despite the international appeal of L'Homme en colère, *it was released theatrically and on video with only a French vocal track. A digital version with English subtitles recently became available.*

PRIME CUTS
MY FAVORITE NEO-NOIR

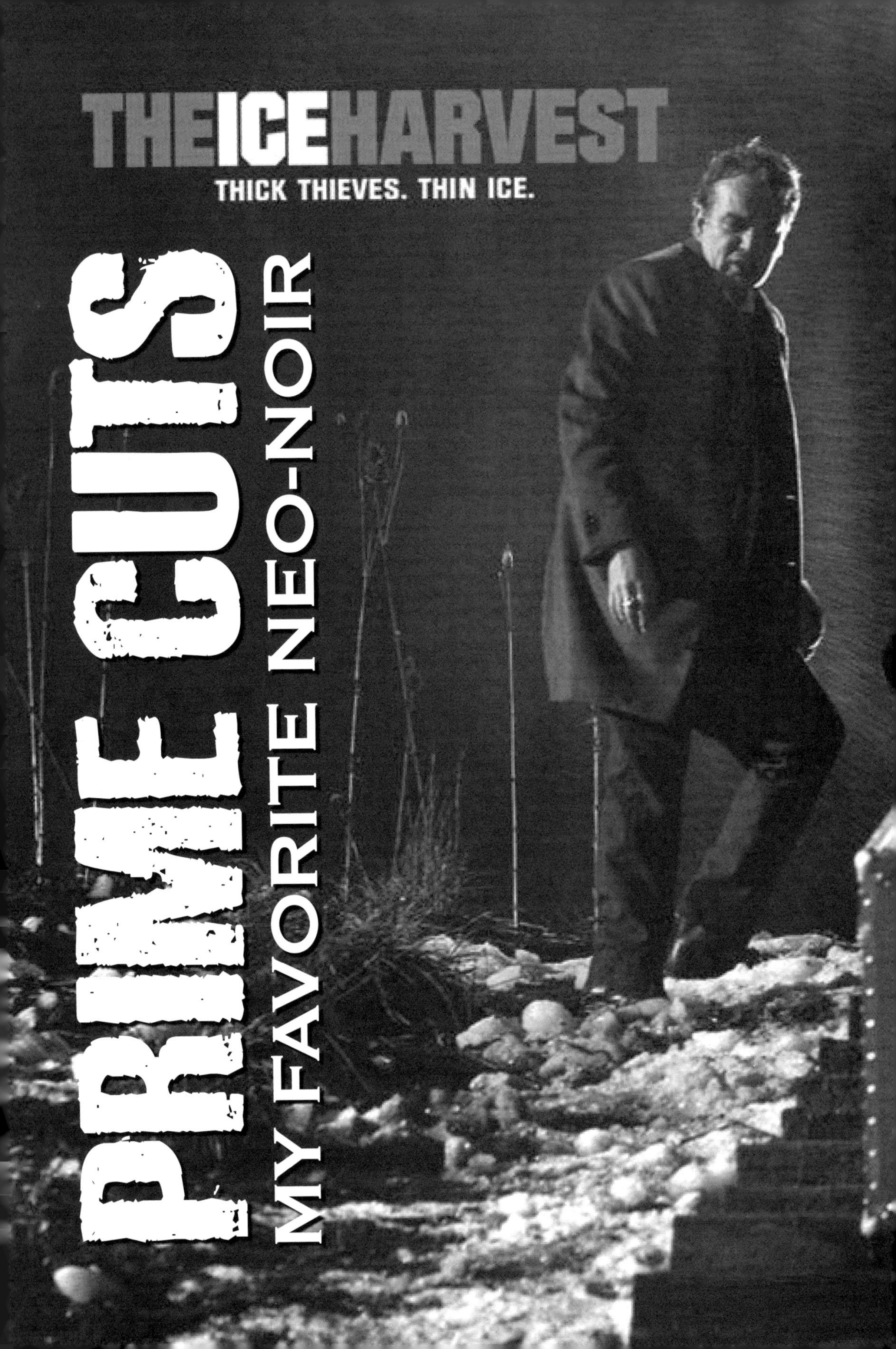

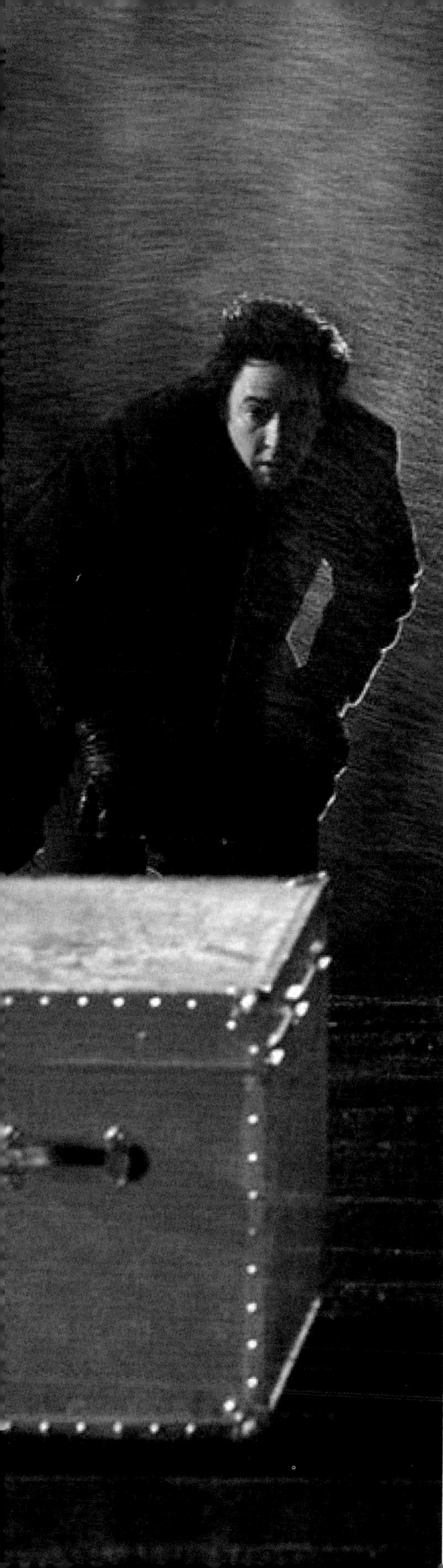

By Sean Axmaker

"People always say there's no such thing as the perfect crime. But I don't agree with that. If you plan things carefully enough, if you think through every last detail, if you have nerves of steel, you can remain calm no matter what happens, there should be no problem you can't handle. It's really just a matter of character. Of course if I had any character, I wouldn't have stolen $2 million from my boss. Christmas Eve. Ho fucking ho."

—Charlie Arglist

Charlie Arglist (John Cusack) has just pulled off a heist that will either set him up for life or end it soon. A Wichita lawyer watching over the strip joints and other local concerns of a Kansas mobster, he sold off his self-respect long ago. Now, he's teamed up with Vic Cavanaugh (Billy Bob Thornton) to rip off their boss and just has to kill the next few hours before splitting the dough and ditching town. But while Charlie may be a moral sell-out, a miserable excuse for a father, and a pushover easily led by Vic, he's not exactly a born thief. He's nervous, anxious, and frankly doesn't trust Vic. (Note to self: was it a good idea to let him keep the money?) And the man has no poker face as he contemplates a new life with his ill-gotten fortune. Renata (Connie Nielsen), proprietor of a rival strip club, notices the sudden jolt of confidence injected into their flirtatious banter. Renata is impressed. Charlie thinks he has a chance, but the night has barely begun.

Set over one long Christmas Eve night, *The Ice Harvest* (2005) is a Midwest winter neo-noir that doesn't get the respect of its brethren *Fargo* (1996) and *A Simple Plan* (1998). It deserves better. Based on (and admirably faithful to) the lean, witty, nastily satisfying debut novel by Scott Phillips, from a screenplay written by multi-Oscar®-winner Robert Benton and Pulitzer Prize-winning author Richard Russo, it's a model of genre filmmaking at its best, straddling the line between rural noir and tawdry small-town portrait with a rich set of distinctive characters and a sly humor built on greed, regret, and self-disgust. Harold Ramis directs with an easy manner that belies the brutality of the situation until it hits Charlie in the stomach and makes him puke his guts out. And it all sneaks up on us. The theft is deceptively easy, just a matter of walking out of the bank with a satchel of cash. It's the consequences that'll kill you. Isn't it always?

"Snowblind noir" is a personal favorite noir

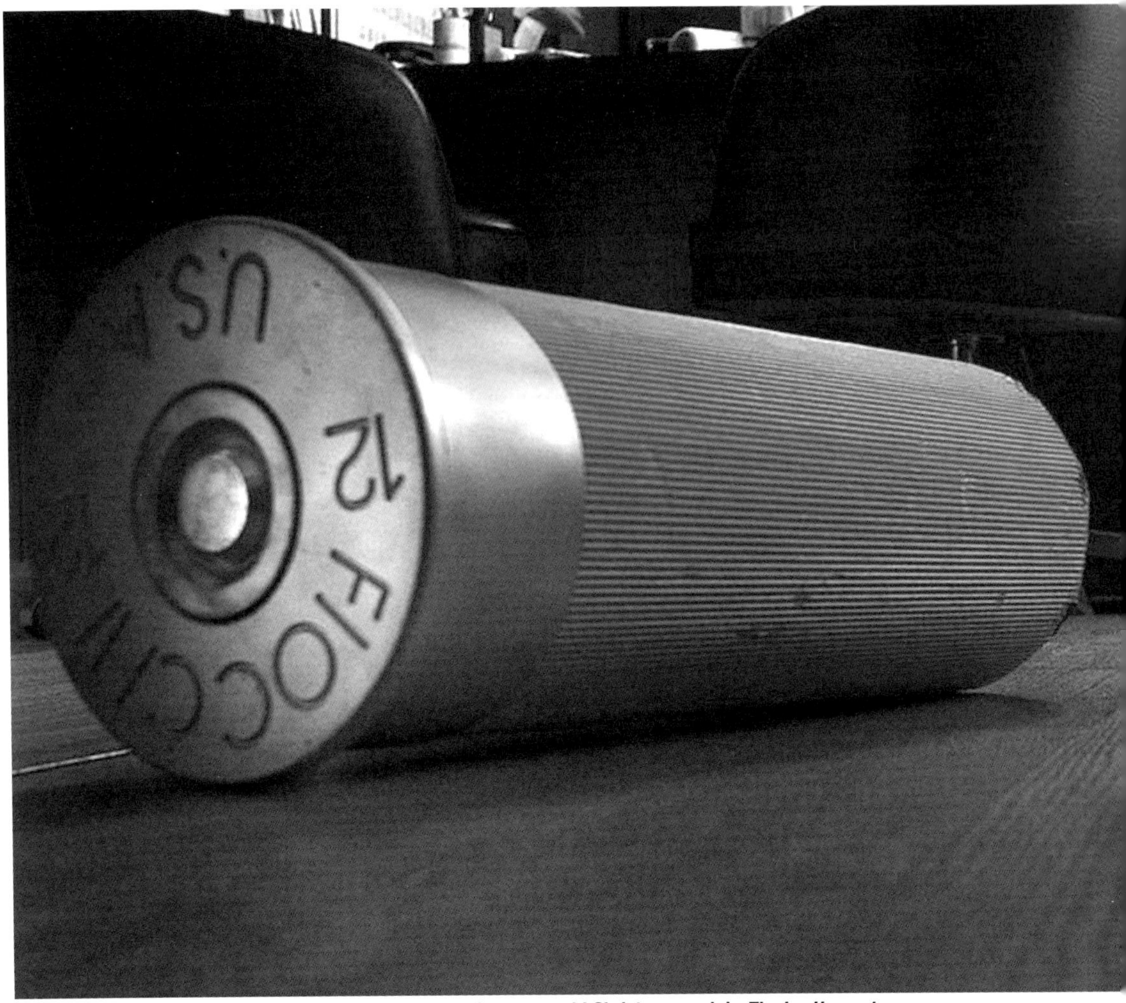

Holiday on Ice: John Cusack as Charlie Arglist tries to heist some cold Christmas cash in *The Ice Harvest*

subgenre of mine, the dark doings set against the white blankets of snow that Hollywood otherwise reserves for innocence and holiday cheer (when it isn't the unforgiving wilderness of a frontier drama or a survival tale). It blasts away the typical shadows of an urban noir landscape and backlights the characters that otherwise merge into the darkness. The stark contrasts create a distinctive backdrop to *On Dangerous Ground* (1951), *Storm Fear* (1955), and *Nightfall* (1956), and neo-noirs *Fargo* and *A Simple Plan*, where violence and greed poison the snow-white innocence of the heartland.

But I digress, for while *The Ice Harvest* is a Christmas Eve noir, this ain't no White Christmas. This holiday is greeted by freezing rain and icy streets and a gray that slips from dim day into the cold dark of night. It's a small but cinematically significant change from the novel, where snow blankets Wichita as Charlie pinballs from seedy strip clubs to tawdry bars. I don't know what the real Wichita is like, but this cinematic incarnation could be a modern take on *It's a Wonderful Life*'s Bedford Falls, only here the hero chooses the town's nocturnal nightmare version. Red and green lights and cheap holiday decorations are tossed up around the edges of the strip clubs where the dancers outnumber the customers; there's no suggestion of any cheer to be found this Christmas.

Benton and Russo collaborated on *Nobody's Fool* (1994), based on Russo's novel, and *Twilight*

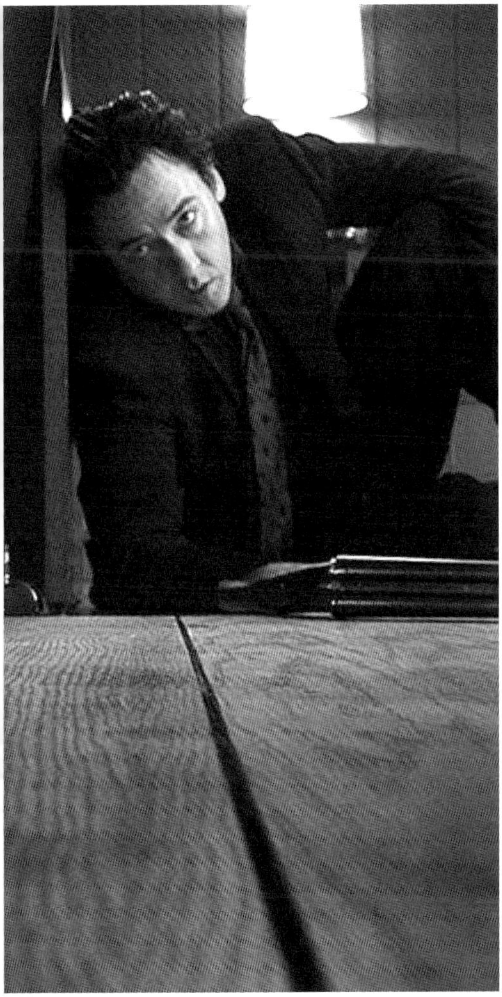

(1998), an original mystery with Paul Newman as the retired private eye pulled into one last case in his sunset years. Benton directed those films but chose to hand the reigns of *The Ice Harvest* over to another and stick to writing and producing with Russo. Their choice was inspired. Harold Ramis is not the first director you'd think of for a project like this. Or the second, or fifth, or… He came from *National Lampoon* and Second City. He wrote *Animal House* and *Stripes* and *Ghostbusters* and directed *Caddyshack* and *National Lampoon's Vacation*. But then Ramis made *Groundhog Day* and *Analyze This*, savvy comedies that plumbed deeper territory than their premises might suggest. Ramis loved Phillips' novel and the script, and he lobbied for the film. He arranged to shoot locations in Waukegan, Illinois, near his Chicago home, and gave the film its signature atmosphere, holiday cheer drowned in dreary gray. As the film goes on, even those colorful flourishes, already distanced from our characters, disappear.

John Cusack, also from Chicago, is perfect casting for Charlie, a smart guy with an amiable manner, little backbone and, as suggested in his opening monologue, even less character. He may be the mastermind of the rip-off, but he's also a relatively passive criminal easily nudged this way and that by Vic or Renata. Cusack, whose boyish face here shows the wear of years, has a geniality and instinctive generosity that's lost on Vic. He's also seriously outclassed in the battle of wills. Thornton plays Vic with the cool arrogance of a guy convinced he's the most ruthless man in the room; his suppressed aggression is all there from the first scene. As Charlie is carried away on the giddy thrill of the steal, Vic grounds him with a terse: "Am I gonna have to slap the shit outta you?" Connie Nielsen's Renata is vamping in a dead-end job in a backwater town, her form-fitted power suit the perfect uniform for the proprietor of a strip club only slightly less seedy than the competition: as sleek as a shark, professional yet feminine, and covering a blouse that could be silky lingerie. She flirts with the practiced ease of a woman who hasn't meant it in years; for all the purring smiles and flirtatious flourishes, she's all business—and business is in trouble thanks to a new zoning law. Charlie robs his company safe for the blackmail photo that his (soon-to-be former) boss uses for leverage, an act of underworld chivalry with an ulterior motive that isn't lost on Renata.

There's one more character, less a player than a reminder of the life he's leaving behind. Charlie stumbles across Pete (Oliver Platt), already sloppy drunk this Christmas Eve, during his clip-joint and cat-house tour of the Wichita underbelly. Pete married Charlie's ex-wife and is as miserable as Charlie once was. It's another savvy change from the novel (here Pete is his ex-brother-in-law) and, rather than create animosity, it gives them a kind of kinship. Whether or not misery loves company, in this case it breeds a special bond of empathy. Pete makes a sport of stirring up shit as he drinks his Christmas Eve away, proclaiming Charlie "the most handsome mob lawyer in Kans-ass" in the way-too-loud voice of the barfly everyone keeps trying to ignore, the holiday-party asshole working a year of misery and suppressed aggression into a single night of unfiltered provocations. Hitting the pick-up bars isn't enough to complete the self-degradation, he has to get himself popped a couple of times and tossed out of the family home.

A MEANNESS IN

REVISITING BRUCE SPRINGSTEEN'S

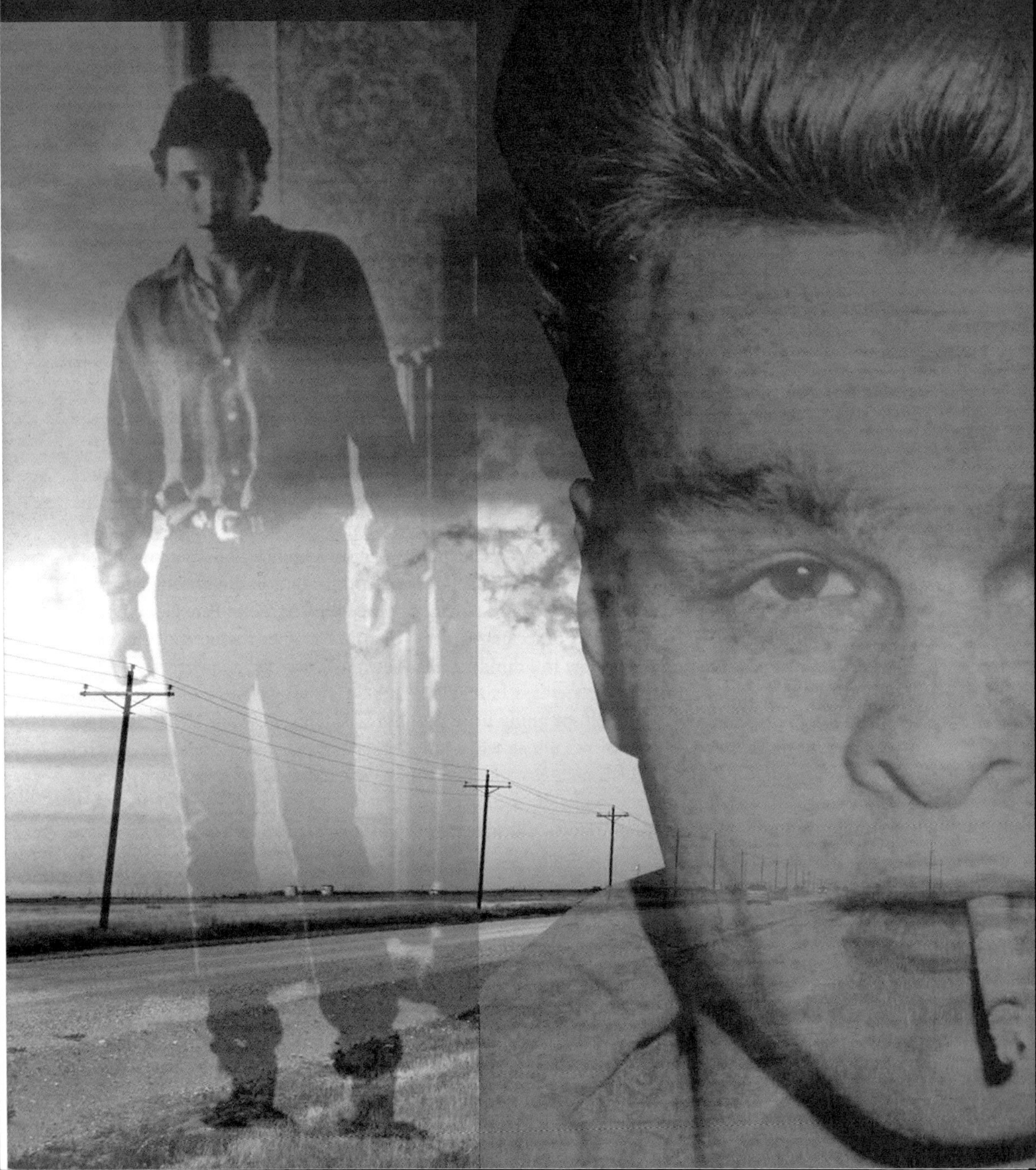

THIS WORLD

NOIR MASTERPIECE

Jake Hinkson

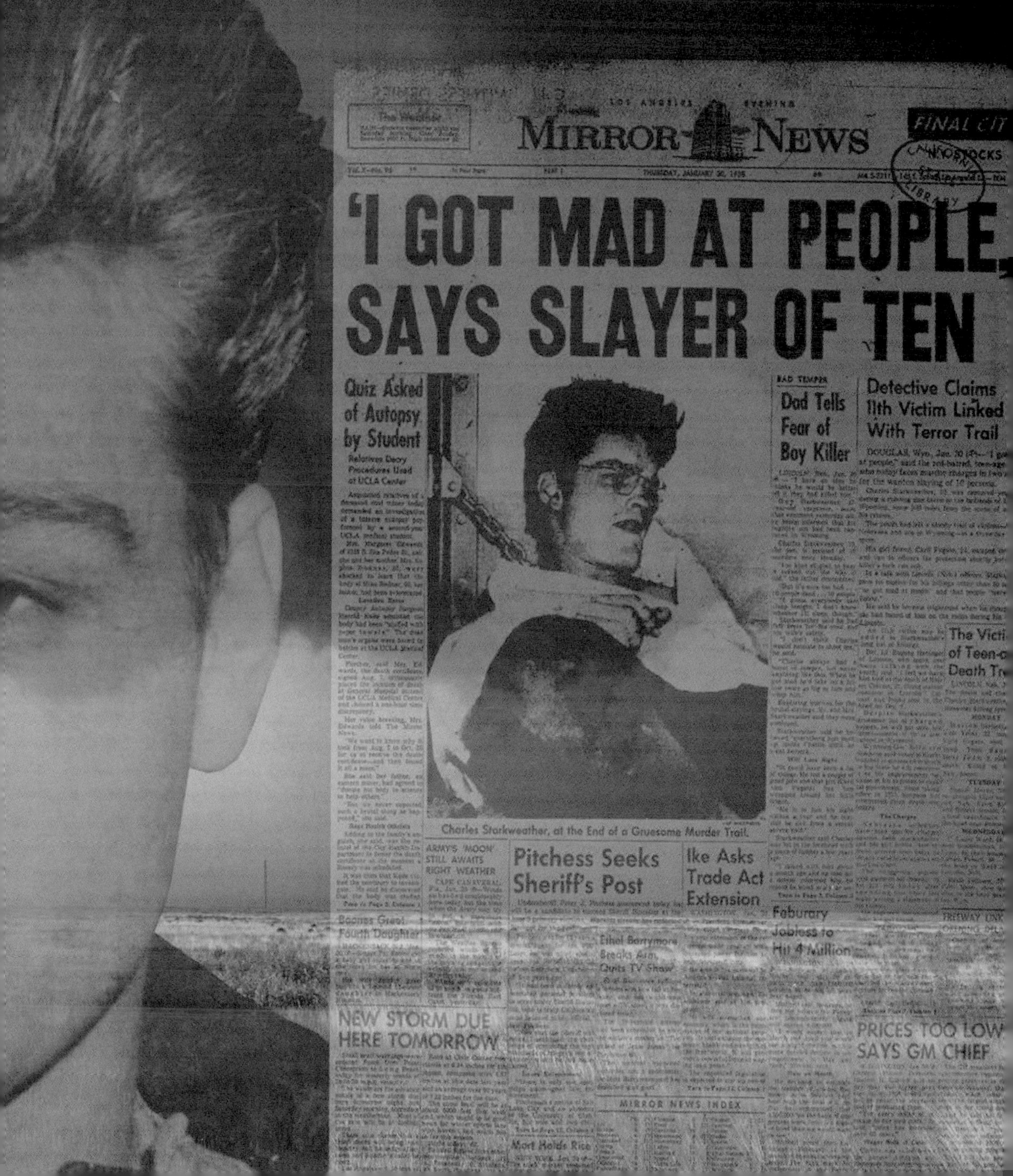

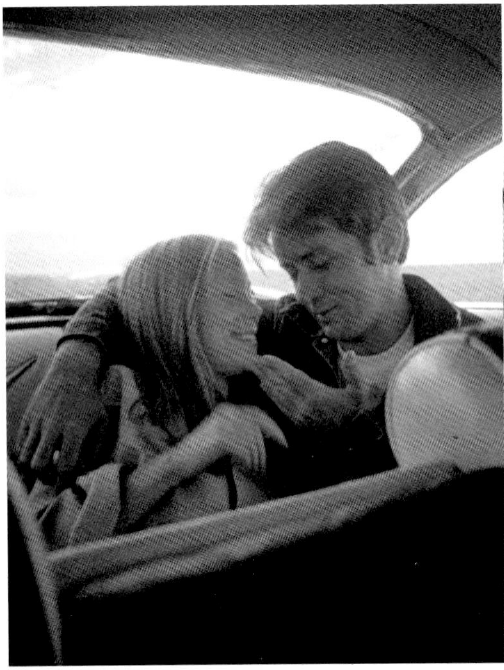

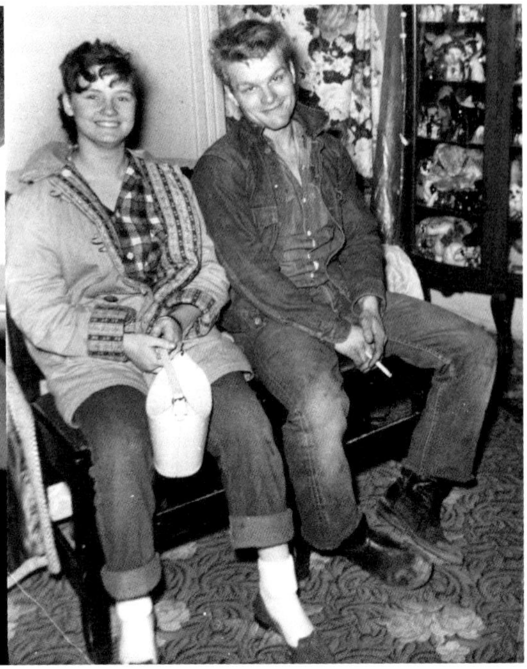

Sissy Spacek and Martin Sheen in 1973's *Badlands*, and their 1950s inspirations, Caril Ann Fugate and Charles Starkweather

N*ebraska* is a storyteller's album. When it was released in 1982, Bruce Springsteen was best known for the working-class operatics of "Born to Run" and "Prove It All Night," stadium-shaking anthems that could bring thousands of fans to their feet. After the success of 1980's blockbuster double-album *The River*, however, Springsteen found himself drawn in a different direction. The new songs he was writing were stripped down melodically, while lyrically they comprised a brooding collection of short stories unified around themes of crime and desperation.

Alone in his bedroom, he recorded the songs that would become *Nebraska* on a TEAC four-track cassette recorder called a Portastudio, creating a soundscape out of nothing but his own voice and a few instruments. He had intended to use these demos to teach the songs to the E Street Band, but upon listening to the intense, almost haunted recordings he realized he had already achieved the perfect sound for such dark and intimate material.

The album's opening track, "Nebraska," is as intense as a Jim Thompson novel. Inspired by the murder spree of Charles Starkweather and Caril Ann Fugate in 1957, the song takes its cue from the opening scenes of *Badlands* (1973), Terrence Malick's movie version of the Starkweather story:

I saw her standin' on her front lawn
just a-twirlin' her baton.
Me and her went for a ride, sir,
and ten innocent people died.

From the town of Lincoln, Nebraska,
with a sawed-off .410 on my lap,
through the badlands of Wyoming,
I killed everything in my path.

Against a dirge-like harmonica, Springsteen's singing is impeccable in its precision, capturing the same bizarre mixture of Midwestern politeness and sociopathic indifference that Martin Sheen brought to his performance as Starkweather surrogate Kit Carruthers in *Badlands*. Springsteen also respects the mystery surrounding the relationship between Starkweather and Fugate, the mystery of whether the young girl (only 14 at the time of the killings) was a victim or an accomplice:

Sheriff, when the man pulls that switch, sir,
and snaps my poor head back,
you make sure my pretty baby
is sittin' right there on my lap.

The most noir moment in this song, however, comes at the end, as Springsteen's Starkweather sums up his tale with the existential clarity of an Allen Baron movie:

They declared me unfit to live,
said into that great void my soul'd be hurled.
They wanna know why I did what I did.
Well, sir, I guess there's just a meanness in this world.

One of the strongest elements of the album is that the songs have a unity of expression and metaphor. The songwriter repeats key phrases, like the polite parenthetical "sir" that pops up throughout and often has a resentful edge to it. Likewise, cars figure prominently on *Nebraska* as symbols of alienation and isolation, from the title song's cross-country rampage to the midnight monologue of "State Trooper":

New Jersey Turnpike,
Ridin' on a wet night,
'neath the refinery's glow,
out where the great black rivers flow.

License, registration,
I ain't got none,
but I got a clear conscience
'bout the things that I done.
Mister state trooper, please don't stop me.
Please don't stop me.
Please don't stop me.

The narrator's plea is half prayer, half warning. Although Springsteen never tells us what the narrator's done, it's clear that his late-night drive is a mission of violence. Over a steady thrumming guitar, he whispers:

Maybe you got a kid,
maybe you got a pretty wife.
The only thing that I got's
been bothering me my whole life.

This isn't a story-song with a narrative arc, it's an elliptical character sketch, a snapshot of a man driving down the New Jersey Turnpike, muttering under his breath that "somebody out there" should "listen to my last prayer."

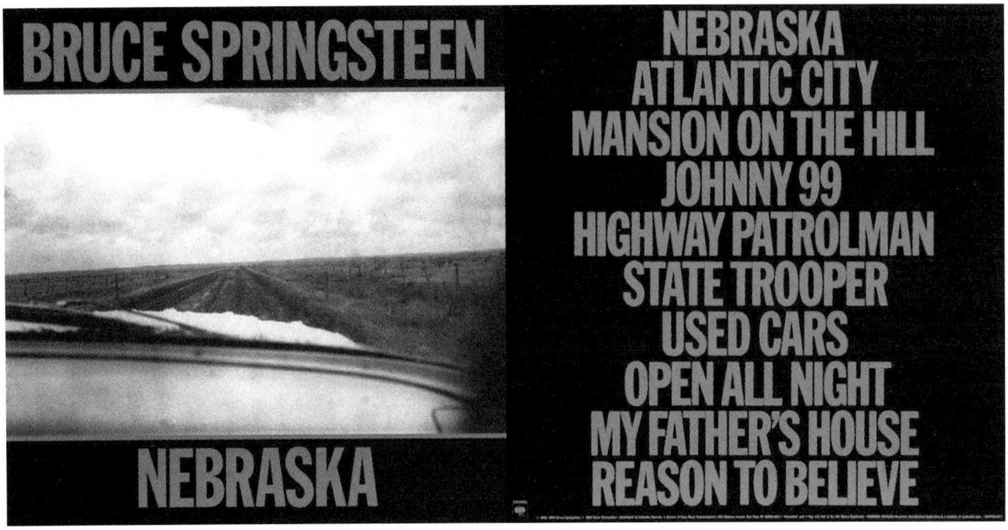

An interesting contrast to the expressionistic "State Trooper" is the laconic "Highway Patrolman," which Sean Penn would later use as the basis for his 1991 directorial debut, *The Indian Runner*. The narrator of this song, Joe Roberts, is a Michigan state patrolman, who tells us bluntly:

I always done an honest job, as honest as I could.
I got a brother named Franky, and Franky ain't no good.

Springsteen gives Joe Roberts a distinctive voice, world-weary, and disappointed. As his Cain and Abel tale unfolds, Joe tells us that Franky served in Vietnam while Joe got married to a girl named Maria and took a farm deferment:

But them wheat prices kept on droppin'
till it was like we were getting' robbed.
Franky came home in '68, and, me, I took this job.

Joe Roberts, the one lawman on an album full of criminals, is more of a failed farmer than a crusader. His main job seems to be looking after Franky, who stays in trouble, drinking too much and getting into bar brawls. Joe bails him out time and time again, though he tells us:

Well if it was any other man, I'd put him straight away.
But when it's your brother, sometimes you look the other way.

Things reach a head one night when Franky seriously injures a young man in a fight at a roadhouse. Joe chases his car through the backroads, finally stopping at the border to watch his brother disappear into Canada. There is no resolution to be had, just the weight of familial obligation. A man who would turn his back on his family, Joe decides, "well, he ain't no good."

"Highway Patrolman" isn't the only song on *Nebraska* that takes place in an America of dimming economic fortunes. Even on songs where the narratives don't turn to lawbreaking, the characters seem trapped in conditions that could lead to crime. Songs like "Mansion on the Hill" and "Used Cars" are both told from the point of view of working class kids caught up in the dawning realization that they belong to a permeant underclass, the existence of which belies the optimistic notion of upward mobility. The title "Mansion on the Hill" echoes Ronald Reagan's famous metaphor, in his 1980 election eve address, of America as "that shining city on the hill." In Springsteen's song, however, that gleaming hilltop crest is more taunting than aspirational:

There's a place out on the edge of town, sir,
rising above the factories and the fields.
Now ever since I was a child I can remember
that mansion on the hill.

In the day, you can see the children playing
on the road that leads to those gates of hardened steel.
Steel gates that completely surround
the mansion on the hill.

On "Used Cars," Springsteen uses the title's subject as a metaphor for deferred dreams. A young boy narrates the story of his family's visit to a used car lot, the salesman "telling us all about the break he'd give us if he could, but he just can't." The family buys the car, but the secondhand vehicle fills the child with shame. Resenting the gulf between his family's labors and their material conditions, he notes:

Dad, he sweats the same job from morning to morn.
Me, I walk home on the same dirty streets where I was born.

Now, mister, the day my number comes in
I ain't ever gonna ride in no used car again.

Elsewhere in the song, the narrator dreams of winning the lottery, his hopes for better material conditions not predicated on his labors—after all, he's seen what's come of his father's sweat and toil—but on blind, dumb luck. A society that offers more hope from the lottery than from honest work is a society poised to explode.

We see that explosion on "Atlantic City," which begins, appropriately enough, with a literal explosion—the March 1981 bombing of Philip "The Chicken Man" Testa, a Philadelphia mafia figure. Over a ferociously strummed acoustic guitar, Springsteen sings:

Well, they blew up the chicken man in Philly last night.
Now, they blew up his house, too.
Down on the boardwalk they're getting' ready for a fight,
gonna see what them racket boys can do.

This is a strange beginning for a song that is, of all things, a heartbreaking love ballad. The narrator is a poor working man caught up in the swirl of events. With war breaking out between the different factions in town, a fight that we infer is sweeping up the unions and the rackets, the narrator addresses this lament to his girlfriend:

Everything dies, baby, that's a fact,
but maybe everything that dies someday comes back.
Put your makeup on, fix your hair up pretty,
and meet me tonight in Atlantic City.

The power here comes from the way Springsteen positions his protagonists as lovers in the storm—the storm in this case being a society with increasingly limited options. The narrator "got a job and

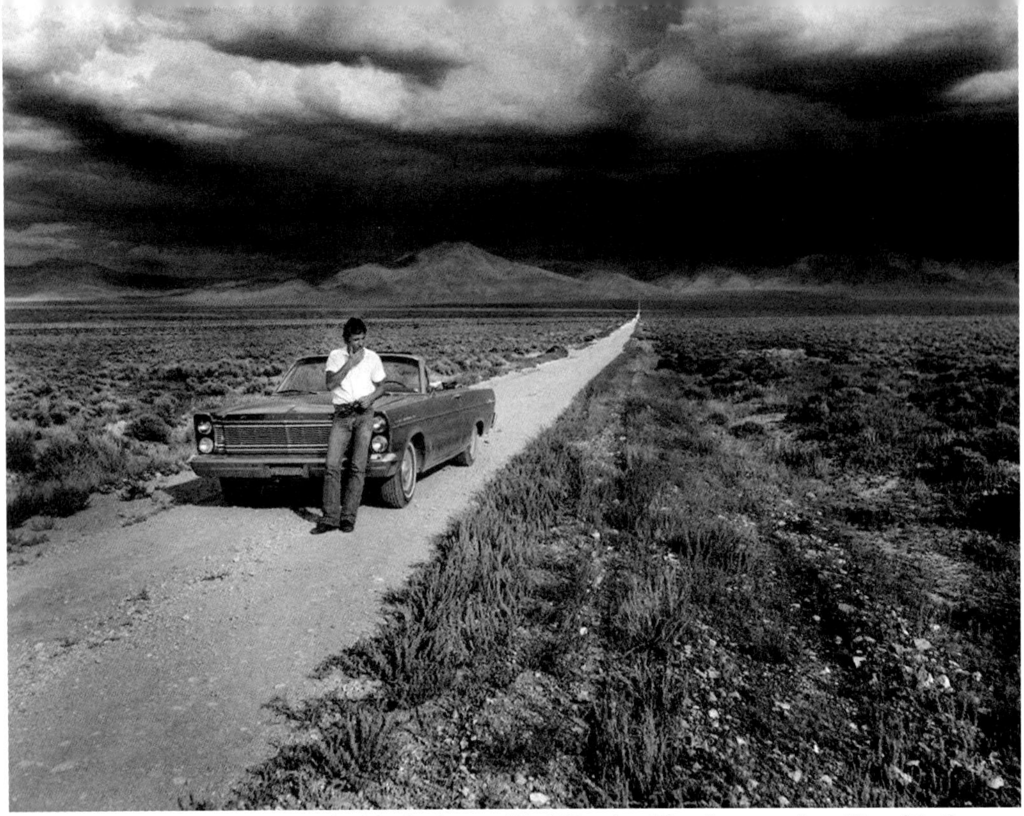

Springsteen's album is rooted in the unforgiving landscape of the Midwest and the grim economic realities of the time

tried to put some money away / but I got debts no honest man can pay," the same work-doesn't-pay lament that forms the undercurrent of much of the album. While a song like "Nebraska" can only shake its head at the unsolvable mystery of Starkweather's sociopathic rage, the rest of the album advances the blunt thesis that crime is the outgrowth of society's moral hypocrisy and economic double standards. "Atlantic City" ends with a surrender to this darkness, as the protagonist ominously tells his lover:

Now I been lookin' for a job, but it's hard to find.
Down here it's just winners and losers and
don't get caught on the wrong side of that line.
Well, I'm tired of comin' out on this losin' end,
so, honey, last night I met this guy,
and I'm gonna do a little favor for him.

A harder and faster brother to "Atlantic City," "Johnny 99" is a barnburner of a song, with Springsteen giving his guitar strings a beating beneath blasts of the harmonica. The song tells the story of a laid-off auto plant worker who gets drunk one night and shoots a night store clerk in a botched robbery. Nabbed by an off-duty police officer, the man is sentenced to "98 and a year" and dubbed Johnny 99. Springsteen links the two songs when Johnny is allowed to make a statement to the court and ends up echoing the narrator of "Atlantic City," albeit with even less hope:

Now judge, judge, I got debts no honest man could pay.
The bank was holdin' my mortgage and takin' my house away.
Now, I ain't sayin' that makes me an innocent man,
but it was more 'n all this that put that gun in my hand.

The air of crime recedes in the album's closing songs. "Open All Night" is *Nebraska*'s one upbeat tune, a rave with an electric Chuck Berry riff sweeping along a joyful celebration of American car culture. The song isn't out of place, though, because Springsteen places its protagonist, a night-shifter worker driving two hours to see his girlfriend Wanda, on the same lonely stretch of the Jersey Turnpike as the brooding narrator of "State Trooper," and he ties these two disparate songs together lyrically with nods to jammed up radio stations and refinery towers. The narrator here is having a good day, but he's swimming against the same tides as the album's other characters.

Interestingly, the lightest song on the album then gives way to the song that is, in many ways, the darkest. In "My Father's House," a man dreams that he is a child lost in the woods late at night. He comes upon a clearing where he sees his father's house "shining hard and bright," and he runs up to the house to collapse in his father's arms. The man awakens from this dream and resolves to go see his father, imagining that "the hard things that pulled us apart / will never again, sir, tear us from each other's hearts." In something of a delirium, he drives through the night to his father's house, only to find people he doesn't know living there, a sudden reminder that his father is dead and gone.

My father's house shines hard and bright.
It stands like a beacon calling me in the night.
Calling and calling so cold and alone,
shining cross this dark highway where our sins lie unatoned.

This isn't a song about crime but sin, of things said and done that can never be taken back. Beautiful and mournful, it is perhaps *Nebraska*'s most effecting song and certainly one of the songwriter's finest achievements.

On the album's final track, the strangely uplifting "Reason to Believe," Springsteen embraces a bruised-and-battered perseverance that previous songs, like "Atlantic City" and "Open All Night" only nodded at. The song ties together four disparate vignettes, beginning with the singer observing a strange scene:

Seen a man standin' over a dead dog by the highway in a ditch.
He's lookin' down kinda puzzled, pokin' that dog with a stick.
Got his car door flung open, he's standin' out on Highway 31
like if he stood there long enough that dog'd get up and run.

"Reason to Believe" is a humanist statement that never seems pat or coy. By beginning the album's final song with the image of the baffled motorist grieving over the dog he's killed, Springsteen creates a fascinating juxtaposition to the sociopathic indifference on the album's opener. When he writes "Struck me kinda funny, seems kinda funny, sir, to me / how at the end of every hard-earned day people find some reason to believe," he's not shortchanging the *hard-earned* part. On the next vignette, a woman loses her lover and spends the rest of her life waiting for him to return. Some musicians would doubtless render this story as a grand romantic gesture, but Springsteen views it as dispassionately as he views the dog in the ditch. The next vignette contrasts the baptism of an infant and the funeral of an old man, the unbroken circle of life and death that is as unceasing as it is ultimately meaningless. "Lord, won't you tell us, tell us what does it mean?" the congregation prays. To their beseeching, however, all Springsteen can offer up is the song's refrain, "At the end of every hard-earned day people find some reason to believe."

The song ends with a groom abandoned on his wedding day, watching a river flow by, indifferent to his worries or sorrows. It's a potent image on which to end the album, an existential summation to a collection of songs about human beings fighting to survive in a world as cold and apathetic as the frozen plains of Nebraska. ■

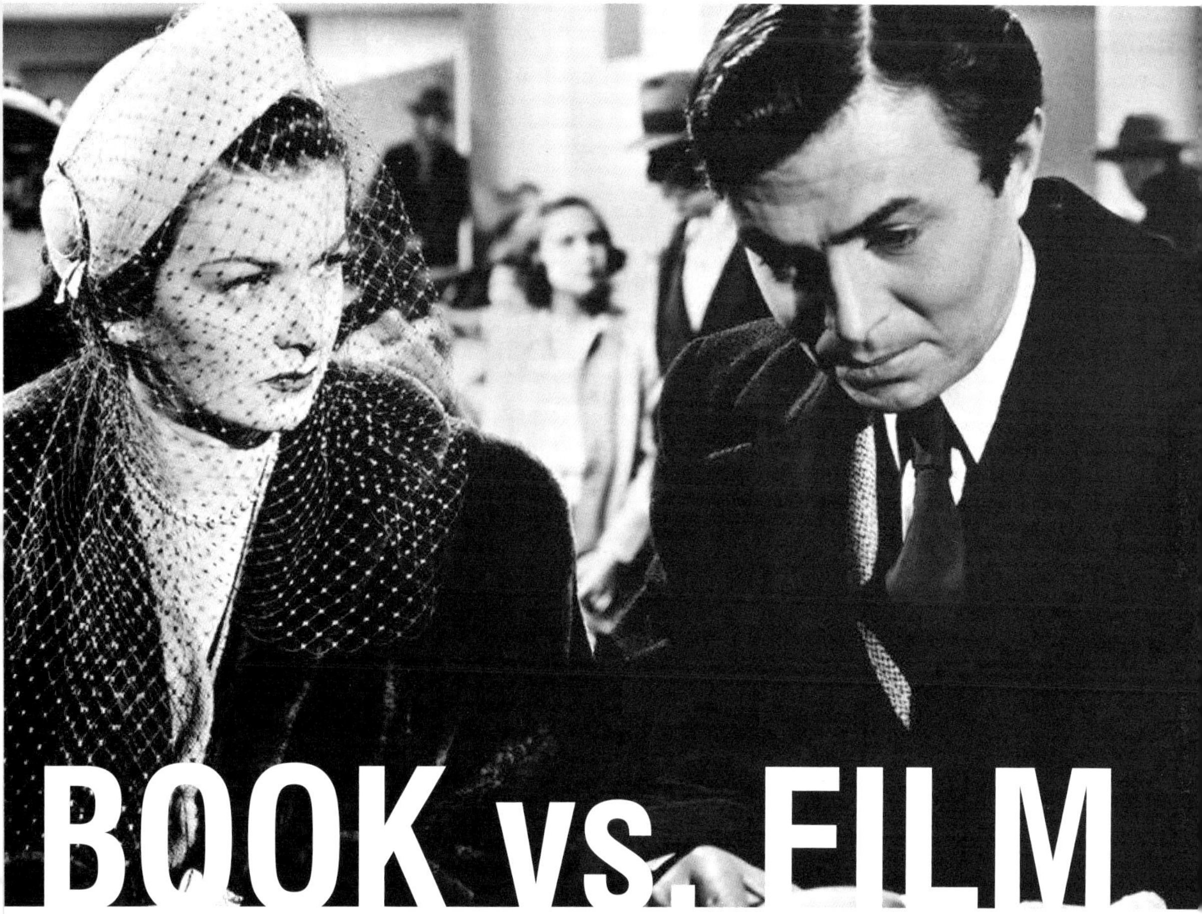

BOOK vs. FILM

SECTION FIVE

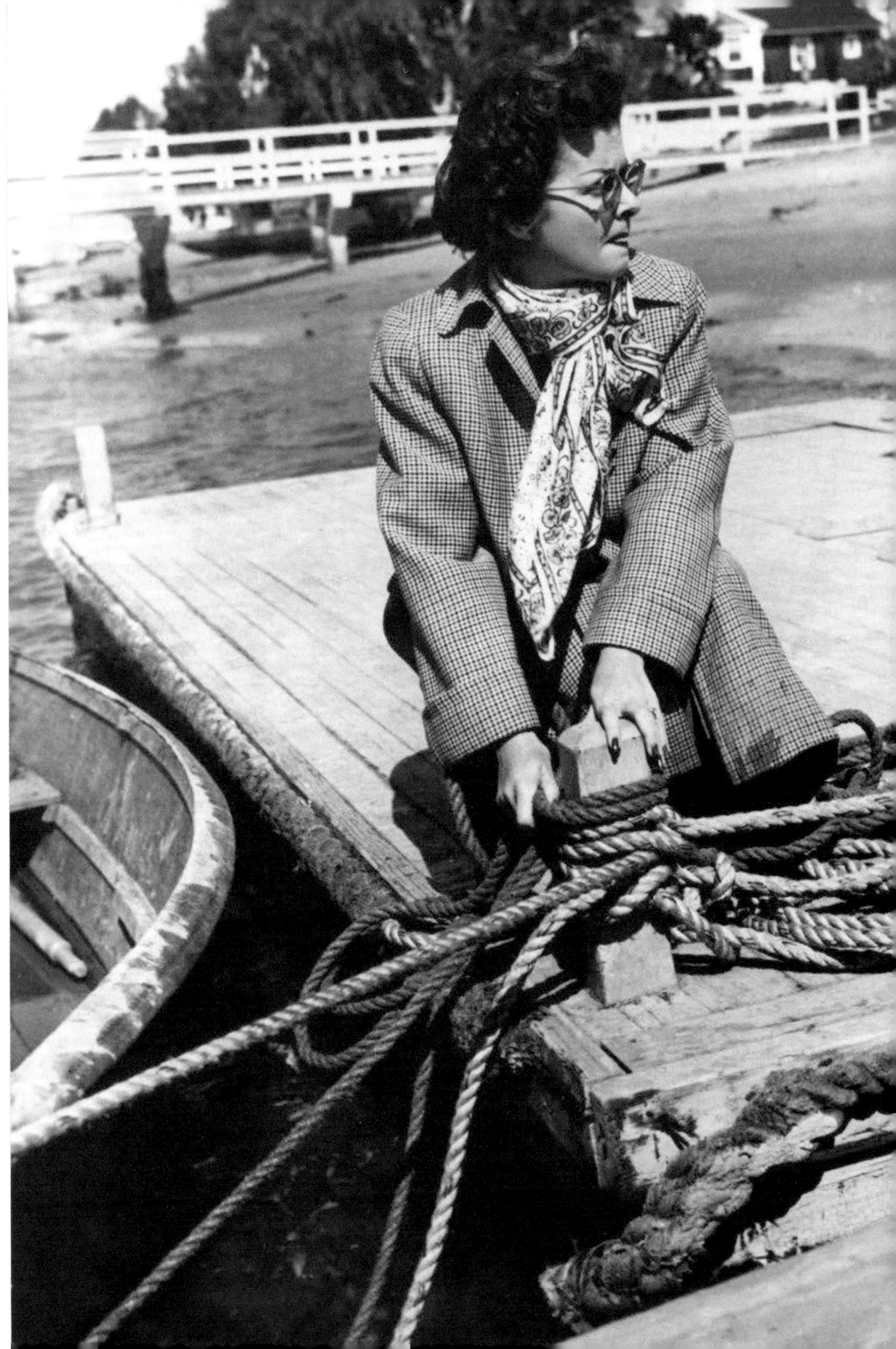

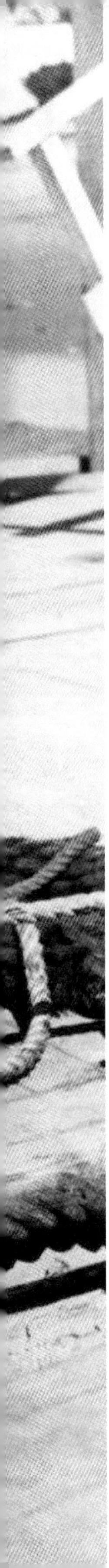

The movie transports the action west, to Balboa, a quiet coastal town in California about fifty miles from Los Angeles. Ophüls and his screenwriters open up the narrative perspective. Whereas the novel stays in close on Lucia Holley (now Lucia Harper), the film lets us see the incident that leads to Darby's death. After Lucia and Darby meet at the cheap hotel, Darby calls Bea (changed from Bee) before Lucia can reach her and sets the girl against her mother. That night, he sneaks up to the Harper's waterside home for an assignation with Bea in the boathouse. Bea's no fool though, and soon enough she sees through Darby's manipulation. A struggle follows, and in a complicated sequence of events, Darby ends up dying without Bea realizing what has happened. She runs back to the house, swears to her mother that she's through with Darby, and goes to bed. Early the next morning, Lucia goes for a walk down on the shore and finds Darby's dead body.

The Reckless Moment adds emphasis to Lucia's relationship with the nervous blackmailer Martin Donnelly (played by James Mason), who has love letters written by Bea to Darby. He wants $5,000 (a heady sum in 1949) or the letters will go to the police. Donnelly is not a particularly good blackmailer—he's clearly charmed by Lucia, maybe even oddly protective of her—but he's working for a shadowy character named Nagel (Roy Roberts), and, unfortunately, Nagel *is* a good blackmailer. He's not charmed at all by Mrs. Harper.

The Reckless Moment shows Ophüls, known for both his exquisite camera technique and for his sensitive treatment of female protagonists, in full command of his powers as a Hollywood filmmaker. His tracking shots, which are more like tracking glides, were simply the best in the business. Many directors move the camera; Ophüls's camera *floats*. If one only knows his lushly romantic pictures like *Letter from an Unknown Woman* (1948) or his European triumphs like *La Ronde* (1950), one might well wonder if his style could work in noir. That it works superbly is not so much a testament to how much Ophüls adapted to the material, as it is proof of how evocative and fraught with tension his style is to begin with. One look at the opening scenes—the way Lucia's meeting with Darby unfolds in graceful sweeping shots that create, in mere seconds, Darby's *demimonde* in that sleazebag hotel—and know in an instant that this is an Ophüls movie.

With this film, the director delivered another of his great "women's pictures." Holding's novel is a rich, dark story, and Ophüls seized on it as a way to tell the story of female entrapment in the postwar years.

As in Holding's novel, Lucia Harper is boxed in by her family—her daughter, her son, her father-in-law, and even the mysteriously distant husband, Mr. Harper, at work overseas "building a bridge" in postwar Europe. She loves her family (and they clearly love her), but that love only makes the weight of her commitments to them all the heavier. In fact, Lucia's chief difficulty in navigating the blackmail scheme is that her family is always watching her. She keeps stealing away to the city. Strange men keep showing up at the house. Questions arise about money. Exasperated at one point, Lucia tells Donnelly, "You don't know how a family can surround you sometimes."

"You never get away from your family, do you?" he replies.

Staring out the window, she quietly answers, "No."As Lucia, Joan Bennett gives a stunning performance, all the more surprising if a viewer only knows her as the sexy bad girl from *The Woman in the Window* (1944) and *Scarlet Street* (1945). To see her trapped in Lucia Harper's world of tortured middle-aged motherhood and bourgeoisie asphyxiation might be a shock, but it's a bigger shock how well she pulls it off. She sinks into this role, portraying Lucia as a frantic, unhappy, but ultimately resourceful woman. Wanger intended the film as a showcase for her acting chops, and it is one hell of a showcase.

Joan Bennett, playing against her *femme fatale* image, gives one of her greatest performances as Lucia Harper in *The Reckless Moment*

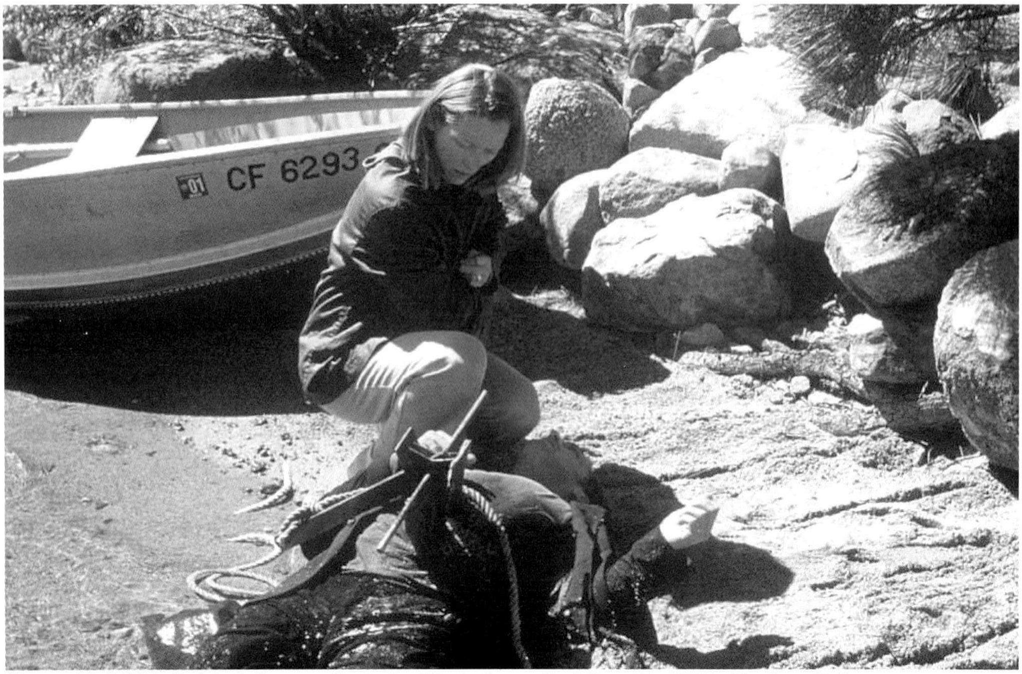

Margaret Hall (Tilda Swinton) discovers the body of Darby Reese (Josh Lucas) in 2001's *The Deep End*

The Deep End (2001)

Lucia Holley is such a great role for an actress, perhaps it was inevitable that she would return to the screen. In 2001, Scott McGehee and David Siegel adapted *The Blank Wall* as *The Deep End*. Their impressive remake stays remarkably close to the original, with the significant exception of changing the focus of the mother's worries and fears from her daughter to her son.

Tilda Swinton (in the role that brought her to a wide American audience) stars as Margaret Hall, a mother of three, caring for her children and aging father-in-law while her husband is serving on a ship "somewhere in the Pacific." As the film begins, her teenage son Beau (Jonathan Tucker) has been in a drunk driving car wreck, the result of a wild night with an older man named Darby Reese (Josh Lucas).

McGehee and Siegel have moved the action to Nevada, with Margaret rushing from her home in sunny Lake Tahoe to seedy Reno where Darby owns a nightclub called The Deep End. The filmmakers start the story in the same fashion as Holding and Ophüls, with the mother entering the city to warn the older man away from her child. It's a bracing first scene, with Margaret descending from the bathed-in-sunlight streets to the neon abyss of Darby's club.

The Deep End follows the same pattern as the book and previous film: Darby's accidental death, the mother's attempt to cover up the death by submerging the body in the lake, the sudden appearance of the soft-hearted blackmailer, and the inevitable confrontation with Nagel—the second, more vicious blackmailer. The weakest aspect of the film (and, it must be said, the weakest aspect of all three versions of the story) is the relationship between the mother and the blackmailer, here named Alek Spera and played by Goran Visnjic. Spera, even more than the previous incarnations of the blackmailer, never comes into focus as a character of his own, and, as a result, Margaret's sudden (the story unfolds over a few days) attachment to him feels forced. At the end, she is devastated by what happens to Spera after the violent showdown with Nagel, whereas the audience is thinking, "Well, that actually works out pretty good for you." Both film versions soften and sentimentalize the relationship with the blackmailer somewhat, whereas Holding ends the novel on a darker, bleaker note.

The big swerve in *The Deep End*, and in many ways the most interesting change that McGehee and Siegel bring to the material, is to have Margaret and Beau reconnect as mother and son at the end. Though the film is ostensibly about Beau's closeted homosexuality and the danger he faces as a gay teenager in 2001 (and, it is implied, some of that danger may come from his own absent father), mother and son never discuss these issues. Beau is as resentful of his mother's nurturing authority as Bee and Bea were, but his relationship with Darby is buried in an even deeper shame. It also helps that, by 2001, their relationship can be more explicitly sexual. Whereas the previous versions tiptoed around sex with talk of letters that linked the daughter to the dead man, Margaret is blackmailed with a videotape of her son having sex with Darby, a tape Darby shot himself, perhaps with blackmail in mind. By foregrounding these issues, McGehee and Siegel set up the end of the film, where Margaret and Beau reconcile, a scene that has no analog in the previous versions—making *The Deep End* the most redemptive incarnation of the story.

In the showdown between Elisabeth Sanxay Holding and the filmmakers who adapted her novel, everyone comes out a winner. Max Ophüls made one of the great feminist noirs of the classic era, a film that goes on the shortlist alongside works like *Mildred Pierce* (1945) and *Caged* (1950), while Scott McGehee and David Siegel took the 50-year-old material and turned it into one of the most original films of the neo-noir era. Of course, all of this reflects back on the strength of Holding's original masterpiece, perhaps the best domestic noir of the war years, a novel as resonant today as it was 70 years ago. ■

BOOK vs FILM

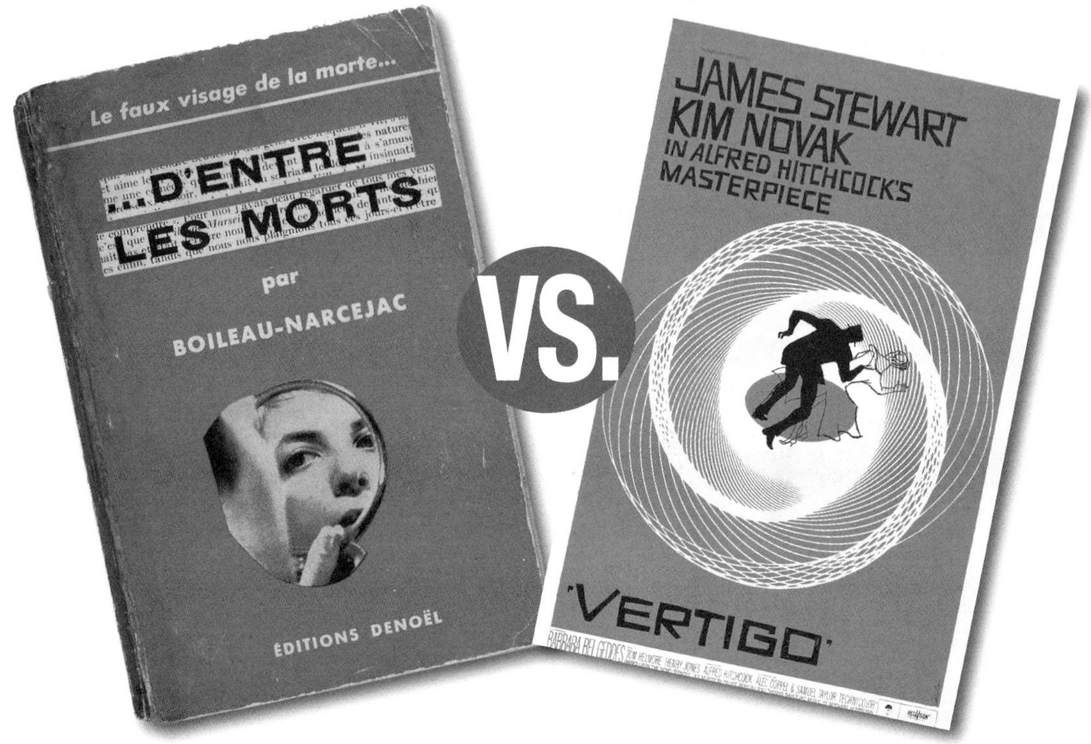

Brian Light

At a 1948 awards banquet in Paris honoring Thomas Narcejac (Pierre Ayraud's *nom de plume*) with the Prix du Roman d'Aventures, given to the year's best work of detective fiction–French or foreign, the author was introduced to the 1938 winner, Pierre Boileau. Both of their acclaimed novels were "locked room" mysteries, a subgenre of crime fiction originating from Edgar Allan Poe's 1841 short story "The Murders in the Rue Morgue." Boileau and Narcejac shared an immediate connection, not only through mutual admiration—both writers felt trapped in their formulaic "locked rooms." Neither was inspired by the American "hardboiled" school of fiction, which had infiltrated the European market in the 1940s. In collaboration, they instead created a new strain of mystery fiction focused on the victim or collaborator in a crime, exploring the psychology, motivations, and actions as that character struggles through dire circumstance. Boileau would construct the diabolical plots and Narcejac would craft the complex characterizations. The partners had one *règle de jeu*: the protagonist must never wake from the nightmare.

Their first collaboration was *Celle qui n'était plus* (*She Who Was No More*) in 1952. In his landmark interview, *Hitchcock/Truffaut*, Truffaut suggests that when Boileau and Narcejac learned

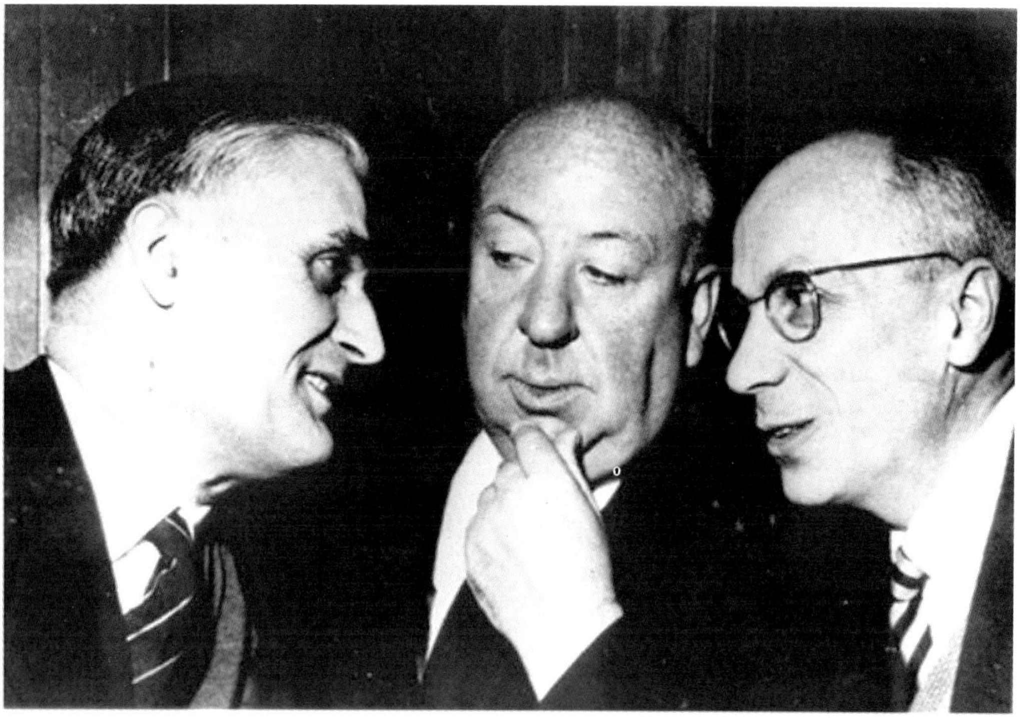

Alfred Hitchcock consults with the authors of *D'entre les morts* — Thomas Narcejac (left) and Pierre Boileau (right)

Hitchcock had tried to acquire the rights to their first book (adapted by Henri-Georges Clouzot and released in 1955 as *Les Diaboliques*) they wrote their third, *D'entre les morts* (*From Among the Dead*) with the director in mind. Hitchcock was quick to dispute this: "No, they didn't. The book was out before we acquired the property." Dan Auiler confirmed this in an interview with Narcejac for his exhaustively detailed book, *Vertigo: The Making of a Hitchcock Classic*. Narcejac said they never intended to write a story for Hitchcock; the idea was sparked in a French cinema as Narcejac watched a newsreel and believed he recognized someone he'd lost touch with during the war.

"After the war," he explained, "there were many displaced people and families—it was common to have 'lost' a friend. I began to think of the possibilities of recognizing someone like this. Maybe someone who was thought dead. ... and this is where *D'entre les morts* began to take shape." The novel came to the attention of Paramount, and Hitchcock, in the form of a plot synopsis in November 1954. When *Les Diaboliques* became a movie-house sensation in 1955, Paramount acquired the rights to *D'entre les morts*. Hitchcock told Truffaut what drew him to the story: "I was intrigued by the hero's attempts to recreate the image of a dead woman through another one that's alive." The English translation of the novel *D'entre les morts*, retitled *The Living and the Dead*, released in the U.S. in April 1957.

The director already had Vera Miles in mind for the role of Madeleine. He had recently directed her in the debut episode of his television series, *Alfred Hitchcock Presents*. "Revenge" was a taut tale of a woman who becomes emotionally unstable after being raped. Hitchcock was so impressed by her performance he cast her again the same year opposite Henry Fonda in his underrated neo-realist thriller *The Wrong Man* (1956). Hitchcock was convinced his next feature would make her a major star...but it was not to be. During preproduction, Hitchcock was beset with health problems and twice went under the knife, each recuperation period pushing back the film's schedule. In the interim, Miles, who was married to *Tarzan* hunk Gordon Scott at the time, became pregnant with their son Michael. After some deliberation, Kim Novak was cast, even though she was under contract to Columbia. A deal was struck in which Harry Cohn agreed to lend the actress for *Vertigo*'s production

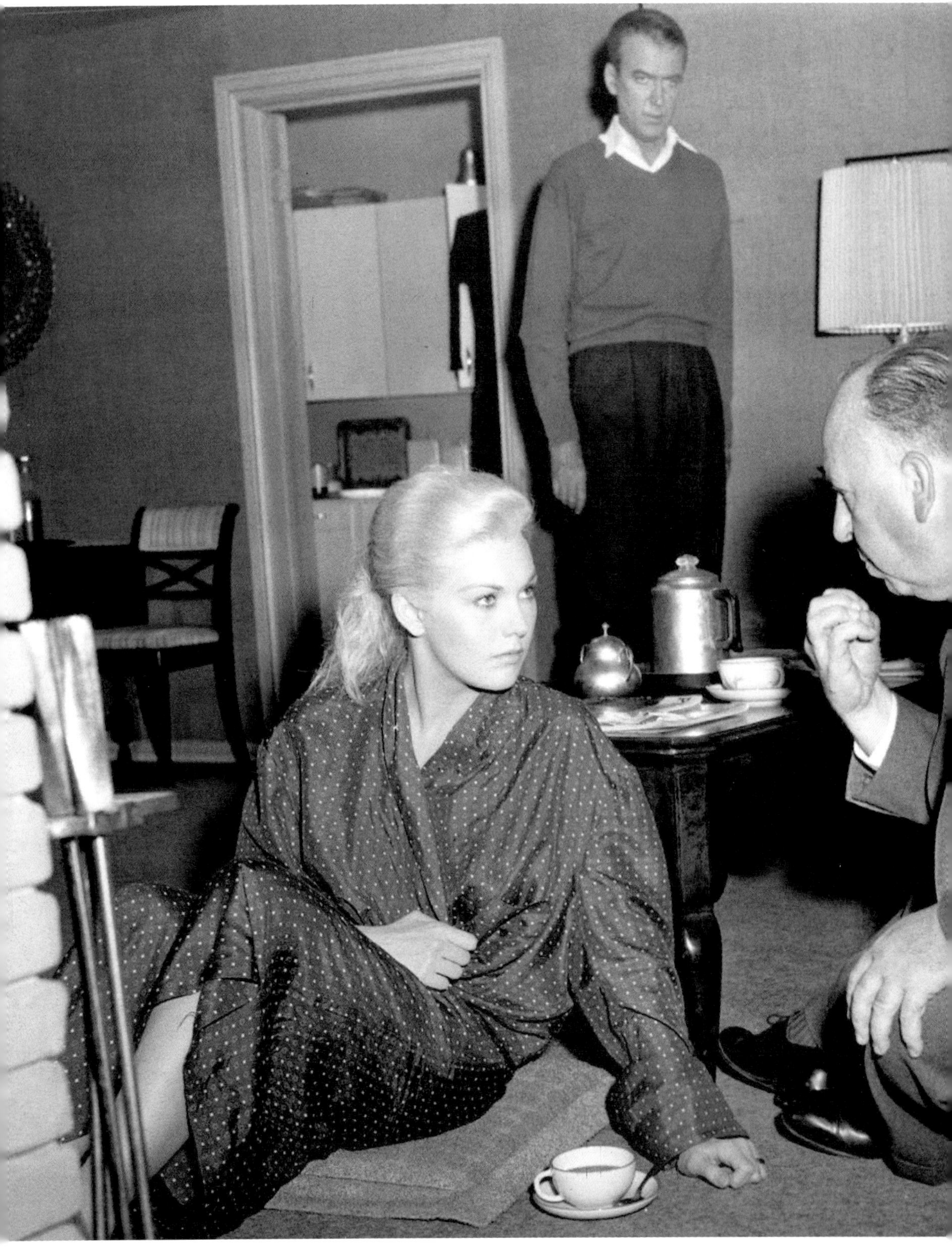

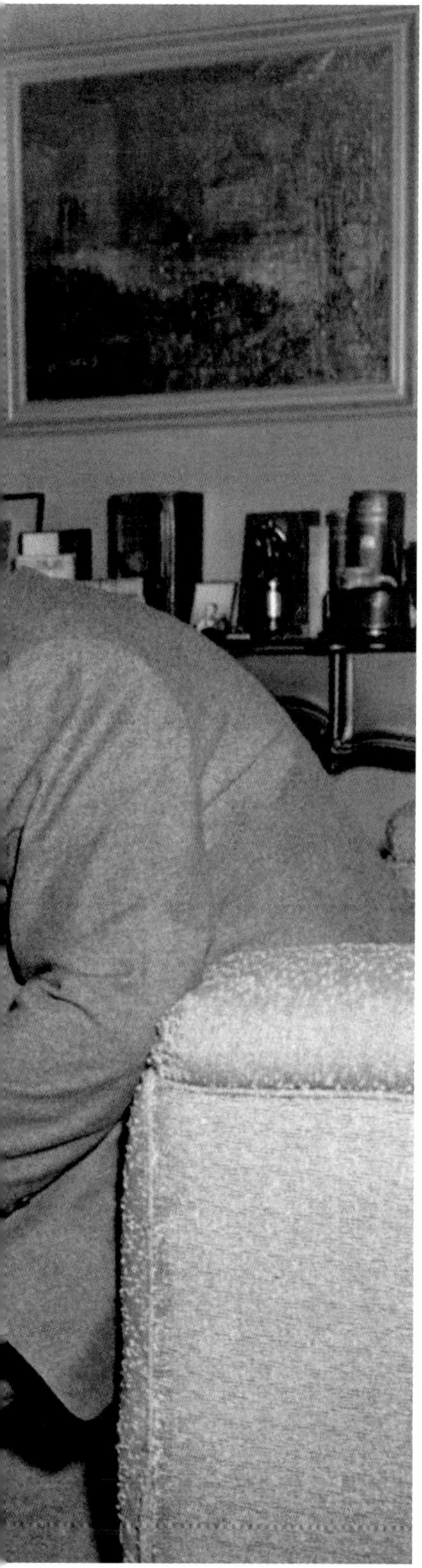

in exchange for Stewart starring (again with Novak) in *Bell, Book and Candle* (1958).

Hitchcock was famous for so thoroughly storyboarding each scene he rarely (if ever) looked through the camera viewfinder on set. But for this film, his preparation and meticulous attention reached new heights of fervency. Prior to the creation of a shooting script, Hitchcock and associate producer (and all-around right-hand man) Herbert Coleman scouted locations in and around San Francisco, a city Hitchcock loved. The shift in period and location were the first significant variations from the source novel, which begins in 1940s France as German forces threaten its borders. The movie eliminates the book's oppressive cloud of conflict and wartime occupation by shifting the story to the late-1950s California. Hitchcock dismissed an early draft by playwright Maxwell Anderson and hired Alec Coppel (already under contract to Paramount) to take a fresh crack at it. Coppel had adapted his own novel for the claustrophobic Brit-noir *The Hidden Room* (aka *Obsession*, 1949), one of two films directed by Edward Dmytryk in England during his U.S. blacklisting. Together, Coppel and Hitchcock devised the opening rooftop chase to explain the source of the detective's titular phobia.

Having already made three films with Hitchcock, Jimmy Stewart was the obvious choice to play Roger Flavières (renamed Scottie Ferguson in the film). Stewart—a creative partner on the film—expressed concern about the surreal tenor of the developing script and felt that it was essential to have at least one aspect of the plot rooted in reality. Hitchcock hired a native San Franciscan, Sam Taylor, to further retool the script. Taylor created Midge (played with sly reserve by Barbara Bel Geddes), an old college friend to whom Scottie was previously engaged. There is no such character in the novel. Midge is a warm but overly maternal companion, a pointed contrast to the mysterious, alluring Madeleine. She is the film's grounding touchstone. Hitchcock's typical *modus operandi* was to extract the essence from the source material and weave his own distinctive story around it, making it very much his own (e.g.: *Rear Window, Strangers on a Train, Psycho).* But in this case, he followed the novel with unwavering fidelity. His imprimatur for this film—its visual texture—directly referenced silent movies, which he considered the purest form of cinema. "Dialogue should simply be...something that comes out of the mouths of people whose eyes tell the story in visual terms." He typically employed to great effect what he referred to as the "subjective treatment," an alternating pattern of shot/reaction shot, which he used to heighten suspense. In *Vertigo*, this technique forms the principle structure of the narrative, intensifying our identification with Scottie's obsession, which ultimately leads to psychosis.

This scene in Scottie's apartment required over a week of shooting and endless retakes until Hitchcock was satisfied with the tone and pacing

The film immediately pulls the viewer in with a title sequence designed by Saul Bass. Hitchcock began his career designing intertitles for silent movies, and he always displayed a keen eye for film's graphics. The first image that appears on-screen is an isolated mask-like face (no less than seven of the titles originally suggested for the film contained the word "mask"). The title—*Vertigo*—slowly emerges from the pupil of the eye. In her essay *Woman as Death: Vertigo as Source*, Barbara Creed connects this image to two René Magritte paintings, *The False Mirror* (1928) and *The Eye* (1932/35). In *Hitchcock on Hitchcock*, the director acknowledged surrealism as "An influence that I experience myself, if only in the dream sequences and the sequences of the unreal in a certain number of my films." Then a series of swirling spirals—a pattern replicated throughout the movie—emerges from and then fades back into the pupil, drawing us into "the mind's eye." Bass incorporated original images from French mathematician Jules Antione Lissajous for this sequence. His collaborator, avant-garde filmmaker John Whitney, skillfully set them in motion, creating the hypnotic effect. As Jennifer Bass and Pat Kirkham detail in *Saul Bass: A Life in Film & Design*, Bass wanted to convey the vertiginous disequilibrium associated with obsessive love. Of the forms themselves, he elaborated:

> *I did not invent them, they already existed, but were not fully recognized for their aesthetic potential since they were mainly seen as scientific expressions. You could say I was obsessed with them for a while—that I had fallen in love with them—so I knew a little of what Hitch was driving at.*

Adding another layer of emotional complexity is Bernard Herrmann's score, which references Wagner's *Tristan und Isolde*, specifically the *Leibestod*, or love-death passage of the tragic opera. As Steven C. Smith notes in *A Heart at Fire's Center, The Life and Music of Bernard Herrmann*: "*Vertigo* is Alfred Hitchcock's most uncompromising film, and Bernard Herrmann's fullest realization of his favorite themes: romantic obsession, isolation, and the ultimate release of death." Paramount initially hired Jay Livingston and Ray Evans to compose a theme song for the film—which Hitchcock wisely discarded.

There follows an abstracted image of a ladder's rung—suddenly gripped by the hands of a criminal pursued by a uniformed policeman and Scottie. Cut to a wide shot of the rooftop, revealing the nocturnal skyline of San Francisco. The "City by the Bay," imbued with nostalgia and romance, is more than a mere backdrop. An underlying motif of dominant men and discarded women will run throughout the film, suggesting the "power and freedom"—a phrase invoked at key points throughout the film—that men enjoyed in the bygone days of early San Francisco.

In addition to establishing the source of Scottie's vertigo, there is another striking facet to this sequence: the lack of a resolution—how does Scottie survive his precariously dangling predicament? As Robin Wood theorizes in *Hitchcock's Films*: "We do not see, and are never told, how he got down from the gutter: there seems no possible way he *could* have got down. The effect is of leaving him, throughout the film, metaphorically suspended over a great abyss." In the novel, there is a parallel scene recounted in flashback by Flavières, but it's already been determined that he has acrophobia. After this establishing scene, the film follows the book to the letter, right down to the novel's bifurcated structure.

Flavières/Scottie meets with an old college friend, Paul Gévigne/Gavin Elster (Tom Helmore, though Everett Sloane was briefly considered for this role). Flavières/Scottie—retired from the police—reluctantly agrees to shadow his pal's potentially suicidal wife, Madeleine, who is obsessed with her great grandmother (Pauline Lagerlac/Carlotta Valdes). Flavières/Scottie trails Madeleine, at first curious and protective. Gradually, a fixation develops and an idealized love takes root. In the novel, the reader is trapped in the confines of Flavières' internal monologue, as he sinks in deeply: "...he had made up his mind to follow Madeleine week in, week out, for months if necessary. ... he wouldn't recover his peace of mind until he got to the bottom of the mystery." At night: "He had thought about her and heard her footsteps in his dreams."

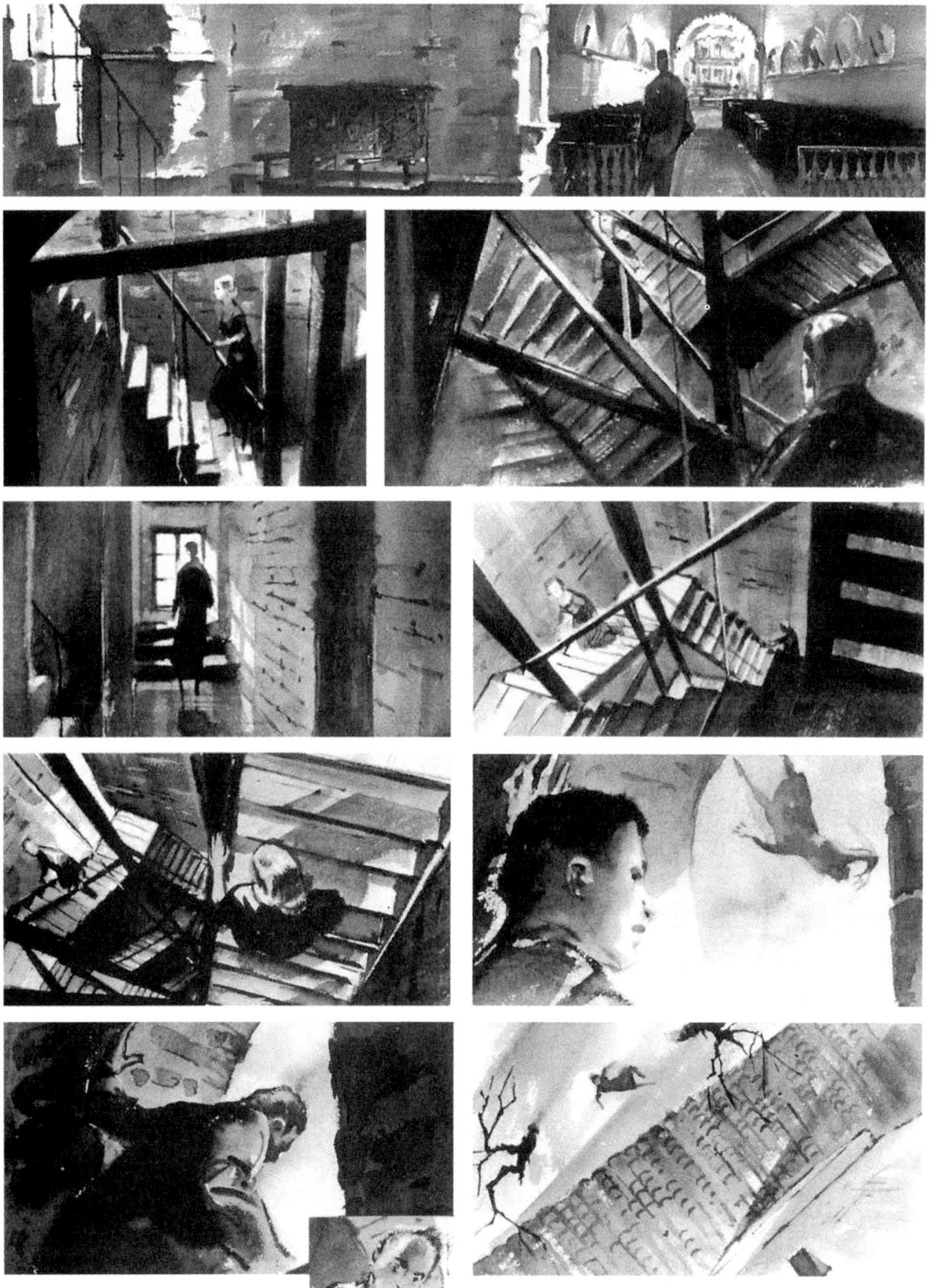

Hitchcock used storyboards and production sketches to lay out every scene in the film before a single frame of *Vertigo* was shot

Scottie's emotional involvement is more gradual, but no less consuming. Hitchcock's languid pacing, the selective use of fog filters by DP Robert Burks, and the absence of dialogue—for a total of roughly 18 minutes—creates a dreamlike ambiance. This somnolent mood is ruptured when Madeleine plunges into San Francisco Bay (the river Seine in the book). After she's rescued, it's the first time we hear her speak. With the hook now in deep, Flavières/Scottie unwittingly takes a more active role in this elaborately choreographed deception—though the protagonists of book and film have different motivations.

Flavières has developed disdain for Gévigne, whom he regards as a wartime profiteer not worthy of Madeleine's affections. He fantasizes that she shares his contempt "...as though there was some common bond between them, as though they were united in a common hostility to Gévigne." He calls her his Eurydice (Orpheus' wife, rescued from the underworld) and he surrenders himself completely: "...he realized the extent to which he was in her clutches. She absorbed literally all his strength. He was a blood donor. No, that wasn't the word. A soul donor."

Scottie's emotions are less complex. He feels he's wandering aimlessly through life and he quickly becomes seduced by Madeleine's offer to "wander" together. Continually distracted by reveries from the past, Madeleine leads Flavières/Scottie to an old, isolated church with a conveniently high tower (at Saintes in the book, San Juan Bautista in the film) and her staged suicide plays out in precisely the same manner on-screen as on the page. In the novel, there is an inquest and Gévigne is suspected, but Flavières refuses to appear, concealing the fact that he was with Madeleine when she died. Flavières is bereft, and a deep melancholia sets in. As the war intensifies, he struggles to conjure memories of Madeleine:

> *Yes, it was good to wander through those shadows. The land of the living was far away. Here were only the dead, solitary figures slinking through the streets, haunted by the bright days of long ago, tortured by a remembered happiness. Some stopped for a moment to look down at the dark river licking its banks, then slunk on again. Were they preparing themselves for the Day of Judgment?*

The first section of the novel ends as Flavières "...with death in his soul, boarded a motor-coach bound for Toulouse."

Hitchcock provided a sharp contrast to the book in the way he concluded the "front story," as he called it. Scottie *does* appear at the inquest and is raked over the courthouse coals for failing to prevent Madeleine's death. After visiting her grave, Scottie experiences a harrowing nightmare. This sequence—which Hitchcock and Coppel worked out in precise detail—was designed with special effects by John Ferren, a contemporary abstract expressionist who had previously consulted on and supplied paintings for *The Trouble with Harry* (1955). He was heavily influenced by artists such as Matisse and Kandinsky, and more specifically their use of color, which he drew from to great effect. Scottie is not simply melancholy, he is broken enough to be institutionalized. In her final scene in the film, Midge comes to visit him—reinforcing her maternal instincts, she soothingly says, "Mother's here"—but even she cannot reach him. As she slowly walks out of the psychiatrist's office and down the corridor, she, and Scottie's tenuous link with reality, gradually fade to black.

The second section of the novel begins with Flavières' return to France (now liberated) after four years in Africa. He discovers the scars of war, and his own past, are ever present:

> *He hardly recognized this Paris, still plunged in the mists of winter, these great empty spaces, these broad avenues along which hardly anything passes but bicycles and jeeps. He hurried along quickly like everyone else. The Arc de Triomphe loomed up distinctly in the grey mist. Everything was the color of the past, the color of memory. What feast of the dead had he come here to celebrate?*

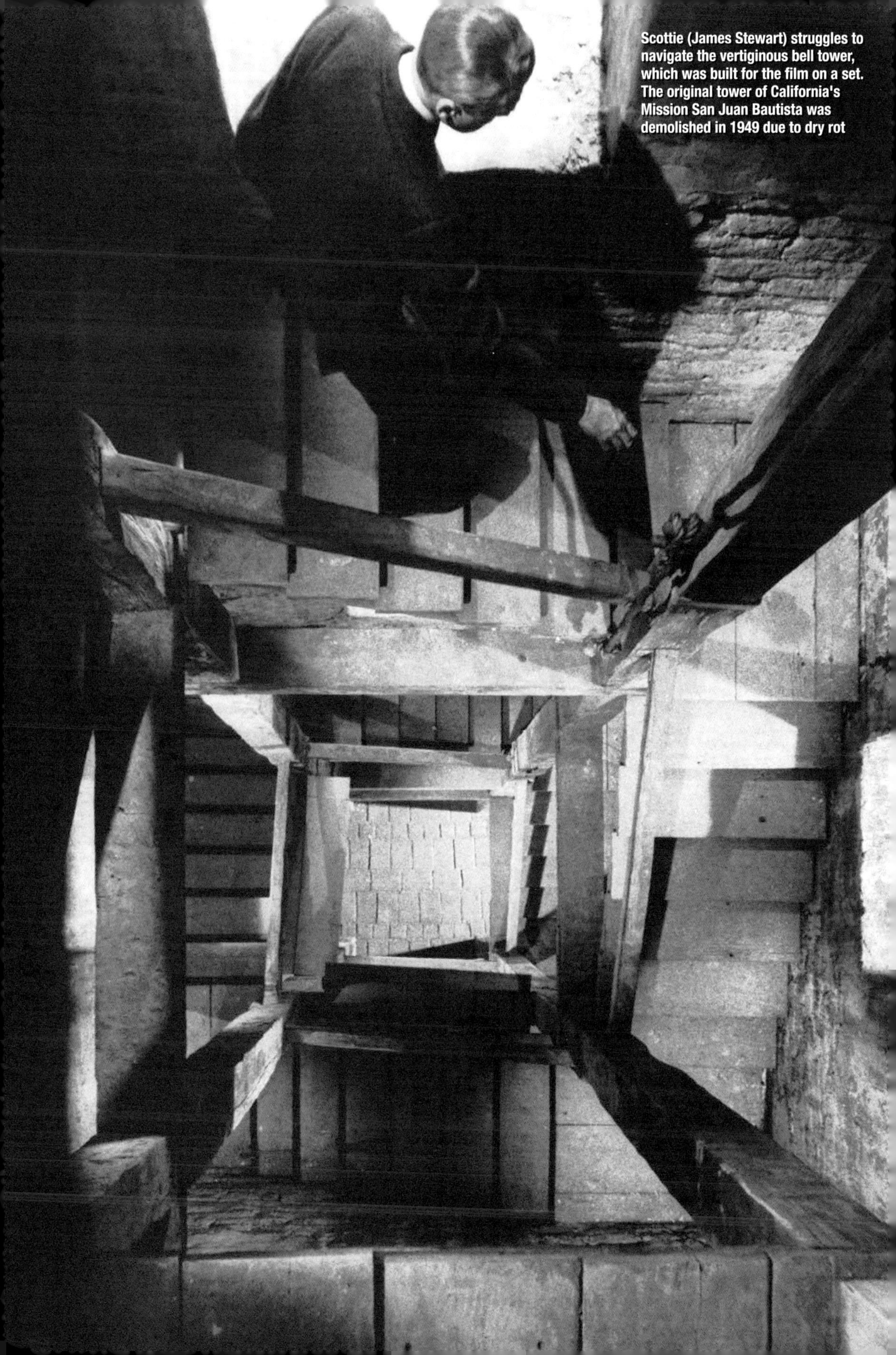

Scottie (James Stewart) struggles to navigate the vertiginous bell tower, which was built for the film on a set. The original tower of California's Mission San Juan Bautista was demolished in 1949 due to dry rot

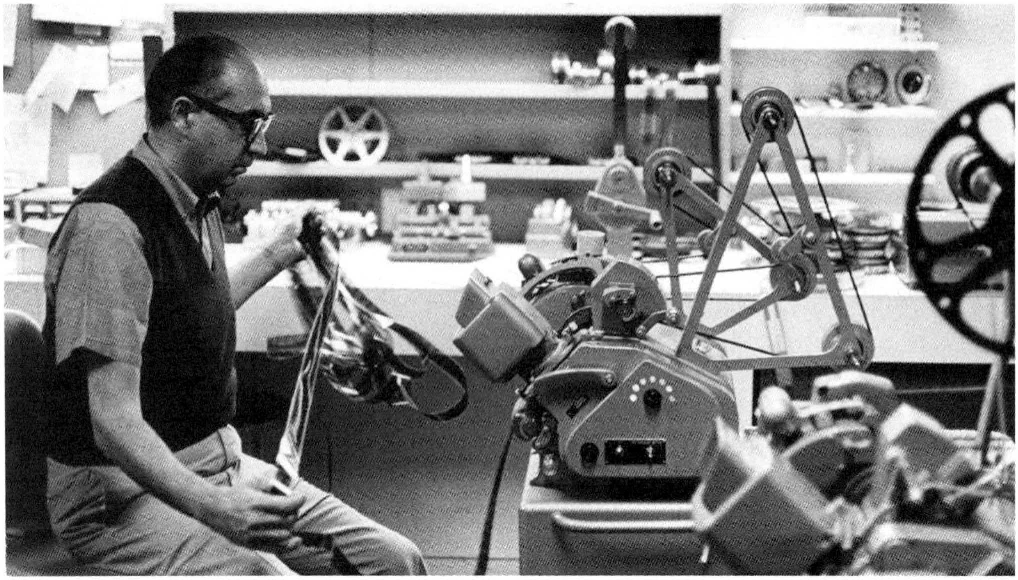

Designer Saul Bass in his workshop

Flavières discovers that Gévigne was killed in the war; on-screen, Elster disappears to Europe with his wife's money. Flavières eventually drifts into a movie theater and during a newsreel spots a girl bearing a striking resembles to Madeleine—Narcejac's real-life impetus for the story. In the film, Scottie has been released from the hospital to resume his solitary wandering, and his chance encounter occurs on a street corner. How Flavières and Scottie pursue this mystery woman provides a sharp distinction between French and American (and Hitchcock's) mores of the time. When Flavières meets Renee (Judy in the film), she's keeping company with a black marketeer. When he "turns her out," Flavières seizes the moment and moves in with her, although he takes little pleasure in the carnal aspect of their relationship. By contrast, Scottie courts Judy in the chaste manner proscribed by the Hollywood Production Code.

Judy's confession—delivered to the audience in voiceover two-thirds of the way into the film—is the most significant change from the novel, which saves this revelation for the climax. Hitchcock asserted sole responsibility for this change, but Dan Auiler gives the credit to Sam Taylor. "It's really a Hitchcockian thing," Taylor told the director, pitching the earlier "reveal." "I said 'This is not pure Hitchcock unless the audience *knows* what has happened,' and he agreed." This is the first time we are liberated from Scottie's POV, making us complicit in Judy's deception in a way the novel does not. This creates a second level of engagement; we now also empathize with Judy.

Drawing inspiration from Edgar Allan Poe, whom he greatly admired, Hitchcock infuses this final section of the film with a chimerical rationale:

I try to put in my films what Poe puts in his stories: a perfectly unbelievable story recounted to readers with such a hallucinatory logic that one has the impression that this same story can happen to you tomorrow. (*Hitchcock on Hitchcock*)

Scottie becomes increasingly disillusioned with Judy because she is *only* an illusion...not Madeleine. Their physical interactions have a palpable awkwardness; unlike Flavières with Renée, he can barely bring himself to touch her. As with Flavières, Scottie's need to recreate Madeleine is deeply obsessive and unrelenting, a "pathological Pygmalion" as critic Andrew Sarris described him. A process that Hitchcock likely identified with as "*Vertigo* has been seen as a mirror of Hitchcock's own insecurities and his desire to manipulate the beautiful women he loved and feared." (*The Dark Side of Genius: The Life of Alfred Hitchcock*, Donald Spoto.) Scottie dresses Judy in the same wardrobe as Madeleine, as Flavières, does in the book; Hitchcock even lifts from the novel the tapered gray suit and the hairstyle (bun at the nape of the neck). When Renée models different ensembles for Flavières, he observes, "Perched on high heels...she looked another person, almost ethereal." This description resonated with Hitchcock, who later bathes Judy's transformation into Madeleine in an ethereal green light. Symbolic of rebirth and eternal life, the color green has been referenced in the earlier scene in the Redwood forest, when Scottie defines *Sequoia Semperviva*—"evergreen," ever living—for Madeleine. This haunting sequence is charged with an undercurrent of forbidding longing—there is no corresponding scene in the novel.

In the film, Scottie struggles to free Madeleine from the specter of Carlotta, thus saving her from the same fate. Flavières' attraction, however, is darker and more complex. He is seduced by Madeleine's preoccupation with death: "Madeleine dreaming in front of Pauline's tomb....Homesick! For the grave! ... No, it was impossible. But who really knew what was possible or not?" Even the perfume she wears reminds Flavières of freshly dug earth, and the decay of withered flowers.

What a long time he had waited for this woman who was not quite at home in the daylight. Since the age of twelve, to be exact, when he had first penetrated into the heart of the earth, exploring the shadows, the country of phantoms, of the dead...

Flavières becomes increasingly invested in the notion of reincarnation. First, Pauline Lagerlac renewed as Madeleine, and now Madeleine in the process of renewal as Renée. "It was all very well for her (Renée) to swear she wasn't Madeleine: he knew she was." In the first of two instances, the authors foreshadow the inevitable, "He would have liked to throw his arms around her, to embrace her: yes, perhaps to suffocate her." In the second instance, Flavières grimly reflected, "For their love was something monstrous, foredoomed to death...To death," an indirect reference to the *Liebestod*. In the film, Hitchcock's reference to this concept is more overt. Scottie can only make love with Judy after her transformation into Madeleine is fully realized—after death comes love. In later interviews, Hitchcock glibly described this as a form of necrophilia, which only serves to attenuate the emotional complexity of Scottie's mental state.

On both page and screen, the incriminating necklace appears accidentally, but for Flavières, this is just another link to Madeleine, whose spirit he believes resides deep inside Renée. He continues to sink deeper into his own myopic (mental) morass as he struggles to convince Renée she really is Madeleine, and who, like his "little Eurydice," has returned from the grave. "He still had a host of questions to ask her. They writhed in his brain like worms. ...He must coax her (Madeleine) back, little by little to the threshold of life. Then...the moment would come when she would remember." When Renée finally reveals the deception, Flavières cannot accept that the woman he loved never existed. Murmuring Madeleine's name beseechingly, and believing she was trapped inside Renée, he strangles Renée to death and is arrested.

Scottie, however, once onto the hoax, puts the duplicitous pieces together himself. He drives Judy to the scene of the crime and literally drags her back up into the bell tower. But he, too, is hopelessly consumed by his own illusive reverie, exclaiming to Judy, "Madeleine, I loved you so." The sudden appearance of a ghostly nun startles Judy, who this time falls from the tower accidentally—and fatally. Scottie finds himself back where he was at the beginning of the film, on a ledge, staring down from a great height—only now his arms extend in a gesture of supplication, as he struggles to comprehend what he has done.

An alternate ending was filmed which showed Midge listening to a radio report indicating that the French police are closing in on Elster. She snaps it off as Scottie walks in to her apartment. She makes him a drink, which he takes to the window, gazing out at the San Francisco night skyline. This coda would have provided a closed loop, leading back to Hitchcock's beloved city, but the director clearly felt he had already expressed a sentiment more crucial, and personal: the impermanence of idealized love. ■

BOOK vs FILM

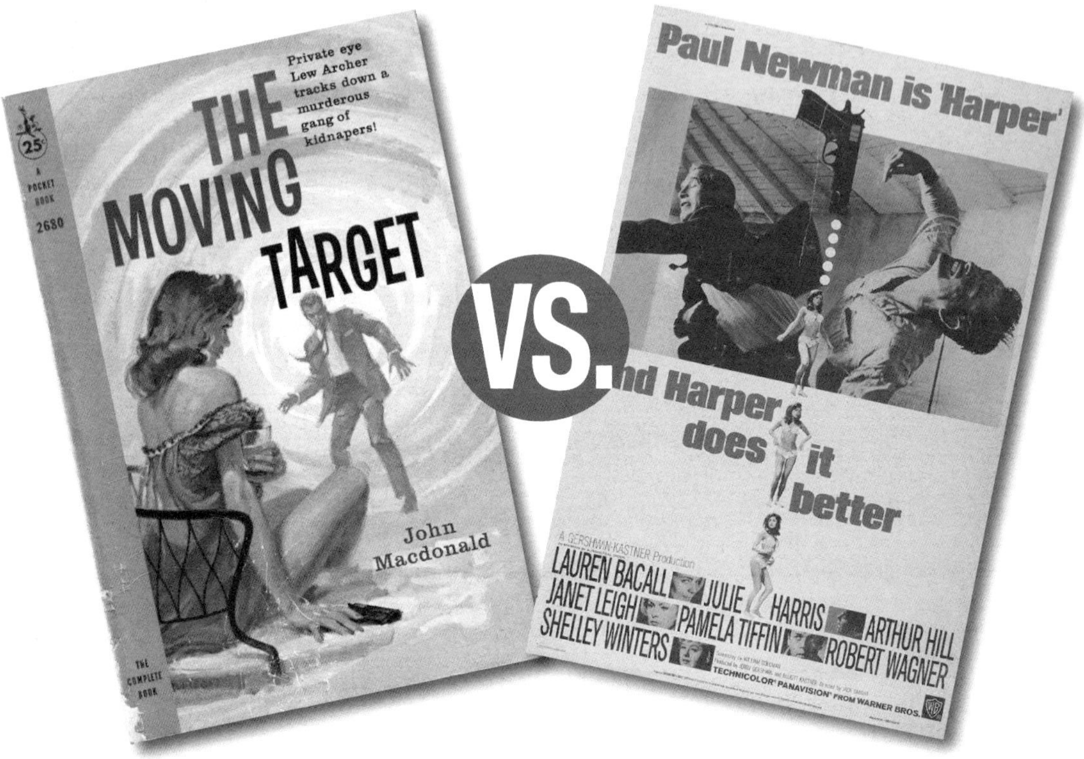

Ben Terrall

Kenneth Millar, better known by his pseudonym Ross Macdonald, differed from most other mid-20th-century American mystery writers in that he gave his characters psychological complexity where others settled for stereotypical affectations. His plots could be complicated, but were never sloppy—they fit together like elaborate, elegantly crafted jigsaw puzzles.

Born in 1915 in Los Gatos, California, Macdonald spent most of his formative years in Canada. After his father abandoned his mother, he grew up in foster homes and with a succession of relatives.

Macdonald's first four novels were published under his real name. The first two were spy novels, *The Dark Tunnel* (1944) and *Trouble Follows Me* (1946). Then came *Blue City* (1947) and *The Three Roads* (1948), written, in the author's words, "in kind of an angry rapture."

Macdonald told an interviewer that artists and musicians "really spoke to me directly and they taught me things to do in writing that you couldn't learn from other writers, you had to learn from musicians and painters. At least *I* did." *Blue City*, written in a month, was influenced by Dashiell Hammett, Nelson Algren, jazz musicians, and painters.

With his next book, *The Moving Target* (1949), Macdonald took the pseudonym John

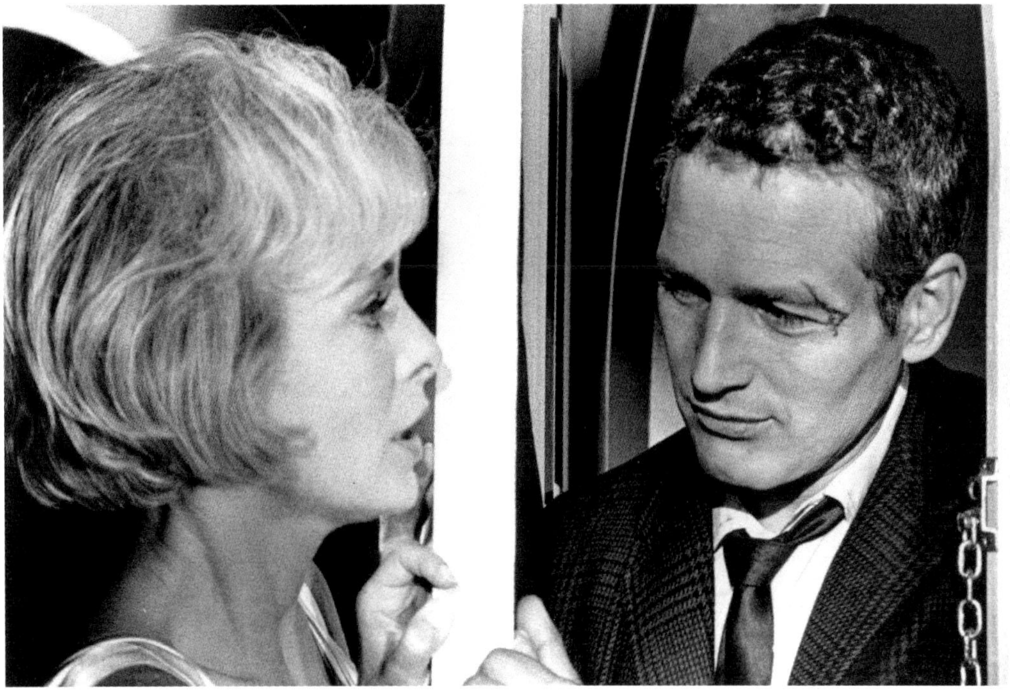

Paul Newman's bruised and battered *Harper* gives a blue-eyed wink and a tentative nod to his estranged wife Susan, played by Janet Leigh

Macdonald, which within a few years became Ross Macdonald to avoid confusion with fellow crime writer John D. MacDonald. *The Moving Target* began a decades-long, amazingly rich series of books featuring private eye Lew Archer. Looking back in 1971, Millar wrote:

The rush of change which the war had started continued and accelerated afterwards, particularly in the empty spaces of California. It seemed that a brave new world was being born here, on the last frontier, and people migrated to it as we had from all over the continent. I wrote about the far side of the brave new world, in a series of hardboiled detective novels begun in 1949 with *The Moving Target.*

Macdonald admitted that "Raymond Chandler is a hard man to follow. He wrote like a slumming angel, and invested the sun-blinded streets of Los Angeles with a romantic presence." In its plays on language and entertaining similes, *The Dark Tunnel* shows the strong influence of Chandler; in one of the book's more memorable lines, the hero tells a dim-witted policeman, "I want to talk to a detective who isn't moribund above the coccyx." But as he began the Archer series, Macdonald "tried to work out my own version of the 'hardboiled' style, to develop both imagery and structure in the direction of psychological and symbolic meaning." (Elsewhere, Macdonald noted, "The term hardboiled is not necessarily connected with violence, it has more to do with a realistic attitude toward life as reflected in the language.")

Macdonald was paid more money for *The Moving Target* than he'd received for any of his earlier books. Though there was only one printing by his publisher, Knopf, the book was reprinted by the Mystery Guild in 1949, and was published in paperback by Pocket Books in the U.S. and Pan Books in England. This first Archer book garnered positive critical responses: the influential *New York Times* mystery critic Anthony Boucher called it "the most human and disturbing novel of the hard-boiled school in many years." Boucher also wrote in *Ellery Queen's Mystery Magazine* that it was "the high point of recent American books ... you can put this on your Hammett-Chandler shelf; it won't be at all out of place in that company." Privately, Boucher told Macdonald, "You can write like a son of a bitch."

Unfortunately for Macdonald, Chandler himself, notoriously cranky and with a snobbish streak a mile wide, was unimpressed. Not flattered by *The Moving Target's* similarities to his classic *The Big Sleep*, Chandler called the "pretentiousness" of Macdonald's phrasing "rather repellant." Chandler described Macdonald as being the kind of writer who is a "literary eunuch ... the sort of mind that keeps avant-garde magazines alive."

Nonetheless, *The Moving Target* was the up-and-coming Macdonald's most successful novel to date. And if, in Macdonald's own estimation, he didn't make "a clean break with the Chandler tradition" until he wrote *The Doomsters* (1958), there were also key differences between Macdonald's and Chandler's approaches. In 1973, Macdonald wrote:

Chandler described a good plot as one that made for good scenes, as if the parts were greater than the whole. I see plot as a vehicle for meaning. It should be as complex as contemporary life, but balanced enough to say true things about it. The surprise with which a detective novel concludes should set up tragic vibrations which run backward through the entire structure.

Macdonald spent months working out the plots of his books, which tend to have many characters spanning two or three generations. *The Moving Target* is no exception. Mrs. Sampson, a rich woman confined to a wheelchair, hires private detective Lew Archer to find her wayward husband Ralph. Archer soon encounters the missing man's daughter, Miranda, and his pilot, Taggert. As Archer begins making inquiries, he finds himself tracking a down-at-the-heels female piano player who once cut some popular boogie records, and he's repeatedly battered by a bruiser named Puddler, who is connected to what turns out to be Sampson's kidnapping. Suffice it to say that numerous other characters crisscross Archer's path, including a classically Californian pseudo-mystic named Claude, about whom Miranda says, "He wears his hair long and never cuts his beard and talks like a bad imitation of Walt Whitman."

The Sampson family is one of the many oil dynasties that appear in Macdonald's fiction. Their corrupting influence on the people around them, and society as a whole, rings especially true in an age when decades of oil company denials of global warming have seriously compromised the future of our species, and when a former ExxonMobil CEO has somehow become the U.S. Secretary of State.

This attention to American class structures is characteristic of Macdonald, who has Archer instinctively side with the underdog: in *The Moving Target*, he observes white attitudes toward Mexicans, "It makes it easier to gouge people if you don't admit they're human." And though divorced, Archer harbors none of the misogyny that taints so many fictional detectives.

When it came to the murderers in his books, Macdonald reflected in a letter to his publisher, Alfred Knopf, that "I would rather understand them than condemn them. I would rather display them in characteristic postures and sum up their lives and their reasons for their lives than cause a self-righteous hero to denounce them or push them around for the sake of action."

In *The Moving Target*, Archer reflects on his earlier life as a policeman: "I believed that evil was a quality some were born with, like a harelip." Archer, the private eye, no longer views the world that way: "But evil isn't so simple. Everybody has it in him, and whether it comes out in his actions depends on a number of things. Environment, opportunity, economic pressure, a piece of bad luck, a wrong friend."

Macdonald had mixed feelings about Hollywood. In *The Moving Target*, when Archer watches the film industry veteran Fay Estabrook, a former silent star, walk off a set, the detective refers to "the evil which hung in studio air like a gas." But Macdonald had been entranced upon his first exposure to motion pictures at the age of seven. Looking back in 1967, he wrote, "One thing that strikes me, over and above a recurrent fascination with Hollywood, is my use of film techniques. *The Moving Target*, in particular, is a story clearly aspiring to be a movie. It was no accident that when Warner Bros. made it into one last year they were able to follow the story virtually scene by scene."

In 1964, William Goldman, who went on to become a highly successful screenwriter, was a Hollywood neophyte. Goldman told producer Elliott Kastner that they should make a movie out of a

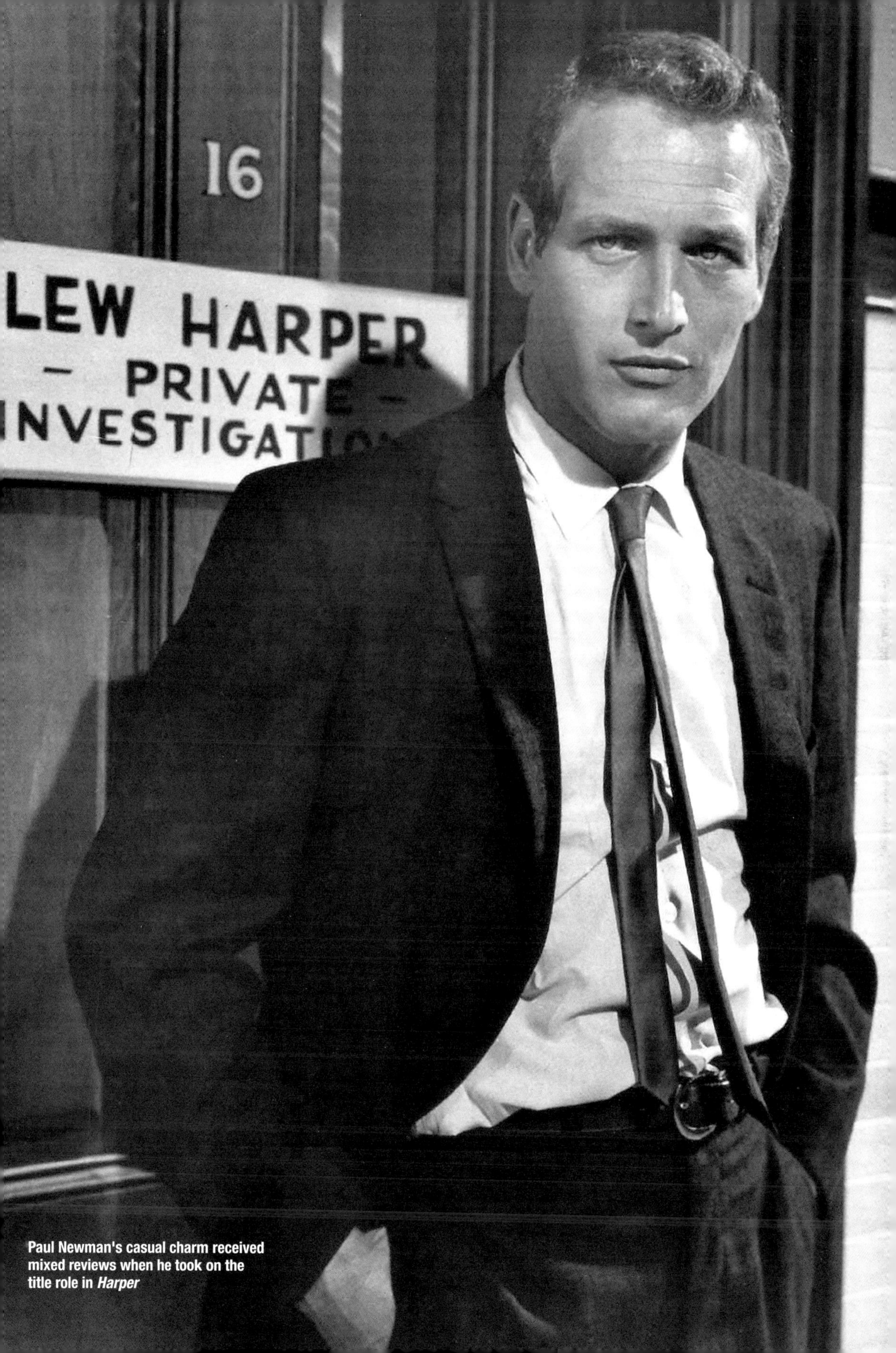

Paul Newman's casual charm received mixed reviews when he took on the title role in *Harper*

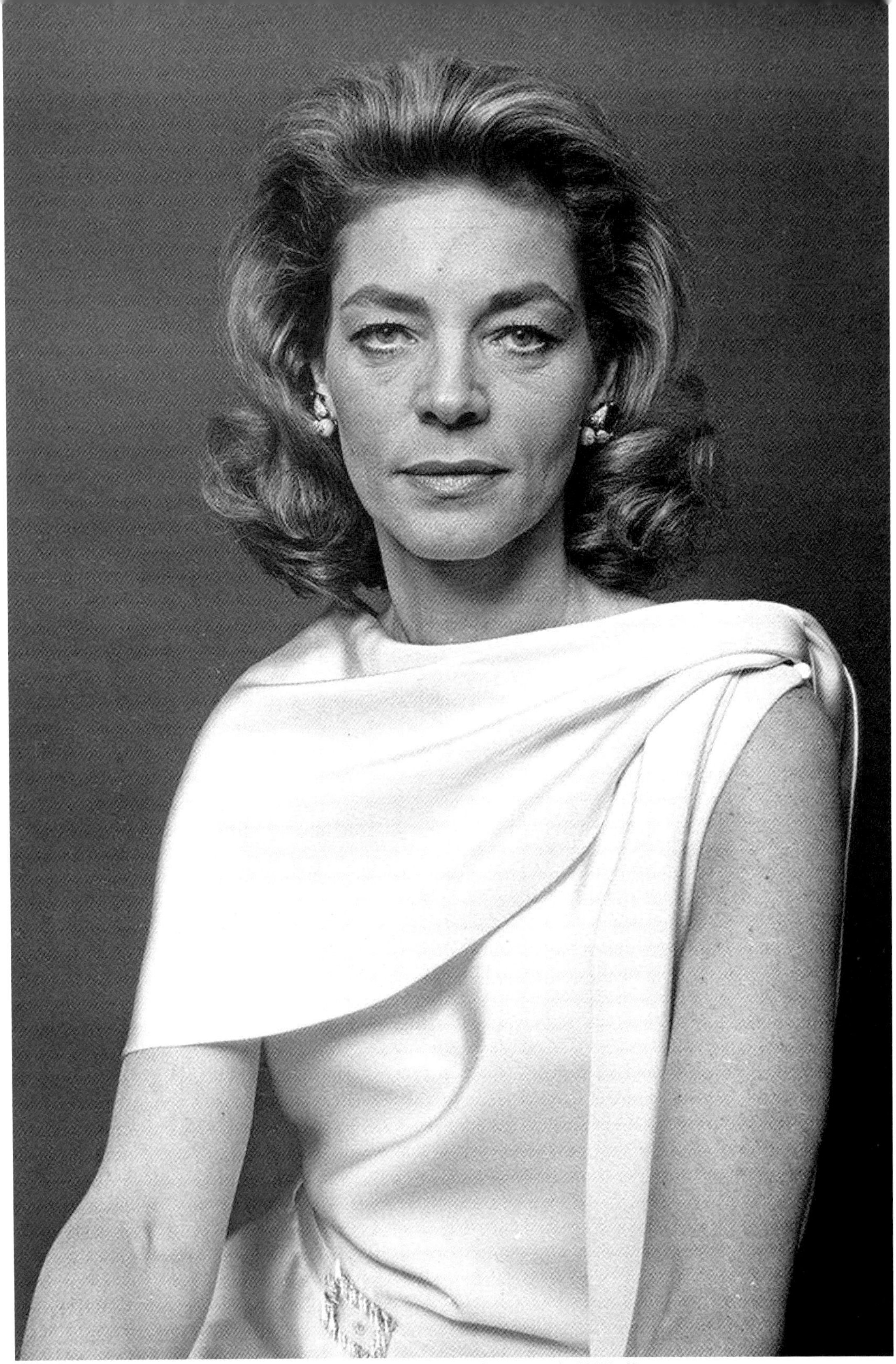

Still the grande dame of noir, Lauren Bacall is sly, sinister, and seductive as ever in 1966's *Harper*

Lew Archer novel. Goldman, who described himself as "a lunatic Macdonald fan," had been reading Archer novels since picking up *The Moving Target* at a bus station in 1950. He set upon re-reading the Archer novels and decided that *The Moving Target* was "the most cinematic." Warner Bros. was enthusiastic about the project, and wanted to make a series of movies about Archer, but when Macdonald asked for the not-that-princely sum of $50,000 for exclusive rights, WB balked. Instead, it simply changed Archer's name to Harper (reportedly with the blessing of star Paul Newman, who felt characters with "H" names brought him good luck). Macdonald did ultimately make enough from the film to buy a new house overlooking the Pacific.

As Macdonald noted, Goldman's script stuck fairly closely to *The Moving Target*. One major difference was that a lawyer who's merely an acquaintance of Archer's in the book becomes a close friend of the detective in the film. That extra dimension to their relationship becomes a key to the film's final scene. Goldman created the character of Harper's estranged wife Susan, effectively played by Janet Leigh. In Macdonald's Archer books, the detective's past as a married man is alluded to, but there's never a carnal encounter with his ex, as there is in the film. Macdonald told critic John Leonard that, "the paperback people wanted me to put in more sex and I started perversely leaving it out."

Goldman said he was thinking of Humphrey Bogart in the title role when he wrote the screenplay. That Paul Newman was ultimately cast as Harper certainly gave the movie box-office clout, but Newman's rendering of the hero isn't exactly in the Bogart tradition. But then, who can do Bogart besides Bogart? Newman is, as usual, charismatic and charming—but maybe too charming. There are occasional lapses into self-consciously jokey lines where Newman's winking and eye-rolling pull the viewer out of the story.

One of the film's greatest strengths is its cast, which Goldman admitted he was "shocked that were able to get." Lauren Bacall, still radiant and sharp, plays the wealthy, duplicitous wife of the kidnapping victim with consummate professionalism; Julie Harris excels as the down-and-out junkie chanteuse; and Strother Martin is hilariously on-target in his portrayal of an all-too-familiar New Age huckster. Even Robert Wagner, not always the most versatile actor, convincingly pulls off a complicated character.

Critics were split on *Harper* (1966). Bosley Crowther of the *New York Times* compared Jack Smight's direction to the work of Howard Hawks, while Pauline Kael called Smight, "a bungler from start to finish." Kael, never one to mince words, also trashed Newman, arguing that his performance as Harper was his worst since the bible epic *The Silver Chalice*.

Despite Kael's pan, *Harper* was Newman's first hit since *Hud*, again putting him in the top ten of the annual exhibitors' poll of box-office stars. The film sparked resurgence in the detective film genre and spawned a sequel of sorts, a less successful feature called *The Drowning Pool* (1975), based on the Macdonald novel of the same name and again starring Newman. For Macdonald, perhaps the best thing about *Harper* is that its release brought the earlier Archer books back into print.

Harper is very much a period piece, with plenty of swinging nightclub scenes of youngsters shaking it on dance floors, and some fairly ridiculous bikini-clad go-go dancing on a diving board. Conrad Hall's cinematography alone makes the movie worth watching, with breathtaking helicopter footage of the gorgeous Southern California coastline and beautifully lit interiors.

Perhaps it's unfair to carp that *Harper* doesn't approach the level of artistry found in *The Moving Target*. Macdonald's work is just too top-notch. He was so good at what he did that in a review of the *The Goodbye Look* (1969), William Goldman called the Archer books "the finest series of detective novels ever written by an American," concluding, "classify him as you will, he is one of the best American novelists now operating, and all he does is keep on getting better." Macdonald kept at the series until he finished *The Blue Hammer* (1976), after which his worsening Alzheimer's made it too difficult for him to continue writing. Macdonald died from the disease in 1983, leaving behind a legacy that will continue to enthrall readers for decades to come. ■

CONTRIBUTORS

Nathalie Atkinson is a Toronto-based freelance culture writer and film critic, and a columnist for *The Globe and Mail*, Canada's daily newspaper; she regularly interviews leading writers, actors, showrunners, and filmmakers (and screen icons like Kim Novak). A member of the Toronto Film Critics Association, Nathalie is also the creator and host of the popular film series Designing the Movies.

Sean Axmaker lives in Seattle with his cats, Hammett and Chandler, and writes the syndicated newspaper column *Stream On Demand* and the companion website at streamondemandathome.com. His work has appeared in *Vulture*, Turner Classic Movies online, *Filmfax*, *Indiewire*, and *Parallax View*.

Eric Beetner is the author of more than two dozen crime novels and more than one hundred short stories. He hosts the *Noir at the Bar* reading series in Los Angeles, as well as the crime fiction podcast *Writer Types*. He works as a TV and film editor in L.A. and has made it a priority that his children watch plenty of black-and-white movies. For more information, visit EricBeetner.com

Gary Deane is a regular contributor to *NOIR CITY e-magazine*. He's been a university film teacher, repertory cinema programmer, syndicated music journalist, and also a professional librarian. But now it's mostly about 'the film noir project.' For more information: noirworthwatching.blogspot.ca; Facebook 'Gary Deane'.

Danny Gardner, when not writing crime fiction, enjoys careers in stand-up comedy, acting, and filmmaking. His short fiction has appeared in anthologies, including *The Obama Inheritance: Fifteen Stories of Conspiracy Noir* (Three Rooms Press, 2017). His debut novel, *A Negro and an Ofay*, is published by Down & Out Books (2017). He lives in Los Angeles by way of Chicago.

Jake Hinkson is the author of the novels *Hell on Church Street*, *The Posthumous Man*, and *No Tomorrow*, as well as the essay collection *The Blind Alley: Exploring Film Noir's Forgotten Corners*. His fiction has been translated into French by Éditions Gallmeister, and his novel *Hell on Church Street* was awarded the 2016 *Prix Mystère de la critique*, the French mystery critics prize.

Vince Keenan is co-managing editor of *NOIR CITY e-magazine*. With his wife Rosemarie Keenan, he writes the Lillian Frost and Edith Head mysteries (*Design for Dying* and *Dangerous to Know*) under the pen name Renee Patrick. He is also the author of *Down the Hatch: One Man's One Year Odyssey Through Classic Cocktail Recipes and Lore*.

Sharon Knolle has written for *Variety*, *USA Today*, AOL Moviefone, and more. She has run a Robert Mitchum site (welcometothebigsleep.blogspot.com) since 1997 and is the editor-in-chief of Moviepaws.com, a site dedicated to animals in the movies.

Steve Kronenberg is co-managing editor of *NOIR CITY e-magazine*. He has served as co-publisher and contributor to the classic horror magazine *Monsters from the Vault*. Steve is co-author of *The Creature Chronicles: Exploring the Black Lagoon Trilogy* and *Universal Terrors: The 1950s*, both published by McFarland and Company.

Brian Light, NOIR CITY Hollywood showrunner, has contributed program notes for various Los Angeles County Museum of Art film series such as *The Naked City: New York Noir and Neorealism, 2012: A Kubrick Odyssey, and Animating the Subconscious*. He has also published a series of articles on the global rockabilly scene for *Billboard*.

Trina Robbins, editor of *Miss Fury, Sensational Sundays, 1941-1944*, and *1944-1949*, has written books and graphic novels for over 40 years, including her 6-part graphic novel series for young readers, *Chicagoland Detective Agency*, her history of San Francisco's Chinese nightclubs '32-'62, *Forbidden City*, and *Tender Murderers* about women who kill. Her memoir, *Last Girl Standing*, was published in 2017 by Fantagraphics Books.

Alan K. Rode, FNF board member and noted film scholar, is the author of *Charles McGraw: Film Noir Tough Guy* and the recently published *Michael Curtiz: A Life in Film*. Alan has hosted and produced the Arthur Lyons Film Noir Festival in Palm Springs, California, for over a decade. Alan produces classic film Blu-ray and DVD content, and has provided commentary for TCM's FilmStruck. Visit alankrode.com

Imogen Sara Smith is the author of *In Lonely Places: Film Noir Beyond the City*. Based in New York City, she writes regularly for the Criterion Collection, *Film Comment*, *Sight & Sound*, *Cineaste*, and other journals, and has guest curated film series for the Museum of the Moving Image and FilmStruck.

John Wranovics is the author of *Chaplin and Agee*. In *NOIR CITY Annual 9*, John reported on the extent of U.S. Intelligence and Psychological Warfare agency involvement in the birth of Italian Neo-Realism ("Spooks Behind the Lens"). John's writing on film and social history has appeared in the New York Times, *Positif*, *Capricci 2011* and various academic anthologies. He blames an early childhood viewing of *The Night of the Hunter*.

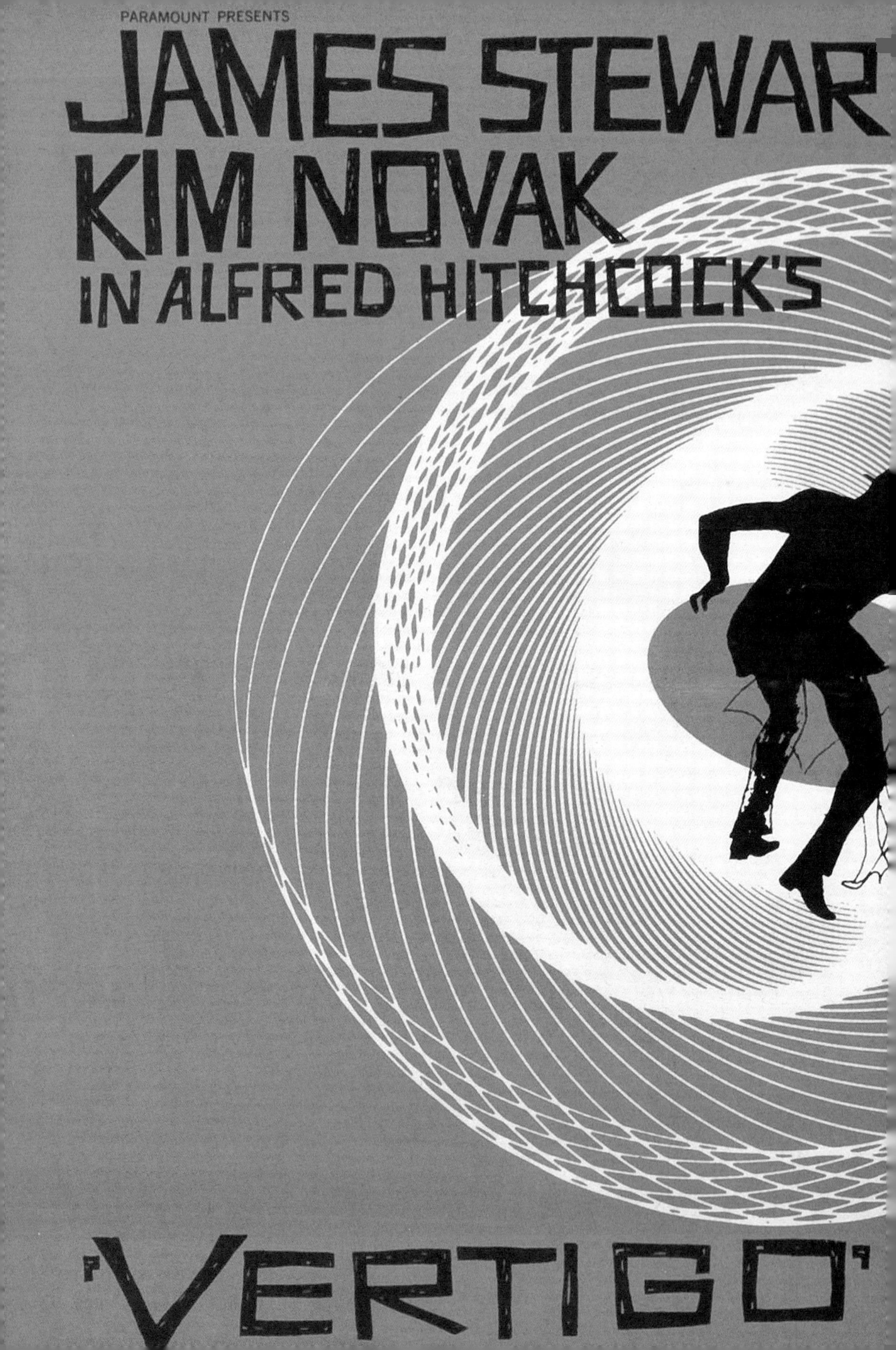
PARAMOUNT PRESENTS
JAMES STEWAR
KIM NOVAK
IN ALFRED HITCHCOCK'S
'VERTIGO'

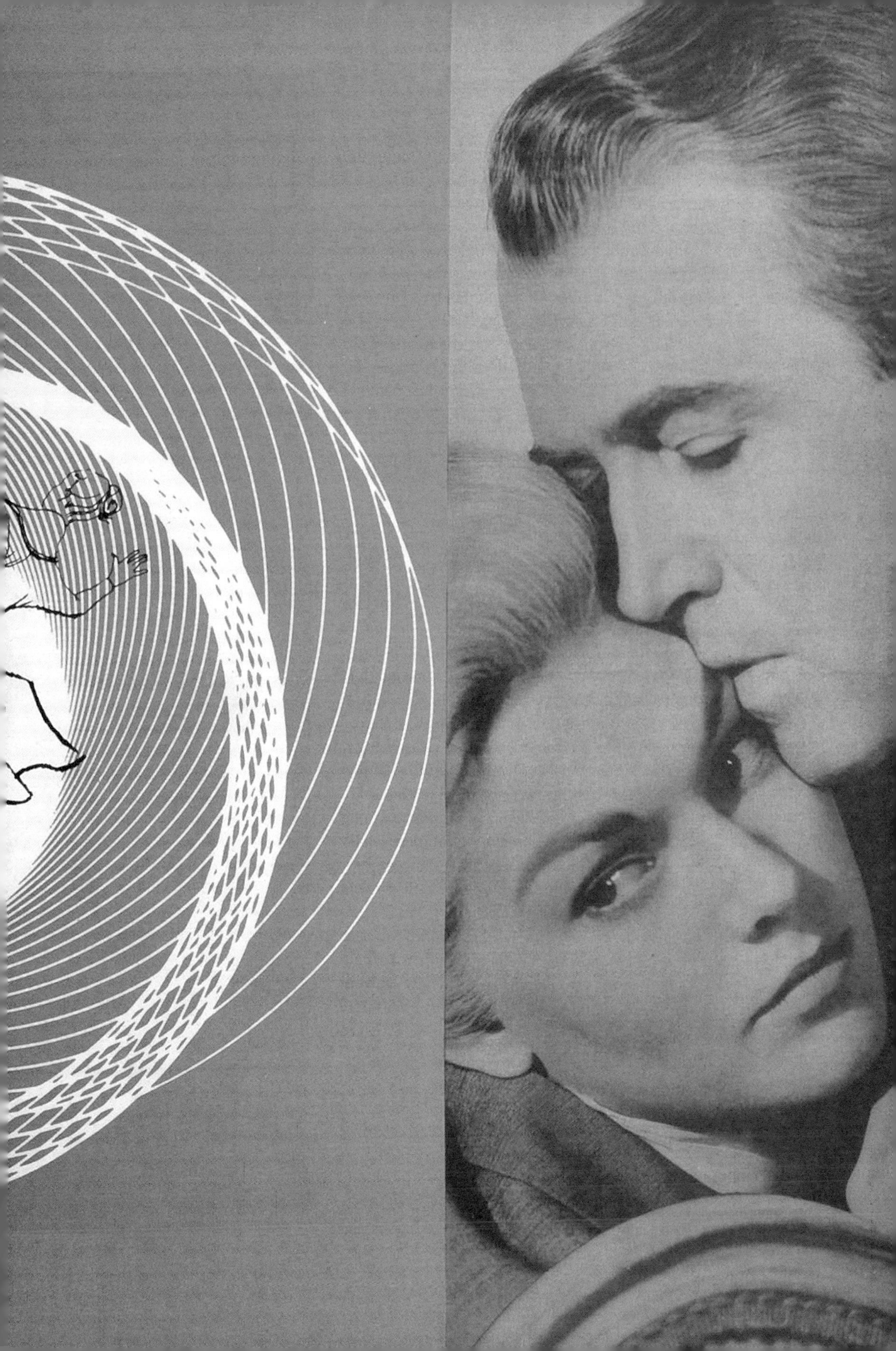

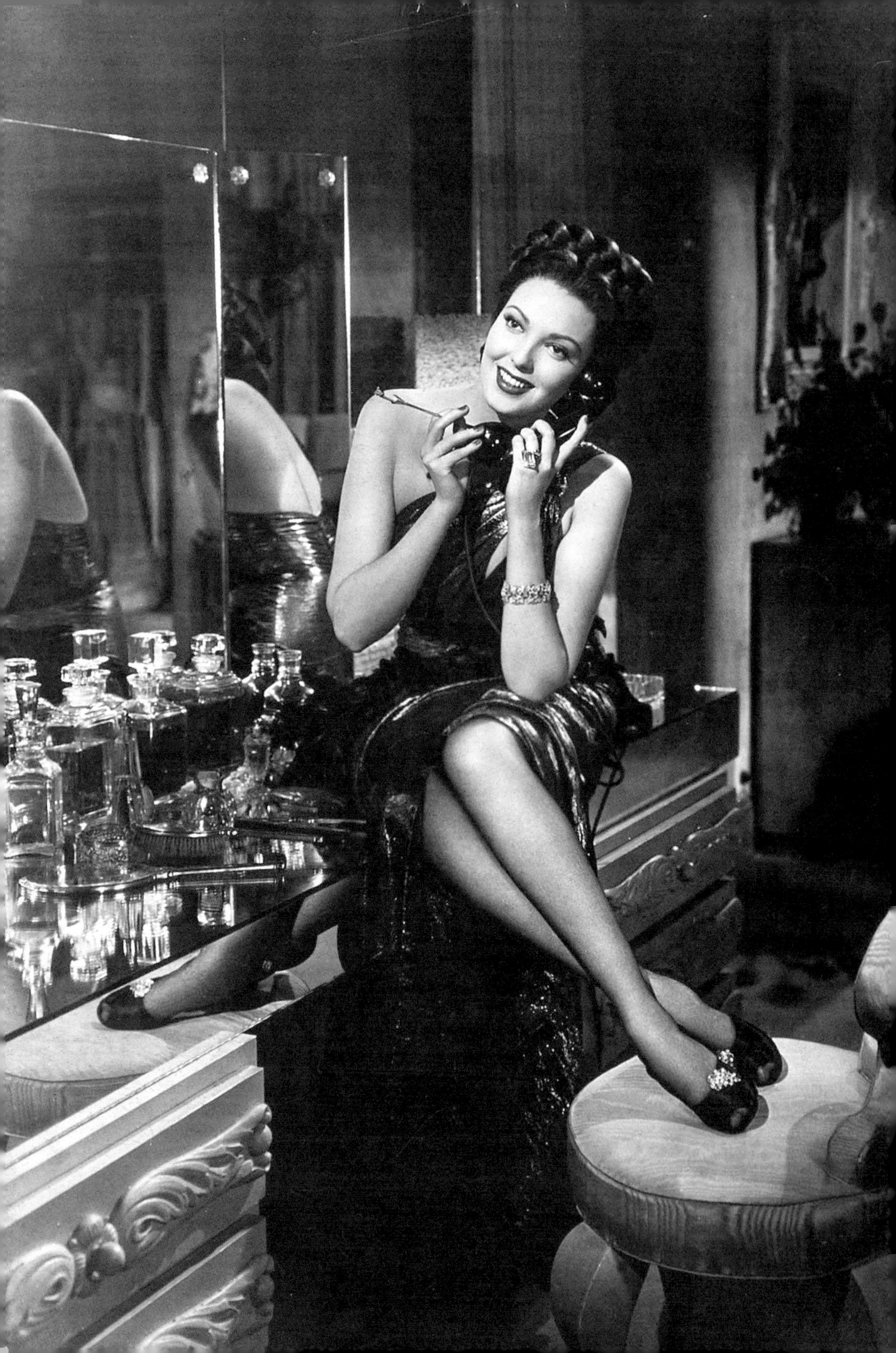